THE
HORSE
ENCYCLOPEDIA

THE HORSE
ENCYCLOPEDIA

DK LONDON
Senior Designer Ina Stradins
Project Editor Miezan van Zyl
Project Art Editor Francis Wong
Editors Gill Pitts, Kaiya Shang
US Editors Rebecca Warren, Margaret Parrish
Jacket Designer Mark Cavanagh
Jacket Editor Claire Gell
Jacket Design Development Manager Sophia Tampakopoulos
Producer, Pre-Production Andy Hilliard
Producer Mary Slater
Managing Art Editor Michael Duffy
Managing Editor Angeles Gavira
Art Director Karen Self
Associate Publishing Director Liz Wheeler
Publishing Director Jonathan Metcalf

Consultant Editor Kim Dennis-Bryan
Project Management Amanda Lunn, Jo Weeks

DK INDIA
Senior Editor Anita Kakar
Project Art Editor Vaibhav Rastogi
Editor Arpita Dasgupta
Art Editors Karan Chaudhary, Yashashvi Choudhary, Debjyoti Mukherjee
Assistant Art Editor Sonakshi Singh
Picture Researcher Sakshi Saluja
Jacket Art Editor Dhirendra Singh
Senior Jacket DTP Designer Harish Aggarwal
DTP Designers Rajesh Singh Adhikari, Syed Md Farhan, Anita Yadav
Managing Editor Rohan Sinha
Managing Art Editor Anjana Nair
Manager Picture Research Taiyaba Khatoon
Managing Jackets Editor Saloni Singh
Pre-production Manager Balwant Singh
Production Manager Pankaj Sharma

Original text by Elwyn Hartley Edwards taken from *Ultimate Horse* and *The Encyclopedia of the Horse* copyright © Mary Hartley Edwards 1991, 1994

First American Edition, 2016
Published in the United States by DK Publishing
345 Hudson Street, New York, New York 10014

Copyright © 2016 Dorling Kindersley Limited
DK, a Division of Penguin Random House LLC
16 17 18 19 20 10 9 8 7 6 5 4 3 2
006—291450—Sep/16

A catalog record for this book is available from the Library of Congress.
ISBN 978-1-4654-5143-9

DK books are available at special discounts when purchased in bulk for sales promotions, premiums, fund-raising, or educational use. For details, contact DK Publishing Special Markets, 345 Hudson Street, New York, New York 10014 or specialsales@dk.com

Printed and bound in China.

All images © Dorling Kindersley Limited
For further information see: www.dkimages.com

A WORLD OF IDEAS:
SEE ALL THERE IS TO KNOW
WWW.DK.COM

CONTENTS

1 INTRODUCTION TO HORSES

2 HORSES AND HUMANS

3 CATALOG OF BREEDS AND TYPES

4 CARE AND MANAGEMENT

CHAPTER 1

INTRODUCTION TO HORSES

The horse family

The only surviving members of the horse family (Equidae) belong to a single genus, *Equus*. There are seven species, two of which are domestic (the horse and donkey). The wild species, most of which are now endangered, comprise Przewalski's horse, the Asian and African wild asses, and the zebras. During the last 56 million years, however, there have been up to 12 different equid genera living at one time, often of quite varying appearance.

For many years, the evolution of the horse was thought to have been a gradual progression: the horse increased in size as the number of toes it possessed decreased, and its teeth gradually altered from being suited to eating leaves and woodland plants to eating grass. Today, the fossil record, though incomplete, reflects a different story of rapid diversification and extinctions. It is now known that, at times, albeit in different habitats, equids with one and three weight-bearing toes coexisted. Those that lived in open woodland areas ate leaves, while those on open plains fed on grass. There were others that ate less discriminately and could live in either habitat.

EARLY EQUIDS

Unlike the equids of the present day, the early "horses" were polydactyl (several toed), browsing animals that lived in forests. Genera such as *Sifrippus* and *Hyracotherium* had relatively short faces, low-crowned teeth and three weight-bearing toes, each ending in a small hoof. *Sifrippus*, which was similar in form to *Hyracotherium*, fluctuated in size—during a 175,000-year period of global warming, it shrank by about 30 percent to the size of a cat. When temperatures fell again, it became larger, attaining a shoulder height of about 19½ in (50 cm). Fossil teeth and bones once attributed to *Hyracotherium* are now thought to be a mixture of species, some of which have equine features and others that do not. Scientists consider only the former to be equids.

Early fossil horses
The feet and teeth of these three extinct equids differ considerably from those of present-day horses. The change in diet, number of weight-bearing digits, and size is thought at least in part to be related to the different environments in which these equids lived.

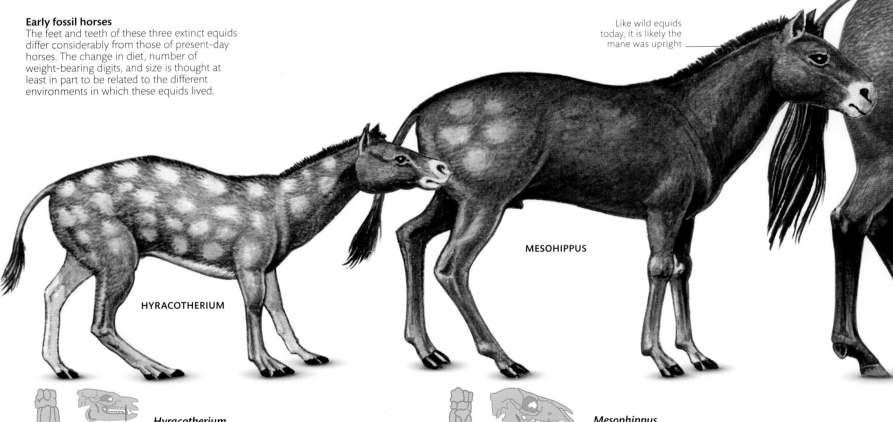

Like wild equids today, it is likely the mane was upright

MESOHIPPUS

HYRACOTHERIUM

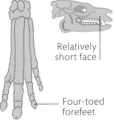

Relatively short face

Four-toed forefeet

Hyracotherium
This early equid lived in forests, where it browsed soft plant material, such as leaves and twigs, using its low-crowned unspecialized teeth. Because it was small and could easily hide among the trees and undergrowth, *Hyracotherium* didn't need to be fast.

HEIGHT
14 in (35 cm)

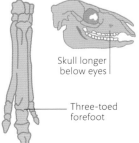

Skull longer below eyes

Three-toed forefoot

Mesophippus
In Oligocene times, the climate became drier. This opened up woodland areas, and equids such as *Mesohippus* appeared. They had longer legs and were fleeter than the forest species. They also had broader cheek teeth to cope with coarser vegetation.

HEIGHT
18 in (45 cm)

INTERIM HORSES

Mesohippus lived in North America about 37 million years ago (MYA). Its name, "middle horse," is derived from the fact that it possessed features of both early and modern equids.

During Miocene times, about 20 MYA, the climate became drier, forests declined and grasslands expanded. As a result, the equids rapidly diversified, some of the new species becoming larger and others smaller. Equids were most diverse toward the end of the Miocene period (5.3 MYA) when there were more than 12 different equid genera.

For a time, the plains of North America were occupied by both single and multi-toed grazers and browsers. However, only those with diets and hooves like those of modern horses survived to modern times.

Merychippus was one of the first grazing horses. It lived 17–11 MYA, stood around 10.2 hh (122 cm) high at the withers, and had a long face, which, like that of modern equids, housed a battery of cheek teeth. Later equids had even longer faces with larger brains and deeper jaws that contained continually growing teeth that could compensate for the abrasive action of silica

in grass. Longer legs, along with fusion of the radius and ulna (see pp.14–15), gave them more energy-efficient speed and endurance, which helped them to escape capture by the newly evolving plains predators.

Stilt-legged horses, such as *Hipparion*, appeared at the start of the Miocene period. Although polydactyl, these grazers also had only one weight-bearing toe. They were a remarkably successful group of equids, surviving some 22 million years, and colonizing Europe and Asia when the opportunity arose. However, they were unable to survive the development of modern equids and predation by hunters, such as cave hyenas.

About 12 MYA ago *Dinohippus*, a single-hooved equid resembling a modern horse, appeared in North America. It was another 8 million years before the first *Equus* species appeared but when it did, rapid diversification followed. When temperatures plummeted during the Late Pliocene to Pleistocene, they, like other equids, crossed to the Old World using temporary land bridges created by the fall in sea levels. At some point after that—and for reasons as yet unknown—all species of equid died out in North America. No equids would be seen there again until modern horses were introduced by Europeans in the 16th century.

Around 10.2 hh (122 cm) in height

MERYCHIPPUS

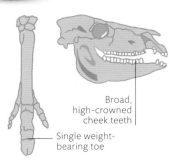

Broad, high-crowned cheek teeth

Single weight-bearing toe

Merychippus
A grazing horse with body proportions not unlike those of a modern horse, *Merychippus* lived in the open plains. Here there was no hiding from predators and speed was essential for survival. Browsing many-toed equids still lived in the wetter wooded areas.

HEIGHT
47 in (120 cm)

Human contact
After crossing from North America to Europe, equids continued to diversify and spread across Europe. Cave paintings at Lascaux, France, showing representations of horselike animals, were made before horses were domesticated.

MODERN EQUIDS

The surviving members of the genus *Equus* can be divided into two groups— the non-caballine zebras and asses, and the caballine horses (see opposite). All are grazers with one functional toe and high-crowned teeth that grow throughout life. Probably the best known of the non-caballine equids are the zebras. There are three species—Grevy's, mountain, and plains—which are easily recognized by their black-and-white-striped coats. Grevy's zebra is the largest and has the narrowest stripes. The smaller mountain zebra from southern Africa is unique in having a dewlap (fold of skin under the throat). The plains zebra has six subspecies or races, each with a different pattern of stripes, depending on where in Africa it comes from.

Wild asses are found in northern Africa, Asia, and the Middle East. Those from north Africa are critically endangered with only about 200 adults remaining. There are only two surviving subspecies—the Nubian wild ass and the Somali wild ass. It is from these African asses that the domestic donkey (see pp.12–13) is derived. The Asian asses comprise the onagers, of which there are four subspecies or races, and the Kiang. Sadly, their numbers too are in decline due to human activities.

Of the caballines, only Przewalski's horse lives in the wild in its original range. Following disappearance of the last truly wild individuals in 1969, it has been successfully reintroduced using captive-bred animals. Another wild form, the tarpan, became extinct in the 19th century.

The tarpan and the domestic horse are genetically more similar to each other than either is to Przewalski's horse. They both have 64 chromosomes (strands of DNA) whereas Przewalski's horse has 66.

Horses were first domesticated about 6,000 years ago (see pp.32–35). Since then, humans have crossbred them with donkeys to produce mules and hinnies, created breeds and types for different purposes, and transported them all over the world. In some places, this has led to thriving feral populations of horses and donkeys (burros) in areas where they never previously existed.

Maintaining wild populations
Herds of the Przewalski's horse survive in the equine's original ranges thanks to a program to introduce horses bred in captivity, such as the two shown here, into the wild.

RELATIONSHIPS OF THE HORSE FAMILY

The horse and its relatives belong to the order *Perissodactyla*, which also includes the tapirs and rhinoceros. This branching diagram shows the relationships of the surviving equids (all members of the genus *Equus*). It is superimposed on a timeline to show the sequential subdivisions as the equid line diversified. Around 4 to 5 million years ago, they divided into two groups—the non-caballine zebras and asses and the caballine horses. Caballine is derived from the Latin *caballus*, which means "of or from a horse." In evolutionary terms, some of the divisions are very recent.

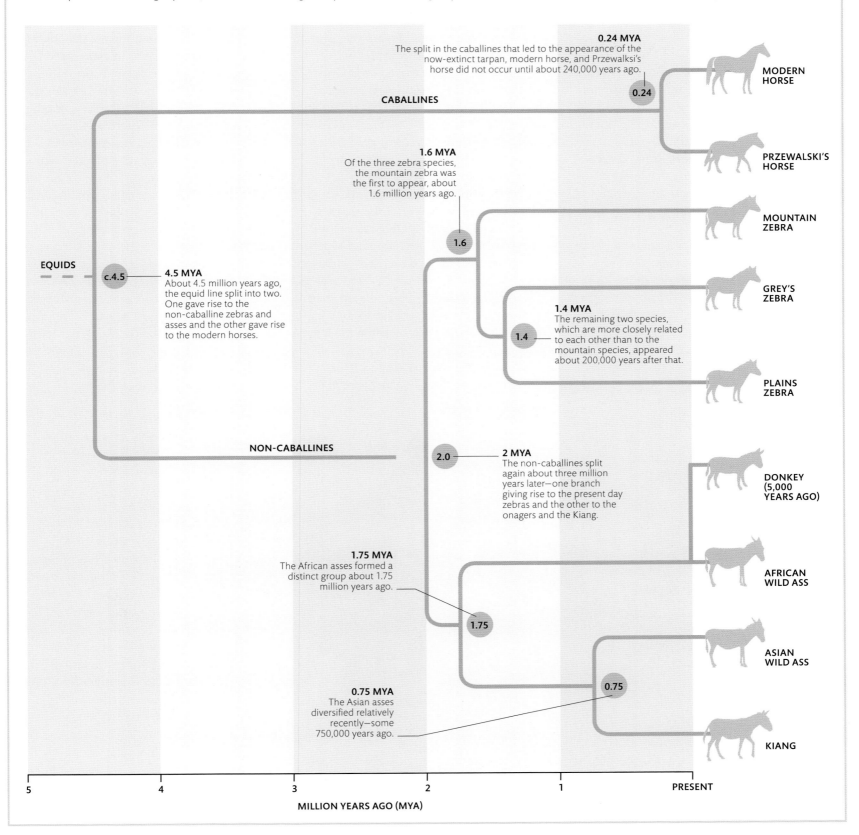

0.24 MYA
The split in the caballines that led to the appearance of the now-extinct tarpan, modern horse, and Przewalksi's horse did not occur until about 240,000 years ago.

CABALLINES

1.6 MYA
Of the three zebra species, the mountain zebra was the first to appear, about 1.6 million years ago.

EQUIDS

4.5 MYA
About 4.5 million years ago, the equid line split into two. One gave rise to the non-caballine zebras and asses and the other gave rise to the modern horses.

1.4 MYA
The remaining two species, which are more closely related to each other than to the mountain species, appeared about 200,000 years after that.

NON-CABALLINES

2 MYA
The non-caballines split again about three million years later—one branch giving rise to the present day zebras and the other to the onagers and the Kiang.

1.75 MYA
The African asses formed a distinct group about 1.75 million years ago.

0.75 MYA
The Asian asses diversified relatively recently—some 750,000 years ago.

MODERN HORSE

PRZEWALSKI'S HORSE

MOUNTAIN ZEBRA

GREY'S ZEBRA

PLAINS ZEBRA

DONKEY (5,000 YEARS AGO)

AFRICAN WILD ASS

ASIAN WILD ASS

KIANG

5   4   3   2   1   PRESENT

MILLION YEARS AGO (MYA)

Asses, donkeys, mules, and hinnies

The familiar gray-coated donkey and the two groups of wild ass (Asiatic and African) belong to the genus *Equus*, while the mule and the hinny are hybrids between a horse and a donkey. All these equines are renowned for their endurance and resilience, as well as for their supposedly stubborn nature.

ASIAN WILD ASSES

Asian wild asses (see p.11) are also called hemiones. They have reddish brown coats that are paler on the belly and legs, and may have a dark dorsal-eel stripe. They have long slender legs in comparison with their body and their ears are longer than those of a horse, but shorter than those of the donkey. All of them are endangered.

The Asian wild ass (*Equus hemionus*) has four recognized subspecies: Mongolian khulan (*E. h. hemionus*) from northern Mongolia, also known as the dziggetai; khur (*E. h. khur*) from the Thar desert in India; kulan (*E.h. kulan*) from Turkmenistan, and Persian onager (*E.h. onager*) from Iran. A fifth hemione, kiang or Tibetan wild ass, is currently a different species, *E. kiang*, but recent genetic research suggests it is another subspecies of *E. hemionus*. The subspecies differ slightly in coat color.

The Mongolian kulan is remarkable for its speed. American naturalist R. C. Andrews, who studied them in the Gobi Desert between 1922 and 1925, reported that when pursued by a car, they set off at speeds of 35–40 mph (56–64 km/h). This is faster than wolves, its natural predators.

DOMESTIC DONKEYS

Donkeys were domesticated from the African wild ass (*Equus asinus*) of North Africa (see p.11). There are two subspecies: Nubian, which may be extinct, and Somali, which stands about 14.3 hh (140 cm) at the shoulder. It is a buff-gray color, turning to iron-gray in winter. The belly and legs are paler in color, and the lower legs have zebra stripes.

A male donkey is a "jack" while the female is a "jennet" or "jenny." The average height of the common donkey is around 10 hh (102 cm) at the withers, but there are many different donkey breeds. These include miniature donkeys, such as those of Sicily and India, which are as small as 6 hh (61 cm), while the Andalusian jack donkey can reach 15 hh (152 cm). In the US, the Mammoth donkey has a current record of 17 hh (173 cm). Donkeys may be black, white, or any shade of gray, and part-colored coats are not unknown. All except the part-coloreds have a dorsal-eel stripe running down their back and a shoulder-cross at right angles to it. Unlike horses, donkeys have no chestnuts on their hindlegs; they have five lumbar vertebrae rather than six; their ears are disproportionately long; the mane is short and upright without a forelock; and their feet are small and narrow. Their tails are tufted like that of a cow, and they have flat withers, which are lower than the croup. Lastly, there is the animal's characteristic bray, which is quite unlike the neigh of the horse.

MULES

All equid species can interbreed, and produce viable offspring, but they are very rarely fertile. The exceptions are crosses between an African wild ass and a domestic donkey, and crosses between domestic and Przewalksi's horses. A mule is a cross between a jackass and a horse. This cross has long been valued, since mules can be seen in Assyrian friezes and other ancient carvings.

Mules resemble their donkey parent at the extremities—the ears, legs, feet, and tail. They have been described as having a horse's body on donkey legs, and as looking like a donkey in front and a horse behind. They are

Mule at work
In India, mules are used for all sorts of work, including drawing heavily laden carts and carrying packs in mountainous areas.

and a horse behind. They are among the most useful working animals when properly treated, and can be highly intelligent. They were particularly prized because they did not need time off for pregnancy or for tending their young.

Tough, adaptable, and resilient, mules are nearly as strong as oxen and much faster. They are stronger than horses, more capable of sustained hard work, and more economical to keep. Moreover, they adapt to heat more easily and are better able to work in hot climates than most horses. In addition, in many parts of the world a mule is more practical than a horse because of its smooth movement under saddle as well as its sure-footedness on mountain trails that would be too steep and rough for horses.

Mules are still essential in Mediterranean Europe, where they plow, carry heavy loads under pack, and can be driven in harness. At one time, they were also worked in huge numbers in the southern states of the US, where they were used for every sort of transportation as well as in agriculture.

A further advantage of the mule is that appropriate types can be created for specific purposes, by selecting suitable mares and putting them to a comparatively small range of jackass types. For instance, the Poitevin jackass, crossed with the Poitevin mare, produces heavy draft mules (see p.73), while the smaller Maltese and Indian jackasses will get lighter or heavier types, according to the mares with which they are mated. The big Poitevin and the American

Mammoth mules may stand at over 16 hh (163 cm), while those employed in pack companies will be around 14 hh (142 cm).

HINNIES

A hinny is the result of a mating between a horse and a jenny. They are usually smaller than mules, perhaps owing to the female donkey being small. Their head is horselike with slightly longer ears and their manes and tails are also often horselike. Their feet are hard but narrow and straight-sided, like a donkey's. Hinnies may be any color, but are usually gray. Hinnies lack the mule's hybrid vigor, and so are less valuable as workers. They are also harder to breed.

Khur
The very swift and enduring khur (*Equus hemionus khur*), also called Indian onager, has an estimated population of 3,900.

Persian ass
The Persian onager (*Equus hemionus onager*), the "wild ass" of Biblical times, is found in Iran and has a tiny population of about 600.

Kiang
The Tibetan wild ass or kiang (*Equus kiang*) lives in west and central China, northeast Pakistan, and northern India and Nepal. Population 60,000–70,000.

African wild ass
The ancestor of the domestic donkey lives in dry areas of the Horn of Africa. There are only a few hundred left in the wild.

Donkey
The donkey has been domesticated for about 5,000 years. There is an estimated population of 40 million donkeys worldwide.

Mule
Sure-footed and hardy, mules are considered highly intelligent and are still bred for work all over the world. Different parents produce mules with different physical characteristics.

The skeleton

The horse's skeleton has the same key components found in all mammal skeletons, but over time these have changed in response to the horse's changing environment. For example, it reflects the fact that they live in the open, feed on grass, and are flight animals.

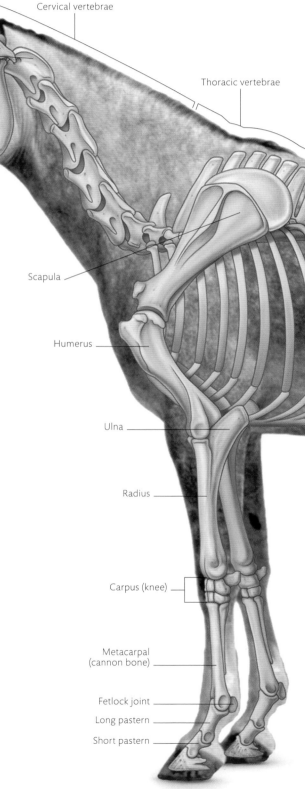

BASIC STRUCTURE

As with all mammals, the horse's skeleton reflects its lifestyle. The long, muscular neck allows the horse to browse on grass and among scrubby plants, which are part of its natural diet. It also helps with balance when the horse moves fast. As well as its distinctive long limbs, the horse has a large rib cage, which houses a big heart and lungs, making it capable of traveling long distances with great speed and stamina.

SKULL

The skull is long and narrow with the eyes set high and at the sides. This position means that the horse can graze while still having good all-around vision for looking out for predators (see p.25). The skull comprises a number of separate bones. These grow by the addition of bone at their margins until the horse is mature, at which point they fuse to form a single unit housing the brain, eyes, and nostrils. The two halves of the lower jaw also fuse together to make the mandible, which can move up and down and sideways. The jaw contains long rows of teeth (up to 40) allowing it to grind down grass into small particles before it is

swallowed. The long muzzle has plenty of space for the sinuses and the other organs required for its acute sense of smell.

SPINE

The horse's body is long and athletic. There are seven cervical vertebrae, making up the neck. The back of the skull fits into a deep cut-like depression in the atlas (first cervical vertebra), creating a joint that allows the horse's head to move up and down. A short peg on the front of the axis (second cervical vertebra) fits into the back of the atlas, and this enables the head to move from side to side. The remaining five cervical vertebrae are linked with shallow ball-and-socket joints that mean the horse can turn its head and scratch at its flanks as well as reach down to graze. Along with the tail (caudal) vertebrae, the neck is the most mobile part of the spine. The horse uses it to alter its center of balance, particularly when cornering at speed.

There are 18 thoracic vertebrae. They have long spines (processes) on their upper edge. At the shoulder, these shape the withers. Facets on the sides of these vertebrae hold the heads of the ribs. The first eight ribs are also attached to the breastbone (sternum), while the remainder are attached to each other in a curve by their cartilages. This

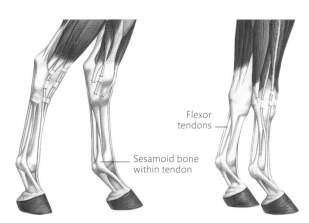

Sesamoid bones
Small bones are embedded in the tendons near the joint surfaces. They move the tendon further away from the joint axis, which reduces friction and increases leverage. They also prevent the tendon flattening when the joint bends.

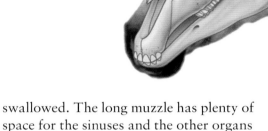

Atlas
Axis
Orbit
Nasal bone
Cervical vertebrae
Thoracic vertebrae
Scapula
Humerus
Ulna
Radius
Carpus (knee)
Metacarpal (cannon bone)
Fetlock joint
Long pastern
Short pastern

Flexor tendons
Sesamoid bone within tendon

creates a strong protective cage for the heart and lungs as well as other organs, such as the liver.

The six lumbar vertebra have long processes on either side, which protect the kidneys. Strong and relatively rigid, this part of the spine enhances the driving force created by the back legs. It also bears the weight of the horse's digestive system (see pp.20–21). The lumbar vertebrae are followed by five sacral vertebrae, which are fused into one bone and to which the pelvic girdle is attached by numerous tough short ligaments.

LIMBS

The forelimbs of the horse are attached to the body by muscles and can move back and forth over the rib cage, which gives the horse a long stride. The movement of the front legs is coordinated with the breathing when the horse moves at speed. The scapula has a flat underside to allow this sliding movement, and a substantial cartilage along the top edge increases the area for muscle attachment. The humerus slopes back from the scapula to the elbow where it joins the radius and ulna. The ulna is reduced in size and fused to the radius, an adaptation that aids rapid flight.

The hindlegs are joined to the pelvis by a ball and socket joint, which enables the horse to take long strides, stepping under its body. The upper limb bones are robust. The femur slopes forward from the pelvis and articulates with the tibia, which has a very reduced fibula running part way down its outer side. The joint between these two bones is called the stifle and it is the site of the largest sesamoid bone—the patella (knee cap). The joint at the base of the tibia—called the hock—is equivalent to the human ankle.

The lower limb bones of the horse have a single "toe" with splint bones (the vestiges of other toes) at either side. Horses have long lower leg bones, which further increases their stride length. Those of the front legs are more robust and shorter than those of the hindlegs because the horse carries more weight on its front end.

The lack of bone in the lower legs makes the horse's limbs lighter and reduces the need for muscle (see pp.16–17). It also makes them more rigid, reflecting the horse's tendency to take straight lines of flight from predators.

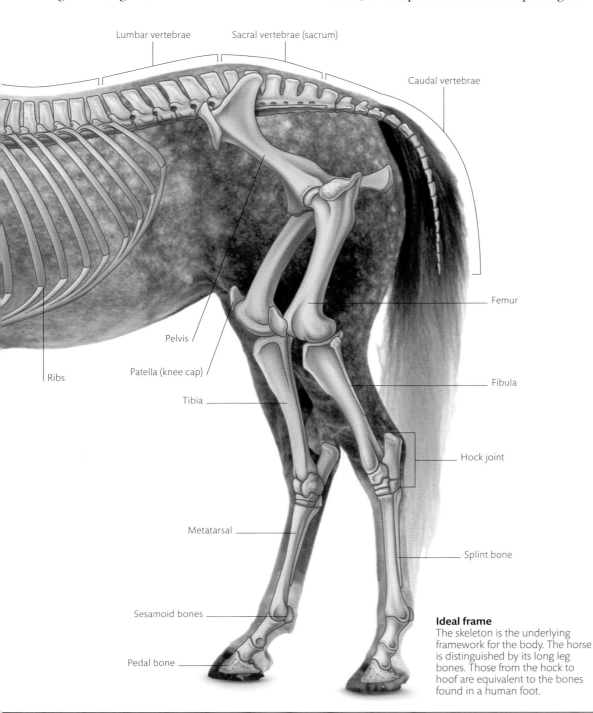

Lumbar vertebrae

Sacral vertebrae (sacrum)

Caudal vertebrae

Femur

Pelvis

Fibula

Patella (knee cap)

Ribs

Tibia

Hock joint

Metatarsal

Splint bone

Sesamoid bones

Pedal bone

Ideal frame
The skeleton is the underlying framework for the body. The horse is distinguished by its long leg bones. Those from the hock to hoof are equivalent to the bones found in a human foot.

HOOVES

Made of tough horn, the hoof wall surrounds and protects the mechanisms and bones of the foot. In both fore and hind limbs, the hoof core is a relatively small wedge-shaped bone, called the pedal bone. In the front legs, it is broad and rounded to take the greater weight of the front of the horse, while in the hinds, it is narrower and more steeply angled to the ground to increase the forward thrust of these legs.

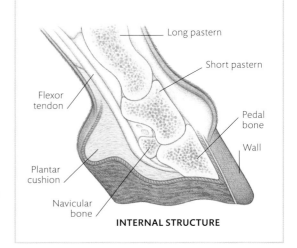

Long pastern

Short pastern

Flexor tendon

Pedal bone

Wall

Plantar cushion

Navicular bone

INTERNAL STRUCTURE

Muscle structure

Muscles are elastic tissues that enable all animals to move and function. Ligaments and tendons are bands of tough, fibrous tissue called collagen. Ligaments hold the bones and joints together, while tendons store and release energy, reducing the work of the muscles.

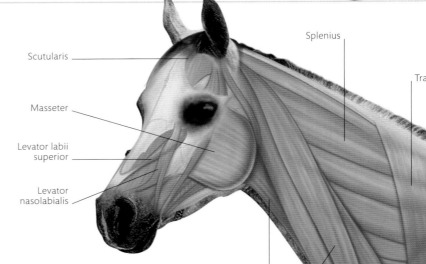

HOW MUSCLES WORK

Muscles can be involuntary, such as those that operate the heart and digestive tract, or voluntary, such as those that make the legs move. Around the joints, muscles work in antagonistic (opposing) pairs. Each pair consists of a flexor and an extensor. In a leg, for example, the flexor contracts to flex, or bend, the joint and move the leg back. The extensor contracts to extend, or straighten, the joint and move the leg forward. When one muscle contracts, the other in the pair relaxes.

The muscles are made up of different types of fibers, which have varying amounts of energy and rates of fatigue. In the horse there are two main types: slow-twitch and fast-twitch fibers. Fast-twitch fibers produce bursts of energy and these give a horse its speed, but this can only be maintained for relatively short periods of time as the fast-twitch fibers fatigue quickly. Slow-twitch fibers can work for longer periods of time without tiring and so have more endurance. There are differences in the ratio of these fibers in the muscles of different breeds of horse. For example, Thoroughbreds—known for their short bursts of energy at top speeds—have a lower proportion of slow twitch muscle fibers compared to Arabs, which are renowned for their ability to travel long distances without tiring.

THE LEGS

Deep muscles in the front legs secure the front limbs to the body (there is no bony connection, see pp.14–15) and support the horse's head and neck as well. This is a considerable task, since two thirds of a horse's weight is at the front end.

The muscles also act as shock absorbers for the limbs. Below the knee, the front legs are mainly tendons and ligaments. The long tendons in the lower legs link the muscles to the bones in the foot and lower leg to allow movement. The lack of muscles in the lower legs reduces their weight, making them more energy efficient, but

Absorbing impact
The horse's leg is capable of withstanding a great amount of stress, or example when galloping or landing after a jump. The muscles, tendons, and joints help absorb the shock and prevent injury.

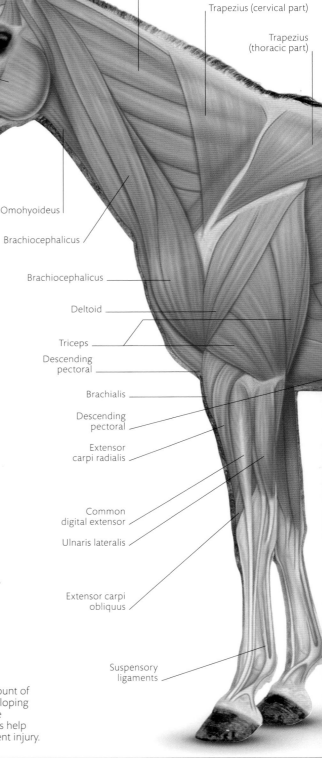

Scutularis

Masseter

Levator labii superior

Levator nasolabialis

Omohyoideus

Brachiocephalicus

Splenius

Trapezius (cervical part)

Trapezius (thoracic part)

Brachiocephalicus

Deltoid

Triceps

Descending pectoral

Brachialis

Descending pectoral

Extensor carpi radialis

Common digital extensor

Ulnaris lateralis

Extensor carpi obliquus

Suspensory ligaments

it also means they are more vulnerable to damage from jarring. There are large muscle masses in the hindlegs to provide forward movement. In the hindlegs, there are no muscles below the hock (see p.15). Again the lower limbs are activated by tendons rather than muscles, which saves energy and reduces weight.

Ligaments are bands of fibrous tissue and are less stretchy than tendons. Ligaments often reduce the movement of a joint or tendon and so prevent over-extension, which would cause injury. In the legs, the check ligament limits the movement of the deep

flexor tendon, for example. However, in horses, the ligaments also perform another role. The suspensory ligament runs down the back of the legs—from the knee to the fetlock in the front legs and from the hock to the fetlock in the hindlegs. The fetlock joint is under permanent downward pressure, and the suspensory ligament prevents it from collapse. Along with the volar annular ligament, which wraps around the entire fetlock joint, and the sesamoid bones (see p.14), it forms the suspensory apparatus, which supports the fetlock when the leg moves. As the foot touches the ground,

the fetlock joint is pressed downward, tightening and stretching these tendons and ligaments. As the horse's weight shifts off the leg, the effect is similar to an elastic band being released, effectively snapping the hoof off the ground.

ENERGY EFFICIENCY
The absence of muscle in the lower legs is one way that a horse is energy efficient, another is the way in which the tendons and ligaments are used reduce the work of the muscles.

In the wild, when a horse lies down to rest, it is vulnerable to predators because its large body takes effort and time to lift off the ground. Although horses do rest by lying down, they have evolved in such a way that they can also sleep standing up, thanks to a system called the stay apparatus. Found in each of the limbs, this a system of ligaments and tendons that can lock the main joints in position, which allows the surrounding muscles to rest. This reduces the energy required for the horse to stand up and avoids muscle fatigue.

Tensor fasciae latae

Superficial gluteal

Biceps femoris

Latissimus dorsi

Semitendinosus

External abdominal oblique

Serratus ventralis (thoracic)

Gastrocnemius

Deep digital flexor

Extensor digitorum lateralis

Deep digital flexor tendon

Extensor digitorum longus

Tendon of extensor digitorum longus

Palmar anular ligament

Movement and support
The voluntary muscles of the body work in conjunction with the skeleton, joints, and tendons to carry and move the horse, and they govern the quality of its actions.

SPINAL SUPPORT

The neck is shaped and supported by the strong, ropelike nuchal ligament, which runs along the crest of the neck above the vertebral column and attaches to the back of the skull. Fibrous, sheetlike branches radiate from this ligament down to the spinous processes of the neck vertebra, creating a strong support system. This ligament is energy efficient, reducing the work of the muscles that raise and lower the head. The supraspinous ligament continues from the nuchal ligament to the top of the tail. Attaching to the top of each vertebra, it stabilizes the spine.

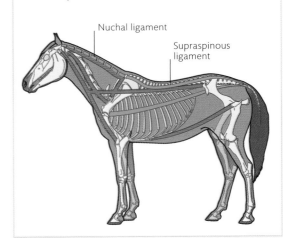

Nuchal ligament

Supraspinous ligament

Gaits

A gait is a particular sequence of footfalls by which a horse moves and alters its speed. Most horses have four natural gaits: walk, trot, canter, and gallop. Some have additional specialized gaits, which usually occur naturally in a breed, but may also be taught or enhanced.

The four natural gaits should be regular and rhythmical. The walk has a distinct four-beat rhythm—each individual footfall can be heard and felt by the rider. The rib cage moves from side to side. The trot is a two-beat gait where the horse puts one pair of diagonal feet to the ground at the same time and then springs onto the other diagonal pair. It is an up-down movement. The canter is a three-beat gait where one of the back feet lands first, then the other back foot and the diagonal front foot land simultaneously, followed by the remaining front foot. It is a rocking forward and back movement. The gallop is usually a four-beat gait, though the beats may become blurred and the sequence varies according to speed. Again the movement is rocking, but very fast.

The walk has an average speed of 4 mph (6 km/h); the trot is about 8 mph (13 km/h); the canter is 10–17 mph (16–27 km/h); and the gallop is 25–30 mph (40–48 km/h), although a horse cannot gallop for an hour.

Walk
Four distinct and regular beats: for example begun with the left hind leg: 1. left hind; 2. left fore; 3. right hind; 4. right fore.

Trot
The trot is a two-beat gait: for example 1. right fore and left hind—moment of suspension (all feet off the ground)— 2. left fore and right hind. In English-style riding, the rider rises out of the saddle in trot.

Canter
Three beats: for example beginning on the left hind, the sequence is: 1. left hind, 2. left diagonal (left fore and right hind touch the ground together), 3. right fore (called the leading leg).

Gallop
Usually four beats, with the sequence varying according to the speed. When the right fore is the leading leg, the sequence is: 1. left hind, 2. right hind, 3. left fore, 4. right fore, followed by suspension when all four feet are off the ground.

SPECIALIZED GAITS

Though largely associated with the American breeds, specialized gaits are also found in Asia and parts of Europe. Most of these are based on the lateral ambling or pacing movement in which the horse moves its legs in lateral rather than diagonal pairs. Some of the Russian breeds pace naturally, and Spain was the home of smooth-gaited horses exhibiting a swift, lateral running walk that was much in demand throughout Europe. The most famous were reared in Galicia and their descendants, the Galiceno of Mexico,

Harness pacer
The American Standardbred is the fastest harness racer in the world. It is a pacing horse, which means that it uses the legs in lateral pairs.

are still noted for their natural gait. Both the Kathiawari and Marwari of western India retain a natural lateral pace, the fast and comfortable *revaal*, but it is in the Americas that the gaits have been refined and perfected. In South America, the famous Peruvian Paso exemplifies the gaited tradition.

The most unique grouping belongs to North America. Along with the Standardbred harness racer, the world's fastest pacing horse, there are the three gaited breeds: the Saddlebred, the Missouri Fox Trotter, and the Tennessee Walker. The three classic gaits associated with these breeds are pace, rack, and running walk. Pacing is a two-beat gait where the legs move in lateral pairs. The Standardbred paces at 145 seconds per mile (1.6 km). The Saddlebred's rack is a fast walk (four beats). This breed can also perform a slow lateral pace (two beats). The running walk of the Missouri Fox Trotter is a four-beat diagonal broken gait, while that of the Tennessee Walking Horse is a gliding four-beat gait of around 6–9 mph (9–14 km/h).

Saddlebred rack
The rack is an expressive gait in which the legs are lifted high with each beat. The footfall is the same as in walk, but the tempo is different.

WESTERN RIDING GAITS

The development of the Western gaits, which are entirely suited to the purpose for which the cow-horse was required and the often inhospitable terrain in which it lived, is an example of how horse and man can work together. The key gaits are a jog, which is a slow, low trot (two beats), very different from the sharp up-down trot seen in Britain, for example. Jog trots, which allow the rider to sit in the saddle, rather than rising, are, however, seen in other European countries. The lope is a slow, smooth canter (three beats), again long and low, with the horse's head carried low. This allows it to canter for long periods without tiring.

Body systems

The horse has long been adapted as a prey animal living on open plains and feeding mainly on grass. Its body has developed a way of digesting tough cellulose, while its organs can supply and sustain tremendous energy at short notice.

HEART AND LUNGS

As with all mammals, the heart is the powerhouse of the horse's circulatory, or cardiovascular, system. In a horse of around 15 hh (152 cm) that weighs 1,000 lb (450 kg), the heart weighs 10 lb (4.5 kg). It has a resting rate of about 30–40 beats per minute, during which time it pumps up to 64 pints (40 liters) of blood.

The horse has a special adaptation for flight. When it is quietly grazing, the red blood cells in its circulation are at about 35–40 percent of their maximum, while the blood in the spleen is 80 percent red blood cells. When it gallops, the spleen is squeezed by surrounding muscles, releasing its oxygen-dense blood into the circulation. This gives the horse a great boost of energy to allow it to flee danger.

The frog of the foot performs an interesting function in the cardiovascular system. As the horse's hoof touches the ground, it acts as a pump to push the blood back up the legs toward the heart.

Although the rib cage of a horse is large, the lungs do not have as much room as might be thought as they share the space with the heart and major blood vessels. In addition, when a horse is moving at a canter or gallop, the diaphragm expands into the rib cage as far forward as the sixth rib, which further restricts room for the lungs. This movement of the diaphragm draws air into and out of the lungs. When a horse is at rest, this work is done by the rib cage. Horses breath in rhythm with their movements, so at a canter

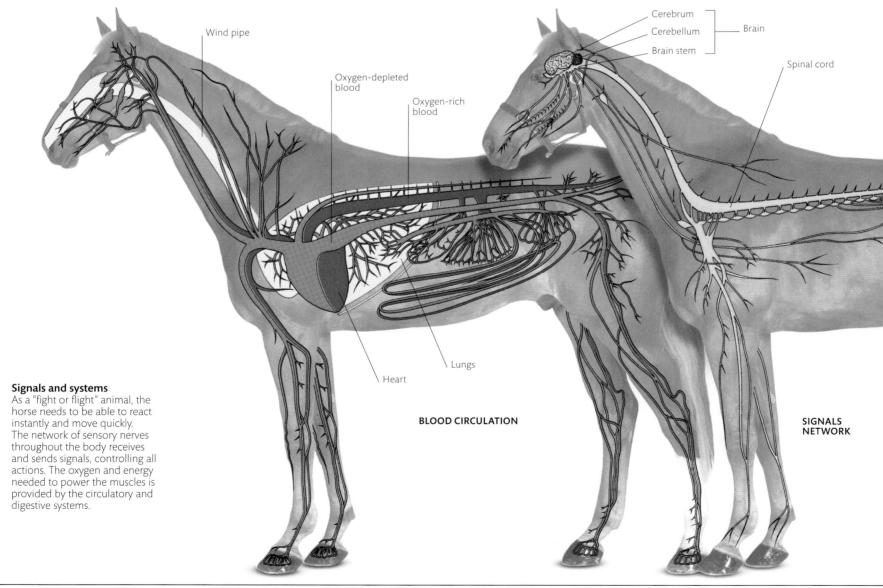

Wind pipe

Oxygen-depleted blood

Oxygen-rich blood

Cerebrum

Cerebellum

Brain stem

Brain

Spinal cord

Lungs

Heart

BLOOD CIRCULATION

SIGNALS NETWORK

Signals and systems
As a "fight or flight" animal, the horse needs to be able to react instantly and move quickly. The network of sensory nerves throughout the body receives and sends signals, controlling all actions. The oxygen and energy needed to power the muscles is provided by the circulatory and digestive systems.

they breath on each stride—comparatively infrequently—and are capable of taking in up to 80 pints (45 liters) of air per second.

NERVOUS SYSTEM

The nervous system coordinates all the activities of the horse's body. It receives information via the senses and sends instructions to relevant systems to perform the required tasks. Most of the nervous system's work is automatic. For example, breathing is an automatic task, which is controlled by the brain stem. The main part of the brain, the cerebrum, does the thinking.

A horse's brain weighs about half that of a human. However, the cerebellum is quite large. This is the part of the brain that controls muscle activity and balance. It gives horses, like all flight animals, the ability to run within an hour of being born.

DIGESTION PROCESS

Horses chew their food well before they swallow it. They have grinding teeth which grow continuously until old age. These have a large flat surface to break down their coarse food. Horses cannot vomit, which makes them vulnerable to poisons, and they can get food stuck in their throat, a condition called choke (see p.346). This is rarely fatal, but is distressing for them.

The horse has a small stomach and must eat continuously to get the nutrition it needs (trickle feeding). The food passes quickly to the small intestine. The horse's main foods are high in cellulose, which is the sugar found in the cell walls of grasses and other plants. Most mammals—including humans—are unable to obtain this sugar through digestion, but the horse has an organ that is devoted to this task. The cecum is found where the

large and small intestine meet and is a large saclike organ, over 3 ft (1 m) long, where the cellulose is fermented by gut bacteria. Even with the help of the cecum, the horse still cannot digest all of its food. However, it is thought that this organ allows horses to graze on a variety of very different plant materials, including bark and twigs. This is in contrast to ruminants, such as cows, which can digest more of their food in their four stomachs—up to 30 percent more—but prefer softer materials. In comparison to cows, horses can also eat more food since it takes 48 hours to pass through their gut, compared to 70–90 hours in a cow.

The digestive system of a horse is very large, with over 65½ ft (20 m) of small intestine and 23 ft (7 m) of large intestine. This has two 180° bends, where food can easily get stuck and cause colic (see p.346).

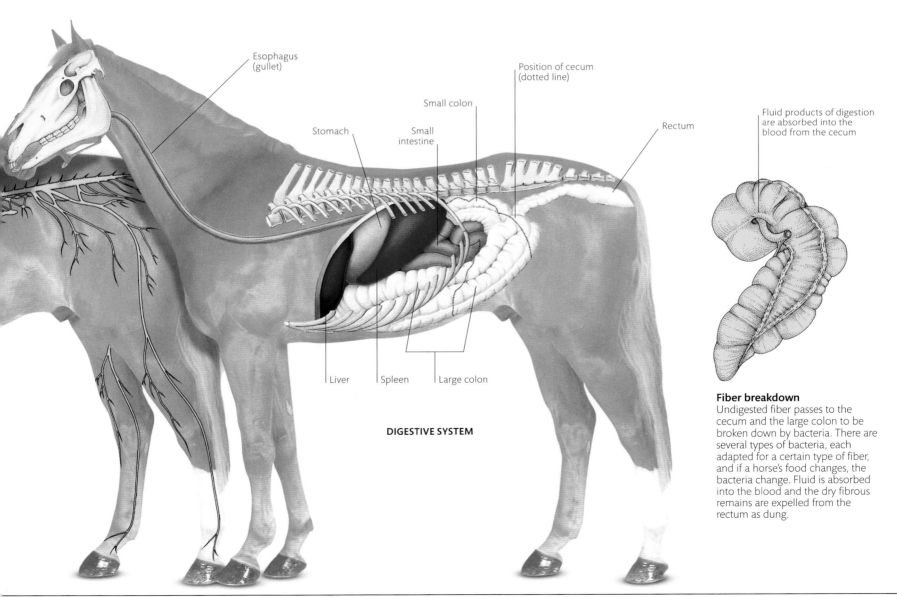

Esophagus (gullet)

Position of cecum (dotted line)

Small colon

Stomach

Small intestine

Rectum

Fluid products of digestion are absorbed into the blood from the cecum

Liver   Spleen   Large colon

DIGESTIVE SYSTEM

Fiber breakdown
Undigested fiber passes to the cecum and the large colon to be broken down by bacteria. There are several types of bacteria, each adapted for a certain type of fiber, and if a horse's food changes, the bacteria change. Fluid is absorbed into the blood and the dry fibrous remains are expelled from the rectum as dung.

Markings and coat colors

Like all its other physical traits, a horse's coat color is determined by its genetic makeup, which is inherited equally from its sire and dam. Unlike wild horses, the different breeds of domestic horse are bred to conform to a breed standard and this often stipulates a particular color or colors.

WHAT MAKES COLOR?

Genes carry the instructions that determine a horse's color and they are found in all cells. These instructions (alleles) are inherited from both parents and may be the same (homozygous), in which case offspring will be the same color as the parents, or different (heterozygous), in which case the dominant color allele prevails and the recessive color allele is effectively masked.

In horses, gray dominates black, bay, and chestnut; bay dominates black; and chestnut is recessive to all colors. Therefore, the combination of a bay allele and a chestnut one will result in a bay foal because the bay allele is dominant. If two offspring of this combination were themselves mated, the two recessive chestnut alleles (one from each animal) might be united to produce a chestnut foal. The mating of two chestnuts always produces a chestnut foal.

Other genes, called dilution genes, can also effect coat color. The recessive allele, when inherited from one parent, lightens the coat. For example, a bay color instruction becomes dun and a chestnut instruction becomes palomino.

Another gene, if dominant, inhibits color formation in skin as well as hair and causes albinism. The genes that influence white marking on horse's legs (called socks and stockings) and faces (see opposite) are not fully understood.

THE EFFECT OF BREEDING

As a result of selective breeding, over time the offspring of purebred horses may only carry genetic coding for particular colors, and so they will breed "true"—always the same color(s). This is even more likely if numbers have fallen very low at any time in the breed's history as a small breeding stock

further reduces genetic variation. Breeds that are predominantly one color include the Lipizzaner and Friesian.

In most cases, horses are not bred solely for their color, but exceptions include palomino (see p.214) and some spotted horses. Breeding for color can be at the expense of other desirable physical traits. Others, and particularly those without a closed studbook or without a studbook at all, usually display greater variation in color (and other traits).

GRAY

Horses that are gray have white hair, often with a few other colored hairs mixed in, and a black skin. They are born a dark color,

Basic colors
Color is important when describing a horse, and its overall color is determined by a combination of coat and skin color, as well as that of its mane and tail.

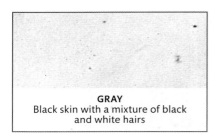
GRAY
Black skin with a mixture of black and white hairs

ROAN
Black or red body, with some white hair

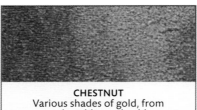
CHESTNUT
Various shades of gold, from pale gold to red gold

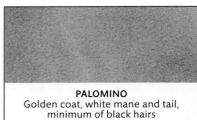
PALOMINO
Golden coat, white mane and tail, minimum of black hairs

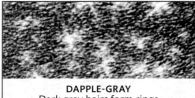
DAPPLE-GRAY
Dark gray hairs form rings on a gray base

PIEBALD OR TOBIANO
Usually large, irregular areas of black and white

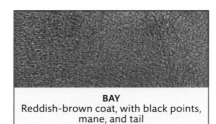
BAY
Reddish-brown coat, with black points, mane, and tail

DUN
Yellow, blue, or mouse, depending on the diffusion of pigment

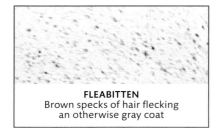
FLEABITTEN
Brown specks of hair flecking an otherwise gray coat

SKEWBALD OR TOBIANO
Large white patches with any color except black

BLACK
Black hair, occasionally with white marks

BROWN
Mixed black and brown hairs, black mane, tail, and legs

such as black or brown, and become paler with age. Gray is a dominant allele. Fleabitten is a variation of gray with heavy flecking in another color.

BAY
This is a horse in various shades of red (as dark as brown) with black mane, tail, and points (lower legs). There is an allele that, if dominant, confines black hair to these areas (see black). Bays that also have a dilution allele have a dun coat with black points.

BLACK
Black is a rare color in horses. It results from the presence of the gene for black hair in combination with the uncommon recessive allele for black points.

CHESTNUT
Horses that lack any black hair are always shades of red (chestnut), from bright to liver. They have manes and tails in various shades of brown to yellow.

PALOMINO AND CREMELLO
These colors are caused by alleles that dilute the basic color, which is red (chestnut). Cremellos have pink skin and often have blue eyes. They occur when the recessive form of the dilution gene is inherited from both parents, rather than from just one parent, as in the palomino. All horses have the potential to have blue eyes.

ROAN
A roan horse has a mixture of dark and white hairs. Like gray, roan is a dominant characteristic, but roans are born with the white coloring. Blue-roans have black hairs with white, while strawberry roans have red hairs with white. The genetics of this coloring is less well understood.

COLORED OR PINTO
Coats with white patches and underlying pink skin are called various names. For example, in the UK there is piebald (black and white) and skewbald (any other color and white) and, in the US, tobiano (white and any color). Colored or pinto horses are born with the white patches and these will remain the same throughout their life. Gene mutations cause these patterns.

WHITE FACE **STAR**

SNIP **STRIPE**

BLAZE

Facial marks
Many horses have white marks on their face. These can vary from a tiny snip to a white face. Some breed standards call for no white markings.

APPALOOSA OR SPOTTED
Coats that consist of many small spots and flecks are called appaloosa, or spotted, and develop as the horse matures, becoming more or less distinct. Spotted horses often also have spotted skin and striped hooves. In these cases, a gene mutation is

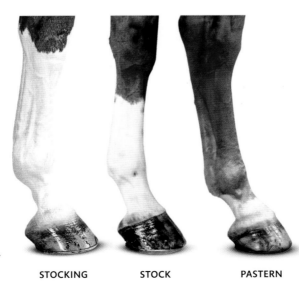

STOCKING **STOCK** **PASTERN**

responsible. The effect of the allele depends on whether a horse inherits the spotted mutation from both parents or just one.

BODY AND FACE MARKINGS
Many horses have one or more patches of white hair on the face. These have been given names to help with identification of individual horses. The main white facial markings are shown above, and they can appear in combination too, such as a snip with a star.

On the legs, the different amounts of white have also been given names (see below). If there is a small amount of white hair at the coronet (see p.44) in an otherwise dark coat, this is an ermine mark. Zebra stripes are dark marks on the legs.

Leg markings
Leg markings include stocking, where the white hair extends over the knee; sock, where it ends below the knee; and pastern, where the white hairs only reach as far as the fetlock. Black marks at the knee and below are called points.

The senses

Like humans, horses have five senses: taste, touch, hearing, smell, and sight. In the horse these senses are far more developed than in humans. There is also that enigmatic sixth sense, a heightened perception, which is apparent in the horse but rare in our species.

TASTE

While very little is known about the horse's sense of taste, we know it is associated with touch and plays an important role in mutual grooming. We presume that horses like sweet things—and feed them sweetened foods for example—but there is no proof to support this assumption. Many horses also appear to relish strong-tasting and even bitter plants, foraging for them in hedgerows and on old pastures. They may even eat tree bark and twigs.

TOUCH

The sense of touch is an important means of communication between horses, and between humans and horses (see pp.26–27). Mutual grooming is concerned with touch and strengthens the bonds between horses in a group. Both the whiskers on the muzzle and the long hairs around the eyes are important for sensing nearby objects. They enable the horse to evaluate by touch objects that he cannot see, allowing him to graze carefully around unpalatable plants, for example. Horse riding relies on the horse's extreme sensitivity in its body and mouth. The leg aids, for instance, exert pressures on the receptor cells on a horse's sides—and a horse can distinguish between slight changes in pressure when being asked to perform different dressage movements.

A rider's hands communicate with the horse's mouth by touch, using the rein and bit.

Horses have an acute sense of touch over their entire bodies, which enables them to detect even a single fly and whisk it away with their tail with incredible accuracy.

HEARING

A horse's hearing is far more sensitive than that of humans. A horse's head may be likened to a sound-box served by the large,

Eating gorse
It is common for horses to eat plants other than grass, including gorse, bark, and leaves. They may simply like the taste or texture, but it could also be an indication that the horse is bored or lacking something in its diet.

extremely mobile ears that can be rotated to pick up sounds from any direction. When a horse hears a sound, it lifts its head high and often looks toward the source without turning its whole body, which would make it less able to run away if the sound turned out to be indicative of danger. The highly

Ears pricked forward

LISTENING AHEAD

Ears back

LISTENING BEHIND

One ear pricked forward and one back

ALERT TO ALL SOUNDS

mobile ears along with the long, flexible neck allow the horse to see and hear what is happening behind it. Horses can also move their ears independently.

The horse is responsive to the human voice, making this a valuable training aid. Our voices can be effective in reassuring and calming a frightened horse or letting it know we are not a threat. Talking to a horse can also be used as a reprimand.

SMELL

The horse's sense of smell is similarly acute and, like hearing, it plays an essential part in a horse's day to day life. It is also an important part of its defensive system. Horses use their smell to recognize each other and their surroundings. It is possible that an acute sense of smell is related to the horse's pronounced homing instinct. It seems likely that they use it in conjunction with their excellent memory to recognize

Whiskers
A horse's whiskers are used to sense nearby objects. Therefore, it is important that you never cut whiskers when clipping a horse, even if the horse is being prepared for a show.

landmarks and so find their way back to their home territory. Smell also plays a part in sexual behavior (see pp.28–29) and social interactions.

Horses also use their keen sense of smell to detect and avoid undesirable items in their food. They are particularly sensitive to the smell of blood, and will often display

SIXTH SENSE

There are numerous examples of horses demonstrating an almost inexplicable perception. The reluctance of horses to pass reputedly haunted places is well documented. They also have an uncanny ability to sense impending danger and they are often hypersensitive in detecting the mood of their rider. Much of this can be explained by their ability to read body language. In the early 20th century, there was a horse called Clever Hans that was claimed to have been able to perform arithmetic and other intellectual tasks. An investigation revealed that the horse was not actually performing these mental tasks, but was watching the reactions of his human observers.

signs of disquiet and nervousness if they have to pass an animal squashed on the road, for instance.

SIGHT

Equine sight is unusual in many respects. The horse's eyes are large in comparison with those of other animals, such as pigs and elephants, suggesting a heavy reliance upon sight. They have nearly 360-degree vision and their eyes are naturally focused on the distance, always on the lookout for approaching predators. They are very sensitive to movement. Horses focus on particular objects by raising and lowering the head, rather than altering the shape of the eye lens. Because the eyes are placed on the side of the head, a horse has wide lateral vision but this is uniocular rather than binocular, which means a horse doesn't have a very good depth of field. When they look forward, they do have a small area of binocular vision.

A horse's eyes see independently of each other, and, when grazing, they have nearly

Field of vision
Horses have almost 360-degree vision and 64 degrees of this is binocular vision, while the rest is 146 degrees monocular vision on both the left and right. This gives horses living in the wild the best chance to spot predators.

all-around vision without needing to raise or turn their head. Although not nocturnal, horses can see quite well in the dark due to the size of their eyes. Horses do, however, have a "blind spot" directly behind them, where they cannot see. It is important to take care behind horses as they may not see you, although they use their other senses to know you are there.

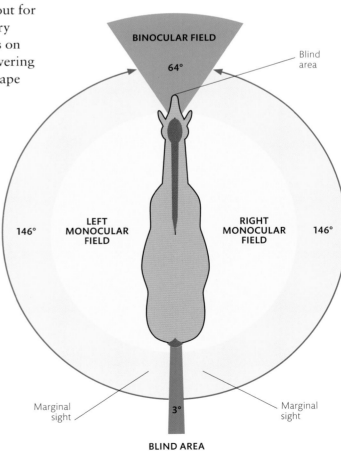

BINOCULAR FIELD

64°

Blind area

146° LEFT MONOCULAR FIELD

RIGHT MONOCULAR FIELD 146°

Marginal sight

3°

Marginal sight

BLIND AREA

Behavior and communication

Horses have a sophisticated language of communication, which involves physical and tactile signals—body language—such as the laying back of ears and mutual grooming. They communicate through smell too. Although horses also make sounds, these are thought to be of lesser importance.

THE IMPORTANCE OF SMELL

Foals instinctively recognize the smell of their dam (mother). Members of a group of horses are identified by what may be a group odor. Smell also plays a significant part in sexual behavior. The pheromone sent by a mare in estrus is a clear message to the stallion that she is ready to mate. The mare also sends physical messages, such as the flashing of the vulva, and the adoption of the mating posture, when she holds the tail to one side. She communicates just as clearly if she is not ready to accept the stallion's attentions, by baring her teeth and attempting to bite or kick him. She may further indicate her displeasure vocally by squealing. Although horses are not as territorial as other animals, stallions do scent-mark their territory with urine and piles of feces. The stallion will also urinate over the urine or feces of mares within his group, which sends a clear message to outsiders that the mares are part of his harem.

FLEHMEN

Stallions check the reproduction cycle of mares by sniffing their vulva and urine. As the mare approaches estrus, the stallion becomes excited and indulges in a form of foreplay where he licks the mare and engages in tactile stimulation. This may be accompanied by flehmen, the peculiar curling back of the upper lip, which enhances their ability to smell (see photo, above). The air is transferred to Jacobson's organ situated above the roof of the mouth at the base of the nasal cavity.

Flehmen is not always associated with sexual excitement. It can be provoked in both sexes by strong and unusual smells and tastes, such as garlic, especially when a horse encounters them for the first time.

VOCAL COMMUNICATION

Horses communicate vocally, although in a limited way. Horses may snort when they see or smell something that interests them particularly or something that is potentially dangerous. Squeals and grunts are usually signs of aggression or excitement. Horses whinny for separated companions, and

Mutual grooming
Grooming each other is common among horses. To initiate a grooming session, one horse usually approaches the other and nuzzles it at the shoulder to suggest grooming might be pleasant.

may whinny out of excitement. A mare will whicker softly to reassure her foal, and both sexes make the same noise in anticipation of being fed or receiving a titbit. Some horses even learn to attract human attention by whinnying loudly if their feed is delayed.

TASTE AND TOUCH

Horses also communicate through the closely related senses of taste and touch. They do this when they groom each other, which creates a friendly relationship. An extension of this is to use their heads to give each other a nudge, which might be a way of saying "get out of the way" or just "I'm here." They will do this to humans too. We seek to communicate or introduce ourselves by touching and patting horses. Grooming is another way to communicate with horses and it builds up a relationship between us and them.

UNDERSTANDING SIGNALS

It is not difficult for us to learn some of a horse's body language. For example, it is easy to understand that a horse standing with a hind foot rested, head down, ears slightly back, lower lip hanging, and eyes partially closed, is in a relaxed state.

The posture of tension is equally easy to interpret. Horses that turn their quarters to a human who enters their stable or field are sending an unmistakable message. Stamping a hind leg, shaking the head and/or swishing the tail are signals of irritation. For example, a horse can get impatient waiting for food or when it is

restricted in a stable, and it may stamp or kick the stable door. A horse that has seen or heard something that worries her will raise her neck and prick her ears in that direction. She may prance around on the spot or shy away. All these are clear signs of fear, interest, and agitation.

Horses' ears give very clear messages, and are perhaps the most communicative part of the horse's body. Ear signals are frequently backed up by other body language. Each ear has a number of different muscles, making them enormously mobile, and the horse can rotate them at will. Their positions reveal the horse's state of mind. Pricked firmly forward, they indicate a strong interest. When relaxed or dozing, the horse

Bonding with your horse
Humans can create a bond with horses by grooming. Most horses enjoy being groomed, but some may be ticklish in places. It is best to groom outside, so that the dust and hairs are blown away.

lowers the ears and allows them to become floppy. Ears that are laid hard back indicate displeasure, temper, or aggression. When one ear is stuck sideways, a horse has probably heard a fly or other irritating noise, although ears cocked to one side can also indicate the horse is paying attention to what a human is doing close beside him. Twitching, mobile ears when a horse is being ridden are comforting because this shows the horse is attentive to his rider.

WHAT HUMANS SAY TO HORSES

One of the ways humans communicate with horses is entirely unconscious communication through the smells we give off. Frightened people—and maybe aggressive ones, too—exude odors that reveal their state of mind to the horse. This causes her to become either apprehensive or aggressive, depending on whether she is a submissive animal or a more dominant one. There is an old saying "a bold man makes a bold horse," which reveals what horse people have long observed: that people with no fear and plenty of self-confidence often get along better with horses than those who are more empathetic to the horses' concerns. However, loud, insensitive people often go too far the other way—it is a delicate balance.

Not now!
This mare is reprimanding her foal, who is asking for a suckle. These encounters sometimes look a bit fierce, but the foal won't be scared or offended.

Reproduction

Mares usually reach puberty between the ages of 15 and 24 months, although it may be later. In nature, they will become pregnant every year and wean the previous year's foal just before the birth of the current year's foal. The average gestation period is just over 11 months.

IN HEAT

From early spring through fall, mares come into season (a condition referred to as being in "heat" or estrus) at regular intervals of between 18 and 21 days. Each heat lasts five to seven days. During heat, a mare will accept a stallion. There are a number of unmistakable signs that indicate a mare is in season, although they do not all occur simultaneously. Mares may appear irritable and unsettled, and will seek the company of other horses more than usual. She will swish her tail almost constantly and she will regularly pass small quantities of urine. Mating occurs two to five days before the end of estrus.

FOAL DEVELOPMENT IN THE WOMB

The foal's presence is apparent from the fifth month of pregnancy, and the foal's movements can be seen from the sixth month. As the pregnancy approaches its completion, the mare's belly drops. Two signs of imminent foaling are the udder enlarging and wax appearing on the teat extremities.

As with all pregnancies, the foal's development in the uterus follows a distinct pattern. At two months, the length of the embryo is approximately 3–3½ in (7–10 cm) from poll to dock. It is possible to distinguish each of the limbs and the sex of the foal can be determined. At four months, the foal weighs about 2 lb (1 kg) and measures 8–9 in (20–23 cm). The first traces of hair occur around the lips and the hooves have formed.

Hair over the body is much more apparent at six months, by which time the external sex organs are formed. The length of the foal will have increased to about 22 in (56 cm) and the weight may be upward of 12½ lb (5.5 kg).

Eight months into the pregnancy, the foal assumes an upright position and has grown its mane and hair along the spine. Weight increases to 36–42 lb (16–19 kg), and length to 27–29 in (68–73 cm). At 10 months,

the coat and long hairs of the mane and tail are fully grown. By this time, the foal weighs up to 74 lb (33.5 kg) and measures between 34 and 37 in (85–92 cm). It soon turns inside the uterus so that it is facing the birth canal. At 11 months, the foal is ready to pass through the pelvic arch. It now weighs 85–107 lb (38.5–48.5 kg) and measures upward of 43 in (109 cm). Its teeth show through the gums.

LABOR AND BIRTH

When left to their own devices, mares give birth quickly and the foal is up on its feet within a short time, feeding and able to move around. Domesticated horses often give birth in the middle of the night, thereby avoiding attention from their owners. Because of this, many breeders have designated foaling stables with closed-circuit TV to ensure that help is at hand should the mare get into difficulties.

Labor has three phases: involuntary uterine contractions as the fetus is positioned for expulsion, and the cervical and associated structures relax; voluntary expulsive effort when the foal enters the pelvis, passes through the cervix, and is born; and, finally, the expulsion of the afterbirth.

Pregnant mare
It is difficult to predict when exactly a mare will give birth, but—on average—a normal pregnancy lasts around 340 days.

Labor can last up to six hours, during which time the mare will be restless and frequently get up and lie down again. After the water breaks, the mare lies down and will strain to give birth. Next to appear are the membranes that contained the fluid in which the foal has developed inside the uterus.

Bonding after birth
The mare usually licks the foal shortly after the birth to warm the foal and to develop a bond. The foal is still covered in the caul membranes.

INTRODUCTIONS

The foal's relationship with humans begins almost as soon as it is born. When the foal is no more than three days old, it should be possible to handle it with the help of someone holding the mare. The mare is placed alongside the stable wall and the foal needs no persuasion to come up along the nearside of its mother. The trainer or owner can then place the right arm around the foal's rump and the left around the chest. In a few days, the young animal will consent to stand quietly within the embracing arms so long as it is allowed to be close to its mother, its flank touching her side to give it confidence. From the second week, the foal should be made used to being touched and stroked all over by humans.

The forefeet and legs of the foal follow with the head of the foal lying flat against them. The caul—a transparent membrane—still surrounds the young animal. Once the shoulders appear, the heaviest part has been delivered and the rest follows. The membranes over the nose break and breathing starts.

As the foal kicks free from the mare, the umbilical cord may break. If not, the mare will break it as she rises when the birth is complete. She licks the foal to dry and warm it. After half an hour, it will be nuzzling the mare for food. The colostrum, the first milk the foal receives, is essential to its well-being. It functions as an antibiotic and also ensures the passing of the meconium in the first bowel action. The meconium is made up of amniotic fluid and other material the foal has swallowed while in the uterus. It builds up in the rectum of foals during gestation and is expelled soon after birth.

FEEDING AND CARE

If the grazing is good, and the mare is well fed, her milk and the grass will be ample food for the foal. Along with good nutrition, a foal's other needs are plenty of sleep (rather like a human baby), as well as the company of other horses and enough space to romp in.

It is usual for colt foals, other than those intended for use as stallions, to be gelded before weaning takes place. Gelding can be carried out later, but yearling colts may become incredibly boisterous if left entire. Gelding is a quick and fairly straightforward procedure. Apart from sterilizing the foal, it has a calming effect. Geldings are docile and easy to handle. They are happy to live together and with mares. Stallions on the other hand usually retain all the inbuilt behavior of a wild horse, which means they have to be treated and handled with care.

WEANING

Left to her own devices, a mare begins to stop feeding her foal about a month prior to giving birth to her next foal, when her hormones are changing to signal the development of colostrum. At this stage, her foal will be about 10 months old. It may take her only a few days between initially showing her reluctance to feed the foal and actually stopping him from drinking. Weanlings maintain the close bond they have with their dam (mother). Once the mare has her new foal, the weanling will develop bonds with other herd members, most likely other youngsters, but their dam will still be a comfort zone when the youngster is unsure or frightened.

In studs, a mare and foal are usually weaned at about six months, although some breeders leave it until the foal is eight or nine old months because it can be a traumatic experience.

A kind way to do it is to give the mare and foal a gentle companion. Keep all three (or more) together for a few weeks and then start to separate the mare from her foal and the companion for short periods (starting with 30 minutes then progressing to longer periods of a few hours). Removing the mare but allowing the foal to still see her makes the separation easier.

Mare and foal
Within half-an-hour of birth, foals are on their feet and, in a short space of time, they are able to keep up with their dams—a necessary feat in the wild.

CHAPTER 2

HORSES AND HUMANS

Domestication

From the early days of domestication, to modern times when it is mostly kept for leisure and competition, the key quality of the horse has been its adaptability. Humans began by seeing horses as prey, then realized that they had other uses.

Cave carvings
Images of people and horses are among the 30,000 ancient rock carvings found near the village of Chilas in the Karakoram mountain range of northern Pakistan.

The domestication of horses was a gradual process. Initially, people hunted wild horses for food. Later, they realized they could keep them in enclosures for the same purpose. However, at this point the horses were not handled, as such, or cared for. It was only when people learned how to control horses, that domestication came about. People paid more attention to their welfare because they needed to be healthy to work effectively.

EARLY DAYS
When horses were hunted for their meat and hides, it is likely that foals were occasionally taken alive and these may have then lived with people. However, keeping horses was not common practice until about 6,000 years ago.

As horses are grazing animals, it is hardly surprising that the first evidence of their domestication is on the steppes of Eastern Europe (in modern-day Ukraine), southwest Russia, and western Kazakhstan. The people who lived in these areas were not farmers, but they could not survive harsh winters in settlements of any size simply by hunting for their food. It seems likely that they raised horses for food as well as hunting them, and there is plenty of archaeological evidence to support this. Most of the animal bones found in this area are from horses, and they have obvious butchery marks.

Eurasian steppe
A young rider herds cattle on the plains of Mongolia. Here, his ancestors would have originally hunted wild equines for food before horses were domesticated.

There is also evidence of fenced enclosures most likely used to keep horses and of equine milk proteins on pottery remains.

As people began to domesticate horses, they learned to control them. Such control would have been limited at first, and the use of force rather than training was probably commonplace. Horse welfare would have been virtually nonexistent. However, horses gradually became more important in human life and people learned that taking good care of their charges was as vital as training them well.

PULLING POWER

As the practice of animal domestication spread further afield and farmers started to grow crops, horses were employed as

War machines
The invention of the spoked wheel and the development of light chariots meant that horses were increasingly involved in battle, rather than just the transportation of soldiers, weapons, and provisions.

draft animals. They had the advantage of being hardier than oxen and they did not need rest periods to ruminate (chew the cud). With the invention of the wheel around 3200 BCE, the importance of horses to human society increased. They were used to pull carts as well as plows. These early wooden vehicles had solid wheels and a central pole to which a pair of horses was crudely harnessed. Control of the horses was not very refined, which limited the vehicles' maneuverability, and the lack of a swiveling wheel axle made cornering difficult. As a result, two- rather than four-wheeled carts were the most frequent means of transportation.

People also found another use for their domesticated animals: for centuries horses have been used in battle. At first they simply transported men and weapons from place to place but the advent of the spoked wheel around 1900 BCE led to the development of chariots, which were faster and lighter than previous vehicles and so could be used in battle. Speed and pulling power were increased by adding a second pair of horses, one on either side of the first pair. The Persian and Chinese armies also attached scythes (horizontal blades up to 3 ft/1 m long) to the hubs of the chariot wheels, turning them into a weapons in their own right. The main drawback was still a lack of maneuverability. To be effective as weapons, chariots needed plenty of space to turn around and so battles had to be fought in flat, open country.

Although the Bronze Age provided a more effective means of controlling horses with reins attached to bridles by metal bits, the presence of spiked cheek pieces suggests that pain was commonly used to steer them. However, as soon as soldiers could fight effectively on horseback, chariots were replaced by cavalry (mounted horsemen).

RIDING HIGH

Warfare on horseback was not commonplace since riders could easily be dislodged. Horses (and donkeys) have probably been ridden since early times, but riding was not a widespread activity until about 1000 BCE. Horses at this time were small. They were ridden bareback or with a saddle pad. There were no girths, so riders were not very secure or comfortable.

Bridles with metal bits gave better control, and by the 3rd century BCE Central Asian archers were sufficiently skilled in battle to engage their enemies successfully. The cavalry of the late Roman Empire was the first to use treed saddles. The saddles had no stirrups, but there were various projections against which the soldiers could brace themselves, which made them more secure and made the use of other weapons possible.

Stirrups were first seen in at China the start of the 4th century CE. It is likely that soft materials had already been experimented

Chanson
The armor worn by knights meant that their mounts became targets too. This lead to the development of barding, or armor for horses, such as this chanfron from Germany, which protected the horse's head.

with elsewhere but they are not preserved. It was the appearance of stirrups that paved the way to modern horsemanship. Initially only a mounting stirrup was used, presumably because horses were now getting bigger, some possibly exceeding 14.2 hh (147 cm). Two stirrups followed and, as well as making riders more secure, they gave additional mobility, allowing riders to stand or crouch down in the saddle.

By now horses had become essential to armies and farmers, and riding and carriage driving in general was increasing in popularity too and with it the importance of the horse to every aspect of people's lives. Horses, therefore, had significant value and so looking after them properly became even more important.

HORSE CARE

Knowing how to keep horses healthy and fit for whatever work they were required to do was key to completing their domestication. Some of the earliest known examples of horse care and crossbreeding are seen in the Assyrian friezes that date from the 9th century BCE. The carvings clearly show horses being fed and groomed and mules (created by crossing a mare with a male donkey) being used as pack animals.

Horses revered
The great Tang emperor Taizong (599–649 CE) ordered images of his six favorite horses to be carved in stone. He also composed a poem to these horses, which were chosen from the mounts he had ridden in battle. Shown here is the emperor with Autumn Dew.

Viking stirrups
This stirrup was used by Vikings between 850 and 1050 CE. It is said to be a triangular shape because it uses less iron than a rounded shape. The point along the side of the stirrup might have been used as a spur.

The need for greater control may have promoted the practice of gelding stallions. It is thought the Scythians were doing this as early as the 8th century BCE. It was probably carried out because it made horses more manageable in battle: geldings are less likely to behave badly in the company of others.

Speed was also important and its association with breathing has been known since early times. Nose slitting was carried out in an attempt to improve performance by increasing the amount of oxygen reaching the lungs. This practice is still carried out in some countries today though more effective surgical techniques are used in most places when the need arises.

In the wild, a horse's feet are subject to normal wear and tear and their tough keratin hooves provide adequate protection for their feet. However, once domesticated and put to work, additional care is needed if a horse is to remain sound. The earliest preserved shoes are Roman and comprise a metal sole held onto the horse's hoof by leather straps. Shoes secured by nails appear much later—in the 10th century CE—but by medieval times they were commonplace throughout most of Europe.

Breeding horses for specific tasks is a relatively recent development. Different regions had horses that exhibited particular characteristics and gradually the idea developed to breed horses for those characteristics best suited to doing specialized tasks, such as draft work. This in turn led to the development of breed standards.

Closed studbooks record only purebred individuals of a breed, regulated by a breed standard to which they must conform. They began appearing only in the last couple of hundred years (see pp.44–45).

THE MODERN HORSE

For centuries, horses were an essential part of our existence; today in many countries, they are kept only for competition and leisure purposes. There are hundreds of breeds and types ranging from giant draft horses over 20 hh (203 cm) high to tiny miniaturized horses that stand as little as 12 in (30 cm) or so at the withers. They are well handled as foals and usually trained carefully to work willingly for humans, rather than broken in with a combination force and fear.

The range of equipment now available for riding and driving as well as generally caring for horses is enormous and changes all the

Working horse
For a long time, horses were essential for agricultural work. Mechanized equipment made them redundant in most of the developed world, though they are still used in some places.

time as new materials and styles become available. Feeding horses and creating and maintaining their fitness is now almost a science in its own right, as is horse behavior. Horses are cared for by a suite of people including owners, grooms, trainers, vets, dentists, osteopaths, and chiropractors. Our relationship with these wonderful animals has come along way from its early days 10,000 years ago on the plains of Ukraine.

Romanian horses
With the exception of the Australian Brumbies and American Mustangs, there are very few truly wild horses. Most equines have owners, including these in the Rodna Mountains of Romania.

The horse in war

Almost as soon as they had domesticated horses, people realized they could use them in warfare. The way horses were employed changed through the centuries, but they remained a vital tool up to and including World War I and they also played a role in World War II.

FIGHTING ON HORSEBACK

Before the advent of saddles, warfare on horseback was rare because it was not easy to fight and stay on the horse (see p.33). The Parthians (247 BCE–224 CE) developed the tactic of galloping up to the enemy and then retreating while turning their bodies to shoot—the origin of the phrase "parting shot." Avoiding physical combat meant avoiding being pulled off your horse. However, as tack design improved, so fighting on horses increased.

KNIGHTS IN ARMOR

There is very little written information about medieval horsemanship, and surviving armor with long spurs and tack with harsh bits indicate it was probably rather brutal. It seems that knights practiced skill-at-arms

Shining knight
This 14th-century bronze model depicts a knight in full armor, sword raised, charging into battle.

from an early age and, during peacetime, tournaments were regular events in castle grounds. Tournaments could result in the injury and death of the knights, so it seems unlikely that there was much concern for the welfare of the horses. Although there are images of knights fighting on horseback, because of the weight and bulk of armor, it is possible that much of the combat took place on foot and horses were used for transportation to the battleground and pursuit afterward. Horses were protected with armor and colored banners were used to distinguish knights in battle.

EMERGENCE OF CAVALRY

The European cavalry derived largely from the methods of Charles Martel and his Frankish knights in the 6th century, who

relied on the momentum of the charge by heavily armored horsemen in tightly closed ranks. However, the hit-and-run tactic remained in use for centuries. In the 13th century, the Mongols, who were primarily horse-archers, were renowned for it.

Two hundred years later, the Hussars, were also exceptionally mobile. Preferring the element of surprise to the set-piece battle, these light horsemen hit swiftly and with devastating effect. They were adept at pursuing a broken enemy. The loose, open formations they adopted made counterattack difficult. Their tactic became known as the "coup d'huzzard." The Hussars rode in short stirrups, their bodies leaning forward, knees bent—the antithesis of the long-leg, braced seat that heavy cavalry had used since the Battle of Poitiers in 732 CE.

DEVELOPING IDEAS

The 17th and 18th centuries saw commanders whose handling of the cavalry was exemplary. Among the most innovative was Gustavus Adolphus of Sweden who perfected the shock tactic in the Thirty Years' War (1618–48). Keeping his troops under tight control, he had them trot to the enemy, fire their pistols, and then "fall on" with the sword. Frederick II of Prussia added a new dimension to the battlefield by introducing galloping horse artillery to support the cavalry. The light guns, drawn by six horses, kept up with the cavalry and could be used to disperse any threatened action against them.

LAST DAYS OF THE CAVALRY

Cavalry was employed on a huge scale in the 19th century, despite the increasing effectiveness of small-arms fire and the

The Battle of Hastings
The Norman cavalry were a fearsome fighting force and their presence at the Battle of Hastings on October 14, 1066 contributed to William's victory. Harold's English army consisted almost entirely of infantry and a few archers.

The Battle of Waterloo
The Scots Greys was one of three heavy brigades that routed an infantry corps, a whole cavalry brigade, and overran many French field batteries, suffering many casualties during the action.

more sophisticated use of artillery. The Battle of Waterloo in 1815 represented the last major European engagement of large bodies of cavalry handled in a copybook manner. Napoleon had 16,000 horses at his disposal, while Wellington, not including the horses of the Prussian allies, had 13,000.

Despite an inevitable impetuosity, the British cavalry behaved magnificently. The French were equally heroic. Under Marshal Ney, they launched repeated attacks on the British infantry squares and were repeatedly repulsed, leaving walls of dead and dying horses and men piled in front of Wellington's stubbornly resolute infantry. Ney himself had five horses shot from under him, and both sides suffered terrible casualties. Much credit for the victory belonged to the Horse Gunners (Horse Artillery), whose support of the infantry was crucial. Despite the carnage at Waterloo, cavalry was to remain integral to warfare long after Napoleon's defeat by the combined forces of Europe.

During the Boer War (1899–1901), the British cavalry was finally compelled, by the inexperienced Boer commandos, to adopt the tactics of the colonial mounted infantry. This followed the practice of the cavalry of the American Civil War (1861–65), many of whom rode to battle and dismounted to fight as infantry.

WORLD WARS
Millions of horses were used for cavalry and transportation during World War I and 8 million died in appalling conditions. Because of the use of trench warfare, the cavalry was of limited use. However, cavalry and horse transportation survived into the World War II. Losses were almost as bad as in World War I, and in one horrendous battle in 1941, 2,000 horses and riders of the Mongolian Cavalry were killed within minutes of launching an attack on a German infantry division.

The use of horses has continued in conflicts up to the present day, although few have frontline duties. In the Bosnian War (1992–95), people fleeing the conflict took what they could on small pack ponies, and in the Soviet-Afghan War (1979–1989), the Mujahideen depended on their horses to cross difficult terrain.

CEREMONIAL WORK
Today, horses have a role to play in the ceremonial guard in many countries. For example, the Kings Troop, Royal Horse Artillery is much appreciated by tourists in London. Mounted police also perform ceremonial duties as well as being used for crowd control.

World War II
Horses were used to draw fire engines and carry other firefighting equipment in British cities during the Blitz. Civilians, including air wardens, and horses wore gas masks during the bombing raids.

Riding as art

Anyone who has ridden a well-trained horse that is ready to go in any direction and at any speed, simply at the touch of the heel or a twitch of the reins, knows how intense that feeling of connection can be. Riding as an art has its roots in the works of Xenophon (*c.*430–354 BCE). One of the first of the great horse masters, he was also the first to advocate reward-based training.

THE BENEFITS OF TRAINING

From the ancient skills of battle to modern-day dressage, through the classical riding era of the 16–18th centuries, riding as an art has always had many practitioners. It makes good economic sense to train horses properly and make them fit, as well as attentive to the rider's commands. This work is also vital for horses taking part in all the competitive disciplines. Good training ensures that riding does not tire either the rider or the horse. If a horse knows the meaning of each command and submits willingly to it, it will avoid injury and stress.

A BRIEF HISTORY OF THE ART

Xenophon's treatise *On Horsemanship* is one of the first works on the equestrian arts. It covers everything from correct care and grooming to the equipment required for going into battle. Many of the techniques he discussed are still practiced today. He understood how to persuade a horse to perform movements such as rearing and "prancing," that showed off its athleticism and grace. Xenophon was unusual for his time in that he also considered the comfort of the horse, asking the rider not to use the spur or whip or pull on the reins.

Tournaments began in the 11th century and were originally intended to train knights for battle. By the 15th century, these events had become more about men of status wanting to impress each other with their skills on horseback. Although they continued into the 17th century, other non-contact equestrian sports began to take over, including skill-at-arms, such as tent

pegging (see pp.118–19). During these later centuries, riding schools had set up in various European countries to educate riders in the higher equestrian skills. One of the first was the Neapolitan riding school, inaugurated in 1532, whose most famous master was Federico Grisone.

His pupil, Giovanni Baptista Pignatelli, developed the first training formula for manège (school) riding.

In the French court, the riding master was highly respected. The post was usually occupied by cultured men of aristocratic birth, such as Antoine de Pluvinel de Baume

Spanish Riding School
Located in Vienna, The Spanish Riding School is famous as a center for classical dressage. Members of the Spanish Riding School also go on tour around the world.

(1555–1620). He created a system of gymnastic exercises designed to increase the suppleness and agility of the horse, and largely discarded the coercive methods of the time. He is generally credited with the invention of the pillars between which the horse is taught collection and the levade—the first of the airs above the ground.

François Robichon de la Guérinière (1688–1751) was equerry to Louis XIV from 1730 to 1751.

Andalucian
Spanish horses, such as this Andalucian (see pp.140–41), have a great talent performing for High School airs.

De la Guérinière refined the principles of equitation as a rational science and developed exercises, including shoulder-in and the flying change, to increase suppleness and balance. His stated objectives were to make the horse calm, light, and obedient so that it was a pleasure to ride and comfortable in all its paces.

Perhaps the best-known exponent of riding as an art, and now the oldest, the Spanish Riding School of Vienna was established in 1572. It is named after the horses used from the very beginning. Now called Lipizzaner (see pp.202–203), the breed was founded on Spanish horses imported to the court stud at Lipizza in 1850. Initially, the school used a wooden riding arena; the famous Winter Riding School was commissioned in 1729. Today, the school is maintained by the Austrian Republic and performances are open to the public.

ADVANCED MOVEMENTS
Basic riding—walk, trot canter, gallop, and jumping—is a skill that is relatively easy to master and highly enjoyable. However, riding as an art is a lifetime's commitment. The horse and rider must master movements that require enormous amounts of energy, balance, control, and submission on the part of the horse. It is said that nothing can be taught to a horse that it doesn't already do in the field when excited, scared, or full of energy, but teaching the horse to do these movements on command takes time. Although they are usually called dressage, many of these movements are also seen in various forms of Western riding. Dressage training is done in a rectangular arena and takes the form of many different gymnastic

Western riding
Though it shares some similarities and movements with the European practice, Western riding is more relaxed and informal. It also has a unique system of saddlery.

exercises based on circles and parts of circles. Once the horse has learned how to balance, often with many different lateral (sideways) movements, it is taught to collect (shorten) and extend (lengthen) its stride in both walk and trot. It is also taught to elevate its action (lift the hooves higher at each step).

As the training progresses, the horse is taught to "engage" its hindquarters to maintain powerful forward movement. This is called impulsion. The beautiful movement of piaffe and passage require a great deal of impulsion. They are based on the two-beat diagonal gait of trot, slowed to the speed of a march and with the feet lifted high for each beat. Piaffe is done on the spot, while passage moves forward.

Advanced canter movements include flying change, where the horse swops its leading leg without breaking the three-beat rhythm of the canter (see p.18), and tempi changes, a more advanced version, where the horse is asked to change the canter lead every fourth, third, second or even every other stride. This requires incredible fitness and balance. When done well, these advanced movements are like an elegant dance.

Dressage
The very popular equestrian discipline of dressage dates back to classical Greek horsemanship, but the principles of dressage training today are all derived from the Spanish Riding School in Vienna.

Horses in legend and culture

For centuries, humans have relied on horses for food, work, transportation, and sometimes even companionship, so it's not surprising that history abounds with myths, legends, and true stories about horses and our relationships with them. The idea of the partnership between horse and rider is captured in a vast number of paintings and sculptures, while novels and films about the feats of horses are part of modern culture.

MYTHICAL CREATURES

The ancient Greeks and Romans had many tales of mythical horselike creatures. It is impossible to know their source, but it is likely that they have their origins in the earliest days of domestication. For example, it has been suggested that the idea for the centaur—half man, half horse—might have stemmed from non-riding cultures coming across horses being ridden for the first time. It seems unlikely that they would have been mistaken for long, but you can imagine the later fireside tale-telling that might have exaggerated these first encounters, especially if fighting was involved. Although the centaur is clearly a mythical beast, it is interesting to note that the Roman philosopher Lucretius (1st century BCE) wrote a poem in which he said that as horses and humans mature at different rates (a three-year-old human is still a baby, while a horse is mature at three), the hybrid was impossible.

The unicorn is another example. The Greeks believed it could be found in India, which at that time was suitably far away and mysterious to be the land of almost any creature of the imagination. Unicorns are not always entirely horselike—they can also be

The Lady and the Unicorn
This 14th-century tapestry is one of a series of six woven in Flanders of French design, all featuring a noblewoman with a lion and a unicorn. It is though to represent "love" or "understanding."

goats—but they always have a single long horn spiraling out of their forehead. In the Middle Ages, the unicorn became a symbol of purity that could only be tamed by a virgin. In heraldry, it symbolizes a proud beast that would rather die than be captured and is found on many flags and coats of arms.

The Greeks also told tales of Pegasus, the pure white, winged stallion whose sire was Poseidon, god of the sea, and whose dam was the monster Medusa with her crown of serpents. Wherever he touched the earth, a spring of water erupted. His rider was Bellerophon, who eventually fell off him trying to reach Mount Olympus. Also related to water is the Kelpie of Scottish folklore, a shape-shifting water-dwelling spirit that can adopt a human form, but always retains its hooves. It is not always an attractive or pleasant creature, and has often been used in tales to keep children safe from the dangers of water.

Winged horse
This silver coin depicting Pegasus is from the ancient city-state of Corinth, where his rider Bellerophon was born.

Naresuan the Great
One of Thailand's national heroes, King Naresuan ruled the Ayutthaya kingdom from 1590 until 1605 after liberating his people from Burmese rule. The statue at his monument depicts Naresuan on his warhorse.

HORSES IN LITERATURE

The story of the Trojan horse, in which the Greeks entered and overthrew Troy, is one of the oldest horse tales. The symbol of Troy was a horse, which was what inspired the Greeks to build their massive wooden statue. It is hard to imagine that the Trojans fell for such a trick, but maybe the beauty of the horse was just too tempting?

Much more recently, in 1877, Anna Sewell published what is probably the best known horse tale ever. *Black Beauty* is all the more notable because it is told from the horse's point of view in an era when animals were not given much thought by their owners. It is an almost unbearable story of both the cruelty and kindness of humans. In its day, it highlighted the plight of working animals and spurred animal-rights legislation in both the UK and US.

War Horse is also told from the point of view of the horse and is another moving study of the bond between horse and human. *War Horse* was written as a novel

for children in 1982 by Michael Morpurgo and has since been turned into a play and a film. It tells the story of the relationship between a young boy called Albert and his horse Joey. They are wrenched apart by World War I and Joey suffers great hardship throughout the war. Morpurgo wanted to honor the enormous debt owed to the millions of horses that were used during the fighting and highlight the cruel fate that most of them met at the end of the war.

HORSES IN ART

In portraits, kings and war heroes are often shown riding their horses. Somehow being astride a mighty charger lends gravitas and spirit to the human being honored. A walk around almost any city in the world will reveal statues of famous men—and occasionally women—on horseback: Richard I and the Duke of Wellington in London; Charlemagne and Joan of Arc in Paris; and Genghis Khan in Ulan Bator, Mongolia, to name just a few.

In the US, there are portraits of war commanders on horseback, but other equestrian statues are, perhaps, more notable for the anonymity of the rider. For example, *Appeal to the Great Spirit*, sculpted by Cyrus Dallin in 1909, depicts

an American Indian, arms out in supplication, while Alexander P. Proctor's *Bronco Buster* is of a cowboy riding a bucking horse. Since the horse no longer occupies this place in our culture, sculptors have been left with the task of creating impressive statues without the aid of these magnificent creatures. In most cases, a motor vehicle doesn't have the same effect.

HORSES IN FILM

Although there are films about horses, both fictional and real—*National Velvet, The Horse Whisperer, Seabiscuit*—more numerous and more popular are Westerns, which nearly always feature horses in a secondary role. Although now past its heyday, this genre was about the biggest box-office draw for 50 years, from the late 1930s, and was the making of stars such as John Wayne and Clint Eastwood. The romance of the American West was lived out time and again in movies such as *Stagecoach* (1939), *Rio Grande* (1950), *A Fistful of Dollars* (1964), *Pale Rider* (1985), and *True Grit* (1969 and 2010). There were numerous TV series as well, including *Rawhide, High*

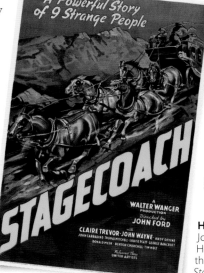

Hollywood hero
John Wayne's breakthrough role in Hollywood was as "The Ringo Kid" in the widely lauded John Ford Western *Stagecoach*.

Chaparral, and *The Virginian*. The height of cool was actors like James Stewart, Burt Lancaster, Gary Cooper, Charles Bronson, and many others riding into town on their horses, spurs jangling, guns at the ready.

The working horse

For centuries, the economy of most countries depended upon horse power. This dependence lessened with the advent of engines and motorized vehicles, but there are still parts of the world where horses remain an essential element of working life.

COACHING AND TRANSPORTATION

Until the late 15th century, people walked or rode, or used carts or heavy carriages to get around (see pp.32–35). The development of the coach in Kocs, Hungary, revolutionized wheeled transportation. It had a light body, which was suspended on springs, and could carry up to eight passengers.

Stage coaches, as these vehicles were called, were drawn by horses or mules (see p.13) in teams of between two and six. In 19th-century Britain, the network of coach roads was vast and people could travel up to 70 miles (112 km) a day. The "stage" was the distance a team of horses would work before being changed for a fresh set—usually at a coaching inn. The American equivalent was based on the famous Concord coaches.

These covered long-distance routes, often at speeds of 15 mph (23 km/h). They were introduced into Australia in 1853, where they provided a service covering 6,000 miles (9,655 km) in New South Wales and Queensland. This era was also notable for the number of private driving vehicles, of many shapes and sizes, that were owned by wealthy members of society.

The first public transportation in cities was provided by enclosed vehicles called omnibuses drawn by horses, and later by horse-trams running on rails. The first omnibus service was run in Paris as early as 1662 by Blaise Pascal. However, it was short-lived and it was not until 1828 that a regular passenger service, also in Paris, was set up. The French service was copied in London in 1829. By 1890, there were 2,210 omnibuses in London and the service employed 11,000 people and twice that number of horses.

TRAINS AND CANALS

In the 18th century, canals were used for transporting both freight and passengers. The canal barges were drawn by horses called "boaters," although sometimes mules or even donkeys were used. In spite of the development of the railroads in the early 19th century, barges continued to be used.

Light and fast
The development of light coaches made traveling over long distances faster and easier. "Four-in-hand" rigging allowed a single driver to control four horses at the same time—previous rigs required two drivers for a four-horse carriage.

There were a few still at work in the 1950s. Horses hauled freight and passenger trains over short- and medium-distances before and after the advent of the steam train. The first horse-drawn train, connecting Wandsworth with Croydon, in outer London, started operating in 1803. A similar branch line in Northern Ireland terminated at Fintona Station. The latter continued in use until 1957. There were similar lines throughout Europe. There is no record of horse-drawn railroads in the US, but tracks were laid in the big lumber camps and teams of six or eight horses hauled lumber up steep inclines.

COMMUNICATION

From transferring important documents to sending simple letters, horses made written communication possible. As long ago as the 3rd century BCE, the Persians had developed a highly efficient mail system that stretched from Egypt to Asia Minor and from India to the Greek Islands. The civilizations of Greece and Rome had similar arrangements, while in the 13th century, Genghis Khan had the Yam, a reliable courier system that enabled him to govern his huge empire. Until the 19th century, pack trails were commonplace. In mountainous areas where there were few proper roads, people continued to use pack transportation into the 20th century.

Continuing traditions
Concerns about the environment have led to a resurgence in the use of horses in forestry. They are ideal for selective removal of trees from dense woodland.

INDUSTRY AND AGRICULTURE

The British Industrial Revolution (1789–1832) had an effect on the framework of international trade. Although machines took over work that had been done by hand for centuries, industry was still highly dependent on the efforts of horses. The main source of power was coal: at the pitheads, horses turned the windlass of the hoist, moved heavy machinery, and hauled coal wagons. Ponies worked underground in the mines.

For hundreds of years, oxen were used in agriculture rather than horses. In the 18th century, changes in farming methods, coupled with the invention of agricultural implements, meant that horses, which were faster and did not need time to ruminate became more popular. Jethro Tull's seed drill, used from 1731 onward, was one of the first implements developed specifically for a horse. Significant improvements were also made in the design of the plow, culminating in the Arbuthnot swing plow. It was lighter than any other plow and turned the soil cleanly and easily. Tests proved that when drawn by two horses, an Arbuthnot could till a greater area in one day than six oxen pulling the older type. By the middle of the 19th century, threshing machines, corn grinders, elevators, multi-furrowed plows, special sub-soiling plows, reapers, cutters, binders were all in use. And, in the US, there huge and heavy combine harvesters pulled by teams of 40 horses. Indeed, American expertise in the operation of multi-horsed agricultural implements was unrivaled. By 1914, the horse population of the US was 25 million. Almost as quickly as horse power had risen, it died. By 1940, tractors had taken over and thousands of horses were made redundant.

Horses are, however, still used every day in a large number of industries. Whether that is in remote areas, where they are cheaper to obtain and maintain than heavy machinery, or for transportation, tourism, and haulage. The horse remains an important part of working life around the world.

THE PONY EXPRESS

The legendary Pony Express carried the mail between Missouri and San Francisco from April 1860 and October 1861. Epitomizing the frontier spirit, the service covered a distance of 1,966 miles (3,164 km) in 10 days. A series of riders took the mail in relays, each man riding 60 miles (96 km). Each pony was galloped for 10 miles (16 km) between stations where the rider would be given a fresh mount. The Pony Express was not profitable and soon closed down, but it had pioneered the most practical route across the continent, which was subsequently followed by the famous Wells Fargo Overland Stagecoach.

Developing breeds and types

After domestication, the evolution of the horse into the breeds and types of today accelerated, but most of the changes have only occurred in the last few hundred years. For the most part, the modern horse is the product of selective breeding, supported by advances in feeding, management, and veterinary care.

DELIBERATE BREEDING

Once people began to realize that different types of horse were better suited to different sorts of tasks, they began to breed deliberately for particular characteristics. For example, they looked for little feathering in the legs of what became the Suffolk Punch (see pp.54–57) because they noticed that horses with less hair on their legs coped better with the heavy clay soils of Suffolk, and horses that were narrow in their hindquarters were more suitable for walking and plowing a furrow. Riding horses with sloped shoulders gave a more comfortable ride and well defined withers made the saddle more stable. These aspects of a horse's make up came to be called conformation. Gradually conformational "faults," such as cow hocks (see opposite), were identified and attempts were made to avoid them when breeding. The definition of good conformation can vary between breeds, depending on what the horse is used for.

With increased knowledge of the part genes play in physical characteristics, such as coat color, for example, it was realized that performance might also be heritable. So, more recently, there has been a focus on attempting to improve jumping or racing ability by carefully breeding particular bloodlines. Breeding of Europe's competition warmbloods (see opposite) and the Thoroughbred (see pp.120–21) is done on the basis of pedigrees, assessments, and performance records.

HEAVY HORSES, LIGHTER HORSES, AND PONIES

Although there were always differences between horses, breeding for specific purposes began to emphasize these traits.

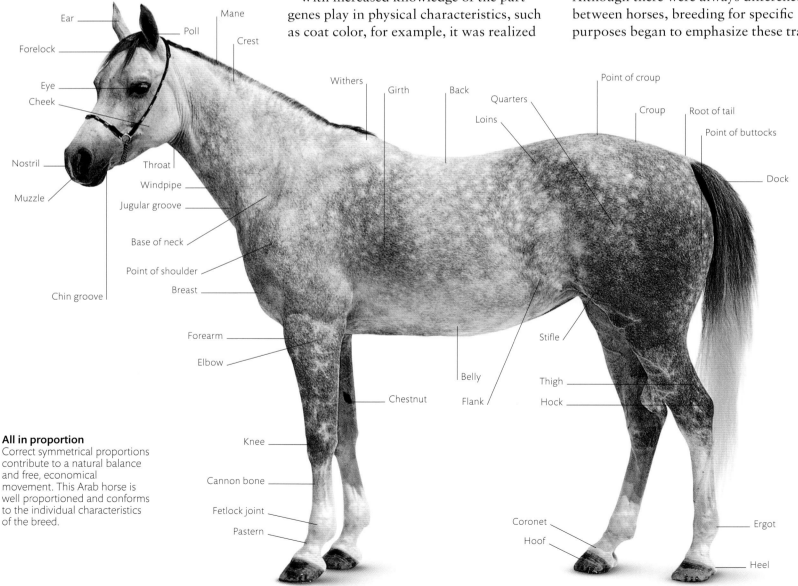

All in proportion
Correct symmetrical proportions contribute to a natural balance and free, economical movement. This Arab horse is well proportioned and conforms to the individual characteristics of the breed.

Ear
Poll
Mane
Crest
Forelock
Eye
Cheek
Withers
Girth
Back
Quarters
Loins
Point of croup
Croup
Root of tail
Point of buttocks
Nostril
Throat
Muzzle
Windpipe
Jugular groove
Base of neck
Point of shoulder
Chin groove
Breast
Dock
Forearm
Elbow
Stifle
Belly
Thigh
Chestnut
Flank
Hock
Knee
Cannon bone
Fetlock joint
Coronet
Ergot
Pastern
Hoof
Heel

Heavy horse
The proportions and the broad, thick structure of the heavy draft horse allow for great strength at slow speeds. They tend to have upright shoulders, producing a high action.

Lighter horse
The Thoroughbred horse is the definitive lighter horse. Its shape is characterized by long limbs and a narrow body. Their shoulders are notably sloped, which allows for a long stride.

Pony
Ponies have a long body in comparison with their height at the withers; its depth equals the leg length. They may have upright shoulders, making their gait rather choppy.

Nowadays, horses are classified into three basic types based on build: heavy horses, lighter horses, and ponies. Heavy horses have large bodies, short, stocky legs, and big hooves. Their heads tend to be large and plain with small ears. The model for the lighter horse is the Thoroughbred. Lighter horses usually have a narrower body than a heavy horse, finer legs, and a more refined head with ears that are more in proportion. Ponies are usually breeds and types below 15 hh (152 cm). Compared to lighter horses, they have a deeper body and shorter legs in relation to their height.

HOT, COLD, WARM
Another distinction is made between "hotbloods," "coldbloods," and "warmbloods." The Arab (see pp.92–93), and the Barb (see pp.94–97), along with their derivative, the Thoroughbred, are traditionally called "hotbloods," a reference to their pure bloodlines. "Coldblood" refers to the heavy draft horses of Europe. Horses that have a percentage of hot blood as well as cold are called "warmbloods." Most of the best competition horses today are warmbloods.

STUDBOOKS, BREEDS, AND TYPES
"Breeds" are horses that are registered in a studbook. They have been bred selectively over a long enough time to ensure that youngstock share common and defined characteristics such as size, conformation, action, and possibly color—the breed standard. In horses, amount of "bone"

is sometimes seen as a requirement. For example, "8 in (20 cm) of bone is required." This refers to the circumference of the cannon bone, and is thought to be an indication of the strength of legs.

Breeding animals (mares and stallions) often have to pass inspections and performance trials in order to be entered in the studbook, thus ensuring that certain standards are maintained. A closed studbook is one where no new blood is allowed. For example, when developing a breed, to remove conformational shortcomings, breeders might cross some of their stock with quality horses known to pass on their good physical traits, such as Thoroughbreds or Arabs. Once they have achieved the desired result, they close the studbook so that only members of the same

breed can be entered into it. This ensures all offspring share similar characteristics, so breed true, but can also reduce the gene pool.

"Types" are horses that do not qualify for breed status because they lack a fixed character and are not entered in an accepted breed studbook. Notable examples are polo ponies (see pp.238–39), hunters (see pp.124–25), hacks (see pp.128–29), and cobs (see pp.130–31).

In the catalog of horses in this book (pp.46–327), breeds and types are included together, but heavy horses, lighter horses, and ponies are in separate sections. Because the difference between a horse and a pony can be arbitrary, a horselike pony might be in the horse section or a pony-like horse might be found in the pony section.

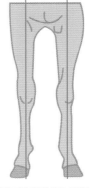

FORELEGS   **HINDLEGS**

Correctly aligned limbs
If the foreleg is straight, a vertical line dropped from the point of shoulder will pass through the center of the knee, fetlock, and foot. Deviations are regarded as faults because they can cause lameness in working horses.

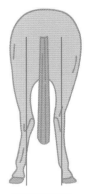

TOES TURNED OUT   **COW HOCKS**

Conformation faults
If a horse's toes are turned out, it may dish when it moves. Dishing is the round circular action when the toe is thrown outward. With cow hocks, the points of the hock are carried close together, and the lower limbs incline outward, producing uneven wear in the joint and reducing speed potential. In some heavy breeds cow hocks are a desired feature.

CHAPTER 3

CATALOG OF BREEDS AND TYPES

HEAVY HORSES

Heavy horses are also known as coldbloods or draft horses. There are a number of different breeds, with varying characteristics, but they all share a similar conformation and overall proportions. They also share the traits of strength, patience, and a docile temperament. This has made them very easy to handle, despite their great size, and useful for a range of jobs, such as agricultural work, forestry, and pulling carts, drays, and canal barges. Heavy horses have a broad, dense structure and short, strong limbs, which enables them to exert great power at slow speeds.

◄ **Born to work** As well as their use in agriculture, heavy horses play a vital role in forestry, where they can haul timber in situations where the use of machines is uneconomic.

Clydesdale

HEIGHT AT WITHERS	ORIGIN	COLORS
16.2–18 hh (168–183 cm)	Scotland	Bay, brown, or chestnut, but grays, roans, and blacks also found

These large horses are known for their style and elegance, which comes from a freedom of movement.

The Clydesdale originated in the Clyde Valley, Scotland, and dates from the mid-18th century. The breed was founded when the 6th Duke of Hamilton imported Flemish horses to improve and increase the size of the native draft stock. At the same time John Paterson of nearby Lochlyoch also brought in Flemish horses, probably from England, and established a strain that became a major influence at least until the mid-19th century. Around this time, Shire (see pp.52–53) blood was introduced by Lawrence Drew and David Riddell, local men dedicated to improving the breed.

Today, the Clydesdale is renowned for its high-stepping action and is carefully bred to have hard-wearing and good quality hooves. This makes it well suited to working on city streets, but less suitable for plowing as the feet can be too big to fit in the furrow. The modern Clydesdale is lighter than its predecessors and is distinctive in type and appearance. Breeders aim for "close" movement, with the forelegs placed under the shoulders and the hindlegs close together, which makes cow (close together) hocks acceptable.

The Clydesdale is among the most successful of the heavy breeds, and has been exported worldwide, even though the heavy white markings and feather, which can cause an eczema-type condition on the legs, have been a disadvantage in some markets. They are found in Russia, Germany, Japan, South Africa, Canada, the US, New Zealand, and Australia, where they earned the title "the breed that built Australia."

BUDWEISER CLYDESDALE

In the US, Clydesdales are used by the Anheuser-Busch Brewing Company to promote Budweiser beer. Smartly turned out teams of eight horses pull wagons advertising the brand. Only bay geldings with four white legs and a white blaze are used. They are at least four years old and stand 18 hh (183 cm) high. This tradition first began in 1933 to celebrate the repeal of the prohibition laws that banned the consumption of alcohol. The Clydesdales travel widely each year and are very popular with the public.

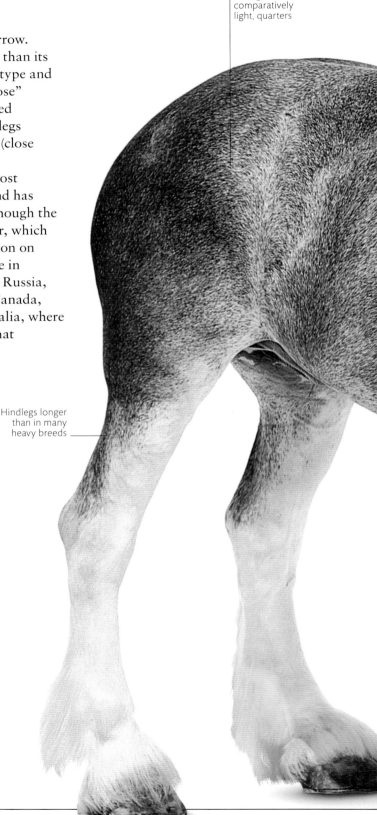

Strong, but comparatively light, quarters

Hindlegs longer than in many heavy breeds

Straight profile with wide forehead

CLYDESDALES **CAN PULL 5,950 LB (2,700 KG), THREE TIMES** THEIR **WEIGHT.**

Clearly defined withers higher than croup

Sloped shoulders

Ears are exceptionally mobile

Shaved and decorated tail, a feature of show horses

Flat knees

Strong hock joints; cow hocks acceptable

Heavy, silky feather on lower limbs

Somewhat flat but hard-wearing feet

Long neck
runs into deep
sloping shoulders

Short back

Medium-sized
head

Slightly Roman
(convex) nose

Wide
quarters

Clean, hard, and
muscular legs

Hindlegs are
close below
the hocks

AT AN EXHIBITION
IN ENGLAND IN 1924,
A PAIR OF **SHIRES**
EXERTED A PULL
CAPABLE OF MOVING
55 TONS.

Open, solid, perfectly
shaped feet

Shire

 | **HEIGHT AT WITHERS**
More than 17 hh
(173 cm) | **ORIGIN**
England | **COLORS**
Mostly black, also bay,
brown, and gray

Considered by many to be the supreme draft horse, this "gentle giant" has a straight action and a kind disposition.

The Shire got its name in 1884 from the Midland "shires" (counties) of Lincoln, Leicester, Stafford, and Derby, where it was originally bred, and may have its origins in England's Great Horse, although the connection cannot be proven.

When the Great Horses were no longer required in warfare, they were put to work in the farms, eventually developing into powerful draft horses. These horses were improved by various outcrosses, with the heavy Flemish, or Flanders, horse being the most influential. During the 16th and early 17th centuries, Dutch contractors draining the English fenlands imported these strong horses, which later bred with the local horses. Another import, the Friesian (see pp.164–65) had a refining effect and produced a freer movement.

The foundation stallion of the Shire is the Packington Blind Horse who sired numerous colts between 1755 and 1770. The English Cart Horse Society was formed in 1876 and produced the first studbook two years later. It became the Shire Horse Society in 1884. The American Shire Horse Association was created in 1885.

The modern Shire is more like the type developed in the Midlands than the coarser Fen strains. Its powerful musculature exemplify the strong structure of an ideal draft horse.

While the Shire no longer plays a major role in agriculture, it participates in plowing matches. In cities, it can occasionally be seen hauling laden brewers' wagons and drawing coaches in street parades.

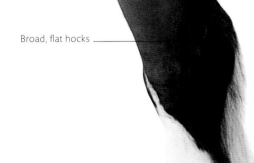

Broad, flat hocks

Heavy, silky feather on lower legs

RACING SHIRES

The first recorded Shire race in the UK took place in 2013 and was won by Joey, ridden by Mark Grant. The race is now an annual event, with Clydesdales also taking part. These events are showcases for these lovely animals and provide great family entertainment.

Suffolk Punch

HEIGHT AT WITHERS	ORIGIN	COLORS
16–16.3 hh (163–170 cm)	England	Shades of chestnut

An endearing "short, fat fellow," the Suffolk Punch is the oldest of Britain's heavy horse breeds.

The Suffolk Punch was developed as a farm horse in East Anglia, UK, from the 16th century onward. While the early origins of this pure breed remain obscure, all Suffolks alive today can be traced back to a single chestnut stallion, foaled in 1768. Owned by Thomas Crisp of "Ufford" (Orford), this short-legged, large-bodied, chestnut stallion was advertised as "good stock for coach or road."

All Suffolks are chestnut (traditionally spelled chesnut). The Suffolk Horse Society, formed in 1877, recognizes seven shades, the most common being a bright reddish brown.

The Suffolk matures early and enjoys a long life. Despite its stamina and power, it thrives on less feed than is needed by other heavy breeds. These robust trotters have very strong quarters and enormous pulling power. A horse's strength used to be tested at fairs in Suffolk by hitching it to a fallen tree. Even if the horse did not manage to

move the tree, it was considered to have passed the test as long as it got right down on its knees in what is considered the typical Suffolk "drawing" action. Its exceptional pulling power can be attributed to its low shoulder, a feature developed by early breeders.

Suffolks are suited to working on heavy clay soil. The lack of feather on their legs means they pick up less soil when working in muddy conditions. In the past they were much in demand for heavy draft work in towns and cities as well.

This horse has a sharp, swinging walk and a unique, rhythmic trot, with only a modest degree of knee action. As a result of the distance between its forelegs, the Suffolk can have a slight dishing action (the front legs circle out sideways as they move).

Well-shaped back end

Large, strong, circular feet

SUFFOLK PUNCH TRUST

Dedicated to preserving the unique history of the Suffolk Punch, the Suffolk Punch Trust owns the Hollesley Bay Colony Stud in Suffolk. Dating from 1759, this is the world's oldest Suffolk Punch stud. The trust was established in 2002 to take over the farm from its previous owners, the UK prisons service, which had used it to help rehabilitate offenders since 1938. Today, the farm is open to the public and visitors can enjoy guided tours and meet examples of this wonderful breed.

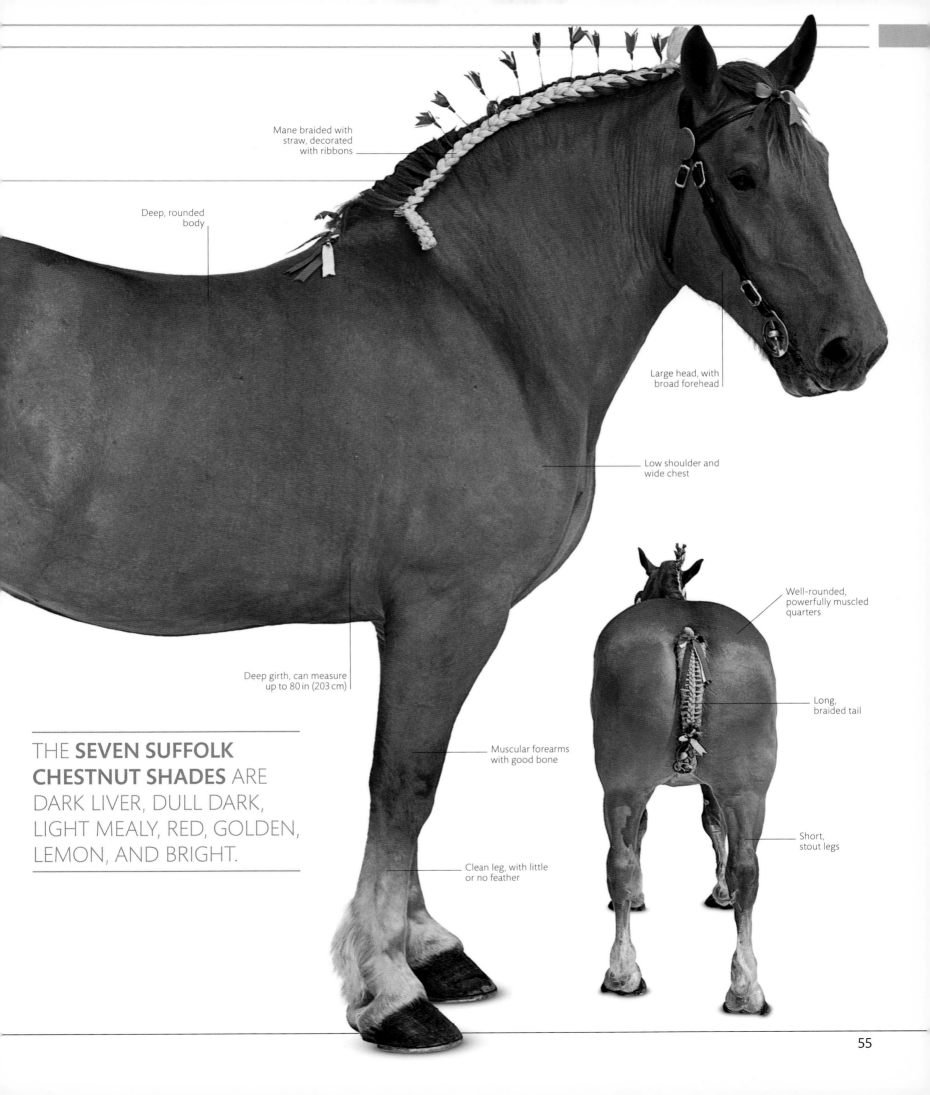

Mane braided with
straw, decorated
with ribbons

Deep, rounded
body

Large head, with
broad forehead

Low shoulder and
wide chest

Deep girth, can measure
up to 80 in (203 cm)

Well-rounded,
powerfully muscled
quarters

Long,
braided tail

THE **SEVEN SUFFOLK
CHESTNUT SHADES** ARE
DARK LIVER, DULL DARK,
LIGHT MEALY, RED, GOLDEN,
LEMON, AND BRIGHT.

Muscular forearms
with good bone

Short,
stout legs

Clean leg, with little
or no feather

Combine harvesting
Heavy horses, such as these Suffolk Punches, were once a common sight in the crop fields of Europe and America. Now, they are confined to a few farms, where the old traditions live on.

Noriker

HEIGHT AT WITHERS
16–17 hh (163–173 cm)
ORIGIN Austria
COLORS Chestnut,
black, brown, and spotted

This powerful workhorse derives its name from the Roman province of Noricum— roughly equivalent to present-day Austria. For hundreds of years, the horses in this area transported goods through the Alps to the Adriatic. Around 400 years ago, breeding became more regulated, and, later, crosses with other European stock increased the Noriker's size, and the introduction of Spanish blood helped to refine the breed. The Pinzgau-Noriker is a spotted strain, resulting from early crosses with Spanish horses. Today, all Noriker breeding follows strict guidelines.

Norikers are strong and good-natured horses. Excellent under harness, they are widely used for sleigh racing.

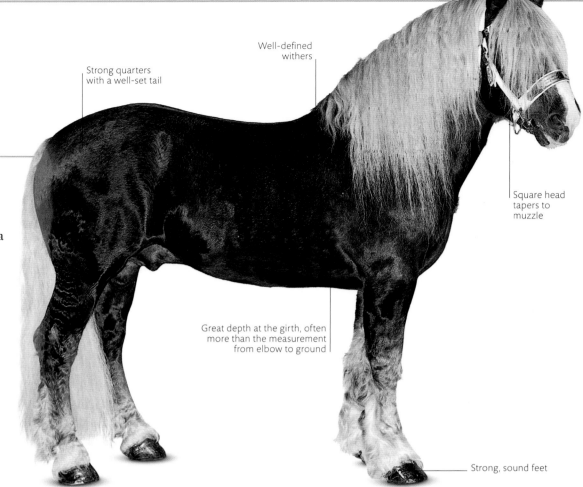

Strong quarters with a well-set tail

Well-defined withers

Square head tapers to muzzle

Great depth at the girth, often more than the measurement from elbow to ground

Strong, sound feet

Black Forest Horse

HEIGHT AT WITHERS
14.1–16 hh (145–163 cm)
ORIGIN Baden-Württemberg, Germany
COLORS Dark chestnut with flaxen mane and tail

Germany's oldest state stud at Marbach in Württemberg is probably best-known for breeding Arabs, but it is also home to stallions of an older coldblood breed, the Black Forest Horse. Established around 200 years ago, the horse—as its name suggests—was used around the Black Forest to haul timber and do farm work. With the mechanization of these industries the breed's numbers declined, but its strength and willing temperament were put to good use under harness. It is an increasingly popular riding horse as well.

Since 2001, Black Forest Horses have been bred in the US and a registry is being established.

Liver chestnut with flaxen mane and tail is a typical characteristic

Strong, muscular second thigh

Large, clean joints

Avelignese

HEIGHT AT WITHERS	ORIGIN	COLORS
Up to 14.3 hh (150 cm)	South Tyrol, Italy	Chestnut or palomino

AUSTRIAN OR ITALIAN?

The Haflinger has a strong following outside of its Austrian homeland while the Avelignese is confined to its Italian roots. Any key differences between the two may be revealed in the future, as DNA sequencing is more widely used. Both are reliable workers in harness and under saddle. The Avelignese is usually heavier in build, but both have attractive heads clearly showing the Arab influence.

The Avelignese is a strong reliable worker in harness and also a popular riding horse.

The Avelignese originates from the mountain village of Hafling in the South Tyrol. Like the Haflinger (see pp.194–95), the Avelignese is technically a coldblood, but both the breeds share an Arab foundation sire, El Bedavi XXII so there is strong underlying eastern blood. The base stock of both breeds is thought to be the now extinct Alpine Heavy Horse as well as the horses the Goths left behind in the Tyrolean valleys.

Slight differences can be seen between the Haflinger and the Avelignese. The latter is somewhat larger than the Haflinger. Although a breed of very old origins, the Avelignese was not officially established until 1874. It was developed with great care, particularly in Bolzano, and became the ideal agricultural workhorse and pack animal for farmers in the high alpine pastures and for forestry. Still used as a draft animal where machinery is impractical, it is now also a much-loved riding horse. The breed is reliable and docile, and its steadiness on Alpine paths makes it ideal for trail riding and other tourist activities in this popular region. Today, the Avelignese is bred in the mountainous areas of northern, central, and southern Italy.

THE AVELIGNESE HAS **VERY STRONG HOOVES** AND SO IS **RARELY SHOD.**

Alert, neat head reflects Arabian influence

Heavy, short neck

Broad back with low withers

Broad and muscular chest

Well spaced apart forelegs

Lightly feathered lower limbs

Italian Heavy Draft

HEIGHT AT WITHERS	ORIGIN	COLORS
15–16 hh (152–163 cm)	Italy	Mostly dark liver chestnut, but can be roan and chestnut

Fairly long, tapering head

Short, strong neck

This Italian favorite has a smallish stature, long walk, and energetic trot, which make it ideal for farm work.

The most popular heavy horse in Italy is the Italian Heavy Draft horse, sometimes called the Italian Agricultural horse. It is bred throughout northern and central Italy, but chiefly around Venice.

Its development dates from a time when Italian farmers required a quick-moving horse of smaller proportions to carry out general light agricultural work. To improve the rather poor local stock, breeders imported the massive and energetic Brabant (see p.75) from Belgium. The resulting crosses produced powerful offspring, but they were also too heavy and too slow. A more successful cross was with the Breton, especially the lighter, quick-moving Postier-type (see p.68). This was renowned for its swift trotting action, which came via its connection with the Norfolk Trotter (see p.157). When crossed with Italian mares, the progeny was compact and relatively fast-moving. Powerful animals with kind, docile temperaments, they were hardy and

also economical to keep. Their speed, much appreciated by Italian farmers, accounts for the Italian name for this breed, *Tiro Pesante Rapido*, which means quick heavy draft.

There is some coarseness in the appearance of the Italian Heavy Draft, the legacy of the less well-made Italian mares. In particular the limbs can be poor. They often lack bone, the joints are small and rounded, and the pasterns are upright, while the feet are boxy. The overall conformation shows the benefits of the Breton influence and the head is unexpectedly fine for a heavy breed. There is also more than a suggestion of the smaller and lighter Avelignese (see p.59), which, as a close neighbor, may well have been involved in the otherwise nondescript base stock. Today the Italian Heavy Draft is bred for its meat as well as its working qualities.

Powerful and rounded quarters

Long hindlegs

SYMBOL OF VERONA

The brand mark of the Italian Heavy Draft is a five-rung ladder within a shield. This is similar to the symbol of the city and province of Verona (pictured here) and emphasizes the breed's close historical links with this part of Italy. Youngsters undergo two assessments to ensure that they are a good example of the breed. The first is at between two and seven months old. If they pass, they are branded on their left quarter. The second is at 30 months and a brand is then added on the left side of the neck.

Light-colored mane

THE **ITALIAN HEAVY DRAFT** HAS A **STRONG FOLLOWING** IN **ITALY.** IN 2010, **REGISTERED HORSES** EXCEEDED **6,300.**

Brand mark indicates the origin

Short back

High-set tail

Deep girth

Muscular limbs with large joints

Lower limbs covered with coarse feather

Boxy feet

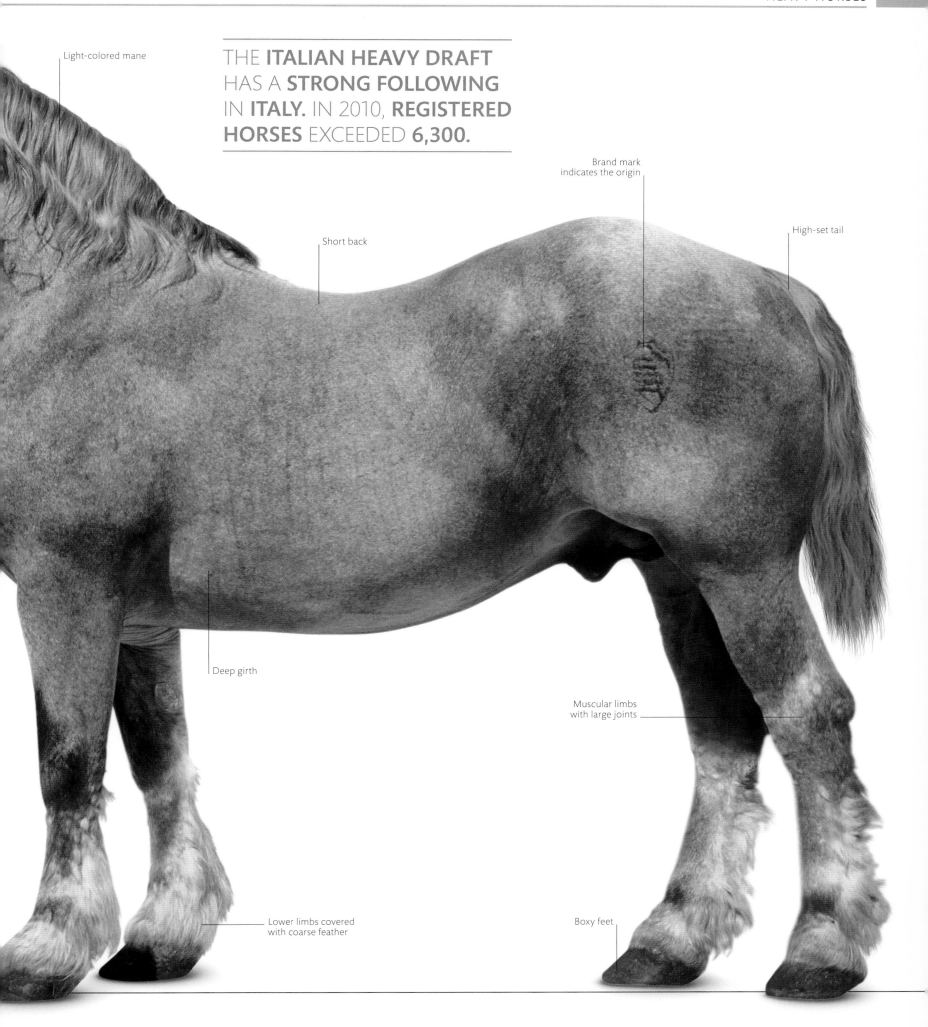

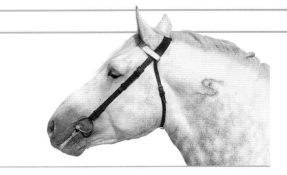

Percheron

HEIGHT AT WITHERS	ORIGIN	COLORS
16.2 hh (168 cm)	Normandy, France	Dapple gray. Black is permissible, and the French accept bay, chestnut, and roan

Said to be the most elegant of the heavy horse breeds, the Percheron is also one of the most enduring.

The best years for breeders were between 1880 and 1920, when Percherons were being exported to North and South America, Australia, and South Africa. The US was the principal market at the time. It is estimated that in the 1880s, 5,000 stallions and about 2,500 mares were imported, and by 1910 registrations had risen to 31,900.

Exceptionally obedient, the Percheron is very willing and capable of doing any sort of work. This adaptability is the result of careful breeding done in response to specific market requirements. Over the years, it has served as a warhorse, coach horse, farm horse, gun horse, and even a riding horse. Thousands of Percherons from America and Canada served on the battlefields of World War I. Of the 500,000 British horses that died during this conflict, a large percentage were Percherons or of Percheron type.

The breed is attractive and is known for its distinctive and stylish action, which is long, free, and low. It is able to adapt to different climates more easily than other heavy breeds—a characteristic often attributed to its Arab ancestry—and it makes an excellent base stock for crossing for specific tasks.

In the harsh conditions of the Falkland Islands, Percherons are crossed with Criollos (see p.236) to produce tough range horses, while in Australia, they are outcrossed to produce stock and competition horses. They remain popular and many countries, including Japan, have their own Percheron society.

Sloped, powerful quarters

Little feather on lower limbs

AMERICAN CREAM DRAFT

A draft horse that originated in Iowa in the early 1900s, this breed is cream with pink skin and amber-colored eyes. It is known for its willingness to work and its unflappable nature. The American Cream Breed Association was founded in 1944. One of the most influential stallions was Eads Captain, a horse that is seen in about one-third of the breed pedigrees. The American Cream was initially used for agricultural purposes in the wheat belt, but as horses were replaced by machines, their numbers fell dramatically. Renewed interest in the early 1980s saved the breed from extinction. Today it is seen being driven in parades and in displays at rodeos. It is also now used as a riding horse.

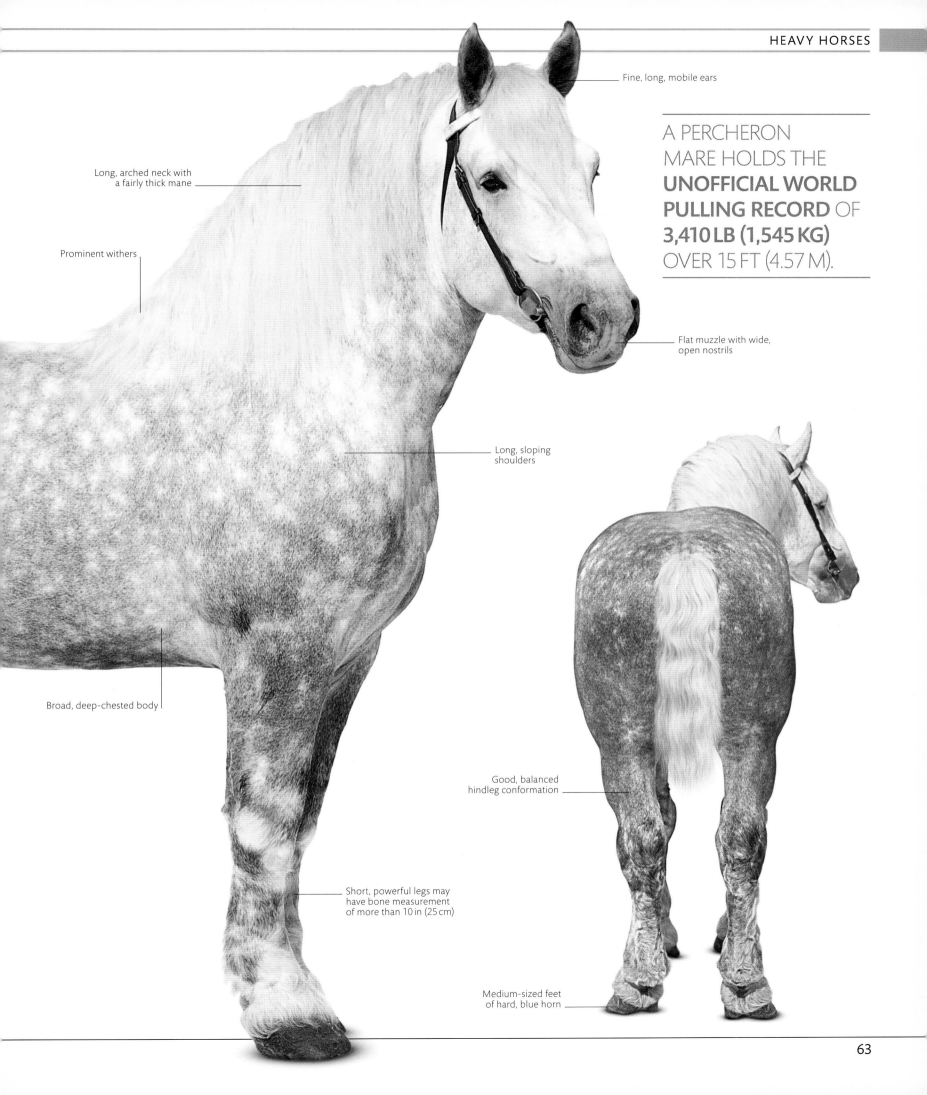

Fine, long, mobile ears

A PERCHERON MARE HOLDS THE **UNOFFICIAL WORLD PULLING RECORD** OF **3,410 LB (1,545 KG)** OVER 15 FT (4.57 M).

Long, arched neck with a fairly thick mane

Prominent withers

Flat muzzle with wide, open nostrils

Long, sloping shoulders

Broad, deep-chested body

Good, balanced hindleg conformation

Short, powerful legs may have bone measurement of more than 10 in (25 cm)

Medium-sized feet of hard, blue horn

Ardennais

HEIGHT AT WITHERS	ORIGIN	COLORS
15.3 hh (160 cm)	Ardennes region, France and Belgium	Roan, red-roan, iron gray, dark or liver chestnut, and bay. Can be bay-brown, light chestnut, and palomino

A massive European breed, the Ardennais is known for its huge frame, incredible strength, and extreme docility.

Originally, Ardennais were stocky, lively horses that were both ridden and used for light draft work. During the French Revolution in 1789, and in the following years of the Empire, they became renowned as the best artillery horses in Europe. They were used to transport guns and food supplies during Napoleon's disastrous Russian campaign in 1812, withstanding the rigors of the winter retreat from Moscow. At the start of the 19th century, in an effort to increase its energy levels, the Ardennais was crossed with Arab blood and later with the Percheron, Boulonnais, and Thoroughbred. Over the years, with changing agricultural demands, three distinct types of Ardennais evolved: a smaller type, nearest to its ancestor, the bigger Ardennais du Nord, or Trait du Nord as seen here, which resulted from outcrosses to the Belgian Draft Horse (see p.75), and the powerful Auxois (see box, below).

In the early 20th century, the Ardennais was popular for improving other breeds, such as the Russian Heavy Draft (until 1937, when the breed had been reestablished), the Comtois (around 1905, to improve the legs and increase its strength), and the Polish Sokolsky.

The overall impression of the breed is that of power. Once described as being "like a tractor," the Ardennais is more thick set than any other cart breed. It has a massive bone structure and very strong muscles. Its legs are short, thick, and strong. It has exceptionally good shoulders, leading to a free, animated, and straight action in the smaller types.

The Ardennais has adapted to the harsh climate and severe winters of the French Ardennes. As a result, it is hardy and has a strong constitution. It is a willing and hard worker, with excellent stamina and endurance. Yet, it is calm and gentle, docile enough for even children to handle.

While the Ardennais are still used as heavy draft horses, they are now mostly bred for the meat market.

AUXOIS

The Auxois from Burgundy is a contemporary of the Ardennais. The impact of the 19th-century Percheron and Boulonnais crosses are evident in this offshoot of the Ardennais. Although it has retained its red-roan color, it is less massive in the legs and quarters than the Ardennais du Nord. It is bred in France, largely to supply the meat industry. Despite its calm temperament and great endurance, it is not reared in other countries and, despite efforts by the French government to encourage its breeding, it has also become rare in France.

BOTH JULIUS **CAESAR** (C.100–144 BCE) AND GREEK HISTORIAN **HERODOTUS** (485–425 BCE) **ADMIRED HORSES FROM THE ARDENNES.**

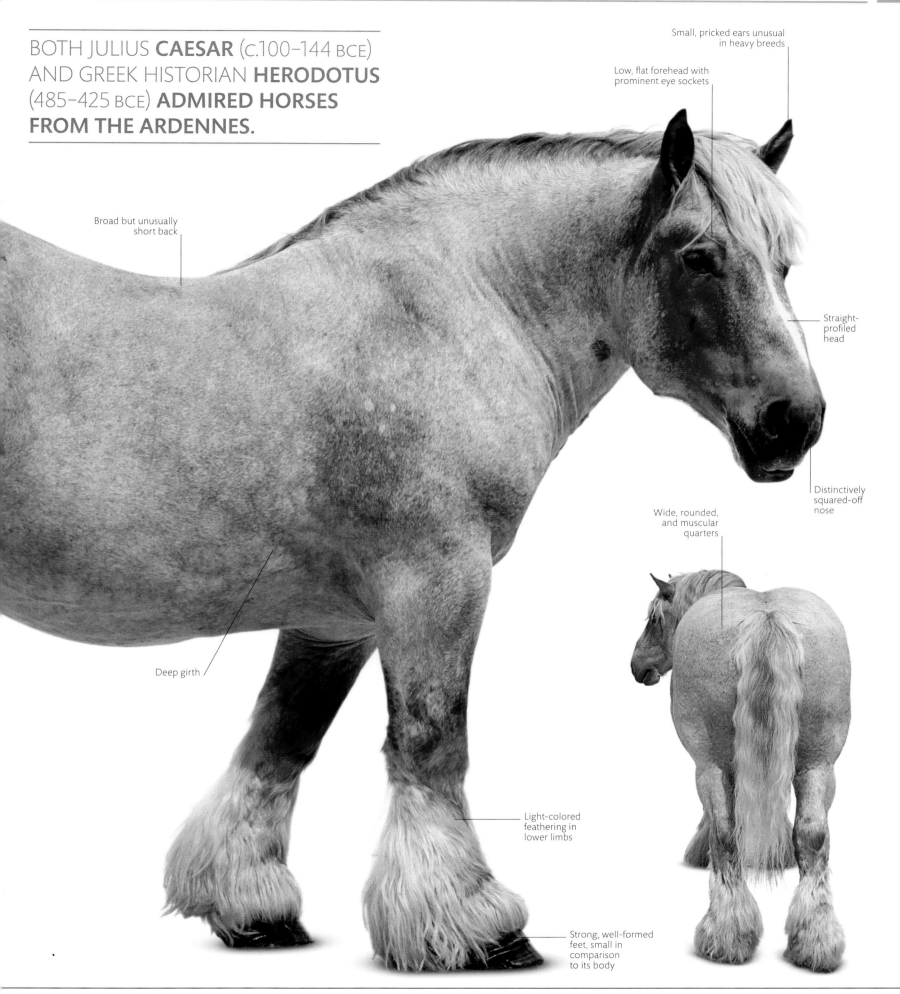

Small, pricked ears unusual in heavy breeds

Low, flat forehead with prominent eye sockets

Broad but unusually short back

Straight-profiled head

Distinctively squared-off nose

Wide, rounded, and muscular quarters

Deep girth

Light-colored feathering in lower limbs

Strong, well-formed feet, small in comparison to its body

Comtois

HEIGHT AT WITHERS	ORIGIN	COLORS
14.3–15.3 hh (150–160 cm)	Franche-Comté, France	Chestnut, occasionally silver-dapple

MEETING THE STANDARD

Colts must pass a series of tests before being registered as Comtois stallions. An examination is carried out by a representative of a local stud farm (Haras) and at least one representative of the breed registry. In addition to being checked against the breed standard, the colt must also have four registered grandparents. If it passes, it is branded with an interlaced TC.

This hardy, powerful horse from the Jura is now bred in the mountainous regions of France.

This mountain horse was originally derived from horses brought to the area from the adjacent region of Burgundy. In Franche-Comte, it was bred with draft horses and was traditionally an all-purpose farm horse, used for plowing and hauling timber in this remote area, as well as working the vineyards around the wine-producing town of Arbois.

In the 17th century, the Comtois was a cavalry mount, and was used as an artillery horse by Napoleon in the 19th century. Around this time, the blood of other heavy French breeds, including the Percheron (see pp.62–63) and Boulonnais (see opposite), was introduced. From 1905, Comtois mares were crossed with small bay-colored Ardennais stallions to improve the breed and a stud was established in 1919 at Besançon.

Today, the Comtois is still used as a draft horse but the focus now is on producing a lighter horse for leisure pursuits, and for drawing carriages and sleighs. A quick learner, the breed is noted for its free action and willing temperament. It is the most numerous of the French heavy breeds, with close to 4,000 mares being registered at the beginning of the 21st century.

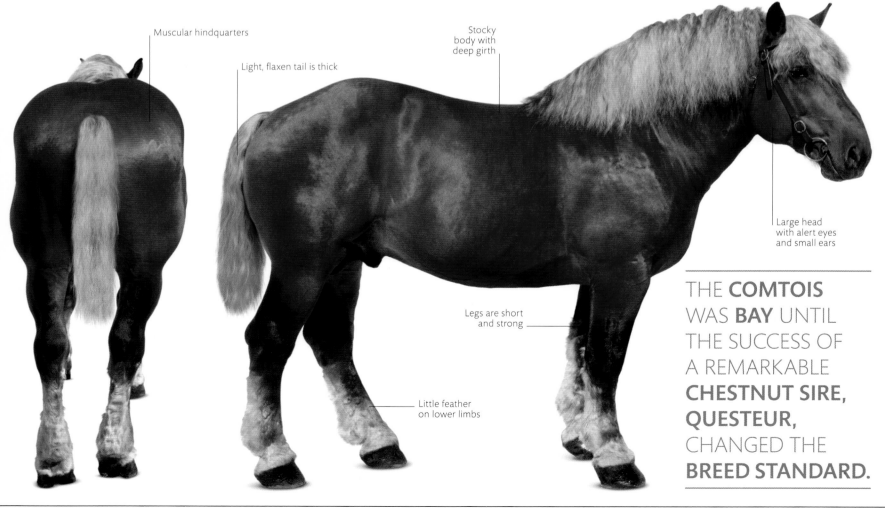

Muscular hindquarters

Light, flaxen tail is thick

Stocky body with deep girth

Large head with alert eyes and small ears

Legs are short and strong

Little feather on lower limbs

THE **COMTOIS** WAS **BAY** UNTIL THE SUCCESS OF A REMARKABLE **CHESTNUT SIRE, QUESTEUR,** CHANGED THE **BREED STANDARD.**

Boulonnais

HEIGHT AT WITHERS
15.1–17.3 hh
(155–180 cm)

ORIGIN
Pas de Calais,
northern France

COLORS
Usually gray,
occasionally chestnut

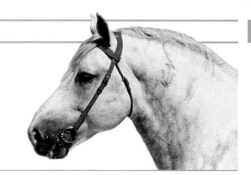

THE ROUTE DU POISSON

Inaugurated in 1991, this 24-hour endurance harness race held in France is a celebration of the historical express transportation of fish from the French port of Boulogne to Paris. Despite its popularity, the race has been canceled in recent years due to financing problems. It is hoped that it be held again in the future.

Elegant and beautiful, the Boulonnais is sometimes called the "Thoroughbred" of draft horses.

A native breed of northwest France, the striking Boulonnais developed from heavy horses in the Boulogne-Calais region. Its fine, Arab-like features are, however, the result of infusions of eastern blood. Numidian (Algerian) cavalry divisions of the Roman army stationed in northern France may have been the origin of the first introduction of eastern sires. During the Crusades, aristocratic French breeders introduced more eastern blood, then in the 14th century the forerunner of the Boulonnais was crossed with heavier breeds to bring it up to the weight and size required for a warhorse. When Spain occupied Flanders in the 16th century, there were crosses with Spanish horses that had already been subject to desert-horse influence (see pp.98–99).

The breed became known as the Boulonnais in the 17th century, and two distinct types emerged. The smaller, quick-trotting type, the *mareyeur* (fish merchant), was ideal for the swift transportation of fish from Boulogne to the Paris markets. The bigger, heavier type was an agricultural workhorse. During the two world wars, the breed almost disappeared. Today, there is a drive to safeguard it by promoting it as a good choice for driving competitions.

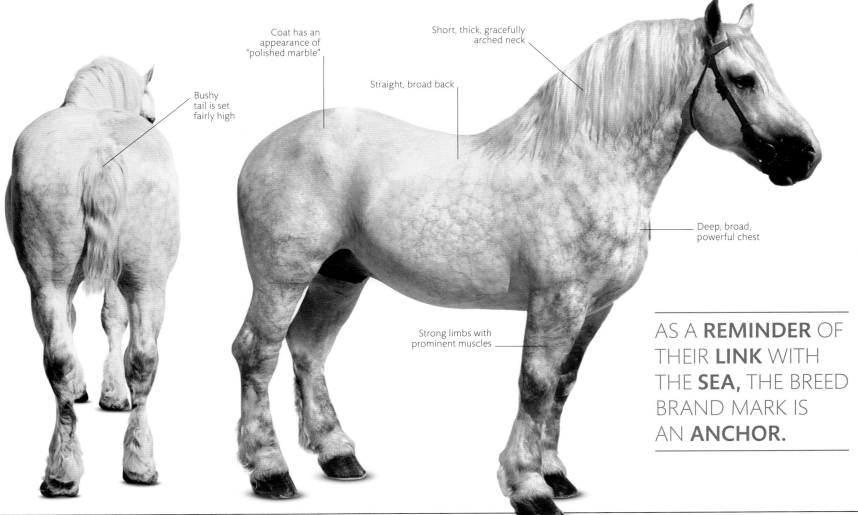

Bushy tail is set fairly high

Coat has an appearance of "polished marble"

Straight, broad back

Short, thick, gracefully arched neck

Deep, broad, powerful chest

Strong limbs with prominent muscles

AS A **REMINDER** OF THEIR **LINK** WITH THE **SEA**, THE BREED BRAND MARK IS AN **ANCHOR**.

Breton

	HEIGHT AT WITHERS	ORIGIN	COLORS
	15.1–16 hh (155-163 cm)	Brittany, France	Red-roan and chestnut, can also be bay and gray

BRETON POSTIER

Once the pride of the French Horse Artillery, Breton Postiers are an active, almost clean-legged type of the Breton breed. They display exceptional energy at trot, and are ideal for light draft and farm work. To qualify for admission in the studbook, they must be of Postier parentage and pass a performance test in harness. Nowadays, test days are like festivals with local people joining in the celebrations.

Brittany's horse breeders pursue the development of the Breton with enthusiasm bordering on obsession.

Bretons have often been crossbred with other native breeds to meet the changing needs of the local population. At one time, there were four types: two pacers (amblers), a general-purpose ride-and-drive, and a heavier draft. Today, there are two main types: the Breton heavy draft and the slightly smaller Breton Postier (see box, left). Both have shared a studbook since 1926. It was closed to outcrosses in 1951.

The Breton heavy draft is a massive, early maturing horse created by the addition of Ardennais (see pp.64–65), Boulonnais (see p.67), and Percheron (see pp.62–63) blood. It is an attractive horse with a short, square body and strong limbs. It is hardy, with great stamina and strength, making it suitable for all kinds of agricultural work. It is used extensively in the vineyards of the Midi-Pyrénnées in southern France. It is also valued for meat due to its fleshy frame.

The Breton's excellent constitution, along with its engaging temperament and attractive appearance, makes it a suitable and popular outcross for less-developed stock. A popular horse in France, the Breton is exported as far as Japan and Brazil. In the UK it is appreciated not only for its own sterling qualities, but also in crosses to produce riding cobs (see pp.130–31), which are required to be powerful and hard-working with a calm outlook.

The Postier is lighter in build and less common (see box, left). It was produced using Norfolk Roadsters in the late 19th century. There is also a version of the riding type, developed using eastern stallions and Thoroughbreds. Called the Cheval de Corlay, it is now very rare, but at one time it was fast enough to be raced at local meetings.

Small, mobile ears

Powerful quarters

Short, thick, arched neck

Compact, barrel-shaped body

Sloping shoulders

Hard, well-shaped feet

Square outline with a deep girth

Lower legs carry little feather

Short, thick, strong legs

IN INDIA, BRETONS WERE USED TO **PRODUCE MULES** AND, **WHEN CROSSED WITH ANGLO-ARABS,** CARRIAGE HORSES.

Crested neck

Shoulder is sloped
giving a free action

Short, strong
back

Appealing
cob-style head

Powerful
quarters

Stocky frame

Well-set
hocks

Short, very
muscular limbs

Light feather
at heels

ANCESTORS OF THE
NORMAN COB HAD
A GREAT **TROTTING
ABILITY** AND DREW
MAIL COACHES
OVER ROUGH ROADS.

Norman Cob

HEIGHT AT WITHERS	ORIGIN	COLORS
15.3–16.2 hh (160–168 cm)	Normandy, France	Chestnut, bay, or bay-brown; occasionally red-roan or gray

Powerful and stocky, the Norman Cob was developed as an all-around agricultural horse.

Tail is set high

The Norman Cob is a medium-weight heavy horse whose ancestors have been bred in Normandy for several hundred years. It owes much of its development to two of the great French royal studs (see box, below). However, as early as the 10th century, Normandy was established as one of the world's best horsebreeding areas, its limestone sub-soil and abundant grass pastures providing the ideal nursery for rearing horses. The Norman breeders were famed for a warhorse that nowadays would be called a draft type, although it was not as heavy as the massive heavy horses of Flanders. In the 16th and 17th centuries, outcrosses to Arab (see pp.92–93) and Barb (see pp.94–95) horses resulted in a lighter horse. By the beginning of the 20th century, breeders were making a distinction between horses that were suitable as

cavalry mounts and those of lesser quality and sturdier build that could be used in light draft on small farms. The term "cob" was used for these stocky horses because they closely resembled the English Cob (see pp.130–31), and soon the *Cob Normand* was recognized as a breed in its own right.

In the late 20th century, various reorganizations of the registry focused attention on the breed, which was suffering the same decline in numbers as many agricultural horses. In 1992, a new studbook was created and breed enthusiasts worked to tailor the Norman for driving and recreational riding. Today, numbers are stable at around 320 births a year. The Norman Cob is not a true heavy since it is a warmblood and lacks the massive proportions of the heavy draft horse. It could also be classed as a heavyweight riding horse, suitable for light draft.

ROYAL STUDS

The royal studs of Le Pin and Saint-Lô (pictured here), both in the French region of Normandy, were set up to meet the demand for vast numbers of horses for military purposes. For centuries they have produced a variety of horses from French Trotters (see pp.156–57) to Percherons (see pp.62–63) as well as the very popular Norman Cob. At Le Pin, the first stallions were installed in 1730, while Saint-Lô was set up in 1806.

Heavy head, covered
with wiry hair

Thick and coarse hair
in mane and tail

THE POITEVIN IS ONE OF
THE **MOST ENDANGERED**
OF FRENCH BREEDS. IN 2013,
ONLY 61 FOALS WERE BORN.

Long back with
undefined withers

Straight shoulders

Low-set tail

Large body covered with
rough hair in winter

Thick limbs with
round joints

Coarse, heavy hair
on lower legs

Large, platelike,
flat feet

Poitevin

 HEIGHT AT WITHERS
16–16.2 hh
(163–168 cm)

ORIGIN
Poitou,
France

COLORS
Dun, gray,
black, bay

The plain-looking Poitevin is not much of a worker, but it is one parent of the very useful Poitevin mule.

The Poitevin is descended from Dutch, Danish, and Norwegian draft horses brought by Dutch engineers to southwest France in the 17th century. Here, they were used to help drain the marshes of Poitou along with those in the neighboring Vendée. These imported horses interbred with tough local animals to produce the Poitevin, which—with its large, platelike feet and slow movement—is well suited for work in soft wet ground. Along with the feet, the Poitevin has retained many other primitive characteristics from its distant forest horse ancestors, such as the dun coloration with dark zebra stripes around the lower limbs. It has a strong constitution and can survive harsh conditions, but little care has been taken with its breeding and many conformational faults persist. These include the tendency to a long body, and a heavy coarse head with thick ears that have limited mobility. The quarters are strong, however, with plenty of muscle and the hindlegs are broad and thick. In addition, it has a calm and sober temperament.

The mares are crossed with the Baudet de Poitou (see box, below) to produce the Poitevin mule. Known for its versatility and strength, this mule is useful in both agricultural work and under saddle. These willing workers can manage on basic rations in inhospitable terrains with a working life of up to 25 years.

In the 1990s, partly due to the production of the more favored mule, there were fewer than a hundred purebred Poitevin mares in France, so a plan was put in place to ensure the breed's survival. Numbers have increased but still remain very low. The future continues to look doubtful for this breed.

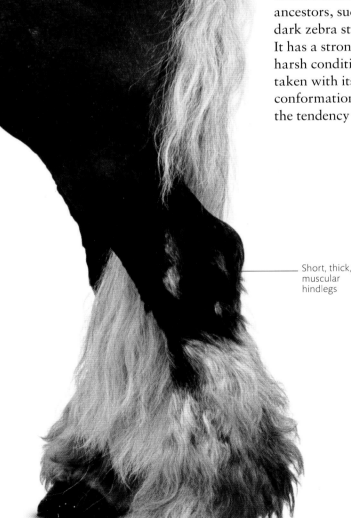

Short, thick, muscular hindlegs

BAUDET DE POITOU

The Poitou donkey, better known as the Baudet de Poitou, is crossed with the Poitevin mare to produce the Poitevin mule. Unusually hardy for a donkey, the Baudet de Poitou stands almost as tall as the Poitevin at 16 hh (163 cm). It has a quick action and an unexpectedly good stride length due to its size, long limbs, and the set of its shoulders. Its head—described as having a pleasing expression—is enhanced by its large ears.

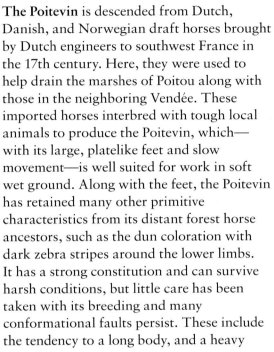

Jutland

HEIGHT AT WITHERS	ORIGIN	COLORS
15–16.1 hh (152–165 cm)	Jutland Peninsula, Denmark	Chestnut with a light-colored mane and tail

CARLSBERG GIANTS

Danish brewery, Carlsberg, has kept Jutlands to pull its drays since it was founded in 1847 in Valby, just outside Copenhagen. At that time the brewery kept more than 300 horses to distribute beer throughout Denmark. Not all were Jutlands, however; some Frederiksborgs were also used. Seven Jutlands still work at the brewery, which is doing its bit to conserve this endangered breed. It estimates the contribution these beautiful horses make to its success is worth €200,000 a year.

The attractive Jutland has a powerful body and a kindly character, both vital traits in a working horse.

Bred on the Danish Jutland Peninsula for hundreds of years, this breed's ancestors may date back to the Viking period. During the Middle Ages, horses from Jutland were exported, where they may have influenced the Suffolk Punch (see pp.54–55), whom the modern Jutland most closely resembles.

During the 18th century, the Jutland was crossed with the Danish Frederiksborg (see p.178) to improve its paces. As trade continued to develop between England and Denmark in the 19th century, Cleveland Bay (see pp.122–23) blood was also introduced, not very successfully. However, it was the Suffolk Punches imported by German dealer Oppenheimer for the Mecklenburg state stud that exerted the strongest influence. One Suffolk stallion in particular, Aldrup (or Oldrup) Munkedal—descended from

the chestnut Oppenheimer LXII bought to Germany in 1862—founded the Jutland's most important bloodline. Most existing Jutlands are said to be descended from two of Munkedal's sons, Hovding and Prins af Jylland. The Jutland, in turn, is the foundation ancestor of the Schleswig (see pp.78–79). The first Jutland breeders' association was formed in 1888.

The modern Jutland differs from the Suffolk Punch in that it has feathering on its legs—a feature Jutland breeders are trying to reduce. Coarser than the Suffolk, the Jutland has retained the compact, roly-poly body and the appealing roundness of the British breed. The active, enduring Jutland is still used for draft work to a limited extent and is popular at horse shows.

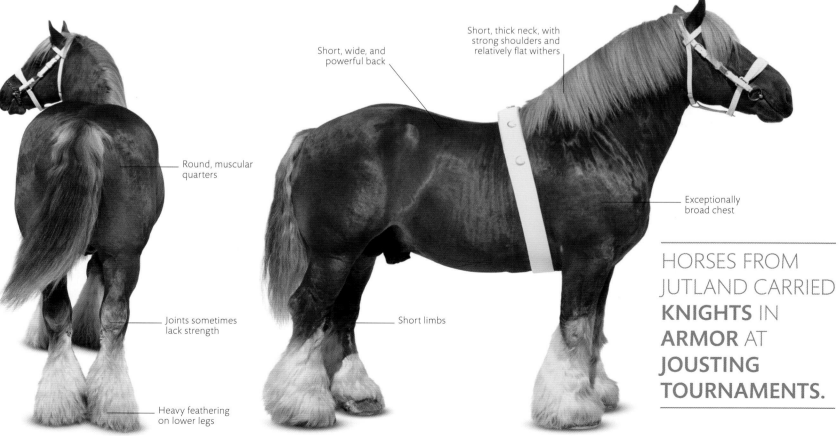

Short, thick neck, with strong shoulders and relatively flat withers

Short, wide, and powerful back

Round, muscular quarters

Joints sometimes lack strength

Heavy feathering on lower legs

Short limbs

Exceptionally broad chest

HORSES FROM JUTLAND CARRIED KNIGHTS IN ARMOR AT JOUSTING TOURNAMENTS.

Brabant

HEIGHT AT WITHERS
16.2–17 hh (168–173 cm)
ORIGIN Brabant and
Flanders, Belgium
COLORS Bay, black
and chestnut

Also called the Belgian Heavy Draft,
the Brabant is a massive breed. Historically
known as the Flanders Horse, it played an
important role in the development of other
heavy breeds, including the Clydesdale
(see pp.50–51) and the Shire (see pp.52–53).
Belgian breeders produced a unique working
horse suited to their climate and heavy soil
by excluding foreign blood and following
a policy of strict selection. The resulting
Brabant—which is also known as the
cheval de trait belge—is more versatile
than most heavy draft breeds and is quite
exceptional in terms of power. Today, the
Brabant is also bred in the US, where it
has a strong following.

Short, thick, and strong
neck suited to heavy
draft work

Croup is
characteristically
"double-muscled"

Broad chest

Heavily muscled
second thighs

Thick and
compact body

Short legs are
extremely strong
and hard

Medium-sized,
well-formed feet

Dutch Draft

HEIGHT AT WITHERS
16 hh (163 cm)
ORIGIN Netherlands
COLORS Chestnut, bay, and gray

The Dutch Heavy Draft Horse is usually
known simply as the Dutch Draft. It was
developed from the Brabant (see above)
after 1918 using Dutch mares of the old
Zeeland type and an occasional outcross
to the Belgian Ardennais (see pp.64–65).
A massive horse, it is still one of the
Netherlands' principal working horse
breeds and is employed in farming and
forestry, as well being used as a carriage
horse. The Dutch Draft possesses a
calm temperament, is free-moving,
and has great stamina. Bred for
working on mixed farms, this
slow-paced horse is known for its
easy-going nature.

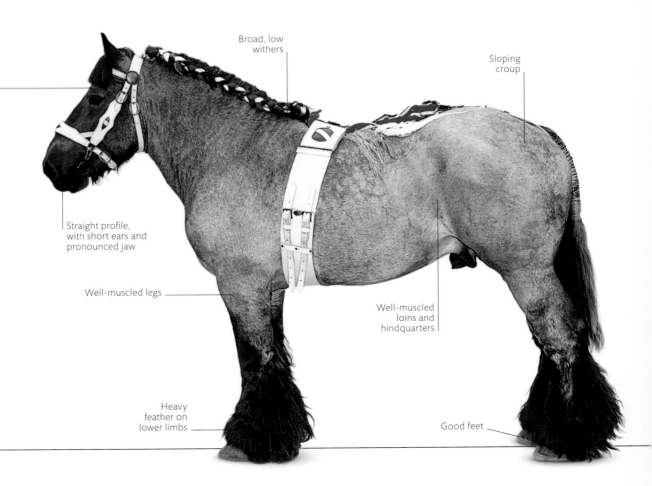

Broad, low
withers

Sloping
croup

Straight profile,
with short ears and
pronounced jaw

Well-muscled legs

Well-muscled
loins and
hindquarters

Heavy
feather on
lower limbs

Good feet

Amiable characters
These two mares and their foals are typical of the Dutch Draft breed. Their placid nature can be seen in their facial expressions and their build is heavy and compact.

Schleswig

HEIGHT AT WITHERS	ORIGIN	COLORS
15.2–16 hh (157–163 cm)	Schleswig-Holstein, Germany	Chestnut, gray, and bay

The origins of this strong, placid breed can be traced back to one particular Jutland stallion.

The Schleswig breed developed from the sturdy Jutland (see p.74), which in turn bears a close resemblance to the British Suffolk Punch (see pp.54–55). The breed's foundation is said to go back to a Jutland stallion named Aldrup Munkedal 839, and to his inbred descendants—the horses Prins of Jylland and Høvding. Initially, the Yorkshire Coach Horse and even the Thoroughbred (see pp.120–21) were also used to improve the soft and somewhat coarse native Schleswig. From 1860 onward, however, selective breeding based on the Munkedal line was practiced. In 1888, a breed standard was recognized and three years later the Society of Schleswig Horse Breeding Clubs was formed. By the end of the 19th century, the Schleswig had become a medium-sized draft horse and was in great demand for pulling buses and trams.

The early Schleswig was predominantly chestnut as a result of the Jutland influence, but gray and bay coats were seen in later years. Outcrosses to the Jutland were made

regularly to maintain the breed until 1938, when strict selection was practiced in an effort to eradicate some notable conformational deficiencies. These included flat ribs, an over-long body, and soft, flat feet. At the end of World War II, the breed reached its height of popularity, with over 25,000 mares and 450 stallions on the register. At this time, a move was made to improve its conformation and a Boulonnais (see p.67) and a Breton (see pp.68–69) stallion were brought in to accelerate this process, with the Boulonnais having the greater influence on the Schleswig's development. Numbers of Schleswigs, like those of its ancestor, the Jutland, then declined with the advent of increased mechanization. Inevitably, the traditional functions of this strong, placid breed, such as agricultural work, hauling timber, and transporting people, were taken over by machines.

BREED SOCIETY

The Society of Schleswiger Draft Horse Breeders (Verein Schleswiger Pferdezüchter) was founded in 1891 and the brand mark V.S.P. within an oval and placed on the back leg was introduced. This society closed in 1976 when the number of horses registered had dropped to 35 mares and 5 stallions. The breed's records were continued by the Schleswig-Holstein Horse Stud Book in Hamburg. The Society of Schleswiger Horse Breeders was founded in 1991 and has about 190 members. Some 200 mares and 30 stallions are registered.

Short limbs with plenty of bone

LIKE **MANY HEAVY HORSES**, THE SCHLESWIG IS **ENDANGERED**. IN 2014, THERE WERE ONLY **25 STALLIONS** AND **160 MARES**.

Short, straight profile

Long back

Short, thick neck

Round, muscular quarters

Good depth through the girth

Heavy feather on legs

Feet are relatively good

Døle Gudbrandsdal

HEIGHT AT WITHERS	ORIGIN	COLORS
15 hh (152 cm)	Norway	Black, brown, and bay

Wide forehead

This general purpose horse is compact and well-made with a good, free action at walk and trot.

Bred in the mountain valleys of Norway, the Døle Gudbrandsdal was developed as a strong, hardy horse which could be used for both agricultural work and as a pack animal. Døle Gudbrandsdal horses serviced the country's overland trade route, which ran through the Gudbrandsdal valley in central Norway, and connected the Oslo region with the North Sea coast.

In the 19th century, a growing interest in harness racing in Norway led to various outcrosses, with the aim of increasing the trotting speed of the horses. Of these, the most notable crosses were made with the English Thoroughbred Odin, imported in 1834. The result was a lighter type of horse, which had a longer, more economical stride at trot. However, the need for the heavier agricultural horse remained. The quality of this heavy type was maintained by the skill of the Norwegian breeders and the influence of one stallion in particular, Brimen 825.

After World War II, agriculture became increasingly mechanized and interest in the breed waned until state breeding centers were established in 1962.

Nowadays a lighter Døle Gudbrandsdal is usually bred. It has an average build, though it can exert a remarkable tractive power in relation to its size, a trait common to many breeds with a packhorse background.

The Døle Gudbrandsdal has features in common with Fell (see pp.272–73) and Dales (see pp.274–75) ponies, both of which were packhorses. It is likely that they share common ancestry.

Wide quarters

Short, thick, and strong legs

Abundant feather at the heels

ST. OLAV'S WAY

The old packhorse route of the Døle Gudbrandsdal from Oslo to Trondheim overlaps with an ancient pilgrim's route called St. Olav's Way, also called the King's Way. There were several different routes through the valleys of Gudbrandsdal and Lågen and over the Dovrefjell mountains, ensuring they could be followed in winter or summer. Horse riders (and walkers) can still take these paths over the mountains and it is an excellent way of enjoying the spectacular Norwegian scenery.

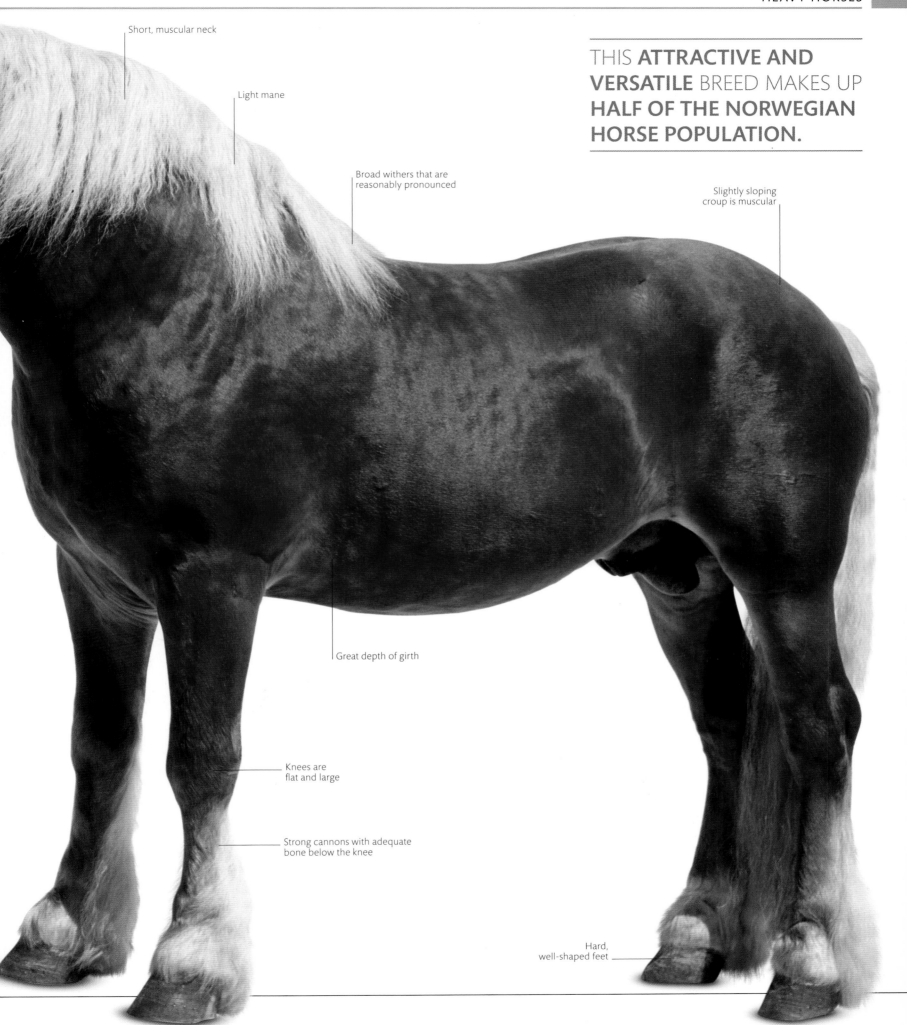

Short, muscular neck

Light mane

Broad withers that are reasonably pronounced

THIS ATTRACTIVE AND VERSATILE BREED MAKES UP HALF OF THE NORWEGIAN HORSE POPULATION.

Slightly sloping croup is muscular

Great depth of girth

Knees are flat and large

Strong cannons with adequate bone below the knee

Hard, well-shaped feet

North Swedish Horse

	HEIGHT AT WITHERS	**ORIGIN**	**COLORS**
	16 hh (163 cm)	Northern Sweden	Any solid color, usually brown or black

JÄRVSÖFAKS

This Swedish Trotter is a part-bred Swedish coldblood. Foaled in 1994, he started racing at 3 years old. He won 201 of his 234 races and broke the world coldblood trotting record, doing 0.6 miles (1 km) in 1 minute 17.9 seconds, in July 2005. He was awarded many titles in Sweden during his working life, including Horse of the Year (three times) and Coldblood of the Year (12 times). Since retiring from racing, Järvsöfaks has had a successful career as a breeding stallion, siring 874 foals.

A compact breed with a remarkable capacity to pull heavy loads and withstand harsh climates.

In Northern Europe and Scandinavia, horses bred for use in agriculture and forestry were expected to be exceptionally hardy and work in difficult conditions. The North Swedish Horse, however, is not simply a "heavy" horse in the European tradition. The growing interest in competitive trotting in Scandinavia also encouraged the breeding of lighter horses that were strong yet could trot at speed.

Regarded as a coldblood, the North Swedish has its origins in the older Scandinavian breeds and is closely related to the Døle Gudbrandsdal (see pp.80–81) of Norway. Until the end of the 19th century it was not a breed as such, but rather a mixture of several imported breeds. Following the formation of a breed society, efforts were made to achieve greater uniformity. At Wången, the principal stud set up in 1903, there was a policy of strict selective breeding as well as rigorous hauling tests over rough ground. These were devised to ensure performance was tailored to the requirements of the forestry industry, which continues to use horses today.

In addition to its strength and endurance, the North Swedish also boasts a cheerful temperament, is exceptionally long-lived, and is said to be very resistant to many common equine diseases. Crosses with the Døle led to the breed being sub-divided in 1966 and the development of a lighter horse that was more suitable for harness racing. This lighter-bodied trotting horse, the world's only coldblood harness racer, is agile with longer limbs and is often known as a Scandinavian Coldblood Trotter. Coldblood Trotters are virtually unknown outside of Scandinavia.

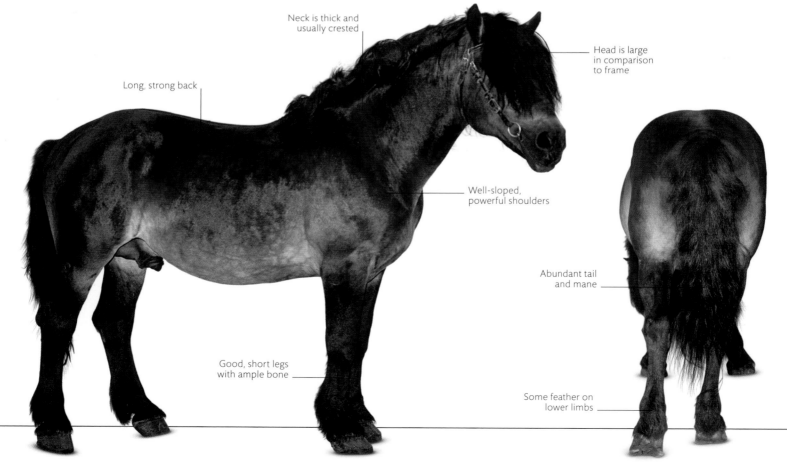

Neck is thick and usually crested

Head is large in comparison to frame

Long, strong back

Well-sloped, powerful shoulders

Abundant tail and mane

Good, short legs with ample bone

Some feather on lower limbs

WÅNGEN IS THE NATIONAL CENTER FOR **HARNESS RACING**, AND VITAL FOR THE **SURVIVAL OF THE NORTH SWEDISH.**

THE **FACE** HAS AN **ALERT EXPRESSION** WITH **LARGE, KIND EYES,** HINTING AT THE BREED'S **ARAB HERITAGE.**

Lightly built, attractive head

Withers are clearly defined for a heavy breed

Body not massive or wide

Muscular forearms

Depth through the girth

Second thighs are well-muscled

Limbs are light but with hard joints

Hocks are well-positioned

Slight feather at heel

Medium-sized feet

Mur아közi

HEIGHT AT WITHERS	ORIGIN	COLORS
16 hh (163 cm)	Southern Hungary	Chestnut; also bay, black, and gray

This Hungarian breed has the flaxen mane and tail of its Austrian Noriker ancestors.

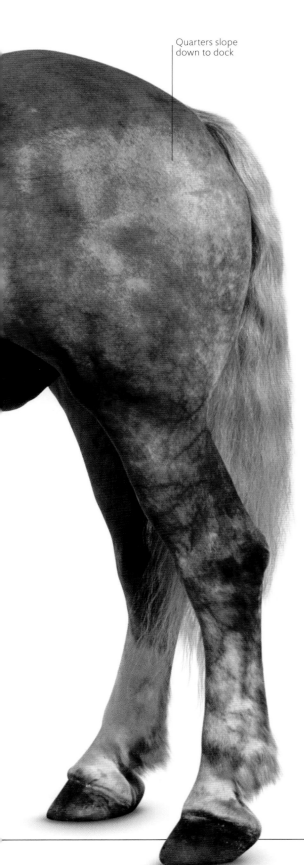

Quarters slope down to dock

Hungary developed many quality light horse breeds between 1870 and the outbreak of World War I in 1914, but excellent heavy drafts were also being produced. At Muraköz, on the river Mura in southern Hungary, the breeding program focused on these agricultural horses, which were vital to the country's rural economy. The early foundation stock was sometimes referred to as Mur-Insulan, which means "confined to the Mura region." To create a new breed, Noriker (see p.58) mares from Austria were put to Arab stallions. Later, good-quality Hungarian stallions were used, and both Percherons (see pp.62–63) and Ardennais (see pp.64–65) were added to the mix.

The breeding program produced a quick-moving, alert horse that was ideal for general farm use and strong enough for intensive arable farm work on heavy soils. The Muraközi was in great demand after World War I when arable farming increased

dramatically in Central Europe. However, World War II had an adverse effect on the breeding stock so Ardennais stallions—already a significant element in the Muraközi's genetic make-up—were imported from France and Belgium to revitalize the breed, which was reestablished in a very short time. It continued to flourish in Hungary up to the late 1970s.

A distinctive horse, possibly owing to the Arab influence in its ancestors, the Muraközi is still classed as a coldblood and can be divided into two types: a heavy horse and a lighter, smaller, more active, general-purpose animal. Both have a calm temperament and their physical constitution is similarly dependable. The breed is also very economical to keep and is noted for its efficiency in converting food into energy. Muraközi horses are bred in Poland and in the countries of former Yugoslavia, as well as in Hungary.

HEAVY TYPE

The heavier Muraközi is very similar to the lighter type, except that it is more heavily built and, as a result, lacks some of the quickness of movement and activity in the paces. As with so many other heavy breeds, Muraközi horses have declined in numbers now that they are no longer needed for agriculture. However, they are gaining popularity as a useful, steady type of riding horse that can be worked in harness if required.

Weeding vegetables
A Muraközi, wearing a traditional Hungarian breast harness, draws a hoe through a young crop. The breed's quick action and calm outlook makes it ideal for the job.

Vladimir

HEIGHT AT WITHERS	ORIGIN	COLORS
16.1 hh (165 cm)	Northeast Russia	Bay

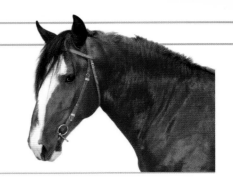

VLADIMIR *TROIKA*

Despite being a draft horse, the Vladimir has proved very handy at drawing the famous Russian *Troika* (see p.110). This is probably thanks to its free and energetic action, and the emphasis placed on keeping its size relatively small for a draft. Its trotting draft record is 6,562 ft (2,000 m) in 4 minutes 34 seconds while pulling 110 lb (50 kg).

Before the revolution of 1917, Russia had more horses per 100 people than any European country except Iceland.

The Vladimir Heavy Draft breed evolved at collective and state farms in the provinces of Ivanovo and Vladimir, east of Moscow. It was based on selective breeding programs using local mares crossed with Clydesdales (see pp.50–51) and Shires (see pp.52–53) that had taken place at the Gavrilovo-Posadsk State Stables in the early years of the 20th century. The principal foundation stallions were three Clydesdales: Lord James and Border Brand, both foaled in 1910, and Glen Albin, who was foaled in 1923. The Shire crosses, though important, were less influential and are found far back in the pedigrees, mostly on the dams' side. The

Shire background is evident in this example, however. By the mid-1920s interbreed crossing was being phased out because a number of good crossbreds had been obtained. Selected crossbreds were then mated to fix the Vladimir's type and character.

Although the selection process continued until 1950, the Vladimir horse was officially recognized as a breed in 1946. Well-built with a deep girth, this is a good-natured animal and combines great pulling power with adequate speed. The horses mature quickly, an important quality for animals that are put to work at 3 years of age.

THE **VLADIMIR** BENEFITED FROM RUSSIAN STATE **BREEDING** POLICIES AFTER **WORLD WAR II.**

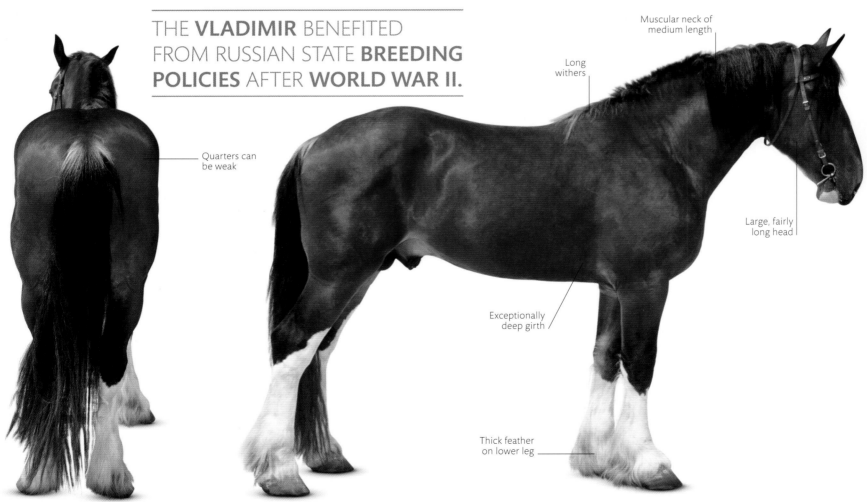

Quarters can be weak

Muscular neck of medium length

Long withers

Large, fairly long head

Exceptionally deep girth

Thick feather on lower leg

Russian Heavy Draft

HEIGHT AT WITHERS	ORIGIN	COLORS
14.2–14.3 hh (147–150 cm)	Ukraine	Strawberry roan, chestnut

KOUMISS

This fermented, mildly alcoholic drink made from mare's milk is thought to have medicinal qualities. It is drunk chilled and traditionally sipped from small bowls. Russian writer Leo Tolstoy (pictured here) drank koumiss regularly and wrote about it in his autobiographical story *A Confession*. Russian Heavy Drafts are used to produce koumiss at an experimental farm in Ryazan, southern Russia.

Known as the Russian Ardennes until the 1920s, this breed began to be registered as the Russian Heavy Draft in 1952.

This comparatively short draft horse was developed around the same time as the Vladimir (see opposite) at the Khrenov and Derkul State Studs in the Ukraine. At first, Ardennes stallions from Sweden were crossed with Ukraine mares and other breeds including the Brabant (see p.75) and some Percherons (see pp.62–63). Orlov Trotters (see pp.110–11) were also brought in to give increased activity. During the 1920s the Russian Heavy was in decline. However, it was saved by a breeding program to produce an amenable horse suitable for general agricultural work.

The Russian Heavy is a smart horse, built like a heavy cob, with a strong frame and lively movement. The head is notable for its lightness and attractive expression, which may be a result of the Orlov cross. The Russian Heavy matures very quickly: it is reckoned to have grown to 97 percent of its full height, and to have reached 75 percent of its full weight, by the time it is 18 months old. The breed has a long life expectancy and is capable of carrying out agricultural work at a fairly advanced age. It is said that the mares are good milk producers (see box, left).

Muscular neck

Strong frame

Thick tail and mane

Chest is wide and short

Head is large and fairly long

Short legs are set well apart

Short feather confined to heels

THE **STALLIONS** MAY STILL BE **USED AT STUD** WHEN THEY ARE **OVER 20 YEARS OLD.**

LIGHTER HORSES

Light horses are primarily used for riding or driving, although some have a background of draft or farm work. They range from the fast-moving Arab and Thoroughbred to the smooth-gaited breeds, such as the Missouri Fox Trotter and Peruvian Paso. One of the largest groups is the warmbloods, most of which have been deliberately produced for competition. Light horses vary greatly in their conformation. Many have long limbs in comparison with their lightweight bodies, but some have short limbs and others have stocky bodies.

◄ **Made for the job** Many lighter horses are the product of years of careful breeding, but others, such as the Camargue, have developed to suit their natural environment.

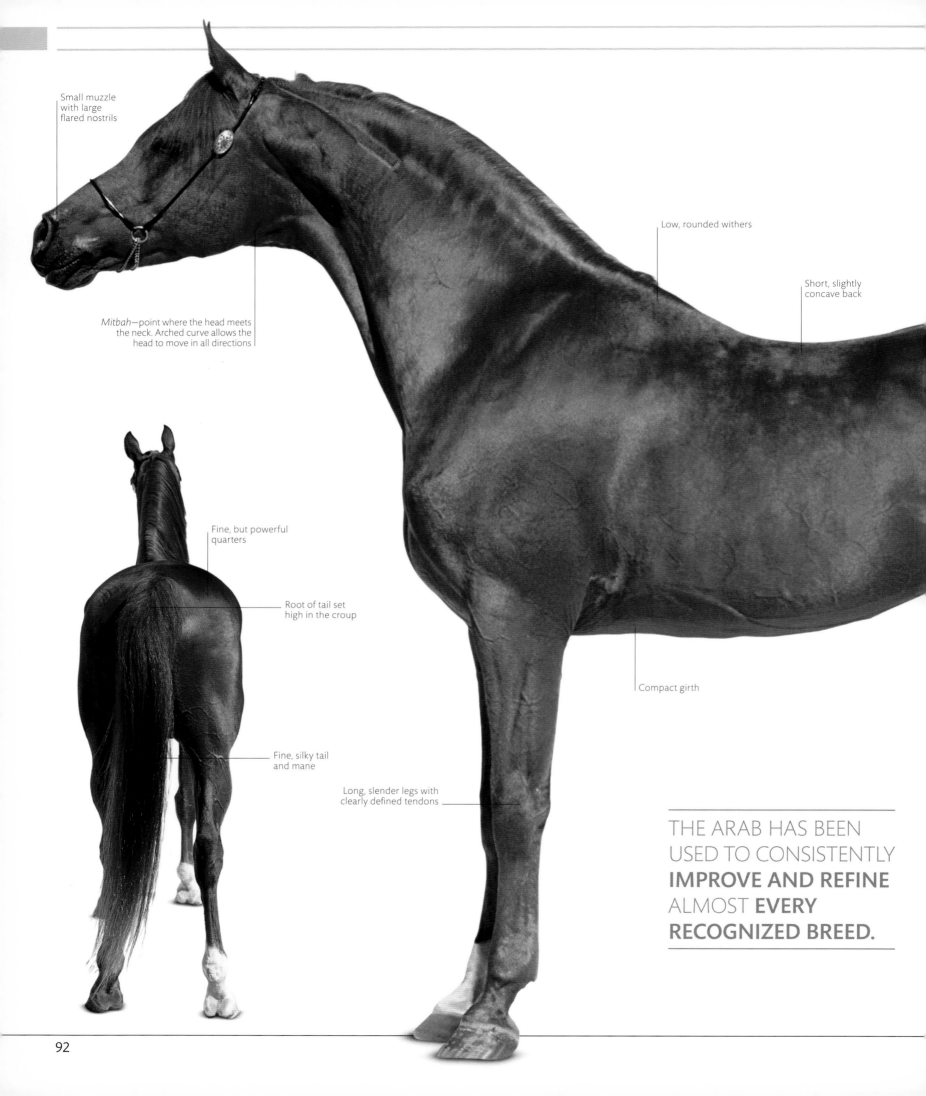

Small muzzle with large flared nostrils

Mitbah—point where the head meets the neck. Arched curve allows the head to move in all directions

Low, rounded withers

Short, slightly concave back

Fine, but powerful quarters

Root of tail set high in the croup

Fine, silky tail and mane

Long, slender legs with clearly defined tendons

Compact girth

THE ARAB HAS BEEN USED TO CONSISTENTLY **IMPROVE AND REFINE** ALMOST **EVERY RECOGNIZED BREED.**

Arab

HEIGHT AT WITHERS	ORIGIN	COLORS
14.3 hh (150 cm)	Arabian Peninsula	Chestnut, gray, bay, and black

Of all the horse breeds, the elegant and distinctive Arab is one of the most instantly recognizable.

Long and level croup

Near perfect feet in terms of shape and size

In 786, Arab historian El Kelbi traced this breed to about 3000 BCE, to a mare named Baz, and a stallion named Hoshaba. Baz is claimed to have been captured in the Yemen by Bax, the great-great-grandson of Noah, tamer of the wild horses.

While these and similar records remain unsubstantiated, they establish the antiquity of the breed. What is known is that when the Moors invaded Spain and Portugal in the 8th century, they brought desert horses with them, so ensuring their spread across the Western world.

The Arab is acknowledged as the foundation of the Thoroughbred (see pp.120–21). It is a popular improving cross, and it is said that Arab blood flows through a greater part of the world's equine population.

While there is no one true type of pure Arabian, there are certain characteristics unique to this breed. A distinctive feature is its short, very fine, "dry" head, which has clearly visible veining. The face is notably concave, or "dished," and the forehead is convex, forming a shield shape called the *jibbah*. The head tapers into a small muzzle. Its large, expressive eyes are widely spaced and are lower than in other breeds.

Arabs have a genetic predisposition to having an extra thoracic vertebra and one fewer lumbar vertebra. It is suggested that this variation contributes to the high carriage of the tail and a distinctive body shape. The Arab has a "floating" action, as if moving on springs.

The modern Arab excels at endurance racing, and its stamina is legendary, but, it is outclassed in many other competitive sports. However, it is still bred in great numbers with rare dedication. It is fiery and courageous, with an exceptionally gentle nature.

MARENGO

French Emperor Napoleon Bonaparte favored the Arab, and had his personal stud of gray Arab chargers. He encouraged the use of Arabs at the French national studs and rode his favorite Arab charger, Marengo, in his last battle at Waterloo in 1815. The horse was named after the French victory at Marengo in 1800.

Arched neck set on prominent withers

Back is short and very strong

Profile is usually straight or convex

Low-set tail

Legs are slender and very hard

ROAN BARBARY, THE **FAVORITE** HORSE OF **RICHARD II** (1377–99), WAS SAID TO BE A **DESCENDANT OF BARB HORSES.**

Barb

HEIGHT AT WITHERS	ORIGIN	COLORS
14.2–15.2 hh (147–157 cm)	Morocco	Usually gray, but also black

The Barb is second only to the Arab as one of the world's great foundation breeds.

Quarters slope from the croup

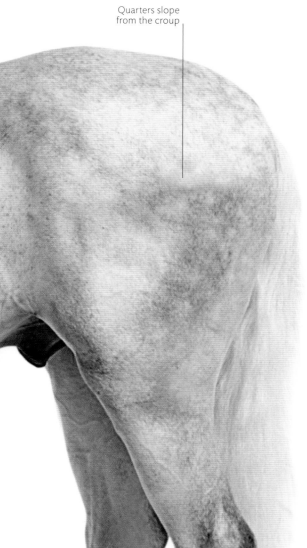

Hindlegs may be cow-hocked

Feet tend to be narrow

The ancestors of this tough desert horse were probably introduced to Europe by Berber horsemen during the Muslim invasion of Spanish territories in the 8th century. Despite the inevitable crossing with Arab stock, this desert-type remained genetically dominant. In most breeds where it has been used as an "improving" cross, the Arab imparts something of its distinctive appearance. However, even today's Barb, with its characteristically long, convex profile, sloping quarters, and low-set tail, betrays little of the Arab's genes. Some authorities hold that the Barb belongs to a desert (Arab) racing strain that resembled the Akhal-Teke (see pp.98–99) prior to domestication, but its definitive ancestry is impossible to establish.

Although its influence is not as widely recognized as the Arab's, the Barb has had a significant effect on European and American breeds. This influence was perpetuated through its most important derivative, the Spanish horse. The Barb also played a major part in the development of the modern version of the Spanish horse, the Andalucian (see pp.140–41), and was influential in the evolution of the Thoroughbred (see pp.120–21) and Ireland's Connemara pony (see pp.264–65). There is also evidence of this desert horse's impact on French stock. The now-extinct Limousin, purpose-bred as a military charger in medieval times, was upgraded using the horses brought to France by the Muslim armies. Today, the various mustang societies of North America, whose object is the conservation of wild horses, place great emphasis on "Spanish Barb" blood. Perhaps because it is less numerous and less attractive than the Arab, the Barb has never received due recognition.

NORTH AFRICAN HORSEMEN

For centuries, desert horses (forerunners of the Barb) were the mount of the North African Berbers. Crossing to Gibraltar in 710, these fierce Muslim horsemen continued their successful campaigns through the north of the Iberian Peninsula and into France, where their armies were defeated at Poitiers in 732. The armies valued these tough little horses for their speed and stamina. Barbs are still found in Morocco, Algeria, Spain, and southern France, but numbers are declining in North Africa.

Modern tournament
Every year in Morocco, scores of Barb horses and Berber riders gather for a display that rivals a medieval joust. In one game, they gallop in a straight line, firing shots in unison.

Short, sparse forelock and mane

Long, thin neck, set almost vertically to the body

Straight profile

High withers

Wide nostrils

Narrow quarters

Chest is deep but narrow

Sparse silky tail

Straight forelegs that can be too close together

Tubelike body with a long back and shallow rib cage

IN 1935, AKHAL-TEKES WERE RIDDEN FROM **ASHKABAD TO MOSCOW,** COVERING **2,580 MILES (4,152 KM)** IN 84 DAYS. ABOUT A QUARTER OF THE JOURNEY WAS THROUGH DESERT, WITH **VIRTUALLY NO WATER.**

Akhal-Teke

HEIGHT AT WITHERS	ORIGIN	COLORS
14.3–16 hh (150–163 cm)	Ashkhabad, Turkmenistan	Bay, chestnut, and dun, frequently with a golden metallic sheen. Can also be black, gray, and silver

One of the oldest and most distinctive breeds, the Akhal-Teke is a long-distance racehorse capable of enduring intense heat.

Thin skin, with an exceptionally fine coat

The Akhal-Teke is a desert breed from Turkmenistan. It is closely associated with the Turkmene (see box, p.113) and it is possible that the two breeds are variants of an ancient common ancestor. Although its origins are not clear, as long ago as 1000 BCE studs at Ashkhabad, Turkmenistan, bred horses famed for their racing prowess. Today Ashkhabad is a center for Akhal-Tekes, so it seems likely that there is a link between the two.

The Akhal-Teke breed has a unique action: it seems to slide over the ground in a flowing movement without swinging its body. In its homeland, it is valued for its speed and endurance but it lacks the conformational qualities sought after in Western racehorses, such as the Thoroughbred (see pp.120–21). It has a long back and narrow rib cage and its second thigh is slight. The long neck may contribute to its tendency to hold its head above the level of the rider's hand. Known as being "above the bit," this reduces the rider's overall control. In addition, the Akhal-Teke is said to be rather obstinate. Despite its negative riding qualities, this horse's eye-catching metallic coat color has ensured it has many fans worldwide.

In modern times breeders have sought to improve the Akhal-Teke using outcrosses to Thoroughbreds and other sport horses. It is now closer to European competition horses in appearance and is the Russian sports horse of choice in the dressage and jumping disciplines. However, Turkoman breeders realizing that this outcrossing also reduces its ability to withstand the harsh desert conditions, have reverted to breeding pure lines.

Long, muscular thighs

Long hindlegs, usually sickle-shaped and cow-hocked

Small, but hard and durable feet

TRADITIONAL PRACTICES

Nowadays, Akhal-Tekes are turned out during the day and stabled at night. Traditionally they were kept tethered in the open all year. They would be wrapped in numerous blankets of heavy felt during the night, to protect against the cold, as well as during the day, the idea being that this would "melt" any surplus body fat. They were fed a high-protein, low bulk diet of lucerne, pellets of mutton fat, eggs, barley, and *quatlame*—a fried dough cake—with the aim of producing a lean body ideal for racing.

Turkmenistan races
Akhal-Tekes are much admired for their racetrack performances. Although not considered as fast as Thoroughbreds, they are quick off the mark and have great powers of endurance.

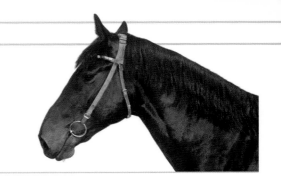

Kabardin

	HEIGHT AT WITHERS 15–15.2 hh (152–157 cm)	ORIGIN Northern Caucasus, Russia	COLORS Bay, dark bay, and black (without any distinguishing marks)

ADAPTED TO THE MOUNTAIN

Herds of Kabardins can still be seen grazing high pastures in Kabardin-Balkar. They begin to climb into the mountains in spring, going ever higher as the snow recedes. These horses are perfectly adapted to their high-altitude home, with strong hearts and lungs capable of coping with thin air and the ability to put on fat to sustain them through the winter. Their abilities as endurance horses are legendary.

Sure-footed and agile, this mountain horse has an uncanny ability to find its way through mist and darkness.

One of the finest mountain breeds of the former USSR, the Kabardin has been recognized as a breed since the 16th century. It has its origins in Mongolian-type steppe horses, improved with the Karabakh as well as horses of Persian and Turkmen blood. In the 1920s, further crosses were made with horses from Kabardin-Balkar and Karachaev-Cherkess studs. This led to a stronger type, suitable for both riding and agricultural work. Later, after the Russian Revolution, further crosses with the Kabardin-Balkar and Karachaev-Cherkess lead to the creation of a stronger type suited both for riding and agricultural work.

Today, the Kabardin is the principal breed of the Kabardino-Balkar Republic, and is used to improve native stock in Armenia, Azerbaijan, Dagestan, Georgia, and Osetia. The best are raised at the Malo-Karachaev and Malkin studs. Though not as fast as the more specialized racing breeds, they are popular for local sporting activities.

Kabardins are very obedient and have a calm temperament. They can work in difficult terrain, undeterred by snow and fast rivers. Their action is energetic and their straight shoulders produce a fairly high step that helps them pick their way over rough ground. They are not fast gallopers, but have an even walk, and the trot and canter are light and smooth. Like many other Asian horses, some Kabardins pace naturally.

Slender neck with defined withers

Small, attractive head

Quarters slope away from croup

Short, straight back

Upright shoulders that can look loaded

Narrow chest

Luxuriant tail

Clean, slender forelegs

Sickle-shaped hindlegs common in mountain breeds

Sound feet that can be worked without shoes

IN A **WINTER TRIAL** IN **1935**, KABARDINS COVERED **1,860 MILES (3,000 KM)** IN **37 DAYS.**

Karabakh

HEIGHT AT WITHERS	ORIGIN	COLORS
14 hh (142 cm)	Nagorno-Karabakh, Azerbaijan	Chestnut, bay, or dun, with a metallic sheen

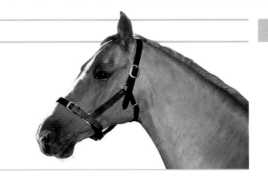

NOVA KHIRGIZ

The eastern part of Kyrgyzstan is said to have been home to the Ferghana horses of antiquity. The Kyrgyz tribesmen from this area perfected their own mountain horse and the Nova Khirgiz evolved here from the 1950s. This refined breed is perfectly suited to the geographical and climatic conditions of the region.

A light riding horse with a calm temperament, the Karabakh is a sturdy mountain breed of Central Asia.

A geographical neighbor of the Kabardin, this breed traces its origins to the Karabakh uplands, between the rivers of Araks and Kura in Azerbaijan. The breed has been heavily influenced both by the Arab (see pp.92–93) horse and by desert horses related to the Arab. The Akhal-Teke (see pp.98–99), from which the Karabakh inherits its striking metallic coat color, has also had a particularly strong effect on the breed.

The Karabakh is said to have strongly influenced the Don (see p.113). The Deliboz, also found in Azerbaijan, is probably a strain of the Karabakh.

The best Karabakh stock are bred at the Akdum stud and they are performance-tested on the race course. The breed is also popularly used in mounted games such as *chavgan* (a form of polo) and *surpanakh* (a type of mounted basketball).

The Karabakh is said to have a calm temperament and good action. But, like many of the other mountain breeds, it has a conformational weakness in the hindlegs, which are often sickle-shaped. While this is unacceptable in the best quality riding horses, it is a common feature in mountain breeds and perhaps contributes to their sure-footedness.

THIS BREED, **MUCH PRIZED** IN ITS HOMELAND, IS **THREATENED** WITH **EXTINCTION.**

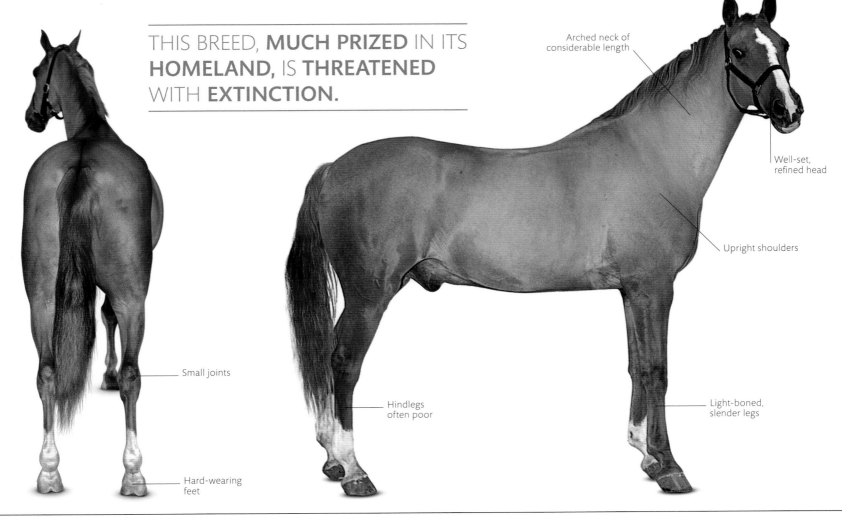

Small joints

Hard-wearing feet

Arched neck of considerable length

Well-set, refined head

Upright shoulders

Hindlegs often poor

Light-boned, slender legs

Karabair

HEIGHT AT WITHERS	ORIGIN	COLORS
14.3–15.2 hh (151–156 cm)	Uzbekistan and northern Tajikistan	Bay, gray, and chestnut. Dun and a dull palomino may occur, but rarely black or piebald

PLAYING *KOKPAR*

One of the toughest Central Asian breeds, the courageous Karabair is commonly used for *kokpar*. This fast and dangerous mounted game has very few rules and involves players dragging a goat carcass to a goal. There are often many casualties. *Kokpar* is the Uzbek version of *buzkashi*, which is the national game of Afghanistan.

This versatile Central Asian breed is a dual-purpose horse that is used both in harness and under saddle.

The Karabair is the product of crosses between unimproved, steppe-type horses and a variety of southern, Asian horses, including Arabs, which passed through the region on ancient trade routes. It is one of the oldest breeds of Central Asia.

Although it shares many desert-horse characteristics with the Arab, this small, quick-moving horse is coarser and less graceful overall. Karabairs tend to have cow- or sickle-hocks, but the limbs are very strong, with ample bone below the knee: the breed standard set by the old USSR authority requires a measurement of 7¾ in (19.6 cm) for stallions, and 7¼ in (18.8 cm) for mares. Karabairs

are known to have a sound constitution, rarely suffering lameness, and have excellent powers of endurance.

The Jizzakh stud at Samarkand is the main center for the breed today, but they also continue to be bred in herds by nomadic Uzbeks living on shrub and desert steppe country. They are alternately kept on mountain and foothill pastures because it maintains their hardiness and adaptability.

They participate in combined competition where they are both ridden and driven in harness. This gives a better indication of versatility, temperament, and stamina. To produce faster racing horses, Karabair mares are crossed with Thoroughbreds.

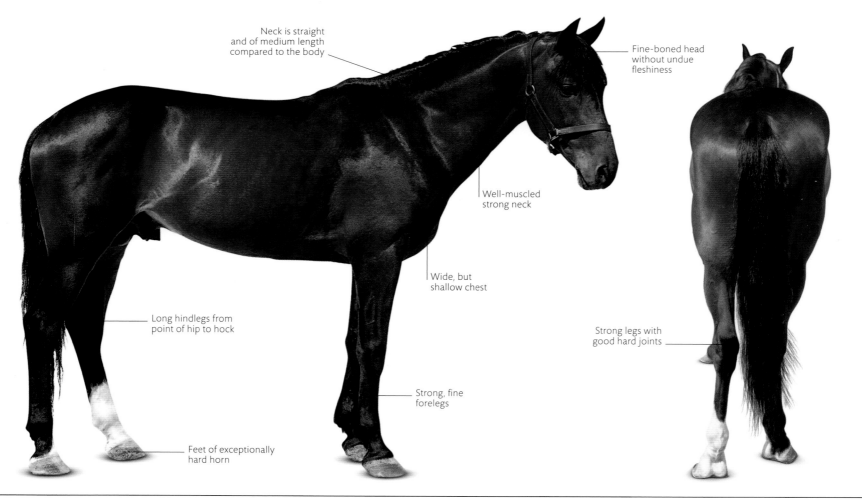

Neck is straight and of medium length compared to the body

Fine-boned head without undue fleshiness

Well-muscled strong neck

Wide, but shallow chest

Long hindlegs from point of hip to hock

Strong legs with good hard joints

Strong, fine forelegs

Feet of exceptionally hard horn

NOMADIC **UZBEKS** REGARD **THIS HORSE** AS THE **EMBODIMENT OF BEAUTY.**

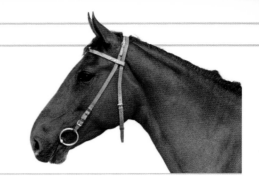

Lokai

HEIGHT AT WITHERS	ORIGIN	COLORS
15 hh (152 cm)	Pamir mountains, Tajikistan	Gray, bay, or metallic chestnut

MOUNTAIN TRANSPORTATION

The tribes of the Pamir mountains still make use of their horses for pack-carrying and for transportation. These steep mountain areas are rarely served by roads, and horses still provide the best means of getting around. The horses often look small and undernourished, and they may appear overladen, but they are valuable to the people, so their health and well-being is paramount.

The ancestors of this sure-footed horse come from one of the world's most inaccessible mountain ranges.

A hardy Asian mountain horse of mixed ancestry, the Lokai takes its name from an Uzbek people. From the 16th century onward, they improved their base stock by crossing it with the Karabair (see pp.104–105), the main Uzbek breed and a true eastern horse with Arab and Turkmene antecedents. More recently, there have been outcrosses to Tersk (see opposite), Arab (see pp.92–93), and Thoroughbred (see pp.120–21) stallions.

The wiry Lokai has very hard feet and is indispensable as a pack- and saddle horse on the precipitous tracks of the Pamir mountains. Located just south of the Tien Shan range, altitudes here range from 6,600 ft to 13,000 ft (2,000 m to 4,000 m). The Lokai is said to be capable of carrying a rider 50 miles (80 km) a day over extremely rough terrain at an average speed of 5–6 mph (8–9.5 km/h). This breed is also the favored mount of Tajik riders in the fierce national game of *kokpar* (which is like polo but uses a goat carcass, see p.104) and it is also raced. The nomadic tribespeople of the Pamirs still maintain herds of Lokai in a traditional way, moving them between lowland winter pastures and mountainous summer ones, and using the mare's milk for food.

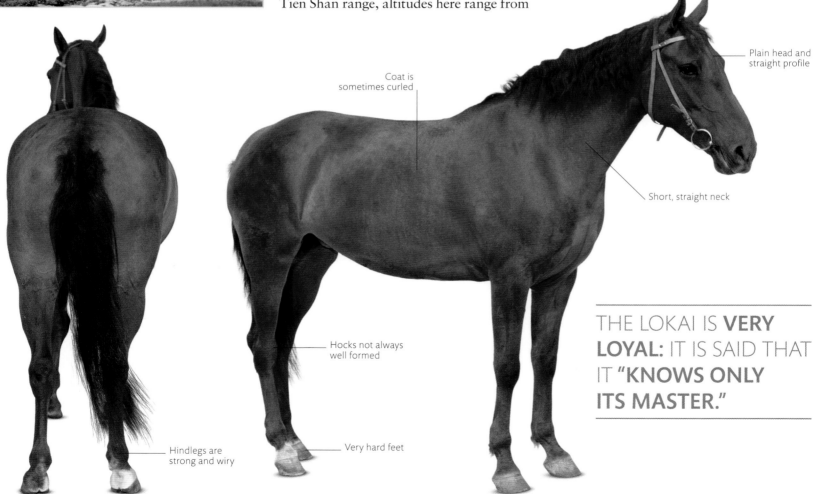

Coat is sometimes curled

Plain head and straight profile

Short, straight neck

Hocks not always well formed

Hindlegs are strong and wiry

Very hard feet

THE LOKAI IS **VERY LOYAL:** IT IS SAID THAT IT **"KNOWS ONLY ITS MASTER."**

Tersk

HEIGHT AT WITHERS	ORIGIN	COLORS
15 hh (152 cm)	Northern Caucasus, Russia	Gray

CRABBET ARABIANS

In 1936, officials from the Tersk Stud visited the famous Crabbet Stud in the UK, looking for some pure Arab blood to improve their horses. Although Lady Anne Wentworth (pictured here) was reluctant to sell her best horses, she agreed to part with six stallions and 19 mares. Among the stallions was Naseem, finest son of the esteemed Skowronek. The purchase was a success and contributed to the Tersk's reputation.

This intelligent and athletic horse excels at a number of equestrian pursuits.

This breed was created between 1921 and 1950 at the Tersk and Stavropol state studs in the northern Caucasus at a time when the Soviet agricultural ministry was determined to re-establish the horse population.

The new breed was planned to replace the Strelets Arabian, which had virtually disappeared in the early 1920s. Only two stallions, both silver-gray, and a few mares survived. These horses were sent to the Tersk stud in 1925 as foundation stock for the new breeding project. No attempt was made to preserve the original Strelets, because the surviving animals were considered too inbred. Three pure Arab stallions were then introduced as well as a number of crossbred mares: Arab-Don, Strelets-Kabardin, and a few crossbred Hungarian Gidrans (see pp.208–209).

The program was very successful and the modern breed is highly regarded. Tersks are distinctly Arab in appearance and have the characteristically Arabian light, elegant movement, while their clean, well-defined paces make them good dressage horses. They are excellent jumpers, bold cross-country horses, and race very successfully against Arabs. The Tersk's intelligence and gentle disposition also ensured its popularity in Russia as a circus horse.

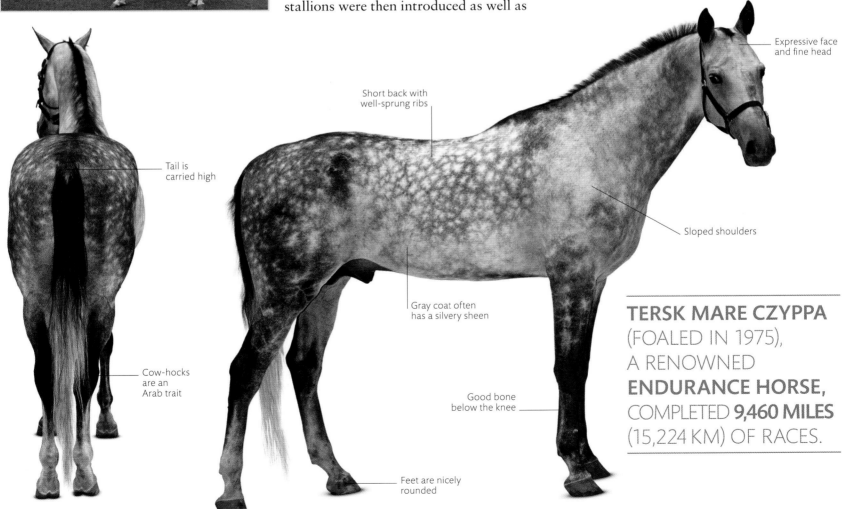

Tail is carried high

Cow-hocks are an Arab trait

Short back with well-sprung ribs

Gray coat often has a silvery sheen

Good bone below the knee

Feet are nicely rounded

Expressive face and fine head

Sloped shoulders

TERSK MARE CZYPPA (FOALED IN 1975), A RENOWNED ENDURANCE HORSE, COMPLETED 9,460 MILES (15,224 KM) OF RACES.

Russian royalty
Tersks have many of the attributes of their Arab ancestors, not least in their fine facial features and gentle expression. They also have the Arab's intelligence and trainability.

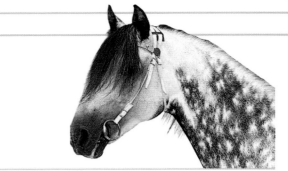

Orlov Trotter

HEIGHT AT WITHERS	ORIGIN	COLORS
16 hh (163 cm)	Central Russia	Gray, dapple gray; also black and bay

One of the oldest and most popular Russian breeds, the Orlov was originally developed as a carriage and racing horse.

At the end of the 18th century, Count Alexis Orlov crossed his white Arab stallion, Smetanka, with Dutch, Mecklenburg, and Danish mares at his Orlov stud outside Moscow. Smetanka left only five offspring in his short stud career, but among them was Polkan I, the result of a mating with a Danish mare of Spanish horse heritage.

Polkan I was mated with a substantial Dutch mare, chosen because she had the freedom of movement and energy levels necessary for trotting. This resulted in the Orlov Trotter's foundation stallion, the gray Bars I—foaled in 1784 and used extensively at the new stud of Khrenov.

From 1788 Count Orlov and his Khrenov stud manager continued to work on the evolution of the Orlov. Bars I served Arab, Danish, and Dutch mares as well as English halfbreds and Arab-Mecklenburg crosses. A policy of inbreeding to Bars and his sons to establish the desired type was then practiced: the pedigrees of all purebred Orlov Trotters show a strong connection to the foundation stallion. Training and a regular program of trotting races were carried out in Moscow from 1834 onward to encourage improvements in the breed and enhance performance.

The Orlov combines height and elegance with a light, powerful build. Ideally, the legs are fine and set square on the body, and there should be pronounced muscular development. There are five basic types within the breed, influenced by the policies of the individual studs. The best is the Khrenov type, which is regarded as the classical Orlov. Improvements continue with emphasis on preserving the height, build, strength of tendons, and the potential to trot at speed.

TROIKA

The word *troika* means triplet or trio. In driving it is when three horses are worked side-by-side often drawing a sleigh. The center horse is usually harnessed with a collar attached to a distinctive shaft bow, rising like an arch above its shoulders. It works at a fast trot, while the out-spanners on either side are in breast harness. They are also kept on tight side-reins, which turn their heads outward, and must canter or gallop to keep pace.

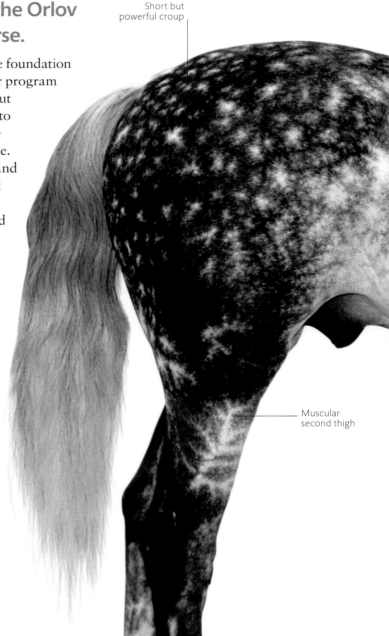

Short but powerful croup

Muscular second thigh

Legs are square-set

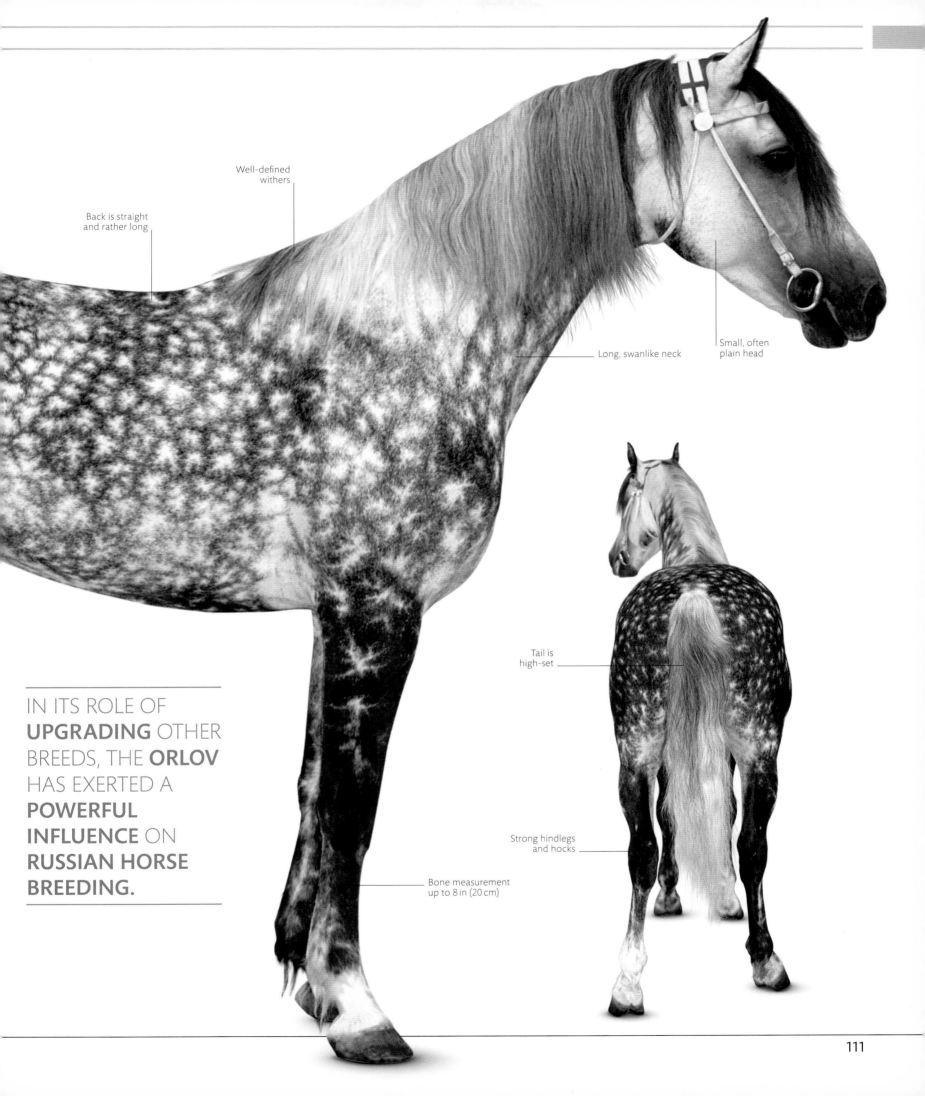

Well-defined withers

Back is straight and rather long

Small, often plain head

Long, swanlike neck

Tail is high-set

IN ITS ROLE OF **UPGRADING** OTHER BREEDS, THE **ORLOV** HAS EXERTED A **POWERFUL INFLUENCE** ON **RUSSIAN HORSE BREEDING.**

Strong hindlegs and hocks

Bone measurement up to 8 in (20 cm)

Russian Trotter

HEIGHT AT WITHERS	ORIGIN	COLORS
15.3–16 hh (160–163 cm)	Moscow, Russia	Bay; also black, chestnut, and gray

TROTTING RACE

The Russian Trotter races in the conventional diagonal trotting gait. A useful performer, and popular in its own country, it doesn't have the supreme speeds of other harness racers, such as the Anglo-Arab (see pp.148–49) or the American trotting breeds. It is faster than the Orlov, but lacks some of that horse's historical cachet. With continued care in its breeding, however, its reputation is sure to improve.

A record holder on the Russian racetracks, this breed is fast enough to compete at international level.

By the second half of the 19th century, the American Standardbred had established its superiority over all the other trotting breeds, so Russian breeders crossed it with the best of their Orlov stock (see pp.110–11) to create the Russian Trotter. Standardbred mares and stallions were imported to Russia between 1890 and the beginning of World War I, including the world record holder of the time, Cresceus, who trotted the mile (1,600 m) in 2 minutes 2 seconds. By the early 1930s, the carefully conceived breeding program had increased the height and improved the frame, body measurements, and conformation of the Russian Trotter.

It had also, in part, regained something of the old Orlov hardiness of constitution. In the late 1970s and early 1980s the popularity of the Russian Trotter, and its consequent export potential, made it necessary to import more American Standardbreds. This further improved the speed of the Russian horses. Modern Russian Trotters are bred principally in the Moscow area and their performance is tested at the Moscow Hippodrome, the city's main racecourse. Although quick to mature, horses rarely attain maximum trotting speeds until they are aged six years or older.

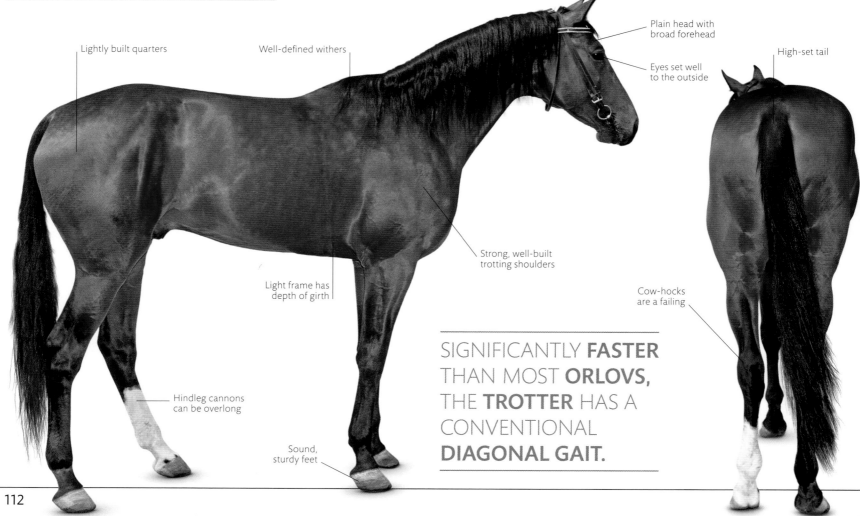

Lightly built quarters

Well-defined withers

Plain head with broad forehead

Eyes set well to the outside

High-set tail

Strong, well-built trotting shoulders

Light frame has depth of girth

Cow-hocks are a failing

Hindleg cannons can be overlong

Sound, sturdy feet

SIGNIFICANTLY **FASTER** THAN MOST **ORLOVS,** THE **TROTTER** HAS A CONVENTIONAL **DIAGONAL GAIT.**

Don

HEIGHT AT WITHERS	ORIGIN	COLORS
15.3–16.2 hh (160–168 cm)	Don steppes, Central Russia	Chestnut and brown

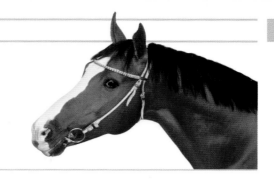

The traditional mount of Russian Cossacks takes its name from the steppes around the Don River.

The Don's ancestors were ridden by nomadic tribes and include the now-extinct Turkmene (or Turkoman) and the Karabakh (see p.103), a mountain horse from Azerbaijan. Dons were reared in herds on the pastures of the Don steppes, northeast of Volgograd, before being improved through outcrosses to the Orlov Trotter, the Strelets Arab, and the Thoroughbred (see pp.120–21). No outside blood has been introduced since the beginning of the 20th century.

Principally employed as an economical, easily kept cavalry horse, the Don is incredibly tough and can live outside all year on a frugal diet and in very harsh conditions. It has also played a significant role in some of the breeds that have evolved at the Russian state studs, in particular the Budenny (see p.114). Intensive selective breeding began in the 1830s and led to the type we see today. Russian breeders place considerable emphasis on performance testing and the Don has been subjected to long-distance endurance tests, at which it excels.

Although attractive, the modern Don does not always conform to the breed standard. It is sometimes a little too long in the leg and with some shortcomings that can restrict movement. However, the breed has been around for a long time and as a willing workhorse with great endurance and an equable temperament, it has proved its worth.

THE TURK

This image shows an idealized Turkmene horse with a light built and strong Asian influence. Some claim that Turkmenes are the ancestors of the Thoroughbred. English soldiers returning from the east brought with them horses called "Turks," but these could have just been horses from Turkey.

Narrow quarters

Intelligent expression

Fairly well-defined withers

Straight, broad back

Fine second thigh

Hocks tend to be sickle-shaped

Shoulders are short and upright

Wide rib cage

Straight legs, with undersized joints

THE DON'S **COAT** OFTEN HAS A **GOLDEN SHEEN**, A REMINDER OF ITS **KARABAKH** ANCESTORS.

Budenny

HEIGHT AT WITHERS	ORIGIN	COLORS
16 hh (163 cm)	Rostov, Russia	Chestnut

CHERNOMOR

The Chernomor, one of the ancestors of the Budenny, was smaller, lighter, and more active than the Don. Originally bred around Krasnodar, north of the Caucasus Mountains, it is descended from horses that were raised by the Zaporozhian Cossacks. The Cossacks were a powerful military and political force from the 16th to the late 18th century, when they signed a treaty with the Russians and were disbanded by force soon after.

The breed is named after Marshall Budenny, a Bolshevik cavalry commander in the Russian Civil War (1917–23).

A Russian warmblood, the Budenny was created by crossing native mares with Thoroughbreds (see pp.120–21) at state studs. In the early 1920s, preliminary selective breeding took place at what would become the Budenny and First Cavalry Army Studs. The aim was to produce cavalry horses to compensate for the enormous losses sustained during World War I, and horses from these studs formed a great part of the Russian cavalry divisions in World War II. The first step in creating this new breed was to cross-select Don (see p.113) and Chernomor mares, both Cossack breeds, with Thoroughbred stallions. The results of the first crossings were known as Anglo-Dons. The best of these horses were interbred, and the foundation stock for the Budenny was carefully selected from their offspring. The breed was officially recognized in 1949. The first studbook was published in 1951. It is technically open, but there are restrictions, such as an upper limit of three-quarters on Thoroughbred, Arab, and Trakehner blood. Before World War II, there was a fairly equal use of Thoroughbred, Don, and Anglo-Don mares, but now most of the mares are Anglo-Dons and the use of Thoroughbred stallions has declined.

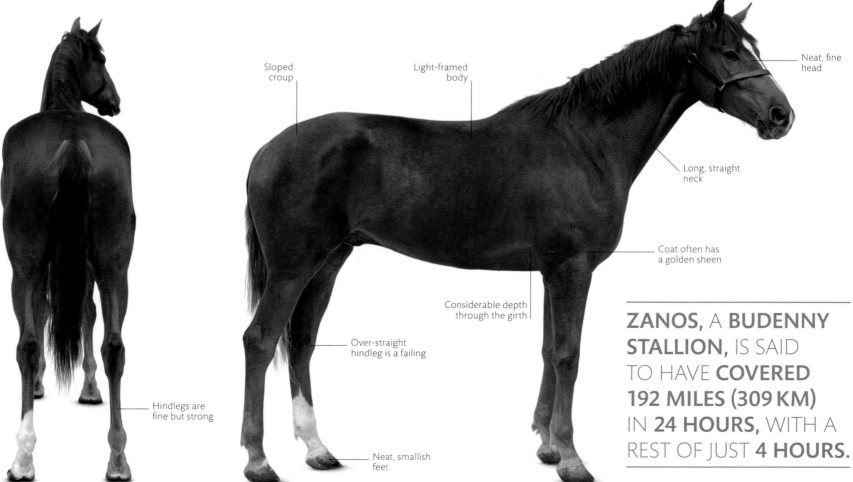

Sloped croup

Light-framed body

Neat, fine head

Long, straight neck

Coat often has a golden sheen

Considerable depth through the girth

Over-straight hindleg is a failing

Hindlegs are fine but strong

Neat, smallish feet

ZANOS, A BUDENNY STALLION, IS SAID TO HAVE **COVERED 192 MILES (309 KM)** IN **24 HOURS**, WITH A REST OF JUST **4 HOURS.**

Ukrainian Riding Horse

HEIGHT AT WITHERS	ORIGIN	COLORS
15.1–16.1 hh (155–165 cm)	Ukraine	Usually bay, chestnut, brown

ORLOV-ROSTOPCHIN

Also called the Russian Saddle (or Riding) Horse, this breed was nearly extinct after World War II. In the 1950s, work was done to recreate it using the Ukrainian Saddle Horse. More recently Trakehners (see pp.186–87) have further improved it. The breed is threatened in its homeland, but it has a strong fan-base in the US, where some were sent after the breakup of the USSR. Barin (pictured here) is a good competition horse with a Orlov-Rostopchin background.

This all-round competition horse is smaller than the Thoroughbred, but it has plenty of presence.

After World War II, Ukrainian studs began to develop this large and strong saddle horse, mainly using Trakehener (see pp.186–87), Hanoverian (see pp.172–73), and Thoroughbred (see pp.120–21) stallions with mares of established Hungarian breeds, particularly Nonius (see p.210), Furioso (see p. 211), and Gidran Arab (see pp.208–209). Breeding started in Dnepropetrovsk and has continued at four additional studs. Where possible, the breeders selected animals with bloodlines that could be traced back to the Russian Riding Horse, also called the Orlov-Rostopchin (see box, left). Coarser mares were crossed with Thoroughbred and Thoroughbred-Hanoverian stallions, while finer and lighter types were crossed with Hanoverian or Thoroughbred-Hanoverian

stallions. More recent breeding is mainly between pure stock with corrective crossing using Thoroughbreds. The Bespechny line consists of horses that are derived from the last Russian Saddle Horse.

The breeders main aim has been to produce reliable competition horses. To this end, excellent diet and intensive training are used to develop the best of the youngstock. Training begins at 18 months old and promising two- and three-year-olds are raced and competed at dressage, cross-country, and show jumping. The most outstanding performers are then used at stud. This careful and systematic breeding has resulted in a versatile and calm riding horse with good bone and a lightly built but powerful body.

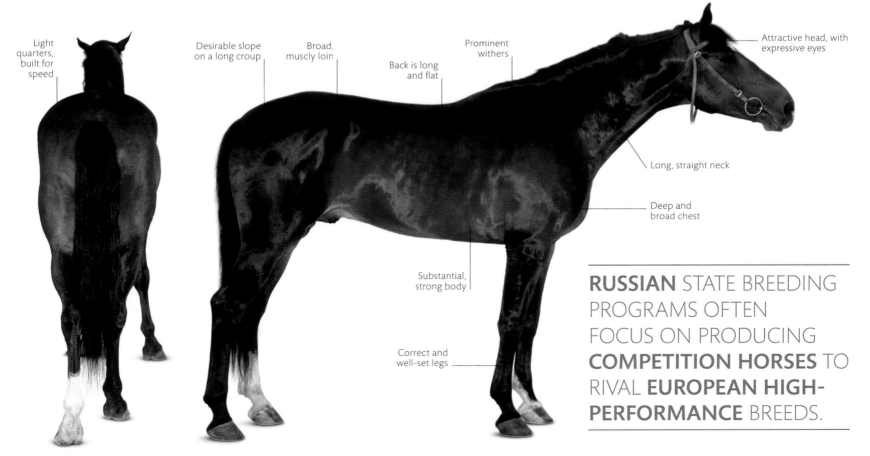

Light quarters, built for speed

Desirable slope on a long croup

Broad, muscly loin

Back is long and flat

Prominent withers

Attractive head, with expressive eyes

Long, straight neck

Deep and broad chest

Substantial, strong body

Correct and well-set legs

RUSSIAN STATE BREEDING PROGRAMS OFTEN FOCUS ON PRODUCING **COMPETITION HORSES** TO RIVAL **EUROPEAN HIGH-PERFORMANCE** BREEDS.

Marwari

HEIGHT AT WITHERS	ORIGIN	COLORS
14.3 hh (150 cm)	Rajasthan, India	Bay, brown, chestnut, and palomino

INDIAN HALFBRED

India's harsh climate is not easy on horses. However, by crossing the hardy native stock with Thoroughbreds, Australian Whalers, Arabs, and other tough breeds, the Indian Army has managed to produce consistently good working horses. The best of these are medium-sized, wiry, and enduring with strong bones that can withstand continuous hard work.

Developed in the state of Marwar (Jodhpur), this breed descends from the mounts of the famous Rajput warriors.

The Marwari bears a definite resemblance to the horses of Turkmenistan and the adjacent territories, although none of those breeds have the Marwari horse's distinctive curving ears. When the Moghuls conquered northern India in the early 16th century, they brought Turkmene-type horses to the area now called Rajasthan, and it is extremely likely that these bred with the Rajput stock. The breed must also be connected to the Kathiawari (see opposite), which has similarly curved ears.

Legends about the Marwari's endurance, courage, and loyalty are part of the Rajput tradition. They excel at High School-style "leaps" (the tradition is older in India than it is in Europe). There is a famous story of Chetak who saved Maharana Pratap of Mewar in 1576 by doing a capriole, although his horse was not a Marwari.

By the 1930s, the breed had deteriorated and was preserved only by the intervention of the Maharaja Umaid Singhji, and the breeding program was continued by his grandson. The modern Marwari is strong, wiry, and well-muscled, with long limbs and very hard feet.

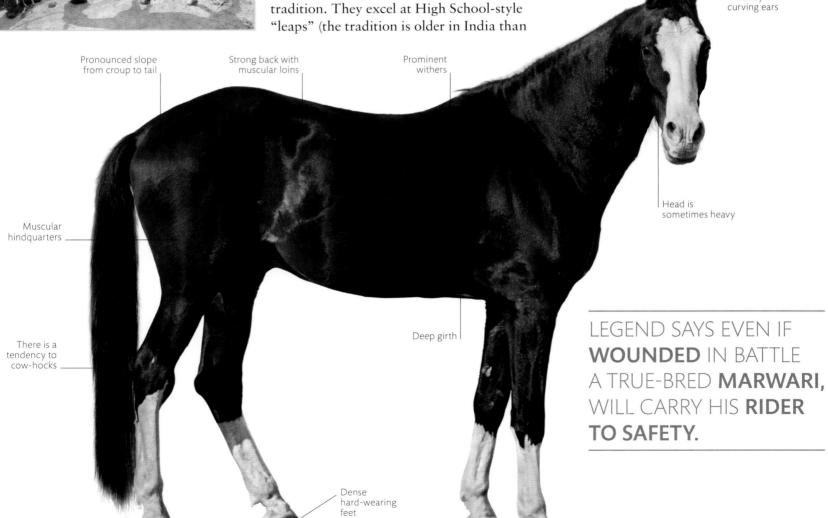

Pronounced slope from croup to tail

Strong back with muscular loins

Prominent withers

Distinctive inwardly curving ears

Head is sometimes heavy

Muscular hindquarters

There is a tendency to cow-hocks

Deep girth

Dense hard-wearing feet

LEGEND SAYS EVEN IF **WOUNDED** IN BATTLE A TRUE-BRED **MARWARI**, WILL CARRY HIS **RIDER TO SAFETY.**

Kathiawari

HEIGHT AT WITHERS	ORIGIN	COLORS
15 hh (152 cm)	Northwestern coast of India	All except black

POLICE HORSE

Kathiawaris are popular among India's mounted police force since they are hardy and tough, and not expensive to purchase. They are widely used for patrol work and urban policing. Tent-pegging, where riders attempt to spear low-level targets (pegs) with a lance, is a favorite sport among police departments and the breed is an excellent competitor, galloping fast and straight to give its rider the best chance of striking a peg cleanly.

For hundreds of years the arid Kathiawar peninsula has been renowned for its horses.

The origins of this breed are not recorded but for centuries India's western coast has had indigenous stock descended from breeds related to steppe and desert horses, such as the Kabuli and Baluchi. Such breeds often have distinctive curved ears like the Kathiawari, and some share its pacing ability. Arab (see pp.92–93) horses imported from the Arabian Gulf and South Africa were crossed with this native stock. Indian nobles bred these horses selectively, each specializing in their own strain and 28 such strains are still recognized.

Treated as favored household pets, the horses acquired a reputation for being intelligent, docile, and affectionate. The Kathiawari was considered a superior cavalry mount and is now employed by police forces throughout India. It is fast and agile, making it a useful polo pony and it excels at mounted games (see box, left).

The Kathiawari's defining feature is its highly mobile ears, which curve inward to touch each other at the tips and can move easily through more than 180 degrees. Like all horse breeds with a desert background, it is resistant to heat and can survive on minimal feed and water. The most interesting coat color is dun, often with a clear dorsal stripe and distinctive "zebra" bars on the legs.

Low-set tail

Fine head with long, curved ears

Neck tapers distinctly toward head

Strong, well-muscled shoulders

Well-sprung ribs

Joints tend to roundness

Slender, straight legs

KATHIAWARIS NATURALLY PERFORM THE *REVAAL*—A SWIFT, LATERAL PACING GAIT.

Skill-at-arms
An old cavalry game, tent-pegging was designed to improve the rider's skill for battle. Fun to do and exciting to watch, it is still widely practiced. This Kathiawari and his rider are in India.

Thoroughbred

HEIGHT AT WITHERS	ORIGIN	COLORS
15.2–17 hh (157–173 cm)	England	Brown, bay, chestnut, black, and gray

The huge and lucrative multinational racing industry was built on the performance of this superb athlete.

This breed was evolved in the 17th and 18th centuries to satisfy the English aristocracy's enthusiasm for horse racing. English breeders imported Arab sires, and crossed them with a native stock of "running horses." Today, the Thoroughbred is the fastest, most commercially valuable breed.

From Henry VIII (1491–1547) onward British monarchs founded studs where horses from Spain and Italy, influenced by the Barb (see pp.94–95), were crossed with stock that included the forerunners of the Fell Pony (see pp.272–73) and the Connemara (see pp.264–65). Under successive monarchs, royal support increased and Newmarket became the headquarters of British racing.

All Thoroughbreds can be traced back to three foundation stallions—the Byerley Turk, the Godolphin Arabian, and the Darley Arabian. The Byerley Turk (imported in 1689) is the sire of the first of the four great Thoroughbred lines: Herod, Eclipse, Matchem, and Highflyer. The Darley Arabian came from Aleppo, Syria, in 1704 and was brought to Yorkshire where he sired the first great racehorse and is the founder of the Eclipse line, Flying Childers. The Matchem line can be traced back to the Godolphin Arabian, which came to Lord Godolphin's Cambridge stud in 1728.

Thoroughbreds are characterized by their long, low, and economical stride. The length of the hindleg from the hip to the hock means they can attain the maximum possible thrust when galloping. They can be highly strung, but possess great physical stamina as well as courage, battling on when other horses would have given up. They mature quickly and are raced from two years old.

Very strong quarters and loins for galloping

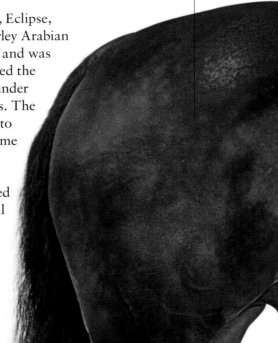

THE GREATEST RACEHORSE?

The American racehorse Secretariat earned $1,313,808 during his highly successful racing career. In 1973, he set records in the US Triple Crown events: the Kentucky Derby, the Preakness Stakes, and the Belmont Stakes. These records are yet to be bettered. This phenomenal racehorse won 16 of his 21 races, coming second in three of the others. After retirement, he sired around 600 foals, few of whom came close to his ability. He died aged 19 in 1989.

Refined,
lean head

Prominent
withers

Graceful,
arched neck

Long, very
well-sloped
shoulders

Large nostrils

Typically
long body

Muscular
forearms

Excellent
hock joints

Long hindlegs

ECLIPSE,
HISTORICALLY
ENGLAND'S MOST
FAMOUS
THOROUGHBRED
RACEHORSE, WAS
NEVER BEATEN.

Cleveland Bay

HEIGHT AT WITHERS	ORIGIN	COLORS
16–16.2 hh (163–168 cm)	Cleveland and northeast Yorkshire, UK	Bay with black points

The Cleveland Bay has enjoyed British royal patronage since the reign of George II (*r.* 1727–1760).

An old name for this breed is the Chapman and, with the exception of native ponies, the Cleveland Bay is the oldest indigenous horse breed in the UK. It was once used as a packhorse for transporting materials excavated from the mines of northeast Yorkshire and was also the mount of "chapmen," the traveling salesmen of the day.

It is reasonable to assume that descendants of the North African Barb (see pp.94–95) played an important role in the development of this breed. The British crown acquired the port of Tangier through the marriage of Charles II to Catharine of Braganza in 1662 and the Barbary Coast horses from which the Thoroughbred evolved began to be imported into Britain. Yorkshire horse breeders were prominent in the sport of horse racing at the time and they probably crossed these imported horses with native Cleveland mares and transformed the breed.

In 1884 when the breed society was established, the Cleveland Bay was acknowledged as the best and most powerful coach horse in Europe, but when the roads were improved with new surfacing techniques in the 19th century, faster journey times were possible and the breed began to be considered too slow. Its popularity as an agricultural horse for pulling heavy loads on deep, difficult ground, however, continued and it also established itself as a heavyweight hunter.

By 1962 there were only four Cleveland stallions in the UK but Queen Elizabeth II bought the colt Mulgrave Supreme, saving him from export to the US, and she made him available for public stud. Mulgrave became a successful sire and numbers of purebred stallions rose dramatically. Crosses with the Thoroughbred have produced good showjumpers and Cleveland Bays have competed in dressage and showjumping at Olympic level. Support for the breed is strong in the UK, US, and Australia and the signs for its continuation are encouraging.

Clean, powerful legs

A MUCH-LOVED HORSE

A recent survey of the number of Cleveland Bays worldwide has found that the breed has a strong fan base. In the UK, the Cleveland Bay Horse Society, which was founded in 1884, is thriving. Its Patron is H.M. The Queen. The Royal Stables use Cleveland Bays in harness as well as a lighter Cleveland Bay cross. The Cleveland Bay Horse Society represents the breed in the US and there are a few Cleveland Bays in the rest of Europe and Australia.

CLEVELAND BAY CROSS IN CEREMONIAL TACK

Mane is
always black

Big, well-ribbed
body

Large, well-set eyes

Profile
shows signs
of Spanish
ancestry

Thick,
luxuriant
black tail

THE **CLEVELAND
BAY** IS ON THE **RARE
BREEDS SURVIVAL
TRUST CRITICAL LIST.**

Short
cannons

Hard, open feet

Hunter

HEIGHT AT WITHERS	ORIGIN	COLORS
15–18 hh (152–183 cm)	Worldwide	Any color is permitted

In the UK, hunting on horseback using hounds dates back to the 16th century.

Hunters are, by definition, horses used in countries where hunting with a pack of hounds takes place. The type of horse varies according to its suitability for the terrain of the country, which means the hunter is not, strictly speaking, a breed. The best examples are those produced in countries with a long hunting tradition, in particular Ireland, the UK, and, to a degree, the US, where the Thoroughbred (see pp.120–21) is a popular choice. Good examples of English and Irish hunters often compete in the sport of eventing.

The ideal hunter is sound and well proportioned, with all the conformational abilities and the natural balance of a top-class riding horse. This is combined with a bold yet equable temperament. Agility, good jumping ability, and a robust constitution are also prerequisites. The main hunting season usually begins in winter, and so horses must be able to cope with challenging conditions, including rough, muddy terrain. They also need stamina for a long day's work and the courage to jump over all kinds of difficult obstacles.

The Irish hunter is often based on an Irish Draft–Thoroughbred cross. While any cross is permissible, the best hunters will always carry a good proportion of Thoroughbred blood, which gives them the necessary galloping speed and jumping ability. The Cleveland Bay (see pp.122–23), for instance, will jump big obstacles and cope with deep, heavy clay. Many good heavyweight hunters have also been bred against the background of the English heavy horse breeds, the Shire (see pp.52–53) and Clydesdale (see pp.50–51) in particular. Crosses and second crosses to the British native pony breeds, such as New Forest (see pp.282–83), Fell (see pp.272–73), Highland (see pp.270–71), or Welsh Cob (see pp.136–37), also produce good hunters with a lively character, stamina, and initiative.

Nicely sloped croup

THE HUNTING TRADITION

Hunting quarry by its scent with a pack of hounds was well known in Ancient Greece; the Greek general, historian, and agriculturalist Xenophon (c.430–355 BCE) wrote at length on the breeding and management of hounds. In Europe, France has the oldest tradition of organized hunting. It was introduced into Britain in the 11th century. The "hunting seat" is a name given to the old-fashioned legs-forward position adopted by riders. Hunting live quarry is banned in the UK, but riding with hounds remains popular.

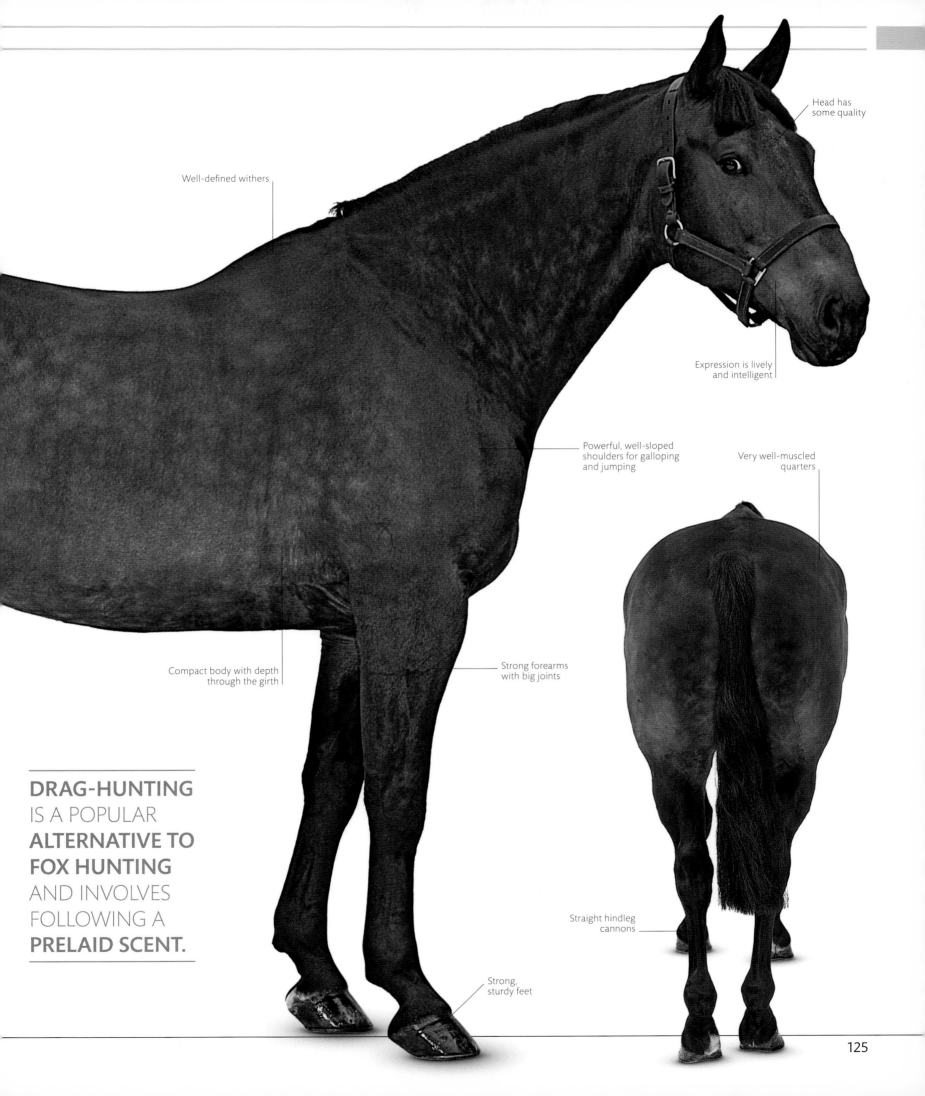

Head has
some quality

Well-defined withers

Expression is lively
and intelligent

Powerful, well-sloped
shoulders for galloping
and jumping

Very well-muscled
quarters

Compact body with depth
through the girth

Strong forearms
with big joints

DRAG-HUNTING
IS A POPULAR
ALTERNATIVE TO
FOX HUNTING
AND INVOLVES
FOLLOWING A
PRELAID SCENT.

Straight hindleg
cannons

Strong,
sturdy feet

Hackney

HEIGHT AT WITHERS	ORIGIN	COLORS
14–15.3 hh (142–160 cm)	East Anglia, UK	Dark brown, black, bay, and chestnut

"Hackney" probably derives from an old French word *haquenée*, which referred to a light riding horse.

The high-stepping Hackney is considered one of the world's greatest and most spectacular harness horses. It has a distinctive conformation and a brilliant, unique action described as "effortless" and "electrical and snappy." In part, this extravagant movement can be taught and refined by skillful training, but much of it is inherited. It is the result of years of careful, selective breeding based on the quality of the foundation stock, the great British trotting horses of the 18th and 19th centuries.

Known as Trotters or Roadsters, the early trotters were noted for their speed and endurance under saddle and were raced long before they were used under harness. There were two types: the Norfolk (see p.157) and the related Yorkshire. They shared an ancestor, Original Shales, a stallion foaled from a "hackney" mare by Blaze, a Thoroughbred stallion (see pp.120–21), grandson of the Darley Arabian. The performance of these horses was often put to the test. Bellfounder, a Norfolk Roadster stallion and a direct descendant of the racehorse, Eclipse, trotted 2 miles (3 km) in 6 minutes, and 9 miles (14 km) in 30 minutes. He was exported to America in 1823, where he contributed much to American trotting breeds.

Today, the regional variations are long gone, and the best Hackney characteristics, including well-muscled quarters and second thighs, good poise, and a light and springy step combine in the modern Hackney. The UK Hackney Horse Society was founded in 1883 in Norwich, East Anglia, and continues to publish the studbook, promote the Hackney, and organize shows where horses wearing the appropriate harness are shown in-hand. Although the Hackney, along with the related Hackney Pony (see p.293), is classified as a rare breed in the UK, it thrives in the Netherlands and enjoys great popularity in the US and Canada.

SHALES HORSE

Finmere Gray Shales (pictured here) traces back to the Darley Arabian acknowledged as one of the three foundation sires of the English Thoroughbred. The Shales horses are direct descendants—and the modern equivalent—of the Norfolk Roadster. This was the pride of 19th-century England and its prepotent blood had a great influence on the breeds of both Europe and the US. The Roadster is in the background of most of the warmblood breeds, many of Europe's heavy horses, and the American Standardbred (see pp.232–33).

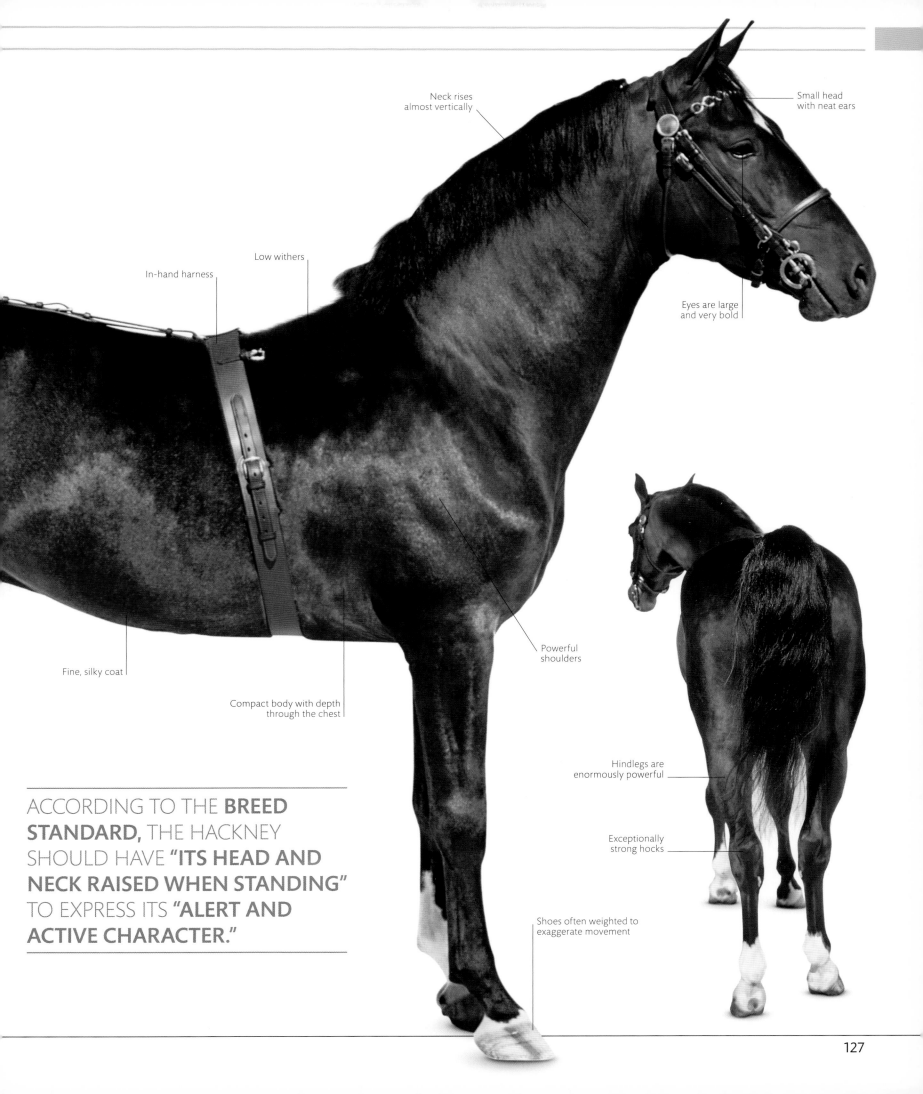

Neck rises
almost vertically

Small head
with neat ears

Low withers

In-hand harness

Eyes are large
and very bold

Fine, silky coat

Powerful
shoulders

Compact body with depth
through the chest

Hindlegs are
enormously powerful

Exceptionally
strong hocks

Shoes often weighted to
exaggerate movement

ACCORDING TO THE **BREED STANDARD,** THE HACKNEY SHOULD HAVE **"ITS HEAD AND NECK RAISED WHEN STANDING"** TO EXPRESS ITS **"ALERT AND ACTIVE CHARACTER."**

Hack

HEIGHT AT WITHERS	ORIGIN	COLORS
14.2–15.3 hh (147–160 cm)	UK and Ireland	Any solid color

Two types of hack were recognized in 19th-century Britain: the "covert hack" and the "park hack."

Hacks are a type rather than a breed. In the 19th century, a hack was a supremely well-mannered horse that was comfortable to ride. On hunting days, well-dressed riders cut a dash on their covert hacks as they cantered to the meet. They then changed to a heavier, sturdier hunter (see pp.124–25) for the day's sport. Elegantly tailored socialites in London rode the more refined park hacks—beautiful, perfectly proportioned, and schooled to perfection.

Covert hacks no longer exist. Their nearest equivalent may be seen in show classes for riding horses. The park hack, on the other hand, corresponds exactly to horses exhibited in today's hack classes. The hack of the modern show ring must be a model of good conformation, not a "blood-weed" (a horse lacking substance). The majority of entrants in hack classes are Thoroughbred (see pp.120–21), although some may be part-bred Arabs and one or two very good ones could be Anglo-Arabs (see pp.148–49).

Hack action must be straight, true, and low to the ground with no tendency toward dishing or lifting the knee. The trot is smooth and floating, the canter is slow, light, and in perfect balance, and the movement is distinguished by a particular brilliance. While the hack is perfectly schooled, the performance is not expected to resemble the disciplined accuracy of the dressage horse. Show classes are for small hacks 14.2–15 hh (147–152 cm), large hacks 15–15.3 hh (152–155 cm), and ladies' hacks 14.2–15.3 hh (147–155 cm). Ladies' hacks are ridden side-saddle (see box, below). Hacks are shown at walk, trot, and canter; they must have impeccable manners at all times.

Perfectly balanced topline

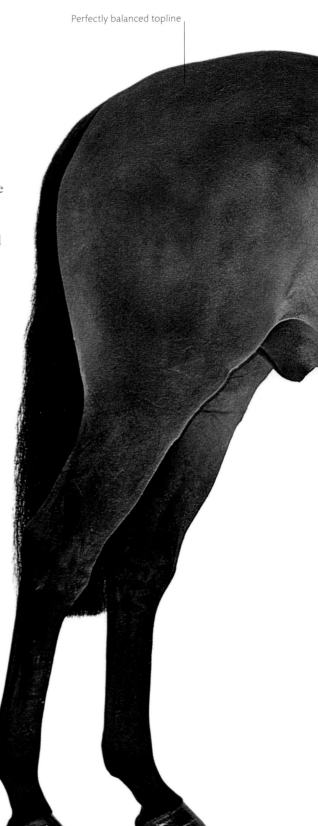

RIDING SIDESADDLE

There was a time when all ladies rode sidesaddle, but nowadays this elegant and skilled form of riding is mainly confined to the show ring. The rider has only a single leg with which to give the aids and on her offside has to rely on her cane, so the horse must be exceptionally well-schooled and responsive. The sidesaddles themselves are very expensive to make and second-hand ones are rare, making it even more difficult for riders wishing to take up this art.

Neck is light, long, and elegant

Prominent withers

The ribs are well-sprung

A neat head tapering to the muzzle

Long, perfectly sloped shoulders

Quarters are rounded

Deep through the girth

Long musculature in second thigh

A **HACK** WAS **ONCE DESCRIBED** AS A HORSE TO BE **RIDDEN WITH ONE HAND** WHILE ITS **OWNER FLIRTED.**

Legs are long and graceful

At least 8 in (20 cm) of bone below the knee

Cob

HEIGHT AT WITHERS	ORIGIN	COLORS
15 hh (152 cm)	UK and Ireland	Any solid color, often gray

Before the invention of the motor car, every country house in England kept a smart Cob for transportation.

Standing four-square on short, powerful legs, this big-bodied horse is built for strength not speed. Unlike the Welsh Cob (see pp.136–37), it is a type rather than a breed, and one without any set pattern to its breeding. Historically, Cobs were used in harness for shopping trips and other errands, they could be ridden around the farm, and would carry the heavier members of the family for a day's hunting. Indeed, the hard-working Cob was said to be the fittest and soundest horse in the stable, as well as being the easiest and most economical to keep. In the UK and Ireland the Cob has long been regarded with great affection, not only on account of its stocky, distinctive appearance, but also because of its ability, intelligence, and character.

In conformation and strength of frame, the true Cob is closer to the heavy horse than to the lighter Thoroughbred (see pp.120–21). With exceptionally well-muscled quarters

that are broad and strong, the Cob is able to carry heavyweight riders. The powerful quarters give good jumping ability and most Cobs make excellent hunters, jumping willingly and carefully. Offering a steady, calm ride, Cobs are supremely dependable and good-natured so make ideal first-time horses as well as reliable mounts for riders of more mature years.

Docking the tail and hogging the mane of Cobs was traditional. Docking was believed to give the horse a jaunty, sporting appearance, while hogging was done to highlight the short muscly neck. In 1948 the Docking and Nicking Act made docking illegal in the UK and it is now considered cruel and unnecessary. Today, the tail is simply trimmed. In the show ring, the classes are divided into lightweight, heavyweight, and maxi Cobs. Working Cobs are required to jump, and no Cob must exceed 15.1 hh (155 cm).

Broad, strong loins

Open feet

GYPSY COB

Also called Romany Cob, Vanner, Tinker, and Irish Tinker, these horses were first bred in the UK and Ireland by traveling people. In the days of horse-drawn caravans, travelers needed a reliable draft horse that could live out year-round, while being easy to handle, calm, and patient. Vanners can be any color, but piebald is popular. They are usually heavily feathered with abundant manes and tails. Honest and hardworking, they are now firm favorites in many non-traveling, horse-loving households. The official Gypsy Cob register was set up in 1996.

Hogged mane

Short, thick, muscular neck in proportion to the head and shoulders

Eyes described as having a "knowing" expression

Compact, stocky body with short back

Good, workmanlike head

Broad chest with wide-spaced forelegs

Muscles of second thigh are well developed and pronounced

Short, strong legs

SOME OF THE VERY **BEST COBS** ARE THE RESULT OF **IRISH DRAFTS CROSSED** WITH **THOROUGHBREDS.**

Horse and caravan
The traditional Vanner is a sturdy, easy-going animal that can tow a caravan, carry children around the campsite, and is happy to graze on a tether at the side of the road.

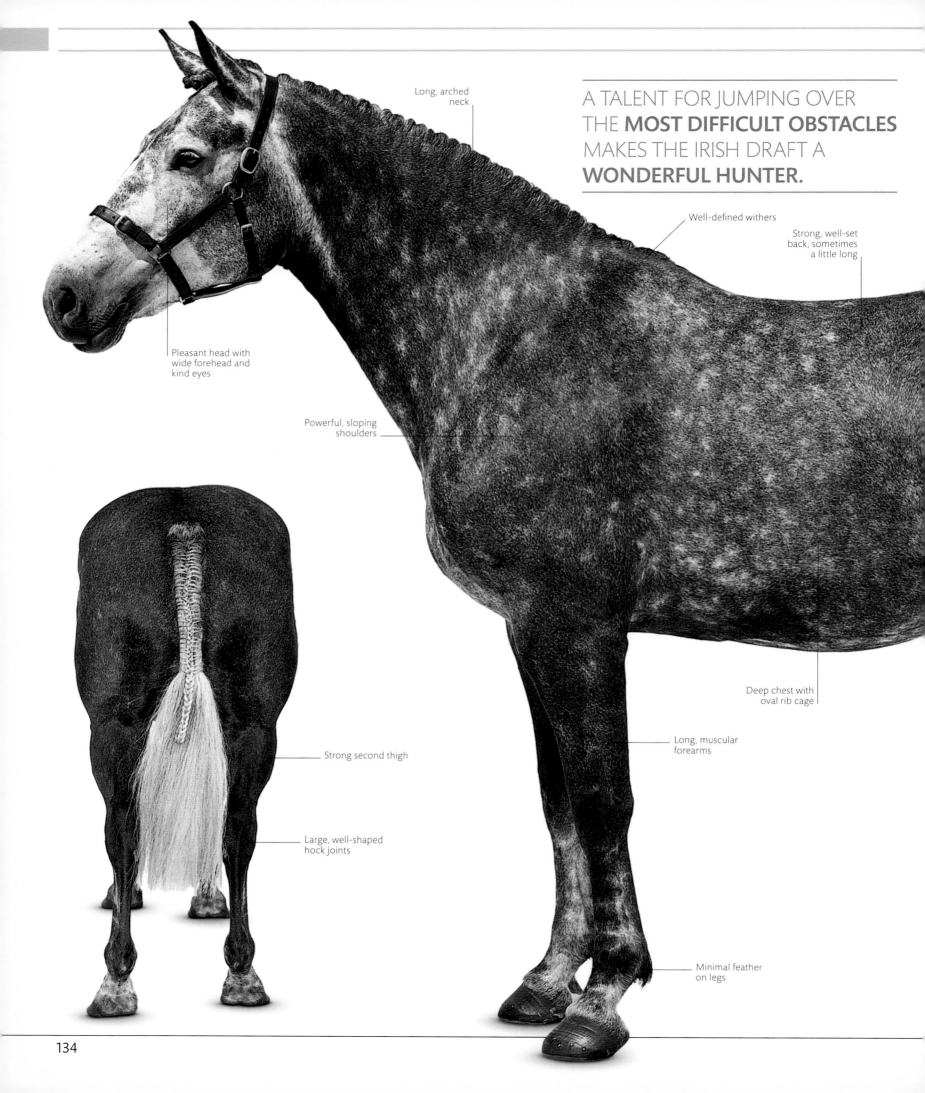

Long, arched neck

A TALENT FOR JUMPING OVER THE **MOST DIFFICULT OBSTACLES** MAKES THE IRISH DRAFT A **WONDERFUL HUNTER.**

Well-defined withers

Strong, well-set back, sometimes a little long

Pleasant head with wide forehead and kind eyes

Powerful, sloping shoulders

Deep chest with oval rib cage

Long, muscular forearms

Strong second thigh

Large, well-shaped hock joints

Minimal feather on legs

Irish Draft

HEIGHT AT WITHERS	ORIGIN	COLORS
15.2–17 hh (158–174 cm)	Ireland	Any solid color

According to the breed standard, the Irish Draft should be "versatile, powerful, and athletic."

Long, gently sloping croup and buttocks

Among the ancestors of Irish horses were warhorses from France and modern-day Belgium, which arrived in Ireland after the Anglo-Norman invasions in the 12th century and were crossed with indigenous breeds. Later, imported horses improved the resulting draft horse. Strong and willing, early Irish Drafts pulled the family trap, worked on small Irish farms, and were ridden.

After the famine of 1847, the number of Irish Drafts declined. Efforts to improve the remaining stock using Clydesdales (see pp.50–51) and Shires (see pp.52–53) were not entirely successful, and Thoroughbred (see pp.120–21) blood was used to counteract some of the resulting problems. Following stallion subsidies in 1904, the breed's fortunes improved and in 1917

A Book for Horses of the Irish Draft Type appeared. Unfortunately, the original records were lost in a fire in 1922. The Irish Draft Society was formed in 1976, followed, in 1979, by the Irish Draft Horse Society.

Today, the Irish Draft is an endangered breed, due to a lack of purebred animals and low genetic diversity. Genetic studies have found it is related to Spanish horses, including Andalucians (see pp.140–41), as well as Orlovs (see pp.110–11), possibly via the Thoroughbred. There was no material available from French breeds.

Thoroughbred crosses were also used to produce the Irish hunter. These added quality and speed without reducing the Irish Draft's inherent hunting skills. Such crosses are now called Irish Sport Horses (see box, below). Irish Drafts are easily managed and have a good temperament. As well as being popular riding horses, they excel at cross-country.

IRISH SPORT HORSE

An Irish Sport Horse is a cross between an Irish Draft and any other breed, usually a Thoroughbred, but now often a European warmblood. Event rider David O'Connor had great success with Custom Made (pictured here) and Giltedge, both Irish Sport Horses. With Custom Made, he won Badminton in 1997, only the second American rider to do so. Among the pair's many other successes was eventing gold in the 2000 Olympics, the first for America in 25 years.

Gracefully arched neck; stallions have a significant crest

Outline is identical to that of the Welsh Mountain pony

Dished face with large eyes and wide, open nostrils

"Middle piece" of the cob is deep, short-coupled, and well ribbed

Some silky feather seen at the heel

THE WELSH COB HAS BEEN DESCRIBED AS **"THE BEST RIDE AND DRIVE ANIMAL IN THE WORLD."**

Welsh Cob

 HEIGHT AT WITHERS	ORIGIN	COLORS
13.2 hh (137 cm)	Mid-Wales, UK	All solid colors

The Welsh Cob is versatile, agile, hardy, and easy to keep, making it an ideal family horse.

Strong quarters

Of the two cobs in the Welsh Pony and Cob Society (WPCS) studbook, the Welsh Cob, or section D, encompasses horses exceeding the height of the section C (see p.291). The Cob's early history is entwined with that of the other Welsh breeds: it was only in 1901 that the four types were formally recognized and each given a separate section in the studbook, based on height. Prior to that, imported stallions had been used to improve the quality of the Welsh ponies; those that were large enough to carry an adult were the forerunners of the Welsh Cob section D.

Modern Welsh Cobs evolved from a mix of Powys stock with 18th and 19th century outcrosses to Norfolk Roadsters (see p.157) and Yorkshire Coach Horses. This ancestry is apparent in the four Welsh Cob lines, as is the addition of Arab blood. The four foundation sires in the WPCS studbook are: Trotting Comet (foaled in 1840); True Briton (foaled in 1830); Cymro Llwyd (foaled in 1850); and Alonzo the Brave (foaled in 1866).

For centuries Welsh Cobs were an integral part of Welsh life, their strength and stamina making them ideal for work on hill farms and hauling slate from the mines. They were also in demand as artillery horses and cavalry mounts, and used as city draft horses by dairies and other trades. The forceful action of the modern Welsh Cob makes the breed ideal for competitive driving, and it is also a sure-footed hunter and a natural jumper. Although spirited, the Cob is easily managed, economical to keep, and very sound.

WELSH CROSSES

The four different Welsh pony and cob breeds have a strong following in countries such as Australia, New Zealand, and the US. They are often used as a cross with other breeds, and their good points come to the fore, but do not dominate. The Welsh Partbred (pictured here) is a promising competition horse. It is usually obtained by crossing a section D with a Thoroughbred. Arabs also make a good cross, producing a good riding pony or horse.

Well-shaped feet made of dense horn

Pride of Wales
Known for their ground-covering trot, Welsh Cobs have great presence and a gentle nature. Although they have a cob-build, they are remarkably agile and have plenty of energy.

Andalucian

HEIGHT AT WITHERS	ORIGIN	COLORS
15–17 hh (152–172 cm)	Andalucia, Spain	Usually gray and bay

The noble head of the Andalucian clearly displays the breed's North African ancestry.

After the Arab and the Barb, Spanish horses have had the most influence on the development of modern horse breeds. They were Europe's premier breed in the 19th century, inspiring the name of the Spanish Riding School of Vienna. Even allowing for regional differences and nuances of type, what is for all intents and purposes the same horse may be called: Spanish, Carthusian (see box, below), Lusitano, Alter Real (see p.142), Peninsular, Zapatero, and Andalucian. In 1912, the Spanish Breeders' Association replaced the name Andalucian with *Pura Raza Española*, or "pure Spanish breed."

The Andalucian probably evolved from a mix of indigenous Sorraia (see p.294) stock and Barb (see pp.94–95) horses. Breeding centered on the Carthusian monastery at Jerez de la Frontera, founded in 1476. The monks preserved the purest strain of Andalucian. Refusing to use heavy Neapolitan outcrosses, they selectively bred the Andalucian and the best lines can be traced to those original horses.

Although not a large horse, the Andalucian has a commanding presence. Its paces are lofty and spectacular. It is well-balanced, supple, and agile and its paces are lofty. Fiery and courageous, the Andalucian is also obedient and intelligent. It is a high-quality riding horse with a natural ability for dressage. In Spain, Andalucians are also used as mounts in the bullring, as well as for cattle work and carriage driving.

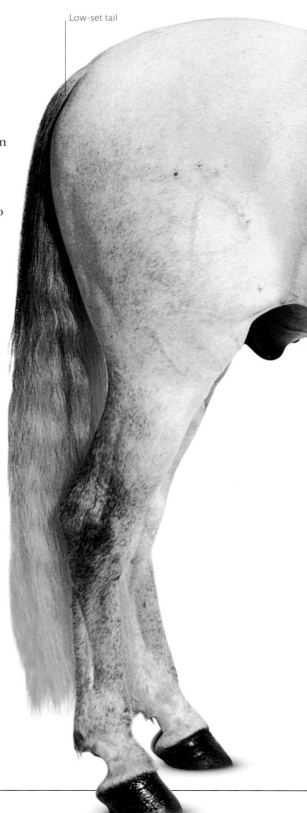

Low-set tail

CARTHUSIAN COUSIN

Said to be the purest strain of Andalucian, the Carthusian, or Cartujano is rare and commands a high price. It is distinguished from the Andalucian by small differences in appearance, such as a tendency to a concave profile. The line dates to the 18th century and a stallion called El Soldado, owned by brothers Andrés and Diego Zamora. A study in 2005 concluded that there is no great genetic difference between the Andalucian and the Carthusian Andalucian.

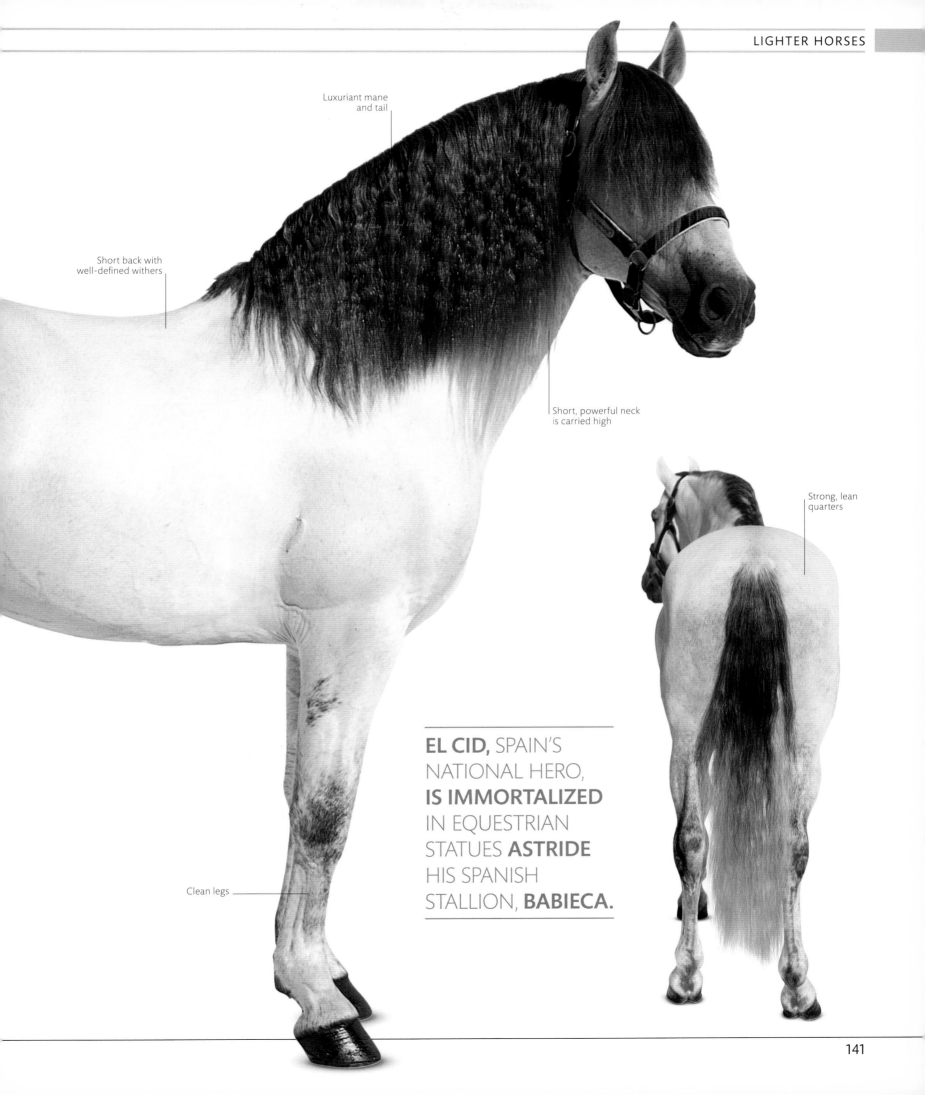

Luxuriant mane and tail

Short back with well-defined withers

Short, powerful neck is carried high

Strong, lean quarters

Clean legs

EL CID, SPAIN'S NATIONAL HERO, **IS IMMORTALIZED** IN EQUESTRIAN STATUES **ASTRIDE** HIS SPANISH STALLION, **BABIECA.**

Alter Real

HEIGHT AT WITHERS	ORIGIN	COLORS
15–17 hh (152–172 cm)	Portugal	Bay or brown

ALTER REAL STATE STUD

Since 2013, the Alter Real stud has been under the control of the Companhia das Lezírias—the organization managing Portugal's national studs. There are around 400 horses at the stud, with around 100 more on loan to equine colleges. The Portuguese School of Equestrian Art currently has 49 bay Alter Reals.

Named after the small town of Alter do Chão, this horse was destined for the royal—*real* in Portuguese—stables.

The royal stud in Alentejo, Portugal, supplied horses for the classical riding academy, and for royal use. In 1756, breeding moved to Alter, and some 300 Andalucian mares were brought from Jerez de la Frontera, Spain. The stud was sacked by Napoleon's troops in the early 19th century, and closed in 1834. Attempts to resurrect the breed through outcrosses to Hanoverians (see pp.172–73), Spanish-Normans, and Thoroughbreds (see pp.120–21) were unsuccessful, as was the introduction of Arabs (see pp.92–93). With the re-introduction of pure Andalucian blood, the Alter Real's fortunes began to improve. The dissolution of the Portuguese monarchy in 1910 and the closure of the royal studs almost finished off the breed. Fortunately, Dr. Ruy d'Andrade (see also Sorraia, p.294) saved a small stock and line-bred to two fine stallions. The herd was handed over to the Ministry of Agriculture in 1942 when the stud was reopened. Today, the Alter Real is considered a strain of Lusitano (see pp.144–45) bred only at the state stud.

The modern Alter Real retains the high, showy action and notable knee flexion suited to High School. A strong, courageous horse, the Alter was the traditional mount of bullfighters. Today, the breed competes in dressage and driving events.

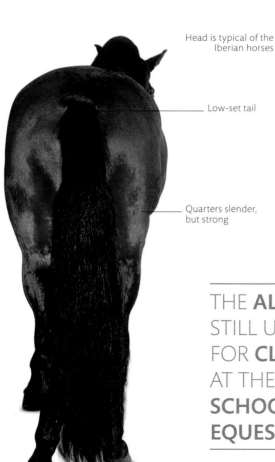

Head is typical of the Iberian horses

Low-set tail

Quarters slender, but strong

Short, muscular neck

Exceptionally deep and broad chest

Short back

Muscular forearms

Short cannons

THE **ALTER REAL** IS STILL USED EXCLUSIVELY FOR **CLASSICAL RIDING** AT THE **PORTUGUESE SCHOOL OF EQUESTRIAN ART.**

Hispano-Arabe

HEIGHT AT WITHERS	ORIGIN	COLORS
Average 15.2 hh (158 cm)	Andalucia, Spain	All solid colors

The Hispano-Arabe combines the Arab's refinement with the substance of the Andalucian.

This elegant breed is the result of judicious crossbreeding between the Andalucian and the Arab or Anglo-Arab to produce a very refined, spirited riding horse. It retains much of the Arab type, particularly about the head, but has the powerful back and quarters of the Spanish horse.

Records of Hispano-Arabe breeding date back to 1778, but the breed's popularity was at its peak in the 1880s when its versatility—as a riding horse and working cattle on the Spanish ranches—was recognized. However, owing to a serious lack of quality stock, the breed declined and by the middle of the 20th century was on the verge of extinction.

In 1986, a studbook was established and the Spanish government initiated a breeding regeneration and conservation program at its military stud farms. Given the small number of Hispano-Arabe mares, pure Arab mares were also introduced to the foundation stallions and a controlled breeding strategy was put in place. Spanish breeders are working to establish a breed standard for the Hispano-Arabe. It is still in demand for livestock work, but efforts are also focused on developing its qualities as a sports horse for show jumping, dressage, and cross-country. It also excels in the equestrian skills sport of TREC.

TRADITIONAL COSTUME

In Spain, *vaquero* (cowboy) attire is often seen in riding competitions and parades. This horse is wearing a vaquera bridle with a *mosquera* (fly fringe) on the *frontalera* (browband). The rider has a Flamenco-style dress, with layers of fabric, and a black sombrero.

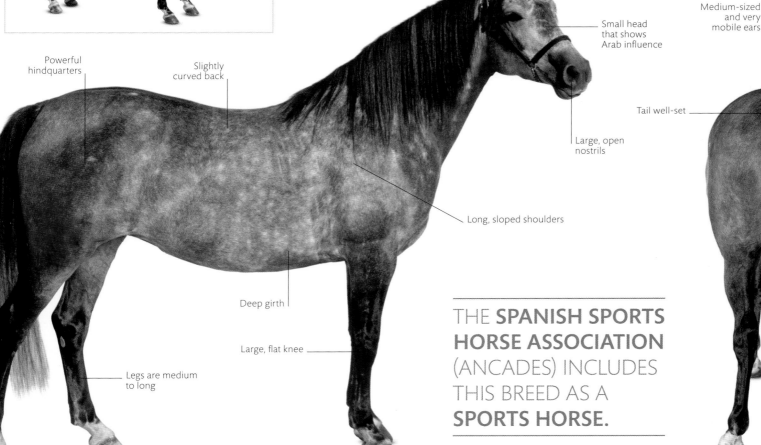

Powerful hindquarters

Slightly curved back

Small head that shows Arab influence

Large, open nostrils

Long, sloped shoulders

Deep girth

Large, flat knee

Legs are medium to long

Medium-sized and very mobile ears

Tail well-set

THE **SPANISH SPORTS HORSE ASSOCIATION** (ANCADES) INCLUDES THIS BREED AS A **SPORTS HORSE.**

NOVILHEIRO, RIDDEN BY UK SHOW JUMPER JOHN WHITAKER IN THE 1980s, WAS A PUREBRED LUSITANO STALLION.

Lusitano

HEIGHT AT WITHERS	ORIGIN	COLORS
15.1–16.1 hh (155–165 cm)	Portugal	Usually gray; any solid color

CAVALRY REGIMENT

Once a month in Lisbon, Portugal, a ceremonial changing of the guard takes place outside Belém Palace, the president's official residence. Mounted on gray Lusitano horses, the National Republican Guard, as well as a body of foot soldiers, perform a series of choreographed marches. The changing of the guard ritual, which includes mounted musicians who perform at the gallop, dates back to the establishment of the republic in 1910.

Finely built but strong and agile, and infinitely trainable, the Lusitano is the pride of Portugal.

Essentially, the Lusitano is the Portuguese version of the Andalucian (see pp.140–41) and is a riding and carriage horse of great quality. There are minor differences between the two—for example, the Lusitano tends to have a more sloping croup and its tail is set lower. The Lusitano is indisputably Iberian in appearance and character. While the precise origin and development of the breed is uncertain, the Lusitano is the definitive Portuguese horse and has been bred selectively in Portugal for over 200 years. However, the name Lusitano (from Lusitania, the old Latin for Portugal) has only been officially recognized since 1966.

The Lusitano probably originated on the plains of southwestern Iberia and was used for light agricultural work, riding, and by the Portuguese cavalry. In the 19th and 20th centuries, foreign blood was introduced to make the breed heavier for draft work, resulting in a loss of quality. Fortunately, a group of enthusiasts produced a strict breed standard and, through a selective breeding program, restored the original qualities of the breed, including its fine balance and superb elevated action.

The Lusitano is the traditional horse of the Portuguese bullring. Agile, intelligent, and courageous, it is the ideal mount for the bullfighter. It is also ridden by the campaneros who tend the bulls bred for fighting. The breed's excellent classical dressage skills have seen Lusitanos compete at the Olympic level as part of the Portuguese and Spanish dressage teams. This versatile horse also takes part in international show jumping and combined-driving events.

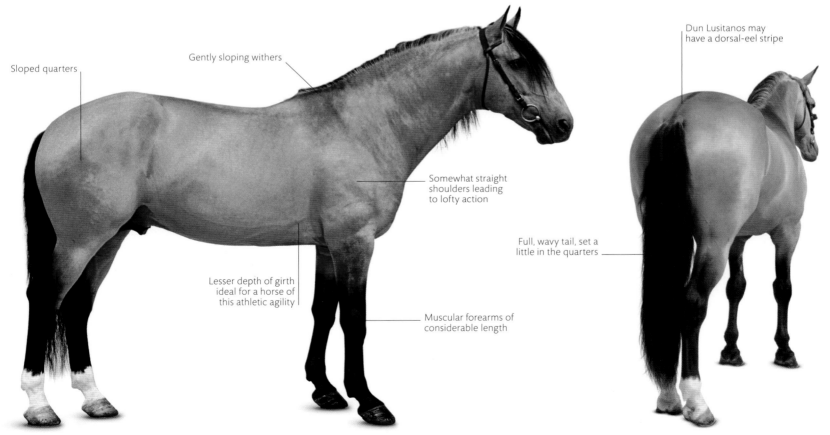

Sloped quarters

Gently sloping withers

Dun Lusitanos may have a dorsal-eel stripe

Somewhat straight shoulders leading to lofty action

Full, wavy tail, set a little in the quarters

Lesser depth of girth ideal for a horse of this athletic agility

Muscular forearms of considerable length

Working cattle
Portuguese *vaqueros* often riding
Lusitanos herd cattle using long poles.
The poles form part of elaborate
horseback displays, and feature in
the sport of working equitation.

Anglo-Arab

HEIGHT AT WITHERS	ORIGIN	COLORS
16–16.3 hh (163–170 cm)	UK and southwest France	Usually gray and bay

The fusion of the Thoroughbred and its ancestor, the Arab, has produced this versatile and athletic horse.

The Anglo-Arab originated in the UK, where the Thoroughbred (see pp.120–21) was originally developed. It was, however, perfected in France, where systematic breeding programs have resulted in Anglo-Arabs that excel at a range of disciplines. The British Anglo-Arab is a cross between a Thoroughbred stallion and an Arab mare, or vice-versa. To obtain entry in the studbook a horse must be able to claim a minimum of 12 ½ percent Arab blood.

In 1836, systematic breeding began at Pompadour in France based on two principal Arab stallions, Massoud and Aslan (described as a Turk), and three Thoroughbred foundation mares: Dair, Common Mare, and Selim Mare. A rigorous system of selection based on performance, stamina, and conformation was built into the early breeding policies

and persists to this day. Additionally, a special racing program for French Anglo-Arabs provides a further criterion for selection.

In theory, the crossing of the Arab with the related Thoroughbred should result in the ideal riding horse, combining the Arab's soundness, stamina, and manageable temperament with the Thoroughbred's speed and scope. The modern Anglo-Arab tends more toward the Thoroughbred in appearance but with a more solid frame. It is a tough, enormously versatile, and athletic horse with pronounced jumping ability. French-bred horses are perhaps slightly less elegant than their British counterparts but have achieved great success in dressage, cross-country, and eventing at an international level.

Exceptionally strong feet with perfectly sloped pasterns

POMPADOUR

In France, the center of Anglo-Arab breeding has long been the national stud at Pompadour in Limousin. The marquise of Arnac originally set up a stud in the castle in 1751 and, at the command of Louis XV, this became a royal stud in 1761. After the French Revolution, it became a national stud in 1872. Napoleon, known to like Arab (see pp.92–93) horses, is said to have brought back several from his Egyptian campaign and sent them to the Pompadour stud.

Mane, coat, and tail
are fine and silky

Well-sloped
shoulders ensure a
long, economical action

Profile straighter than the
Arab, and overall outlook
and expression closer to
the Thoroughbred

Outline tends to
be closer to that of
the Thoroughbred

Long, slender,
well-muscled forelegs

Quarters tend to be
long and horizontal

MANY OF **FRANCE'S INTERNATIONAL** AND **OLYMPIC MEDALS** HAVE BEEN WON BY **ANGLO-ARABS** WITH 25–45 PERCENT ARAB BLOOD.

THESE **BRAVE HORSES** ARE SAID TO WORK BULLS AS **INSTINCTIVELY** AS A **BORDER COLLIE** WORKS **SHEEP.**

Camargue

HEIGHT AT WITHERS	**ORIGIN**	**COLORS**
13–14.2 hh (132–147 cm)	Camargue, France	Gray

With its gray coat and stocky build, this is one of the most distinctive of the French breeds.

Camargue horses are indigenous to the French Camargue, an area covering the Rhône delta—a wild but fragile landscape with scrubby pasture, salt flats, and lagoons. In the past, the horses have been subject to infusions of North African blood as well as horses brought in by other invading armies. This is also apparent from the traditional saddlery, which is very Moorish, with a deep seat and cage stirrups. These are still used by the Provençal *gardians*, who help keep the area's traditions alive. Riding Camargue horses, they round up the black bulls bred on local ranches, driving them through village streets during summer festivals. The *gardians* also show off their horsemanship in the arena at nearby Arles.

The isolation of the area ensured that the gray Camargue remained untouched by outside influences. Today, the breed is protected by the French government and horses are found in semi-wild herds (*manades*). The harsh environment of the wetlands is responsible for the breed's incredible hardiness and stamina. They subsist on tough plants and what they can scavenge from the reeds.

Camargue foals are black or brown. The coat turns gray after about four years. Slow to mature—reaching adulthood between the ages of five and seven—Camargues are long-lived, many reaching 25 years of age. Their paces are interesting, with a long and high walk, a short and stilted trot, and a very free canter and gallop.

DIVERSE WETLANDS

The northern wetlands of the Camargue have been drained for agriculture. But over 315 sq miles (820 sq km) is a nature reserve where Camargue horses roam free. A great way to get to know the area and the horses is to ride for a day. Camargues are sturdy, sure-footed, and good-natured. These "horses of the sea" are often pictured galloping on the shore or wading through water.

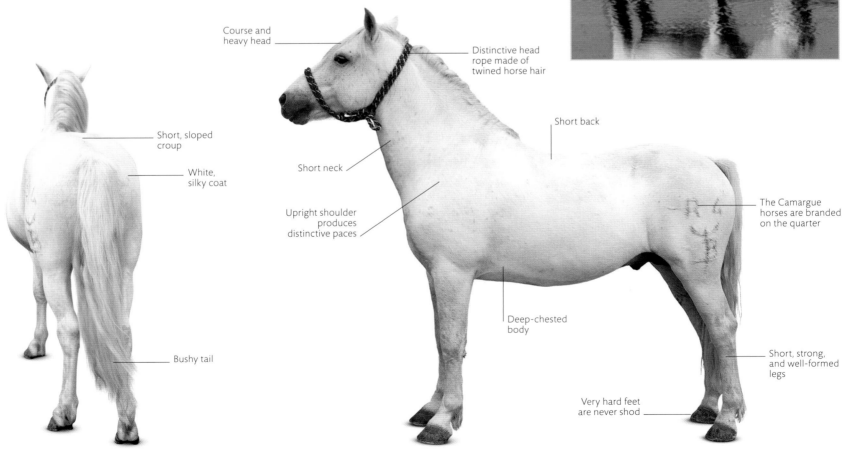

Course and heavy head

Distinctive head rope made of twined horse hair

Short back

Short, sloped croup

White, silky coat

Short neck

The Camargue horses are branded on the quarter

Upright shoulder produces distinctive paces

Bushy tail

Deep-chested body

Short, strong, and well-formed legs

Very hard feet are never shod

At home at sea
The tough Camargue horse has adapted so well to the challenging environment of the Rhône delta in France that it is almost as comfortable in water as it is on dry land.

Selle Français

HEIGHT AT WITHERS	ORIGIN	COLORS
More than 16 hh (163 cm)	Normandy, France	Usually chestnut

Often seen in the French Olympic team, the Selle Français is one of the great international show jumping breeds.

Like all warmbloods, the Selle Français is the result of a mixture of breeds. The term Cheval de Selle Français (French Saddle Horse) came into use in December 1958 to describe French "halfbred" competition horses. Before then, all French riding horses other than Thoroughbreds, Arabs, and Anglo-Arabs, were called *demi-sangs* (halfbreds).

The Selle Français can be traced back to the early 19th century, when the skillful horse breeders of Normandy crossed Thoroughbred stallions, imported from England, and halfbred stallions with their tough all-purpose Norman mares. Many of the halfbreds had a pronounced Norfolk Roadster (see p.157) background. This robust, but now extinct, horse is at the heart of many fast-trotting breeds. The result was two crossbreds: the fast harness horse that split from the mainstream to become the French Trotter (see pp.156–57) and the Anglo-Norman. Of the two distinct types of Anglo-Norman, the draft cob and the riding horse, it was the active riding horse

that was the prototype for the Selle Français. The breed's studbook is, in fact, a continuation of the old Anglo-Norman one.

Although two world wars depleted the population of native Norman mares, breeders managed to conserve some of the best stock. Thoroughbreds from the French national studs were brought in to meet the new demand for a quality riding horse that would combine speed, stamina, and jumping ability. Trotters and Arabs also contributed to the development of the type seen today. Sires included Furioso, whose name appears in the greatest halfbred lines of Central Europe. This Thoroughbred stallion had a brilliant career, topping the ratings for ten consecutive years at the great French national stud, Le Pin. He also produced world-class show jumpers, the principal area of specialization for this agile breed, which has a long-striding movement, a pronounced jumping ability, and more spirit than many other warmbloods.

FRENCH CHASER

A lighter Selle Français is bred specifically for racing under the letters AQPS (Autre Que Pur Sang—Horses Other Than Thoroughbreds). This usually means that one parent is not in the Thoroughbred studbook and often it will have Selle Français blood. The AQPS Stud Book dates from 2005. In practice, most AQPS horses are up to 80 percent Thoroughbred. According to AQPS breeder Henri Aubert, these horses can be distinguished from Thoroughbreds in that "They have a longer racing career, they are stronger and have more stamina, but they are not as quick in a straight line."

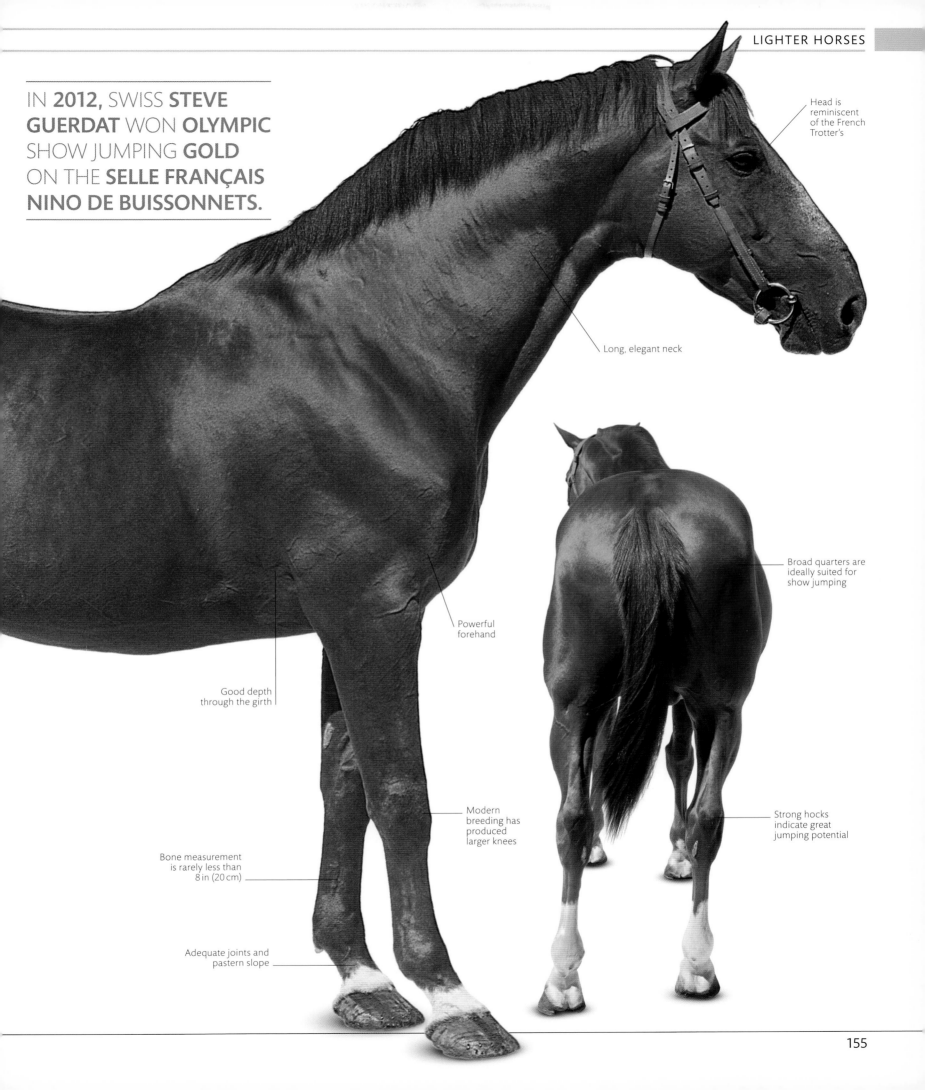

IN **2012**, SWISS **STEVE GUERDAT** WON **OLYMPIC** SHOW JUMPING **GOLD** ON THE **SELLE FRANÇAIS** NINO DE BUISSONNETS.

Head is reminiscent of the French Trotter's

Long, elegant neck

Broad quarters are ideally suited for show jumping

Powerful forehand

Good depth through the girth

Modern breeding has produced larger knees

Strong hocks indicate great jumping potential

Bone measurement is rarely less than 8 in (20 cm)

Adequate joints and pastern slope

Plain head is
set very well
on the neck

No thickness
through the jowl

Very strong shoulders
give good raking action

Muscled second thighs

Withers are defined
but still rounded

Frame is
substantial

Big, flat knees

Typically excellent
legs with good bone

Strong feet

IN FRANCE, MORE
THAN **11,000**
TROTTING RACES
TAKE PLACE
ANNUALLY—
61 PERCENT OF
THE **TOTAL** RACES
WORLDWIDE.

French Trotter

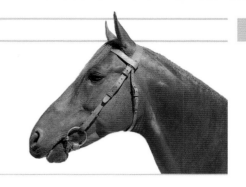

HEIGHT AT WITHERS	ORIGIN	COLORS
16.2 hh (168 cm)	Normandy, northern France	Chestnut, bay, and brown

Capable of taking on the best harness racers in the world, the French Trotter has no equal in trotting races under saddle.

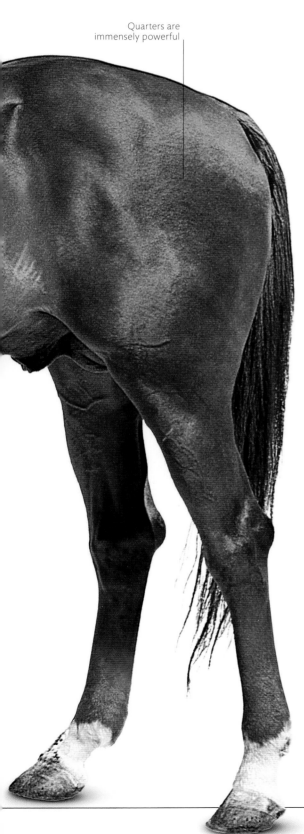

Quarters are immensely powerful

The sport of trotting, both in harness and under saddle, was established in France in the early 19th century; the first purpose-built raceway opened at Cherbourg in 1836. French breeders in Normandy were instrumental in the evolution of the superlative French Trotter which, like the Selle Français (see pp.154–55), developed from crosses with native Norman mares. With support from the powerful French national stud association, they imported Thoroughbreds (see pp.120–21) and, more importantly in a trotting-horse context, English halfbred or hunter stallions, at that time unknown in France. The stallion Young Rattler was one such import. He was a Thoroughbred cross whose dam had Norfolk Roadster heritage (see box, below). Thirty years later, more Thoroughbred stallions, including the Heir of Linne and Sir Quid Pigtail, helped to establish five important bloodlines, to which most

French Trotters can trace their lineage. American Standardbred (see pp.232–33) blood then served to increase the speed of the French Trotter and in 1922 it was recognized as a breed.

Trotting races have encouraged the breeding of a substantial horse with an extremely level action that is able to carry a relatively heavy weight in virtually perfect balance. The primary aim of the Société du Cheval Français, founded in 1864, is to protect this unique character. Breeding has also focused on toughness and great stamina, both necessary for racing success over comparatively long distances on tough courses. At the premier racetrack, Paris-Vincennes, which hosts international events such as the ridden Prix de Cornulier and its harness equivalent, the Prix d'Amérique, a downhill stretch is followed by a punishing uphill gradient over the last 1,000 yds (914 m).

NORFOLK ROADSTER

Now extinct, the Norfolk Roadster, which had an influence of the French Trotter, was a large horse with Thoroughbred blood. It was famed for its trotting abilities in harness and under saddle. Before the advent of good roads, riders would still be able to cover up to 60 miles (100 km) in a day on the best of them. Also known as the Norfolk Trotter, it had close links to the Shales Horse (see p.126), via the stallion known as Old Shales, and the Yorkshire Trotter, which is said to have been the same breed.

Belgian Warmblood

HEIGHT AT WITHERS	ORIGIN	COLORS
16.2 hh (168 cm)	Belgium, particularly Brabant	Any solid color

BIG BEN

At 17.3 hh (180 cm), this Belgian Warmblood was exceptional. Together with his rider, Canadian Ian Millar, he won more than 40 Grand Prix between 1984 and 1999. Big Ben retired in 1999 and died of colic at the end of that year. He won more than 1.5 million US dollars in prize money and the Canadian post office honored him with his own stamp.

In international show jumping, Belgian Warmbloods are among the most successful performers of recent years.

Development of the Belgian Warmblood began in the 1950s with the crossing of lighter-weight Belgian farm horses with Gelderlanders (see opposite). The resulting heavyweight riding horse was solid and reliable but without any great talent or gymnastic ability. Holsteiner stallions (see pp.170–71) and the more athletic Selle Français (see pp.154–55) replaced the Gelderlander in the mix. Both breeds have a strong Thoroughbred background and good paces. Pure Thoroughbred blood was added to achieve the best type of competition horse. Later, Anglo-Arab and Dutch Warmblood crosses fixed the desired temperament.

Also known as the Belgian Sport Horse, the Belgian Warmblood is a powerful, straight-moving horse that combines great agility with the calm nature necessary for the combined stresses of rigorous training, followed by competition at the highest level. There are two studbooks, the Belgian Warmblood Studbook (BWP) and the Studbook SBS, which accounts for the two names for what is essentially the same breed. The BWP is a forward-thinking organization and is undertaking programs to eliminate degenerative disorders from the breeding lines, while the SBS has made its breeding database freely available online.

Broad loins

Well-built, compact body

Neck is short and strong

Plain head with impression of intelligence

Broad, strong quarters

Deep chest

Second thighs are powerfully muscled

THE **MOTTO** OF THE BELGIAN WARMBLOOD **STUDBOOK** (BWP) IS **"BORN TO PERFORM."**

Groningen

HEIGHT AT WITHERS 16 hh (163 cm)
ORIGIN Groningen, northern Netherlands
COLORS Chestnut, bay, brown

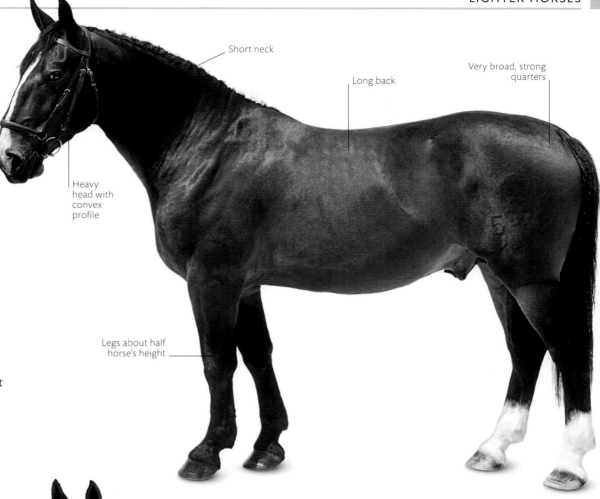

Short neck

Long back

Very broad, strong quarters

Heavy head with convex profile

Legs about half horse's height

Until the end of World War I, the Groningen was similar to the Gelderlander. It developed from breeds along the northern coast of the Netherlands and Germany. Changes in agricultural practice and the two world wars led to the coldblooded heavy Groningen being transformed into a heavy warmblood riding horse through crosses with Holsteiners (see pp. 170–71), Trakehners (see pp.186–87), and Thoroughbreds (see pp.120–21). As a result the old heavy Groningen has virtually died out. The Gelderlander register (VLN) and the Groningen register (NWP) merged in 1969 to form the Royal Warmblood Horse Studbook of the Netherlands.

Gelderlander

HEIGHT AT WITHERS 16.2 hh (168 cm)
ORIGIN Gelderland, Netherlands
COLORS Usually chestnut, often with white markings

Long, curved neck

Low, broad withers

The well-developed quarters are in line with croup

Face is sensible but rather plain

Well-set, strong shoulders

Short, very strong limbs

Hindleg is well made

Legs carry no feather

In the late 19th century Dutch breeders began to develop a carriage horse that could be used for light agricultural work and might also serve as a heavyweight riding horse. Using native mares, they introduced a range of sires including carriage horses, such as Cleveland Bays (see pp.122–23), Arabs (see pp.92–93), and lighter draft horses such as the Orlov Trotter (see pp.110–11) and Hackney (see pp.126–27). The best of the offspring were interbred to obtain a fixed type. The resulting Gelderlander is an impressive carriage horse with a lofty, rhythmic action. Gelderlanders are successful in competition driving and can make reliable, though not fast show jumpers.

Team of four
Competitive and leisure driving has a strong following in Europe and the US. This team of bay Gelderlanders is smartly turned out for a traditional coaching display.

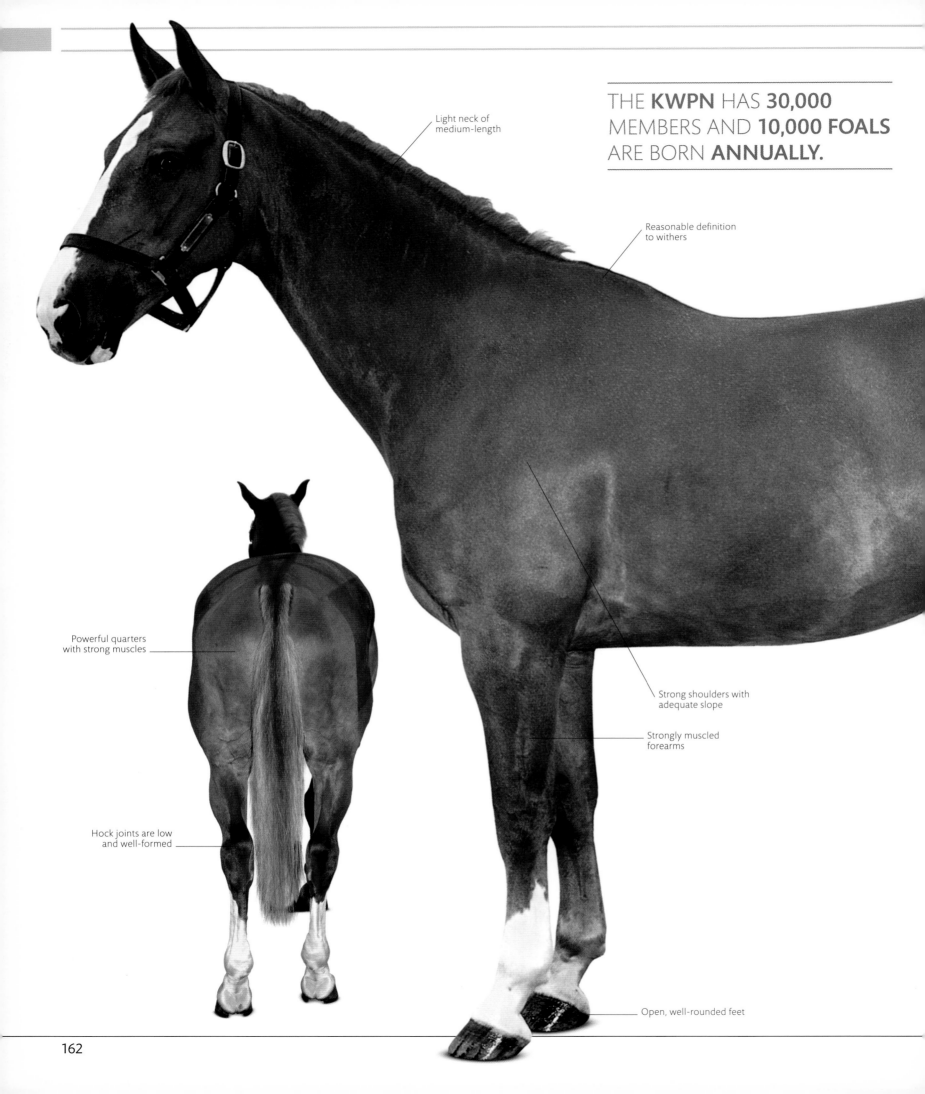

Light neck of
medium-length

Reasonable definition
to withers

Powerful quarters
with strong muscles

Strong shoulders with
adequate slope

Strongly muscled
forearms

Hock joints are low
and well-formed

Open, well-rounded feet

Dutch Warmblood

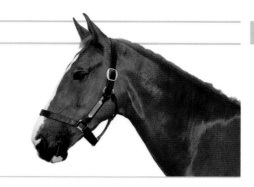

HEIGHT AT WITHERS	ORIGIN	COLORS
16 hh (163 cm)	Netherlands	Bay or brown

In a competitive world populated by talented warmblood breeds, this highly successful breed stands out.

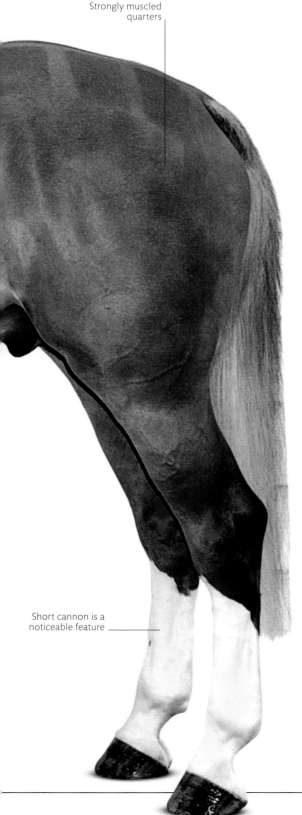

Strongly muscled quarters

Short cannon is a noticeable feature

The Dutch Warmblood owes its success to a selective, strictly controlled breeding program that has been continually adapted to a changing market. The breed has also been strongly supported and promoted by the Dutch state. The governing body for the breed is the KWPN (Koninklijk Warmbloed Paardenstamboek Nederland—Royal Warmblood Studbook of the Netherlands) and its studbook is one of the world's largest and most successful in terms of sport-horse breeds. Dutch Warmbloods are now often referred to as KWPNs.

The Dutch Warmblood is the product of two indigenous breeds—the Gelderlander and the Groningen (see p.159). The heavier Groningen had powerful quarters, but its front was not as good as the Gelderlander's. The two were put together, and the mix was adjusted by outcrosses to create a base for a competition horse. The subsequent introduction of Thoroughbred blood not only eliminated the carriage-horse action

and the long, harness back, but also added refinement and speed. The breeders then went back to related French and German warmblood stock and these were incorporated into the program to ensure the calm temperament was preserved.

This Warmblood excels in competition. Notable performers include Valegro, individual dressage gold medal winner at the London Olympics 2012. At Olympia in 2013, he and his rider Charlotte Dujardin set a new world record score of 93.975 percent. Valegro shows the classic Dutch Warmblood characteristics of good, level paces, straight action, and an even temper. This versatile breed also performs well in international harness-racing competitions.

Dutch Warmbloods undergo a rigorous selection process based on physical assessment and performance testing to ensure that only horses of good conformation, action, and sound temperament are used for breeding.

BORN TO DO DRESSAGE

Dutch Warmbloods are known for their talent for dressage. Their biddable temperament makes them ideal for training, while their elegant and attractive paces make them stunning to watch. Jennie Loriston Clarke (pictured here) has had a long association with Dutch Warmbloods. Dutch Courage, one of her most famous horses, had a background of Gelderlander and Thoroughbred. Born in 1969, he had great presence, but was also known for his cheeky character. It has been said that it was his performances which established dressage as a sport in Britain.

ROMAN HISTORIAN **TACITUS** (55–120 CE) REMARKED THAT HORSES FROM **FRIESLAND** WERE **EXCEPTIONALLY UGLY.**

Friesian

![horse icon]

HEIGHT AT WITHERS
Up to 15.3 hh
(160 cm)

ORIGIN
Friesland,
Netherlands

COLORS
Black

The breed standard stipulates that Friesians must be "jet black with no white markings (only a small star is permitted)."

One of the older European breeds, the Friesian has influenced the development of several other European ponies and horses, including the Oldenburger (see pp.166–67) and the Døle Gudbrandsal (see pp.80–81). Horses have existed in the Friesland area for many hundreds of years—in the 14th century, they were much sought after by the landed gentry for their elegance and high knee action—and have no doubt been influenced by crossbreeding with Spanish horses and others from western Europe.

In its native region, the Friesian was used for farm work, as well as being ridden and raced. Yet despite a studbook being opened in 1879, numbers declined due to competition from heavier breeds. During the world wars, it almost reached extinction, but fortunately some horses surived. In the mid-1960s, there were still just 500 registered mares.

This breed's striking appearance, showy action, and friendly nature has made it popular for film and television work. Dutch actor Rutger Hauer was so impressed by the Friesian he rode in the 1985 film *Ladyhawke* that he bought one. This film increased interest in the breed in the US and was influential in the formation of the Friesian Horse Association of North America.

Today, the powerfully built Friesian enjoys great popularity as a sports horse. It excels in harness racing and dressage.

A HORSE FOR ALL REASONS

With their calm temperament, impressive bearing, and somber coloring, Friesians have long been used to draw hearses in traditional funerals. And a famous team of Friesians used to promote Harrods of London. There are still stables that provide Friesian teams for special occasions in Britain, the US, and elsewhere.

Impressive topline accentuated by proudly arched neck

Sloping croup with a low-set tail

Strong, rounded quarters

Head is long with expressive eyes

Shoulders are very powerful

Tail is thick and luxuriant

Compact, strong, and deep body

Short, thick legs with large, clean joints

Hard feet usually of blue horn

Oldenburger

HEIGHT AT WITHERS	ORIGIN	COLORS
16.2–17.2 hh (168–178 cm)	Oldenburg, Germany	Usually brown, black, or bay

The big, impressive Oldenburger has been continually and successfully adapted to meet changing needs.

The most powerfully built of the German warmbloods, the Oldenburger was developed in the 17th century as a coach horse, largely through the efforts of the Count of Oldenburg. Using native Friesian stock (see pp.164–65) as a base, the count introduced Spanish and Neapolitan horses, both with a background of Barb (see pp.94–95) blood. He also used his gray stallion, Kranich, a descendant of notable Spanish lines. Around 1897, Thoroughbreds (see pp.120–21), the Cleveland Bay (see pp.122–23), and the Hanoverian (see pp.172–73) were also used. The most important influence during this period, however, was that of Normann 700, a French Norman stallion descended from Norfolk Roadsters. Soon, the Roman-nosed Oldenburger coach horse gave way to a more refined carriage horse— one that retained the size, depth, and the early-maturing character of the original.

In the 20th century, the breeding objective changed from the production of a strong, agricultural horse to an all-around riding horse with good paces and greater freedom of action. Condor, a Norman stallion with 70 percent Thoroughbred blood, was a particularly successful sire. More such outcrosses followed. Hanoverians were also occasionally added to the mix.

The modern Oldenburger has retained its powerful build and equable temperament. Although not fast, it has correct and rhythmic paces. From the 1990s, it has excelled in dressage and showjumping.

BONFIRE

Gestion Bonfire was ridden by Dutch dressage rider Anky van Grunsven (pictured here). The pair competed in three Olympic Games and two World Equestrian Games, winning individual gold at Sydney in 2000 and the Hague WEG in 1994. They won seven silver medals as well. Bonfire was famed for his expressive piaffe and passage. When he died in 2013, a statue was erected in his honor at Anky's home town of Erp.

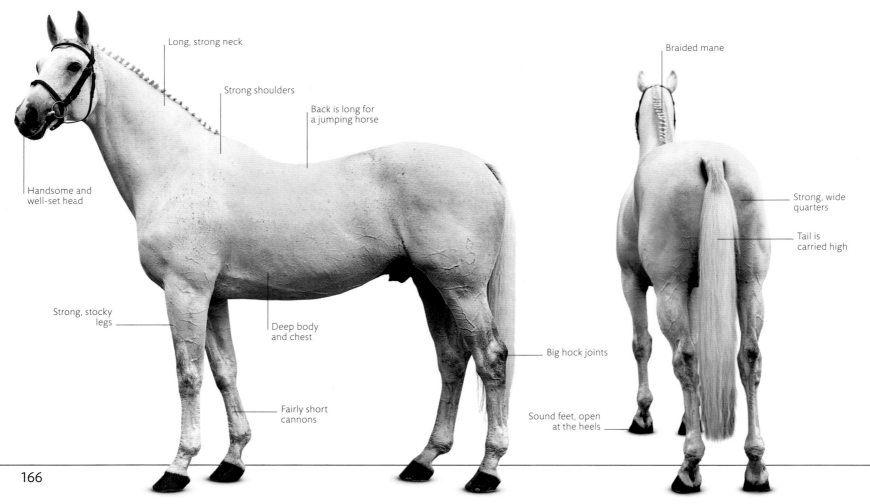

Long, strong neck

Strong shoulders

Back is long for a jumping horse

Handsome and well-set head

Strong, stocky legs

Deep body and chest

Fairly short cannons

Big hock joints

Braided mane

Strong, wide quarters

Tail is carried high

Sound feet, open at the heels

THE MOTTO OF
THE OLDENBURG
BREED SOCIETY IS
**"QUALITY IS THE
ONLY STANDARD
THAT COUNTS."**

Rhinelander

HEIGHT AT WITHERS	**ORIGIN**	**COLORS**
16.2 hh (168 cm)	Germany	Usually chestnut

A FACT OF BIRTH

German warmbloods earn their names from the places they are born and registered: a Rhinelander could be a brother of a Hanoverian or a Westphalian. There are 11 German state studs and, up until recently, these have had a firm control over breeding stock, particularly stallions. Even now, most warmbloods are produced through these studs.

A comparatively new breed, the unpretentious Rhinelander is suitable for recreational or competitive riding.

The best of the German coldblood horses was the old Rhenish-German or Rhineland heavy draft horse, based largely on the Belgian Brabant (see p.75). It was once a popular workhorse in Rhineland, Westphalia, and Saxony, but with the development of modern farm machinery, became redundant. The studbook went from 25,000 mares registered between 1935 and 1945 to almost no entries a few years later. The heavy breed is no longer recognized in Germany. However, the Rhenish Stud Book, founded in 1892, remained open and as the leisure market increased in the 1970s, breeders began using the lighter specimens of the old breed to create a warmblood riding horse—now called the Rhinelander or Rhenish Warmblood.

The breeding work involved crossing stallions from Hanover and Westphalia, in northwestern Germany, with warmblood mares sired by Thoroughbreds (see pp.120–21), Trakehners (see pp.186–87), and Hanoverians (see pp.172–73). From this mix of blood, halfbred stallions were selected to produce dressage and show jumping horses. The aim is for the horses to have a long outline, rather than a square one, and to be "noble" rather than elegant.

Small, plain head

Strong, thick, short neck

Defined withers

Rectangular outline

Sturdy body

Strong, sloping shoulders

Broad chest

Narrow girth

Small, narrow feet in relation to body

THE **RHINELANDER** IS ONE OF THE **MOST RECENT** BREEDS, DEVELOPED IN THE **1970s.**

Westphalian

HEIGHT AT WITHERS	ORIGIN	COLORS
15.2–17.2 hh (157–178 cm)	Germany	Usually black, bay, chestnut, or gray

A USEFUL RIDING HORSE

The focus in Westphalian breeding is to produce useful riding horses for all disciplines. The horses must be willing to learn, but the training of high-performance horses still requires a lot of time and patience. Westphalians have a long history of doing well in competition. Among the most famous are Ahlerich (1971–92) ridden by Dr. Reiner Klimke and Rembrandt (1977–2001) ridden by Nicole Uphoff (pictured here).

The warmblood Westphalian is closely related to the Hanoverian and shares a stud with the Rhinelander.

Warmbloods in Europe have long been developed along similar lines, so it is almost inevitable that they will share ancestry and characteristics. The Westphalian is in effect a Hanoverian (see pp.172–73) although there are sometimes differences in type, with some horses showing more of their coaching background than others.

The state stud at Warendorf, where Westphalians are bred, was set up in 1826 to provide horses for the then Prussian provinces of Rhineland and Westphalia. Initially, the aim was to produce Thoroughbred-type riding horses but demand increased for agricultural

horses and so heavier warmbloods from Oldenburg and East Frisia were introduced. These soon gave way to coldblood horses from Rhineland, which were considered stronger and better suited for agricultural work.

After World War II, heavy horse breeding declined due to the mechanization of farming and, once again, the focus turned to breeding lighter horses. Today, the Westphalian is a very successful competition horse ranking high in dressage and show jumping, but it also makes a good general riding horse, thanks to the careful evaluation and breeding policies of the Westphalian registry.

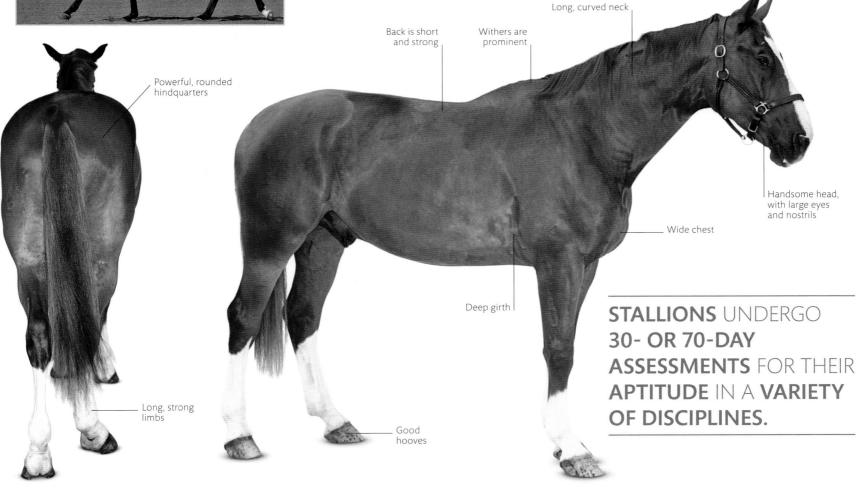

Powerful, rounded hindquarters

Back is short and strong

Withers are prominent

Long, curved neck

Handsome head, with large eyes and nostrils

Wide chest

Long, strong limbs

Deep girth

Good hooves

STALLIONS UNDERGO 30- OR 70-DAY **ASSESSMENTS** FOR THEIR **APTITUDE** IN A **VARIETY** OF **DISCIPLINES.**

Holsteiner

HEIGHT AT WITHERS	ORIGIN	COLORS
16–17 hh (163–173 cm)	Germany	Any solid color

Bold, athletic, and dependable, the Holsteiner is among the world's best show jumpers and suitable for all types of riding.

In the 19th century, most horse breeding in what is now Schleswig-Holstein was done by tenant farmers who could rarely afford good stock. There was a high demand for horses at the time, which had led to a further reduction in quality. In the northern marsh country of the duchy, however, better quality breeding was done by free farmers. In 1883, a new association was created at Krempen Marsh. Called the Holstein Breeding Association, it selected 100 brood mares in its first year. In 1891, all the associations in the area united in the Organization of Horse Breeders in the Holstein Marshes. The goal was to preserve the Holstein breed and develop a coach horse with strong bone and high action, that could also be a heavy-type of riding horse.

In the 19th century, Thoroughbreds (see pp.120–21) and Yorkshire coach stallions were introduced from England, giving the carriage Holsteins greater movement and a calmer temperament. The coarse Roman nose also began to disappear.

After World War II, German breeders wanted a purpose-bred competition horse, and to this end they upgraded again using Thoroughbred blood. Within a short time, they had developed what is now known as the Holsteiner—a lighter, multipurpose riding horse with the ability to gallop and jump. Today, it is an attractive breed and arguably the best eventing prospect of all the German warmbloods.

Gently sloping croup

SHOW JUMPING MACHINE

Holsteiners are renowned for their jumping abilities and Cedric, ridden by American show jumping star, Laura Kraut, is no exception. As part of the US show jumping team, this beautiful gray gelding won gold with Laura at the 2008 Beijing Olympics and was well placed in many other competitions. Laura says Cedric, who is comparatively small at just 15.2 hh (157 cm), is one of the "best athletes in the world." Zeremonie, one of Laura's recent prospects, is also a gray Holsteiner.

THE FAMOUS SIRE **COR DE LA BRYÉRE** PRODUCED A LINE OF HOLSTEINERS THAT HAVE HAD **UNRIVALED SHOW JUMPING SUCCESS.**

Arched, high-set
neck

Small head with fine
features

Clearly defined
withers

Sloping
shoulders

Powerful
hindquarters

Plenty of depth
in the girth

Well-muscled
forearms

Well-carried tail
is not set
over-high

Short, strong
cannons

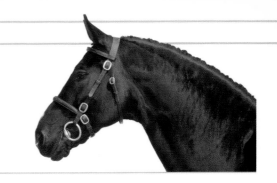

Hanoverian

HEIGHT AT WITHERS	ORIGIN	COLORS
15.3–16.2 hh (160–168 cm)	Germany	Any solid color

WARMBLOOD BRANDING

Warmbloods of similar background and parentage may be registered in different studbooks and so be given different brands and names. The Hanoverian horse, for example, is distinguished by its "H" brand mark. Entry to a breeding studbook is not guaranteed. All warmbloods are rigorously graded and performance tested. This ensures that only high quality animals are used for breeding, which in turn should ensure offspring of the best quality.

Athletic, graceful, and even-tempered, the Hanoverian excels as a show jumper and dressage horse.

The Hanoverian breed was established at Celle, Lower Saxony, in 1735 by George II, Elector of Hanover and King of England. The aim was to provide stud horses for local farmers to use with their mares. The founding sires at Celle were 14 black Holsteiners (see pp.170–71), powerful carriage horses, based on native mares crossed with eastern, Spanish, and Neapolitan blood. Thoroughbred (see pp.120–21) blood was introduced to create a lighter, free-moving horse that could be used in harness and as a cavalry mount, as well as for farm work.

By 1924 Celle had 500 stallions and a second stud was opened at Osnabruck-Eversburg. After World War II some Trakehners (see pp.186–87) arrived at Celle after a long and dangerous trek from East Prussia. They were added to the existing breeding stock and had a distinct effect on the Hanoverian.

From 1945 onward breeding policies were adapted to satisfy the new demand for high-quality sport horses. This led to further use of the Trakehners and more Thoroughbreds, both of which acted as a refining influence, lightening the still heavy-bodied Hanoverian and giving greater scope and freedom of movement.

Today the center of the Hanoverian is still Celle. They are also bred in North and South America, and in Australia and New Zealand.

Muscular quarters

High-set tail

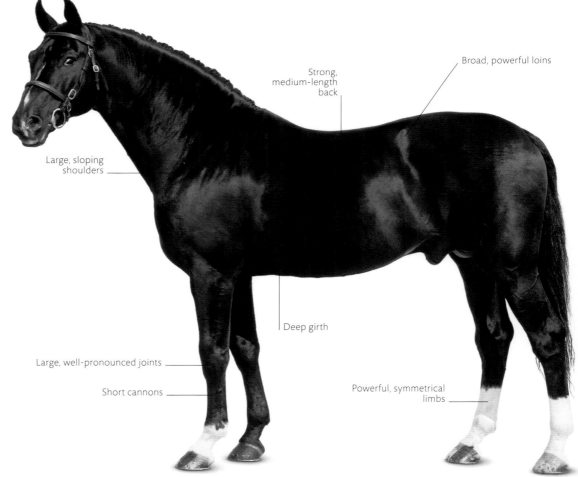

Strong, medium-length back

Broad, powerful loins

Large, sloping shoulders

Deep girth

Large, well-pronounced joints

Short cannons

Powerful, symmetrical limbs

HANOVERIANS COMMAND A **HIGH PRICE:** THE RECORD, **LEMONY'S NICKET,** CHANGED HANDS IN 2008 FOR **$1,130,000** (£700,000).

Württemberger

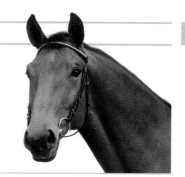

HEIGHT AT WITHERS	ORIGIN	COLORS
16 hh (163 cm)	Germany	Brown, bay, chestnut, sometimes black or gray

BADEN-WÜRTTEMBERG

The Württemberg breed registry, which was established in 1895, encourages breeders in Baden-Württemberg to register youngstock (pictured here), brood mares, and stallions. It records the pedigrees of Württemberger warmbloods and ponies, and the Black Forest horse (see p.58). It states its aim is to "preserve these horses as national treasures." Along with careful evaluation of breeding stock, the registry organizes foal shows and sporting events to promote these breeds.

Among the oldest German warmblood competition horses, the Württemberger is ideal for show jumping and dressage.

Energetic yet sensible, the Württemberger was developed at the Marbach stud in the former state of Württemberg, southwestern Germany. One of the greatest of the European breeding centers, Marbach was founded as a private stud in 1477 and elevated to the status of a court and state stud in 1573. Early in its history the stud had established a reputation for good utility horses suitable for both riding and light harness work. These were produced by crossing the stud's various breeds, which ranged from Spanish horses and eastern stock to heavy horse breeds.

The breed evolved in the 17th century, when local mares were crossed with Arab (see pp.92–93) stallions. Spanish and Barb mares (see pp.94–95) and Friesian (see pp.164–65) stallions were also used. One of the most significant early influences on the breed was an Anglo-Norman stallion of cob type (see pp.70–71) named Faust

(born 1886), who was largely responsible for the Württemberger being officially recognized as a separate breed in 1895.

The early Württemberger was a useful, multipurpose farm horse, but by the 1950s it was decided to breed a lighter, more athletic riding horse. To this end, the Trakehner (see pp.186–87) stallion Julmond was brought to Marbach in 1960. He had a major influence on the development of the breed and is considered to be its foundation sire.

The modern Württemberger has lost some of its earlier stockiness and is more elegant and refined than its predecessor, while retaining its reliability and mild temperament. It is hardy, long-lived, and economical to keep. The action—which is energetic, agile, and true—reveals the Arab influence. Today the Württemberger is still associated with the Marbach stud and is not bred elsewhere.

> FOUNDATION STALLION **JULMOND** WAS ONE OF **1,200 TRAKEHNERS** THAT MADE A **900-MILE** (1,450-KM) TREK FROM PRUSSIA TO **WARENDORF** IN 1948.

Impressive head with a straight profile

Sloping, powerful shoulders

Short, strong back

Broad, muscular loins leading to well-formed quarters

Deep, broad chest

Robust, well-proportioned body

Sound limbs

Short legs with good bone

Well-formed, strong hooves

Knabstrupper

HEIGHT AT WITHERS	ORIGIN	COLORS
15.2 hh (157 cm)	Zealand, Denmark	Spotted

The Knabstrupper dates from the Napoleonic wars, when Spanish soldiers were stationed in Denmark.

This eye-catching breed is descended from a spotted chestnut mare called Flaebehoppen. Believed to have been of Spanish ancestry, she was noted for her speed and endurance, as well as her unusual coloring, which was described as: "dark red with a white mane and tail covered with white snowflakes on her body." When a Danish judge, Major Villars Lunn, bought the mare from a butcher named Flaebe, and put her to a Frederiksborg (see p.178) stallion at his Knabstrup estate, this mare founded a line of spotted horses. Mikkel, her grandson, a celebrated carriage-racer foaled in 1818, is recognized as a foundation sire. Knabstruppers are mainly white with brown or black spots on the head, body, and legs.

The Knabstrupper of the old type, a tough horse with a coarse head, powerful shoulders and a shortish, strong neck, was ideal for harness work. Circus performers also appreciated its broad back for vaulting displays. Unfortunately, ill-advised crossings, including inbreeding, concentrated on the spotted coat alone, regardless of conformation and constitution, leading to a deterioration in the quality of the breed. There was also a disastrous fire at the stables, which killed 22 horses. As a result, the old, heavier-built Knabstrupper declined. The introduction of Appaloosa blood in the early 1970s, followed by crosses to Holsteiner (see pp.170–71) and Trakehners (see pp.186–87), produced the modern Knabstrupper, a versatile and cooperative riding horse used in dressage, eventing, and show jumping. It has the appearance of a quality Appaloosa, but is not bred much outside of Denmark. As Knabstruppers are often naturally small, breeding down has become popular, creating riding ponies, which are naturally popular with children due to their spotted coloring.

Well-set, attractive head

Well-muscled, strong neck

Sparse tail and mane

CIRCUS PERFORMERS

The Guttenbergs (pictured here) performed bareback feats in the Bertram Mills circus in late 19th-and early 20th-century Britain. They used a variety of horses, including spotted ones. Because they are eye-catching, spotted horses are often used for trick riding, but they are not any more suited to the work than other horses. Like teaching a horse to perform airs above the ground (see p.203), this type of training takes time and patience.

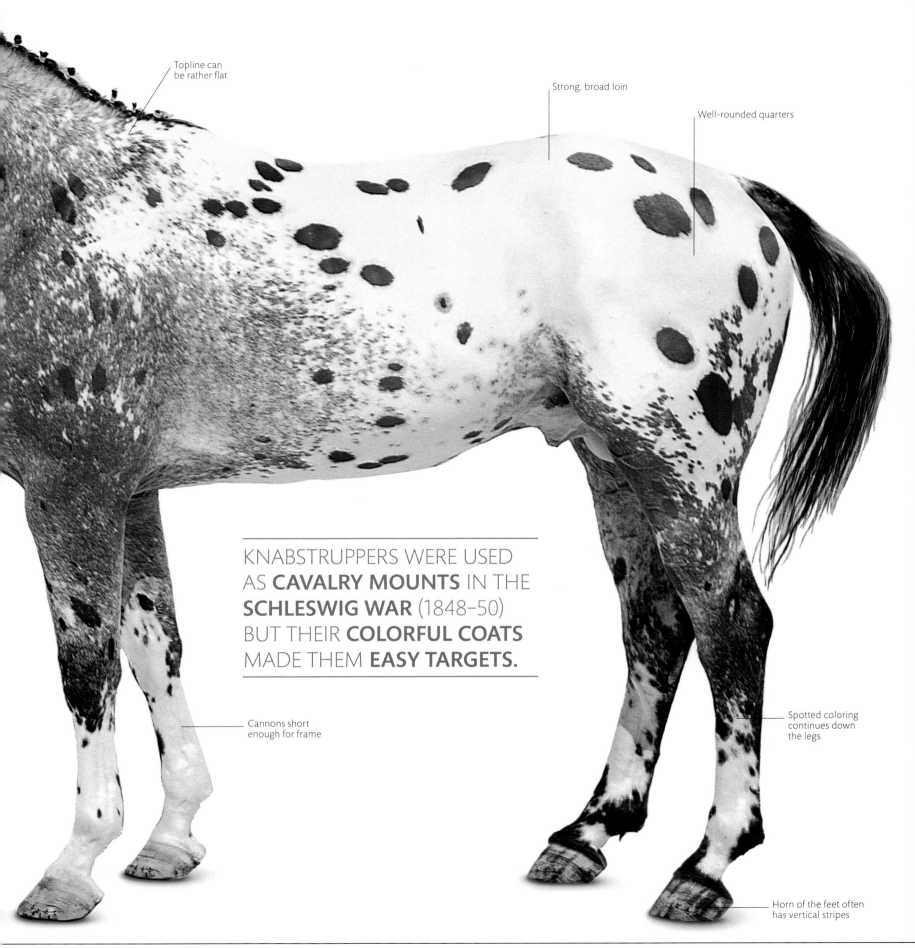

Topline can
be rather flat

Strong, broad loin

Well-rounded quarters

KNABSTRUPPERS WERE USED
AS **CAVALRY MOUNTS** IN THE
SCHLESWIG WAR (1848–50)
BUT THEIR **COLORFUL COATS**
MADE THEM **EASY TARGETS.**

Cannons short
enough for frame

Spotted coloring
continues down
the legs

Horn of the feet often
has vertical stripes

Frederiksborg

HEIGHT AT WITHERS	ORIGIN	COLORS
15.1–16.3 hh (155–170 cm)	Denmark	Chestnut

FREDERIK V

Outside the Amalienborg Palace in Copenhagen is a statue of Frederik V on horseback. It was commissioned by the Dutch East India Company in 1752 and made by French sculptor Jacques Saly (1717–76), who is said to have been inspired by a statue of Louis XV in Paris. Saly modeled 12 different stallions in the Royal Stud in order to produce the ideal of a Frederiksborg.

Although rare today, Frederiksborg horses were held in high esteem throughout Europe for nearly 100 years.

In the 16th century, Denmark was the principal source of elegant saddle and carriage horses that also served as military chargers. The Frederiksborg was developed at the Royal Frederiksborg Stud, during the reign of King Frederik II of Denmark (1534–88). The foundation stock consisted of Spanish horses, and related Neapolitans were introduced later. In the 19th century outcrosses were made to halfbred English stallions and eastern stock, usually Arabs (see pp.92–93). The result was an impressive riding horse with a vigorous, high action. It was used to improve breeds, such as the Jutland (see p.74).

The Frederiksborg's popularity proved to be its undoing. Heavy exportation, including some of the foundation stock, severely depleted the bloodlines. The royal stud was forced to close around 1871. The remaining breeders focused on developing a smart carriage and light-draft horse, so the distinctive riding horse went into decline. More recently, Frederiksborg-type mares have been crossed with Thoroughbreds (see pp.120–21) and Trakehners (see pp.186–87) to develop the Danish Warmblood (see opposite). Today, although numbers are low, Frederiksborgs are used in harness and compete in combined-driving.

PLUTO, A **WHITE FREDERIKSBORG,** BORN **IN 1765,** FOUNDED ONE OF THE **LIPIZZANER** LINES.

Head is held high

Tail set high and carried well

Longish, strong back with low withers

Croup is typically level

Broad chest

Elegant, powerful shoulders are somewhat upright

Proportionate legs, with good-sized joints

Strong, well-shaped feet

Danish Warmblood

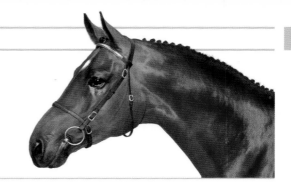

	HEIGHT AT WITHERS 16.2 hh (168 cm)	**ORIGIN** Denmark	**COLORS** Any solid color

With its natural balance, strength, and stamina, this warmblood is ideal for dressage and cross-country.

In the 14th century, most Danish horse breeding took place in Holstein—a Danish duchy until 1864. For many years the policy was to cross heavy North German mares with Spanish stallions, to produce horses like the Frederiksborg (see opposite) and the Holsteiner (see pp.170–71).

Although a Danish equestrian federation existed as early as 1918, it was not until the 1960s that a studbook was opened for the Danish Sports Horse, which has since become known as the Danish Warmblood.

The basis for this breed was the old Frederiksborg stock crossed with the Thoroughbred (see pp.120–21) to produce an active riding horse that, although it retained some of the Frederiksborg's thickness and carriage-horse character, was temperate and reasonably elegant. These halfbred mares were put to Anglo-Norman stallions (mainly Selle Français, see pp.154–55) and to Thoroughbreds, Trakehners (see pp.186–87), and Wielkopolskis (see pp.188–89).

The Selle Français introduced a wiry, athletic quality and improved conformation. The Trakehner and Wielkopolski contributed to their stamina, overall ability, and agreeable temperament, and the Thoroughbred was the refining influence, giving a superior movement and improved quality, speed, and courage.

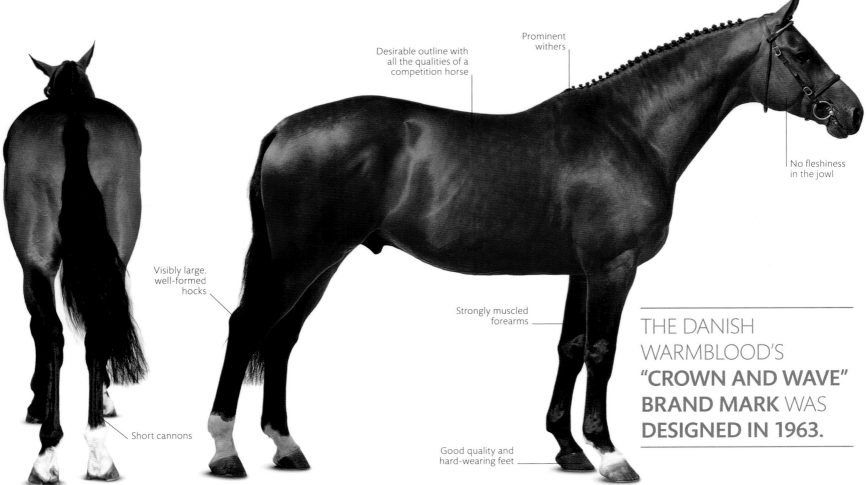

Prominent withers

Desirable outline with all the qualities of a competition horse

No fleshiness in the jowl

Visibly large, well-formed hocks

Strongly muscled forearms

Short cannons

Good quality and hard-wearing feet

THE DANISH WARMBLOOD'S "CROWN AND WAVE" BRAND MARK WAS DESIGNED IN 1963.

Swedish Warmblood

HEIGHT AT WITHERS	ORIGIN	COLORS
16.2 hh (168 cm)	Sweden	Any solid color

Handsome, sound, tractable, and versatile, this quality riding horse excels in many events.

Sweden has a long-standing equestrian tradition and the Swedish Warmblood—now a distinctive and highly successful competition horse—was originally a better-than-average cavalry mount. Its breeding relies heavily on the Thoroughbred (see pp.120–21), so the Swedish Warmblood resembles the best sort of English and Irish middleweight hunter (see pp.124–25).

The Swedish Warmblood descends from horses imported in the 17th century. It was first bred at the Stromsholm Stud, founded in 1621, and at Flyinge, the royal stud established in 1658 in Skåne, southern Sweden, formerly part of Denmark. Neither studs are stallion depots now, but remain respected equestrian centers.

The first of the 17th-century imports came from Denmark, England, France, Germany, Hungary, Russia, Spain, and Turkey and were highly varied. This meant that there could be no fixed type. These imports—most particularly the Spanish horses, Friesians (see pp.164–65), as well as those of eastern ancestry—produced active, strong horses when crossed with the local mares.

In the 19th and 20th centuries, Thoroughbreds, Hanoverians (see pp.172–73), Arabs (see pp.92–93), and Trakehners (see pp.186–87) were introduced into the base stock to create large, powerful horses that were increasingly fixed in type.

The modern type is a good example of riding-horse conformation with easy, straight paces. The best Swedish Warmbloods are well known as dressage horses, show jumpers, and event horses. They are also very good driving horses, and have been exported in large numbers all over Europe and to the US. The breed is performance tested, and is subject to rigorous examination before animals are accepted for breeding.

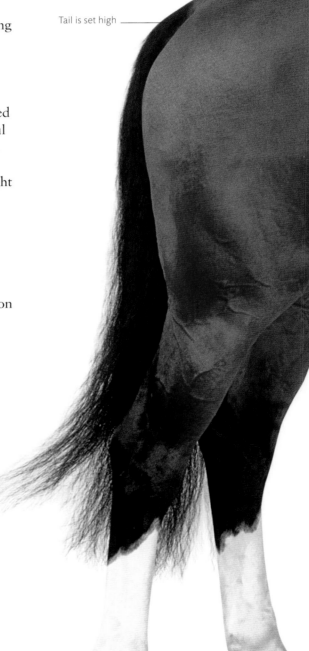

Tail is set high

Solid, well-shaped hoof

BROOD MARES

Swedish brood mares (pictured here) have an important role to play in the production of some of the world's best competition horses. Around 3,000 Swedish Warmblood foals are born in Sweden every year. The Swedish Warmblood Association believes that large pastures with high-quality grazing produce the best youngstock, many of which go on to have excellent careers. Swedish Warmbloods are also bred worldwide, particularly the US, where Swedish Warmblood Association of North America (SWANA) represents the breed, and New Zealand.

Overall outline is of a
quality riding horse

Medium-length back

Handsome head
with straight or
convex profile

Well-muscled,
sloping shoulders

Well-muscled
quarters

Compact body

Large, flat knees

Short, strong
back legs

SWEDEN WAS INSTRUMENTAL
IN THE INTRODUCTION OF
EQUESTRIAN DISCIPLINES
TO THE OLYMPIC GAMES.

Døle Trotter

HEIGHT AT WITHERS	ORIGIN	COLORS
Up to 15.3 hh (160 cm)	Norway	Bay or brown, some black and chestnut; occasionally gray or dun

YOUNGSTOCK

In recent years, the differences between the Døle Gudbrandsdal and the Døle Trotter have reduced again, due to inbreeding. Both are known for their excellent trotting ability. The fact that they are comparatively small, while still being tough and strong, probably also accounts for their popularity. There are about 4,000 horses worldwide—about 175 foals are registered annually.

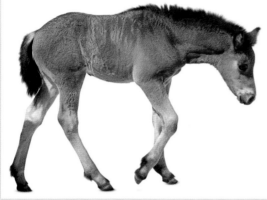

This light and tough sporting horse was developed in Norway in the 19th century.

There are two types of Døle Horse today: the Døle Gudbrandsdal (see pp.80–81), the old "utility" breed of Norway, and the Døle Trotter. Initially, there seems to have been no difference between the heavy draft horses and trotters, but in the 19th century, as harness racing took off in Norway, breeders began to develop horses for the sport. In 1872, the Døle Gudbrandsdal was split into two classes: the heavier agricultural and driving type and the lighter racing and riding horses.

The Trotter, a tough horse with a great trotting ability and capacious lungs, was derived from crossing lighter Døle Gudbrandsdals with imported trotting stallions, which were often Swedish. Thoroughbred (see pp.120–21) blood was also introduced, which can be seen in the length of the Trotter's head. Two stallions—Dovre and Toftebrun—significantly influenced the breed. Dovre, said to be an Arab, is the Døle Trotter's foundation sire.

In 1875, the Norwegian Trotting Association (NTA) was formed to represent the lighter type. In 1902, the first Døle Gudbrandsdal studbook was published, with stallions from both types born between 1846 and 1892. Since 1941 the Trotter has had its own studbook and this was taken over by the NTA in 1965. To qualify for entry, Døle Trotter stallions are performance tested over 0.6 miles (1,000 m).

Long, clean-cut head shows a Thoroughbred influence

Strong, well made quarters

Long, straight back

Neck is short and well-muscled

Tapering muzzle

Forehand is not overly heavy

Short and sturdy legs with little feathering

THE **0.6 MILE (1,000 M) RECORD** FOR A DØLE TROTTER IS **1 MINUTE 21.6 SECONDS,** ESTABLISHED BY **ALM SVARTEN IN 1986.**

Finnish Horse

HEIGHT AT WITHERS	ORIGIN	COLORS
15.1 hh (155 cm)	Finland	Any solid color; chestnut is preferred

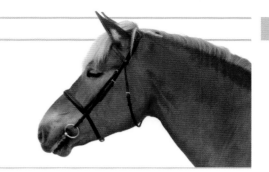

This strong, hardy horse was originally bred for demanding draft work in agriculture and forestry.

The Finnish Horse, like the North Swedish (see pp.82–83), is regarded as a coldblood, but is not a heavy breed. Owing to the growing Scandinavian interest in trotting, breeders concentrated on producing lighter horses that were hardy and sound, and could trot at a fast pace.

Originally there were two types of Finnish Horse: the Draft and the Universal, which was lighter. Neither was noted for its conformational beauty, but both were sound working horses. The Draft was strongly built with quick, active paces and was ideal for forestry and general agricultural work before mechanization. It is still used in some areas for light forestry and landscape work.

In 1907, a studbook was opened for both types and performance testing was also begun. In 1971, a riding type was added.

Nowadays emphasis is given to the lighter Universal type and today's Finnish Horse is a fairly good all-arounder, popular in Finland's riding schools and suitable for dressage and show jumping. It is also raced under harness and competes in the Finnish Trotting Championship. Although relatively small-framed, the Finnish Horse has strong shoulders and great pulling power, together with some speed and agility. It is an even-tempered breed.

Quarters lack muscle bulk

Compact body

Short, squarish head

Straight shoulders

Tail and mane are usually flaxen

Well-proportioned hindlegs

THE **FINNISH HORSE** ACCOUNTS FOR **25 PERCENT** OF THE **TOTAL** NUMBER OF HORSES IN FINLAND.

Estonian Horse

HEIGHT AT WITHERS	ORIGIN	COLORS
Up to 14.1 hh (145 cm)	Estonia	Bay, chestnut, black, gray; some duns

CONSERVATION GRAZING

Along with sheep, goats, and cattle, ponies are used in conservation grazing to clear rough land and encourage diverse plant species to return. Native animals are better suited to survive local conditions. Ponies close graze some areas and leave others untouched, which further contributes to a diversity of plant species.

The small Estonian Horse is an endangered breed, although work is being done to improve its chances of survival.

Once known as the Klepper, the Estonian is a small riding horse originating in the small state of the same name on the shores of the Baltic Sea. Records of horses in this region date back many years. Adam von Bremen, a German chronicler who traveled widely in the 11th century, mentioned the area and its horses. In the 19th century, attempts were made to develop the breed as a harness horse. Breed shows were held, along with trials to test their ability to draw carriages. Later, several studs were founded: Tori on the mainland in 1856, and Uue-Lõve in 1870 and Uue-Mõisa in 1902, both on the island of Saaremaa. These mostly concentrated on developing heavier working horses.

In 1921 the Estonian Native Horse Breeders Society was founded. Thirteen stallions were used to increase the height of the breed, as well as introduce white markings and the color chestnut.

The Estonian makes a good riding horse. It is increasingly used in environmental protection programs (see box, left). Landowners are paid subsidies to use these horses as well.

Medium to long neck

Back can be overlong

Low withers

Wide forehead

Mostly straight, rarely concave profile

Short ears

Croup is muscular with low-set tail

Joints are strong and clean

Legs are short and correct

Hard, well-shaped hoofs

WHEN RIDDEN, THE ESTONIAN IS **ENERGETIC,** BUT **CALM, CHEERFUL,** AND **SENSIBLE.**

Latvian Riding Horse

HEIGHT AT WITHERS
15.3–16.1 hh
(160–165 cm)

ORIGIN
Latvia

COLORS
Bay, brown, black,
and rarely chestnut

The Latvian Riding Horse was developed by crossing native workhorses with a range of imported European breeds.

A breeding program was set up in the 1890s using the Latvian harness horse as a base, and making crosses to a number of breeds, including Oldenburgers (see pp.166–67), Hanoverians (see pp.172–73), and some Holsteiners (pp.170–71). From 1920 to 1940, more Oldenburger stallions and mares were brought in from the Netherlands and Germany. They became the foundation stock.

In 1952, the Latvian Riding Horse was established with work on its development centered on the Okte stud in the Talsi municipality of Latvia. Between the 1960s and the 1970s, Thoroughbred (see pp.120–21) blood was introduced with the aim of producing a finer and much lighter sports horse.

Today, Latvian Riding Horses compete successfully in dressage and show jumping and are also very popular for trekking. The thriving Latvian Equestrian Federation organizes national, regional, and international competitions, and coordinates equestrian sports throughout Latvia. There is also an active Purebred Horse Breeders Association as well as a Latvian Horse Breeders Society with stud farms.

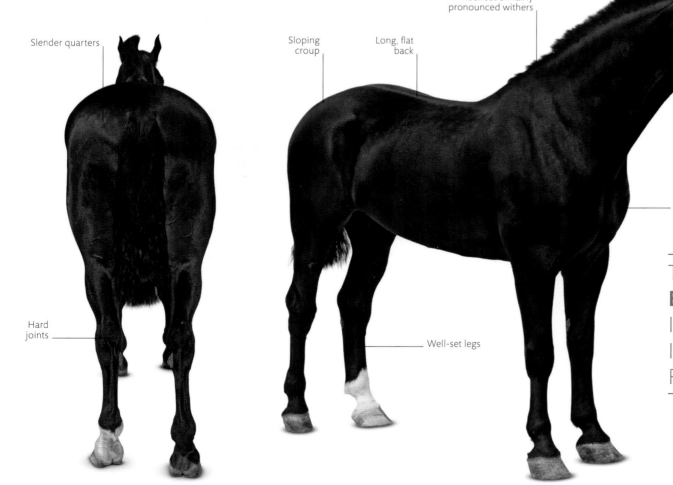

Slender quarters

Hard joints

Sloping croup

Long, flat back

Long, muscular neck set on fairly pronounced withers

Large head with a straight profile

Broad chest

Well-set legs

THE **HARNESS** **BACKGROUND** IS STILL **VISIBLE** IN THE MODERN RIDING HORSE.

Trakehner

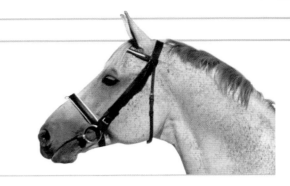

HEIGHT AT WITHERS	ORIGIN	COLORS
15.2–17 hh (157–173 cm)	Prussia (modern-day Lithuania)	Any solid color

Agile and athletic, with natural balance and a willing temperament, the Trakehner is superb for both competition and leisure riding.

In the 13th century, East Prussia (now in Poland) was colonized by the Order of Teutonic Knights. They set up a horse-breeding industry using the local Schweinken ponies as a base. The Schweinken, which may have had Konik (see p.309) roots, was a tough, hardy pony used in farm work. This area is also the birthplace of the Trakehner.

In 1732, Friedrich Wilhelm I of Prussia founded the Royal Trakehner Stud Administration. It became the principal source of stallions for Prussia, and the area soon became renowned for producing an elegant coach horse that combined speed with stamina. Within 50 years, however, the emphasis switched to army chargers and mounts of a quality unsurpassed in Europe.

During the 19th century Thoroughbreds (see pp.120–21) and Arabs (see pp.92–93) were introduced to upgrade the breed further. Over the years, the former became predominant. However, the Arab content always remained a powerful balancing element, to offset any deficiencies caused by the Thoroughbred.

Considered the best cavalry horse, the Trakehner was widely used in World War I. Although its population was halved during the war, it soon recovered. However, at the end of World War II the breed was again under serious threat when the Russians advanced on Poland and sent many horses back to Russia. Thousands of horses were taken by refugees fleeing in the opposite direction. Many of these horses, including several hundred Trakehners, were wounded or died on this perilous winter journey.

The Trakehner has an impressive record in international sports. Trakehners dominated the 1936 German Olympic team, which won every medal at Berlin. In recent years, they have succeeded in dressage, show jumping, and cross-country. Today, they are bred the world over, but mainly in Germany.

Croup shaped for speed

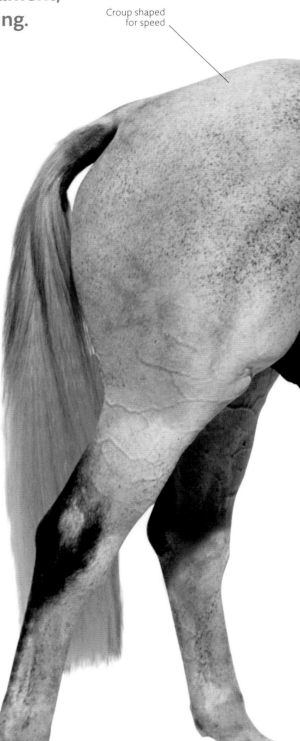

Hard hooves

A HORSE OF GREAT QUALITY

The Trakehner is as near as any to being the ideal, modern, all-around competition or riding horse. Perhaps because of the hardy base stock from which it derives, or the careful use of Arab blood at selected intervals, it seems to have been better able than most warmbloods to absorb the best Thoroughbred qualities while still retaining its own distinct character. Its upgrading influence is evident in many European sports breeds.

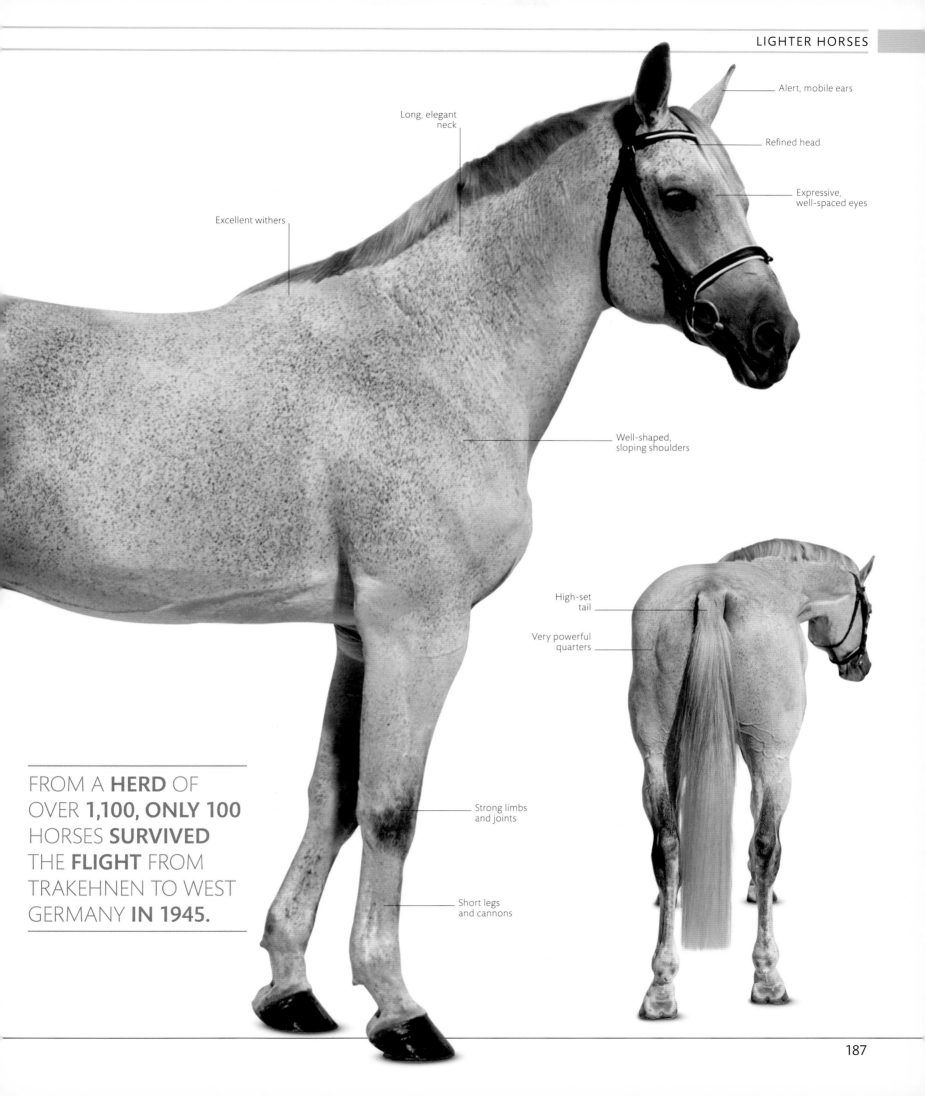

Alert, mobile ears

Long, elegant neck

Refined head

Excellent withers

Expressive, well-spaced eyes

Well-shaped, sloping shoulders

High-set tail

Very powerful quarters

FROM A **HERD** OF OVER **1,100, ONLY 100** HORSES **SURVIVED** THE **FLIGHT** FROM TRAKEHNEN TO WEST GERMANY **IN 1945.**

Strong limbs and joints

Short legs and cannons

THE WIELKOPOLSKI IS THE **WARMBLOOD WITH THE GREATEST POTENTIAL** AS AN **EVENTING HORSE.**

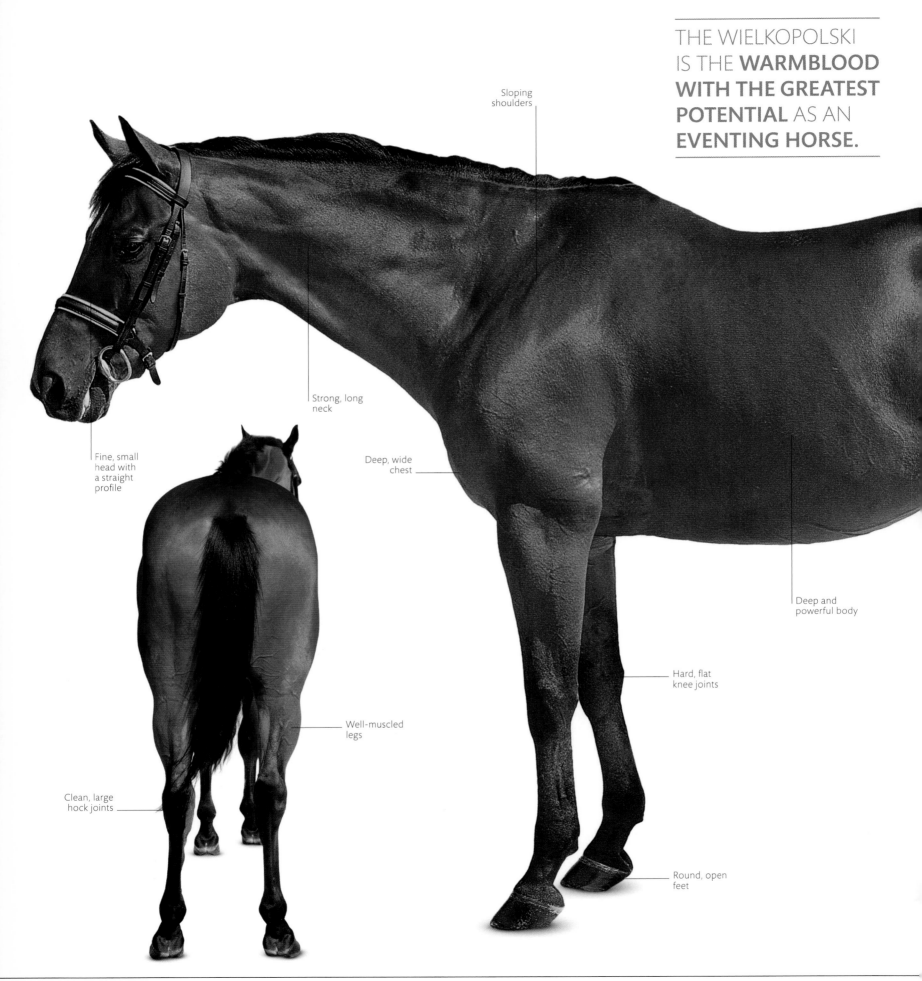

Sloping shoulders

Strong, long neck

Fine, small head with a straight profile

Deep, wide chest

Deep and powerful body

Hard, flat knee joints

Well-muscled legs

Clean, large hock joints

Round, open feet

Wielkopolski

HEIGHT AT WITHERS	ORIGIN	COLORS
16.2 hh (168 cm)	Poland	Any solid color

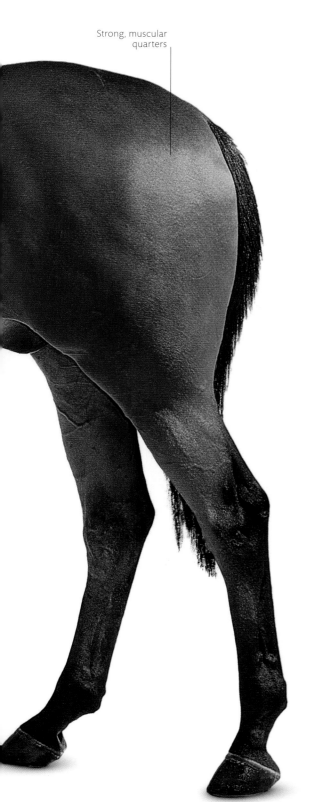

Strong, muscular quarters

A competition horse, the Wielkopolski is very strong and naturally balanced with good paces.

In the 19th century, the Poles (together with the Hungarians) had a tradition of horsemanship unequaled in Europe, and favored Arab (see pp.92–93), or Arab-type horses, to carry their cavalry. Most Polish breeds contain Arab blood, and the Wielkopolski—one of Poland's most important warmbloods—is no exception.

The Arab studs in Poland, which were famous throughout Europe and produced stock of rare and distinctive quality, were created by the Polish nobility. In 1803, Prince Sanguszko was the first to import Arab horses, sending an envoy to acquire horses for his stud at Slawuta. His descendant, Count Potocki, founded the famous Antoniny Stud later in the century. Potocki, a fine horseman and a breeder of great ability, produced notable strains of Arab, as well as spotted and part-colored horses that were Arab in appearance and had the same characteristic action.

Bred mainly in central and western Poland, the Wielkopolski derives from a combination of two Polish warmbloods, the Poznan and Masuren—later crossed with Thoroughbreds (see pp.120–21), Arabs, and Anglo-Arabs (see pp.148–49). Large and well proportioned, the Wielkopolski is a highly practical, dual-purpose horse, going as well in harness as under saddle, and is both easy and economical to keep. The heavier specimens are very active, powerful, and good tempered and make good workhorses. However, today the emphasis is on a lighter, more athletic type of horse that conforms to the requirements of the modern competitive disciplines while retaining the willing temperament.

It is a close relative of the Trakehner (see pp.186–87). Owing to its high percentage of Thoroughbred blood, it is an excellent jumper, with the speed, mental stamina, and courage to go cross-country.

POZNAN AND MASUREN

The Wielkopolski has two Polish ancestors, the Poznan and the Masuren. A well-established breed in the 19th century, the Poznan was originally bred as an agricultural horse with studs in Posadowo, Raçot, and Gogolewo, near Poznan. The Masuren was from the Masury district and was bred mainly at Liski with stallion depots at Starogad, Kwidzyn, and Gniezno. Both these breeds are officially extinct, but their best characteristics can be seen in the excellent Wielkopolski. Like most of the breed, this young horse shows great potential as an all-around competition performer.

Czech Warmblood

HEIGHT AT WITHERS	ORIGIN	COLORS
16–16.2 hh (163–168 cm)	Central Europe	Any solid color

KINSKY

The Kinsky horse has been described as the golden horse of Bohemia, because they come mostly in diluted colors (palomino, buckskin, dun, cremello, and perlino). Sorrels, bays, and blacks do also occur. The breed is linked to the House of Kinsky, a Czech noble family. Kinskys were famous cavalry mounts, and the introduction of top thoroughbred blood made them exceptional at steeplechasing. Nowadays, they are used for sport or hobby riding.

A relative newcomer to the international equestrian scene, this reliable, even-tempered breed is easy to ride and manage.

Sometimes known as the Czech Halfbred, the Czech Warmblood is essentially a mixture of various Central European breeds. The common factor in these horses—and a most important breeding objective—is that of "rideability."

The constituent elements of the Czech Warmblood are the horses bred at the studs in Slovakia and the Czech Republic. The Nonius (see p.210) and Furioso (see p.211), the Gidran Arab (see pp.208–209), and the English halfbreds based on them, all feature in the makeup of the Czech Warmblood, along with the Shagya Arab (see p.205).

Owing to the Czech Warmblood's mixed ancestry, there is no dominant type. In most cases, however, there are discernible conformational features relating to the more prepotent elements in the background. For instance, there is a fairly clear legacy from the Arab, seen in the straight line of the croup, the low, broad withers, and the set of the shoulders. The movement, however, is more like that of a light carriage horse.

The breed is usually strongly built, and has an acceptable, middle-of-the-road, riding-horse conformation. It would be considered an ideal cavalry mount, which was the original purpose for many of them. Moved from the military to the civilian context, the Czech Warmblood is essentially a "riding club" horse. It makes an obedient dressage ride and its paces are of a reasonable quality.

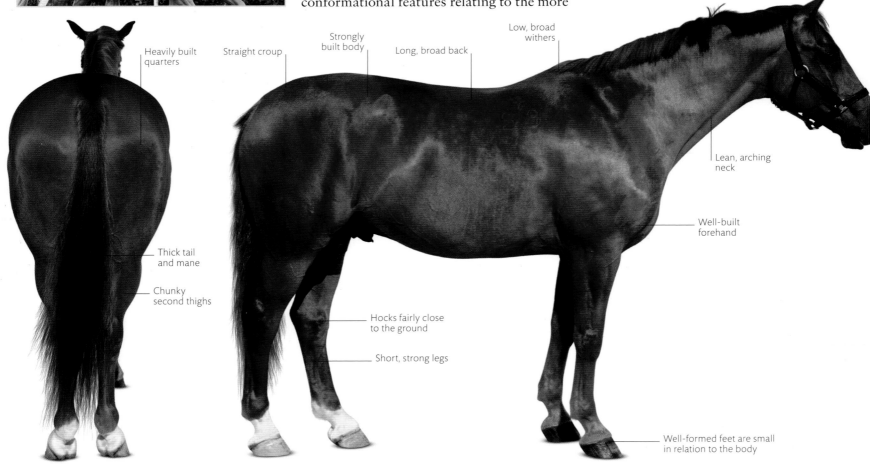

Heavily built quarters

Straight croup

Strongly built body

Long, broad back

Low, broad withers

Lean, arching neck

Well-built forehand

Thick tail and mane

Chunky second thighs

Hocks fairly close to the ground

Short, strong legs

Well-formed feet are small in relation to the body

FROM A VERY **MIXED BACKGROUND,** THE CZECH WARMBLOOD HAS EMERGED AS A **LIKEABLE** AND **RELIABLE** MOUNT.

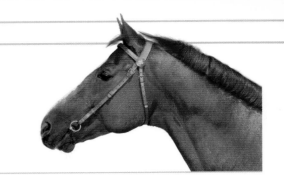

Einsiedler

HEIGHT AT WITHERS	ORIGIN	COLORS
16.2 hh (168 cm)	Switzerland	Any solid color

SWISS HORSE SHOW

Every year the Swiss Alpine town of Saignelégier hosts the Marché-Concours National de Chevaux. This spectacular event was established in 1897 to promote local horse breeds but has now become a general horse-racing weekend and horse sale. Both ridden and harness races are held, and other draws include bareback races and riders in costumes. The show attracts a large crowd of up to 50,000 spectators.

Also called the Swiss Warmblood, the Einsiedler is a large, calm, well-built horse that is a good all-arounder.

Ancestors of the Einsiedler were bred in the Benedictine monastery of Einsiedeln, east of Lucerne, Switzerland. The monastery was known for breeding riding horses using local stock since the 10th century. This breed began to evolve in the late 19th century and is now bred at the Swiss National Stud at Avenches (see box, opposite), near Berne.

In the 19th century, the breed was improved by the introduction of Anglo-Norman mares and a Yorkshire Coach Horse stallion, Bracken, who was imported in 1865. Later, the emphasis shifted to a mix of Holsteiner (see p.170–71) and Norman crosses. Then, in the late 1960s, Swedish and Irish mares were imported to Avenches, where the breed was now being produced. The stallions used were just as varied, and included Anglo-Norman, Holsteiner, and Swedish horses, as well as some native stock.

The selection and performance testing of Einsiedlers is a rigorous process. Stallions are tested at the age of three-and-a-half and then again at five. The tests include jumping, dressage, cross-country, and driving. Conformation is important, and horses only make the grade if their parents have proven performance ability. Mares are tested at three years old, and cannot be registered unless their parents are registered halfbreds.

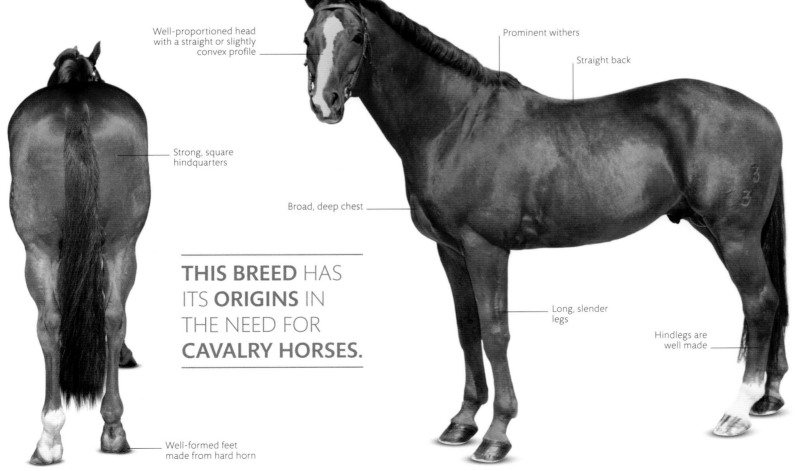

Well-proportioned head with a straight or slightly convex profile

Strong, square hindquarters

Prominent withers

Straight back

Broad, deep chest

THIS BREED HAS ITS **ORIGINS** IN THE NEED FOR **CAVALRY HORSES.**

Long, slender legs

Hindlegs are well made

Well-formed feet made from hard horn

Freiberger

HEIGHT AT WITHERS	ORIGIN	COLORS
15 hh (152 cm)	Switzerland	Usually bay, dark bay, or chestnut with white markings

Originally a mountain-bred horse, the Freiberger is an active mover, sure-footed, quiet, and good-natured.

The Freiberger originated in the hilly Jura region of western Switzerland, on the French border, hence its alternative name of Franches-Montagnes. Powerfully built, with good limbs and feet, it retains the characteristics required of a workhorse for small, upland farms. For generations it was popular with the Swiss Army, which still uses it in small numbers as a pack animal.

Like the Einsiedler (see opposite), the Freiberger is raised at the Swiss National Stud Farm at Avenches (see box, left). Many Freibergers trace to one stallion, Vaillant—a great grandson of Leo I, a halfbred English hunter stallion with Norfolk Roadster (see p.157) connections. Poulette, Vaillant's grandam on both sides, was of Anglo-Norman and Thoroughbred (see pp.120–21) stock. Another Anglo-Norman, Imprevu, produced a second key line through his great-grandson Chasseur.

Other outcrosses to French, English, and Belgian horses had no lasting effect. It was not until after World War II that a new bloodline emerged from Urus, another stallion with Norman blood. Since then, outcrosses have been carefully monitored. Anglo-Normans are usually selected, but Arab blood has also been used. Today, breeders are focused on producing a smaller, lighter Freiberger for riding than the heavier, muscular type used as a workhorse.

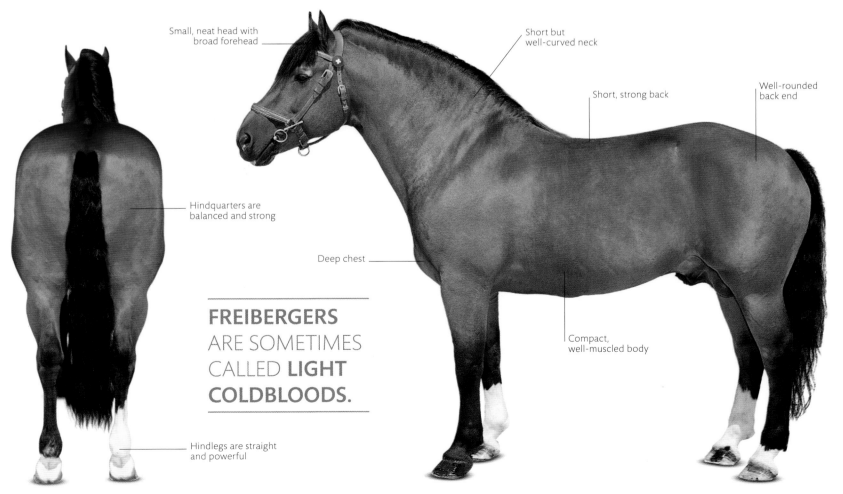

Small, neat head with broad forehead

Short but well-curved neck

Short, strong back

Well-rounded back end

Hindquarters are balanced and strong

Deep chest

Compact, well-muscled body

FREIBERGERS ARE SOMETIMES CALLED **LIGHT COLDBLOODS.**

Hindlegs are straight and powerful

Haflinger

HEIGHT AT WITHERS	ORIGIN	COLORS
13.3–14.3 hh (140–150 cm)	Austria	Chestnut, palomino

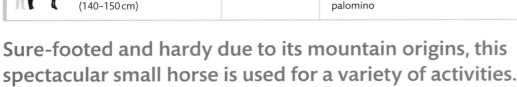

Sure-footed and hardy due to its mountain origins, this spectacular small horse is used for a variety of activities.

Native to the southern Austrian Tyrol, the Haflinger takes its name from the mountain district of Hafling, which is now part of Italy. With its striking chestnut or palomino coat and contrasting, pale flaxen mane and tail, it is one of the world's most attractive horses. Although the Haflinger, and its Italian counterpart the Avelignese (see p.59), are considered coldbloods, they have a strong background of eastern blood: both breeds share a common ancestry in the Arab foundation stallion, El Bedavi. Imported by an Austrian commission in the 19th century, this stallion was crossed with a Tyrolean mountain mare and it is said that the breed's principal bloodlines can be traced back to his sons, grandsons, and great-grandsons.

Haflingers were used as light draft and pack horses on small hillside farms as well as for forestry work. During World War II, however, breeding focused on a smaller, stockier horse for cavalry and heavier draft. Following the reestablishment of the Tyrolean breeding association in 1946, a program to revert to a lighter-framed horse was set up. Since then, strict breeding controls have ensured a fixed type of unmistakable appearance.

Today, the Haflinger is still used for light draft and forestry work where machinery is unsuitable. It is also a good all-around leisure horse for riding and driving, and its calm temperament makes it suitable for young riders. This mountain breed is extremely sound, willing, and can be exceptionally long-lived. The principal Haflinger stud is at Ebbs in the Austrian Tyrol, and the breed has spread to more than 60 countries including America, New Zealand, and Australia.

Nicely shaped croup

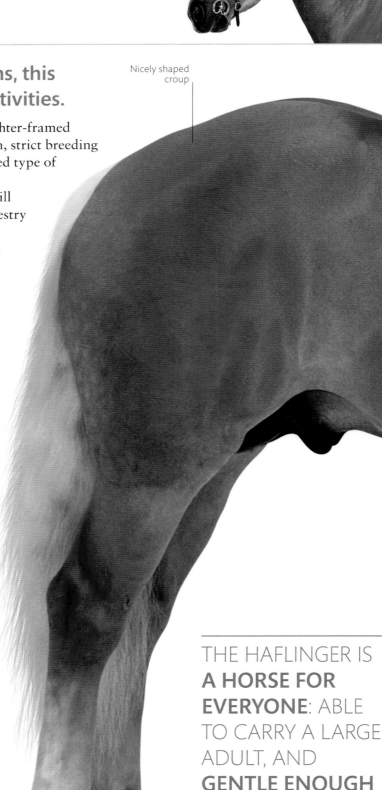

THE HAFLINGER IS **A HORSE FOR EVERYONE**: ABLE TO CARRY A LARGE ADULT, AND **GENTLE ENOUGH** FOR A TIMID CHILD.

MOUNTAIN BREED

Haflingers are traditionally reared on high Alpine pastures where the air is thin. As a result, young Haflingers develop sound hearts and lungs. They also acquire a natural sure-footedness—highly valued by riders and drivers alike—in response to the steeply sloping land. The villages around Hafling are justifiably proud of this breed. All Austrian Haflingers bear the Edelweiss brand mark, with the letter "H" at its center.

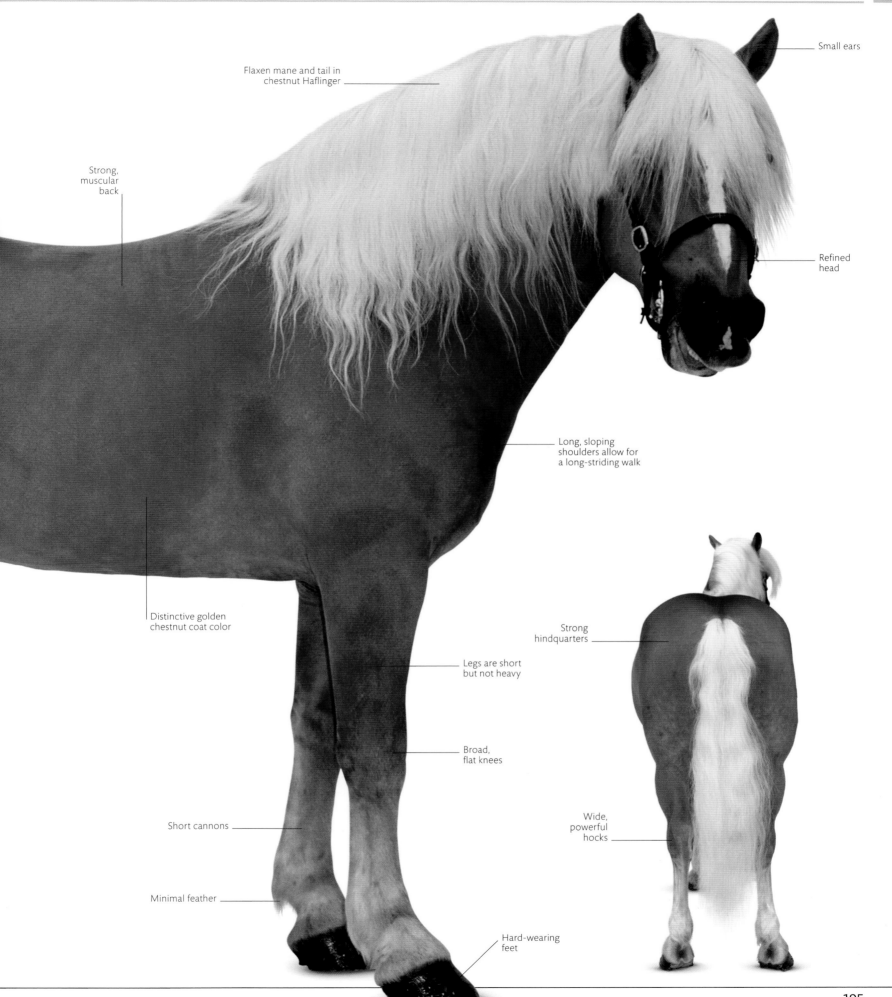

Small ears

Flaxen mane and tail in
chestnut Haflinger

Strong,
muscular
back

Refined
head

Long, sloping
shoulders allow for
a long-striding walk

Distinctive golden
chestnut coat color

Strong
hindquarters

Legs are short
but not heavy

Broad,
flat knees

Wide,
powerful
hocks

Short cannons

Minimal feather

Hard-wearing
feet

SARDINIAN HORSES ARE USED BY MOUNTED REGIMENTS OF THE CARABINIERI (THE ITALIAN POLICE) AND IN TRADITIONAL FOLK FESTIVALS ON THE ISLAND.

Sardinian Anglo-Arab

HEIGHT AT WITHERS	ORIGIN	COLORS
15.2 hh (157 cm)	Sardinia, Italy	Bay, brown, chestnut, gray, and black

This bold, intelligent breed has great speed and stamina, making it suitable for use in many different sports.

For centuries, the Sardinians imported horses from nearby North Africa, basing their island breed on crosses between Arabs (see pp.92–93) and Barbs (see pp.94–95). In the 15th century, a distinctive type began to appear after King Ferdinand II of Spain (1452–1516) founded a stud of Spanish horses (now called Andalucian—see pp.140–41) near Abbasanta. Other studs were later established at Monte Minerva, Padromannu, and Mores. The horses produced became famous as tough, enduring saddle horses.

When Sardinia passed from Spain to the House of Savoy in 1720, horse breeding declined and it was not until 1908 that Arab horses were imported to improve the stock. Later, from the 1920s, Thoroughbred (see pp.120–21) stallions were introduced. In 1967 the breed was officially recognized and breeders aimed for stock to have at minimum 25 percent Arab blood. Thus the best of the modern Sardinian horses have a pronounced Arab or eastern appearance.

The Sardinian Anglo-Arab is a great racehorse, show jumper, and steeplechaser. Most horses in the Palio de Siena (see box, right) belong to this breed. Historically, Thoroughbreds were used, but their long legs were prone to injury on the sharp turns of the racetrack. Sardinian Anglo-Arabs are shorter and sturdier, with stronger legs that are better suited to the conditions. Today, one of the stipulations of the race is that only mixed breeds are used.

PALIO DE SIENA

Twice a year, the main square in Siena, Italy, becomes a racetrack. Jockeys, riding bareback, represent 10 of the 17 *Contrade* (wards) of the city. This fiercely fought race has subterfuge and betting, along with strict rules and role play. Few jockeys win more than once in a lifetime. Animal welfare groups increasingly call for it to be banned, but it continues to be a popular event.

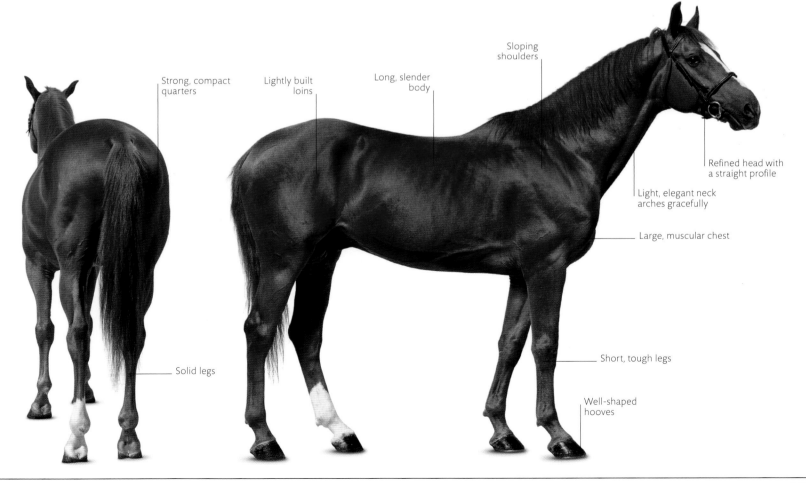

Strong, compact quarters

Lightly built loins

Long, slender body

Sloping shoulders

Refined head with a straight profile

Light, elegant neck arches gracefully

Large, muscular chest

Short, tough legs

Well-shaped hooves

Solid legs

Salerno

HEIGHT AT WITHERS	ORIGIN	COLORS
Over 16 hh (163 cm)	Italy	Any solid color

Probably the best of the Italian riding horses, the Salerno is athletic, strong, and gentle, and has a talent for jumping.

The Salerno originated in the 18th century in the Campania region, southwestern Italy, and is one of the most attractive of the Italian warmbloods. It evolved at the Persano Stud, which was founded by Charles III, King of Naples and then of Spain, in 1763. The horses bred at Persano, known at the time as Persanos, were based on the Neapolitan—a horse bred near Sorrento and Naples and full of Spanish, Arab, and Barb blood. Although coarse in comparison with the Iberian breeds, the Neapolitans were regarded in Italy as one of the best High School horses of the day and were much admired for their fiery action and strong limbs. They were crossed with the local horses of the Salerno and Ofanto valleys, and then with Arab and Spanish imports to produce a distinctive, quality riding horse.

After the Italian Republic was established in 1860, the stud was closed. When breeding was revived in 1900, the old name lapsed and the breed was known increasingly as the Salerno. The introduction of Thoroughbred (see pp.120–21) blood improved the stock, and produced a larger, cavalry-type horse, which is now used in mounted police formations.

Some notable horses were produced at the Morese stud, close to the original Persano stud. These include two of the greatest Italian show jumpers—Merano and Posillipo—both ridden by the Italian ace Raimondo d'Inzeo. Merano and d'Inzeo won the World Championship in 1956, having been reserve to the German rider, Hans Winkler, in 1955. D'Inzeo was riding Posillipo when he won the individual gold medal at the 1960 Olympics in Rome. The Salerno now carries yet more Thoroughbred blood and is even more refined. Despite its many virtues and uses, the Salerno has become a rare breed.

Well-made back end

Hindlegs can lack definition

AHEAD OF HIS TIME

General Raimondo d'Inzeo, an officer in the Italian cavalry, was known for wearing his uniform while competing. In his show jumping career he won six medals—one gold, two silver, and three bronze. However, it was his style of riding that singled him out. In a time well before "natural horsemanship," he believed in working in absolute harmony with his horse, rejecting any idea of domination. His brother Piero was also a successful rider. Raimondo died in 2013 at the age of 88.

Short, strong, well-proportioned back

Long, muscular neck

Light, well-set head shows Spanish influence

Sloping, muscular shoulders

Deep, wide chest

Powerfully built quarters

Well-shaped legs with fine joints

Strong, slender legs

FAMOUS SALERNO RIDER **RAIMONDO D'INZEO** WAS THE **FIRST ATHLETE** TO COMPETE IN **EIGHT CONSECUTIVE OLYMPIC GAMES** (1948–76).

Maremmana

HEIGHT AT WITHERS	ORIGIN	COLORS
15.3 hh (160 cm)	Italy	Any solid color

BUTTERO AND HIS HORSE

At one time, almost all livestock herding was carried out on horseback. In Tuscany, the cowboys, or *butteri*, relied on the Maremmana horse to help them in their work. *Buttero* saddles are deep and comfortable for long days riding. Today, the Maremma Natural Park is home to the last of the *butteri*, who work the long-horned Maremmana cattle with long-stemmed crooks.

The strength, endurance, willingness, and versatility of this "rustic" Tuscan breed make up for its rather plain looks.

Although the origins of the Maremmana are unclear, it is probably derived from Spanish, Neapolitan, Arab (see pp.92–93), and Barb (see pp.94–95) stock. In the 19th century, the local animals were crossed with English imports, notably the Norfolk Roadsters (see p.157) and Thoroughbreds (see pp.120–21), as a means of upgrading the coarse local stock.

Although still somewhat coarse in appearance, the use of better-quality stallions, from the 1940s onward, has resulted in Maremmana offspring with better limb conformation than the old type. A breed association was set up in 1979.

In 2015, 2,652 mares and 122 stallions were registered in the studbook, which is now closed and accepts only horses from four historical lines (Otello, Aiace, Ingres, and Ussero).

The Maremmana is well suited to light agricultural work, and in the past it was also a reliable troop horse, used in large numbers by the cavalry, as well as popular with the police and *butteri* (see box, left). The horses that are used for herding cattle are notable for their strong hock joints. The Maremmana is not capable of any great speed, but its strength and good-natured temperament make it suitable for a variety of purposes.

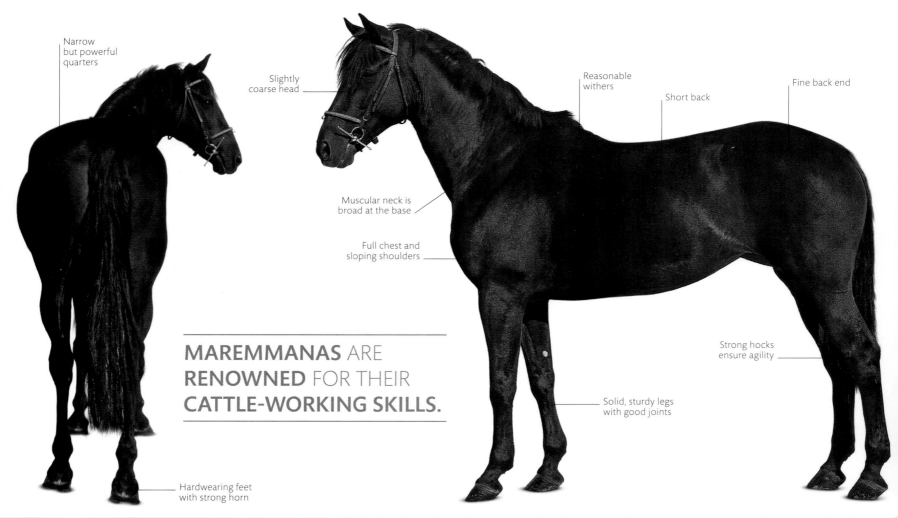

Narrow but powerful quarters

Slightly coarse head

Reasonable withers

Short back

Fine back end

Muscular neck is broad at the base

Full chest and sloping shoulders

MAREMMANAS ARE RENOWNED FOR THEIR CATTLE-WORKING SKILLS.

Strong hocks ensure agility

Solid, sturdy legs with good joints

Hardwearing feet with strong horn

Murgese

HEIGHT AT WITHERS	**ORIGIN**	**COLORS**
15–16 hh (152–163 cm)	Italy	Black or blue roan, occasionally metallic gray

A GOOD ALL-AROUNDER

Like the similar-looking Friesian (see pp.164–65), the large, heavy-set Murgese has presence. This old breed has a small but enthusiastic following worldwide and is popular in its home area of Puglia with in excess of 1,500 animals in the breed register. The stallions are said to have a quiet disposition so gelding is not needed to keep them under control. The metallic sheen on this horse is fairly unusual, with most being black.

This mountain-type breed is extremely hardy and well-suited to the dry, hilly landscape in which it is raised.

The horses of the Murge district in Puglia, southeastern Italy, were in great demand in the 15th and 16th centuries—particularly by the Italian cavalry—as they had a strong constitution and very hard feet. About 200 years ago, interest in them died out and they virtually disappeared. Interest in them revived in the 1920s, but the modern Murgese breed probably does not have any direct relationship to the horses of the past. The new type was basically a light draft horse, similar, but inferior, to the Irish Draft (see pp.134–35). Initially there was a lack of uniformity because breeding was not subject to any control or breed society regulations. This led to conformational faults—flat, muscly withers and upright shoulders—which inhibit free movement.

The herd book was established in 1926, after which breeding became more selective. Granduca, Nerone, and Araldo delle Murge were three of the most successful stallions that formed the main bloodlines of the Murgese. The best specimens are useful as light agricultural horses that can also be ridden. The mares are often crossed with Arab and Thoroughbred (see pp.120–21) or halfbred stallions to obtain better riding stock, and they also produce the strong mules that are still needed in the area.

Slender quarters

Tail may be low

ACTIVE AND ENERGETIC, THE MURGESE IS **AMENABLE, EVEN-TEMPERED,** AND **ECONOMICAL TO KEEP.**

Light head with a slightly convex profile

Withers often ill-defined

Long slope from croup

Sturdy neck is broad at the base

Upright, loaded shoulders

Straight, hard legs

Small, rounded knees

Long hindlegs

Extremely hard hooves

Withers are relatively low

Compact deep and muscular body

Well-shaped head, sometimes ram-like in profile

Shoulders have an adequate slope

Considerable depth through girth

Short powerful limbs

THE BREED **MATURES SLOWLY** BUT IS **LONG-LIVED,** OFTEN STILL WORKING AT WELL **OVER 20** YEARS OLD.

Flat joints with good bone

Hard feet

Lipizzaner

HEIGHT AT WITHERS	ORIGIN	COLORS
14.2–15.2 hh (147–157 cm)	Lipica, Slovenia	White, occasionally bay

This beautiful horse is the mount of the Spanish Riding School in Vienna, a center of classical riding for four centuries.

High-set, fine silky tail

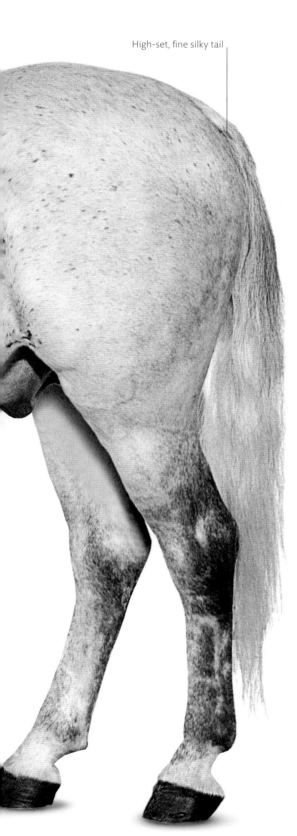

The Spanish Riding School Lipizzaners are raised at Austria's Piber Stud near Graz, but the state studs of Hungary, Romania, and the Czech Republic also specialize in the breed. Because of this widespread breeding, there are variations in type. The Piber Lipizzaner is comparatively small, while Hungary produces a bigger, very free-moving horse. The horses are born black or brown and become white with age. Bay may occur; a bay horse is traditionally always kept at the Spanish School.

The breed takes its name from Lipica (Lipizza), in Slovenia (once Yugoslavia), where it originated and is still bred. The stud was founded in 1580 when 9 Spanish stallions and 24 mares were imported from the Iberian Peninsula at the command of Archduke Charles II of Austria (1540–90). His aim was to supply suitably grand horses to the ducal stables at Graz and the court stable in Vienna. The Spanish School—so called because, from the outset, it used Spanish horses—was established in 1572 to instruct noblemen in classical equitation. The present school, the Winter Riding Hall, was built on the orders of Charles VI (1685–1740) and completed in 1735.

Lipizzaners are based on six principal stallion lines: Pluto (1765), a white Spanish horse from Fredericksborg; the black Conversano (1767), a Neapolitan; the dun Kladruber, Favory (1779); Neapolitano (1790), a bay Neapolitan from Polesina; Siglavy (1810), a white Arab; and Maestoso (1819), a Neapolitan–Spanish cross. Descendants of these stallions and 14 of the original 23 mare lines are still at Piber.

The conformation, particularly in the Piber Lipizzaners, is that of a useful, all-round cob and the action tends to be high rather than long and low. A greater Thoroughbred influence can be seen in the Hungarian type, which has more scope and wider range of movement. Most Lipizzaners are as much suited to harness as to riding.

AIRS ABOVE THE GROUND

The Lipizzaner is known for its ability to perform the High School "airs above the ground." These advanced maneuvers require enormous muscle strength and control. Initially, they are taught without a rider—since that is less taxing for the horse. However, eventually these moves are performed with a rider. There are seven airs. The pesade and levade are controlled rears. The mezair, croupade, ballotade, courbette, and capriole (pictured), involve all four limbs leaving the ground. The capriole, or leap of a goat, is the most difficult air. In this air, the horse is required to raise its forehand, jump up, kick out its hindlegs, and then land on all four legs.

Kladruber

HEIGHT AT WITHERS	**ORIGIN**	**COLORS**
15.3-17 hh (160-170 cm)	Czech Republic	Gray and black

This is the only breed in the world bred specifically as a carriage horse for ceremonial purposes of a royal court.

The Kladruber is a rare breed that originated in Kladruby nad Labem, in the Czech Republic. The stud at Kladruby nad Labem is one of the oldest continually run studs in the world. Though the official imperial court stud was founded only in 1579, an established stud was given to the Habsburg emperor in 1560, and the Lords of Pernštejn bred horses in Kladruby well before 1500.

The breed was established using imported Spanish blood and used solely by the royal court. Although originally there were Kladrubers available in all colors, later only two colors were favored – grays for pulling royal carriages and black horses for carriages of the empire's high clergy and funerals.

After the collapse of the Austro-Hungarian Empire, the breed almost became extinct, but it is now the only living animal treasured as part of the Czech national cultural heritage. Kladrubers are famous for their typical Roman noses, high knee action, willingness to work, and great character.

Today, the Kladruber is used as a carriage horse at the Danish royal court. They are also used by Swedish Mounted Royal Guards, for ceremonies at Prague Castle, and by Czech mounted police, as well as for driving competitions and hobby riding.

SLATIŇANY STUD

Kladrubers come in only two colors, white (gray) and black. The black Kladrubers faced extinction in the 1930s, but horse expert Professor František Bílek saved them by using the remaining stock and introducing some foreign blood. From 1945, the breeding of black Kladrubers took place at Slatiňany stud, where they can still be found. Although it lies some 25 miles (40 km) away, it is now part of the National Stud at Kladruby nad Labem.

Head with typical convex profile

Less pronounced withers

Medium-long back with good loins

Arched, well-muscled neck

Shoulders more upright to allow for high knee action

Powerful hindquarters

Deep and wide chest

Strong legs with good joints

THERE ARE ONLY ABOUT **1,800** **KLADRUBERS** IN THE WORLD TODAY

No feathering on lower legs

Strong, well-shaped feet

Shagya Arab

HEIGHT AT WITHERS	ORIGIN	COLORS
15 hh (152 cm)	Hungary	Mainly gray, but all Arab colors occur

WORLDWIDE APPEAL

The inscription on a statue near the Catholic church in Bábolna proclaims of the Shagya Arab "Most loyal comrade." This rare breed has found admirers all over the world, including the US. Shagya Arab breeding began there in 1986 with foundation stallion Bravo. His parents arrived in America in 1947 on the orders of General Patton, who rescued them from war-torn Europe.

The graceful and tough Shagya has immense stamina, and is and more substantial than Arab purebreds.

Until its collapse in the early part of the 20th century, the vast Austro-Hungarian Empire was equaled only by Poland in the quality of its horse breeding in Europe. Hungary's oldest stud farm, Mezőhegyes, was founded in 1785, and in 1789 the stud at Bábolna was established. Hungary is famous for its superb Arab horses, and Bábolna became the center for their breeding.

After 1816, the Bábolna stud concentrated on the production of purebred "desert" Arabs and on partbreds, which were called Arab Race. Arab Race were the progeny of purebred stallions crossed with mares of very eastern appearance, which carried strains of Spanish, Hungarian, and Thoroughbred blood. This last policy produced the Shagya Arab. The Race was founded on the Arab stallion, Shagya—born in Syria in 1830 and imported to Bábolna in 1836. Cream-colored and big for an Arab, Shagya was the sire of many successful stallions.

The Shagya Arab exhibits all the characteristics of the pure Arab, and may even display more quality and be truer to the original type than some modern purebreds. It is essentially a practical horse, used for every purpose under saddle as well as driven in harness. In the past it proved itself to be a swift, enduring, and very hardy cavalry horse, and today it is popular in sports such as dressage, eventing, and endurance riding.

More prominent withers than in many Arab strains

Large, expressive eyes dominate the head

Typically Arabian head with "dished" profile

Slightly sunken back

Small, tapered muzzle

High-set tail

Long, slender, arched neck

Sloping shoulders

Strong legs with more bone than the purebreds

THE SHAGYA ARAB WAS ONCE THE MOUNT OF THE **HUNGARIAN HUSSAR,** THE *BEAU IDÉAL* OF THE LIGHT HORSEMAN.

Time for fun
Horses like the company of other horses and often spend time together playing or checking their pecking order. These two young Shagya Arabs are enjoying some social interaction.

Small ears

Large eyes

Small, well-set head

Muscular, sloping shoulders

Long back

High-set tail

Symmetrical quarters

Deep girth and well-sprung ribs

GIDRAN SENIOR WAS **"VERY TEMPESTUOUS."** HIS DESCENDANTS ARE OFTEN CALLED—PERHAPS EUPHEMISTICALLY— **"SPIRITED"** AND **"HIGHLY COURAGED."**

Strong, short cannons

Hard feet

Gidran Arab

HEIGHT AT WITHERS	ORIGIN	COLORS
16–17 hh (163–173 cm)	Hungary	Mainly chestnut

Powerful and muscular, this rare Anglo-Arab breed is known for its speed, stamina, agility, and courage.

Powerful back end

Legs well muscled with strong joints

The Hungarian state stud of Mezőhegyes, situated in the extreme southeast of the Great Hungarian Plain, is the oldest of the state stud farms. Founded in 1785, it was responsible for creating the Gidran Arab.

The Gidran Arab is considered to be the Hungarian version of the Anglo-Arab (see pp.148–49). It can be traced back to chestnut Arab Gidran Senior, who belonged to the prominent Siglavy strain (see Shagya Arab, pp.204–205) and was imported from Arabia in 1814. Gidran Senior was put to a Spanish-bred mare, Arrogante, resulting in the birth of Gidran II, in 1820. Gidran II was brought to Mezőhegyes and became the breed's foundation sire. At first he was mated with mares of a

variety of different breeds. Then Thoroughbreds (see pp.120–21) were introduced to improve any faults. However, this cross resulted in temperamental animals so more Arab infusions and Hungarian Kisber stallions were used to fix the type.

The modern Gidran has a bigger frame than the Arab, but has something of the latter's fine, elegant head and high-set tail. The breeding system of allowing each stallion his own small herd of mares and keeping the group at pasture, ensures that the horses are tough and hardy. The Gidran Arab has a good conformation with excellent limbs. With its strong build and ability to gallop, this horse has the qualities of a traditional English hunter. It is used extensively in competitive sport, and the heavier, more robust specimens make good carriage horses. Today, though rare, the Gidran Arab is still bred in Hungary, and also in Romania and Bulgaria.

MEZŐHEGYES STUD

The military stud at Mezőhegyes was established in 1784, by Emperor Josef II, to breed army horses. It was filled with horses—up to 5,000 at one time—from many countries, including present-day Poland, Turkey, Germany, and Spain. They were mainly Spanish or Neapolitan—fashionable at the time—some Arab types, and good local horses. The stud is responsible for developing the Nonius (see p.210), Furioso (see p.211), and Gidran Arab. Today, it is in private hands.

Nonius

HEIGHT AT WITHERS	ORIGIN	COLORS
15.1–16.2 hh (155–165 cm)	Southeast Hungary	Black, dark bay, or brown

A CHANGE OF USE

At the Paris Exposition Universelle in 1900, a Nonius won the title of "Ideal Horse," largely due to its importance as a military harness horse. After WWI, mechanization meant horses were no longer needed by the military. Today, these horses are bred for draft work and riding.

When the Nonius was developed in the 19th century, Hungary dominated horse-breeding in Europe.

Nonius Senior, the foundation sire of the breed, was foaled in Calvados, Normandy, in 1810. His sire was an English halfbred stallion, Orion, and his dam a Norman mare. During the Napoleonic Wars, Nonius Senior was taken from the stud at Rosières-aux-Salines by the occupying Austrian cavalry and sent to Mezőhegyes, then an imperial Austro-Hungarian stud. Nonius Senior had a heavy head, long "mule" ears, a short neck, long back, narrow pelvis, and a low-set tail. He was not much used as a sire, until the breeders realized his progeny did not inherit his deficiencies, surpassing him in conformation.

Initially, Nonius Senior was put to all kinds of mares, including Arab (see pp.92–93), Lipizzaner (see pp.202–203), Spanish, and Normans. During the 1860s, more Thoroughbred blood was introduced, and the breed was divided into two lines. The larger type became a cavalry mount and is still used as a light draft horse. The smaller, heavier type was bred at the Hortobágy stud. The two lines were combined in 1961. The Nonius Breeders Association was set up in 1989. The Nonius is popular under harness and competes in combined-driving championships at international level.

Honest plain head

Well-defined withers

Good, powerful outline

Strong quarters that may be inclined away from croup

Sloping shoulders

Strong, short limbs

Well-made feet

THE **FUTURE** OF THE NONIUS IS **NOT ASSURED,** WITH THE CURRENT **POPULATION** ESTIMATED AT **450 MARES** AND **80 STALLIONS.**

Furioso

HEIGHT AT WITHERS
16 hh
(163 cm)
ORIGIN Southeast Hungary
COLORS Bay, rarely black

The Furioso breed was founded at the Mezőhegyes state stud when Nonius (see opposite) mares were crossed with two English Thoroughbred stallions, Furioso and North Star. Furioso and North Star, imported in 1841 and 1852 respectively. The latter also had Norfolk Roadster blood (see p.157). Both were highly successful and potent sires, and their bloodlines were kept distinct until 1885, when they were crossed—the breed is also known as Furioso-North Star. A quality, hardy riding horse, it is now rare, with only about 500 broodmares and 80 stallions.

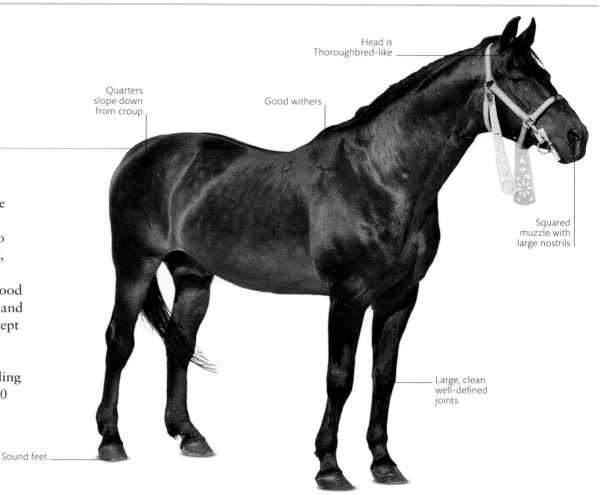

Quarters slope down from croup

Good withers

Head is Thoroughbred-like

Squared muzzle with large nostrils

Large, clean well-defined joints

Sound feet

Hungarian Warmblood

HEIGHT AT WITHERS
16.2–17 hh
(165–170 cm)
ORIGIN Southeast Hungary
COLORS All solid colors

Also known as the Hungarian Sport Horse, this breed was developed at the Mezőhegyes and Hortobágy studs. Nonius and Furioso mares were the base stock. At first they were crossed with Holsteiner (see pp.170–71) and Thoroughbred (see pp.120–21) stallions, and later with other European sport breeds. This is a performance breed, and horses can be assessed for racing, trotting, show jumping, and/or dressage; the tests are different for each discipline. Current breeding aims at improving performance at dressage and eventing.

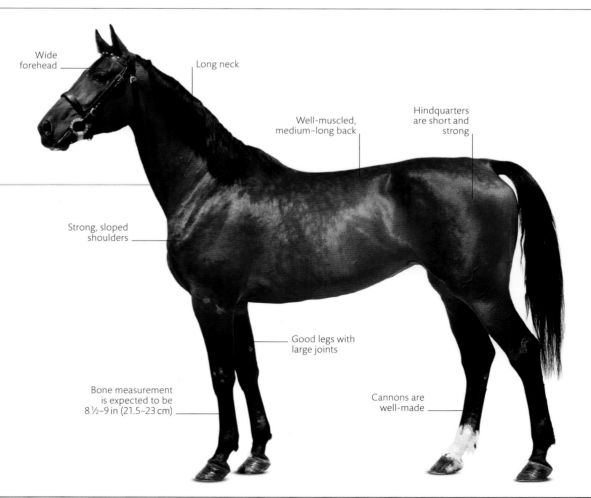

Wide forehead

Long neck

Well-muscled, medium–long back

Hindquarters are short and strong

Strong, sloped shoulders

Good legs with large joints

Bone measurement is expected to be 8½–9 in (21.5–23 cm)

Cannons are well-made

Wide forehead

Short, not very muscular neck

Well-defined withers

Short back

Small muzzle

Long, sloping shoulders

Finely built hindquarters

Low-set tail

Small, well-proportioned body

Straight legs with round knees

THE MUSTANG BECAME A **PROTECTED SPECIES** UNDER US LAW **IN 1971.**

Long cannons

Mustang

HEIGHT AT WITHERS	ORIGIN	COLORS
13.2–15 hh (137–152 cm)	North America	Any

The Mustang is a type of feral horse that roams the open country of western North America.

Long, sloped croup

Mustangs are descended from horses re-introduced to the New World by the Spanish conquistadores in the 16th century. Prior to their arrival, the horse is thought to have been extinct in the Americas for some 10,000 years. After the Spanish had become established, large numbers of their horses escaped or were turned loose and those that survived became feral. Other Mustangs derived from French and German settlers, whose horses escaped or were released when no longer needed. These feral horses later became the mounts of both Native Americans and white settlers alike. At the beginning of the 20th century an estimated 2 million feral horses roamed the western states. However, by 1970 their numbers had been drastically reduced as a result of organized killing to supply pet food and meat for human consumption. As a result of the Mustang's decline, a number of support groups were established to restore the purest possible strains of early Spanish horses and preserve and promote the Mustang through registration and an intelligent breeding program. Numerous welfare groups were also set up, which between them are involved in legislative activities, research work, and practical work in the field. Today, the Mustang population is not as large as it once was, but around 25,000 still live in the western states.

The Mustang is found in a large number of American breeds. Some have retained many of the Spanish characteristics, especially in respect of color. In isolated areas, blood tests have also shown some herds, such as the Cerbat Mustangs in Arizona and the Kiger Mustangs in Oregon, retain significant Spanish blood. There can be no overall description of the breed, since the horses' wide range and lack of selective breeding means that most strains have become adulterated to varying degrees.

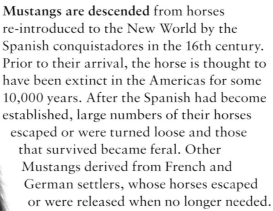

A REMARKABLE JOURNEY

Due to overpopulation in the wild, many Mustangs are rounded up to spend their lives in holding pens, waiting to be adopted. *Unbranded* (2015) is an extraordinary documentary made by four young American men, who used Mustangs to make a 3,000 mile (4,800 km) trip from Mexico to Canada in 2011. They did this partly to highlight the plight of this horse, and also to show that Mustangs can lead useful lives—they are perfectly adapted to the tough conditions found in the wild areas of North America.

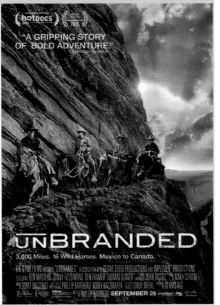

Strong, hard feet

Palomino

HEIGHT AT WITHERS	ORIGIN	COLORS
14.1–16 hh (145–163 cm)	Mexico, US	Palomino

BREEDING PALOMINOS

This mare and foal are at the lightest end of the palomino shades, sometimes called Isabella. Due to color genetics in horses, mating two palominos can result in a chestnut, a palomino, or a cremello. The only way to be sure of getting a palomino is to use a cremello and a chestnut. Palomino breeders also try to get pure colors, with no smutty marks on the body or dark hair in the mane and tail.

Images of horses with golden coats occur in ancient European and Asian art and artifacts.

The Palomino's coloring—a combination of a golden coat with flaxen mane and tail—is found in a variety of horses and ponies as well as established breeds. Horses with Palomino coloring were first imported into Mexico by Spanish conquistadors in the 16th century and spread to North America, where the Palomino is now bred most extensively. However, like the Pinto (see opposite), the Palomino is not a breed, since this is defined by ancestry, but a color type.

In the US, most Palomino horses are registered with the Palomino Horse Association, and through its efforts, the horse has acquired virtual breed status. Horses must meet the association's standards and, while the height and type is not fixed, color is paramount. The color should be "that of a gold coin, but the shade can vary from light, medium, to dark gold." The mane and tail should be "white, ivory, or silver" with not more than 15 percent darker hairs. Palominos are much in demand in Western riding events, and rodeos often feature palomino Quarter Horses. They are also used for a range of activities, including trail riding, show jumping, and as parade horses.

Rich coat color

Hazel or dark eyes—both of the same color

White markings on the face are limited to a blaze, snip, or star

Tail and mane are shining white

White markings must not extend above the knees or hocks

CROSSING A PALOMINO WITH A CHESTNUT PRODUCES THE RICHEST COLOR BUT DOES NOT GUARANTEE A PALOMINO FOAL.

Pinto

HEIGHT AT WITHERS	ORIGIN	COLORS
15–16 hh (152–163 cm)	US	Part-colors

COAT COLORS

In Tobiano the coat is white, with large regular patches of solid color; the legs are usually white. Overo is a colored coat with irregular splashes of white, which do not usually cross the back. The third—Tovero—usually results from crossing a Tobiano type with an Overo. Toveros usually have at least one blue eye. They have dark coloring around the mouth and ears.

Sioux and Crow Indians in the 19th century valued Pintos for their camouflage colors, which made identification easier.

The name Pinto comes from the Spanish *pintado*, meaning "painted," and describes the part-colored, blotched appearance of the coat. In the US, it is also known as the Paint Horse. Like the Palomino, the Pinto could be a descendant of the horses brought to the New World by the Spanish in the 16th century. The coloring can also arise by chance genetically.

In the US, the Pinto comes under the joint aegis of the Pinto Horse Association of America (PHAA) and the American Paint Horse Association (APHA). In simple terms, the Pinto Horse Association prioritizes color

and registers horses with an array of bloodlines. Horses are classified into four types: stock, hunter, pleasure, and saddle. The APHA registers stock-type horses with Thoroughbred, Quarter Horse, and Paint bloodlines.

Pinto coat patterns fall into two main types: Tobiano and Overo (see box, left). The eye-catching patterns of Pintos have made them popular for parades and shows but these well-made horses are very versatile. Noted for their comfortable paces over long distances, they are popular for trail riding.

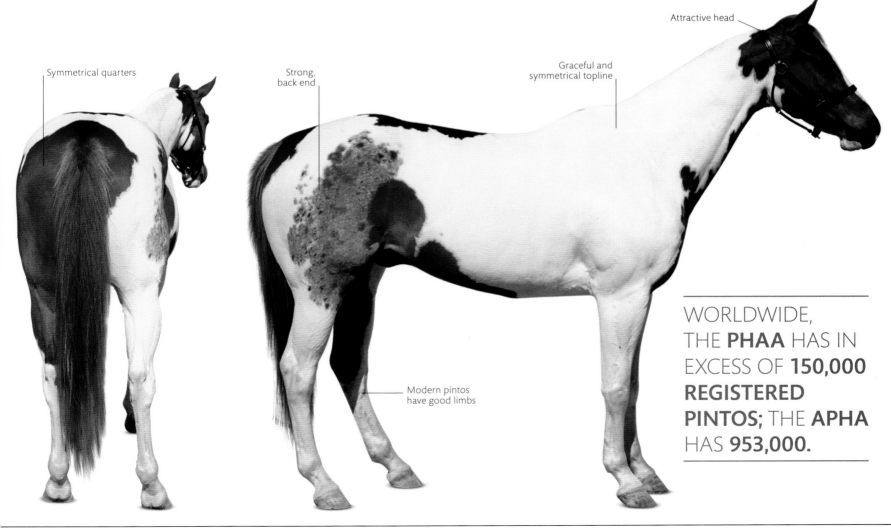

Symmetrical quarters

Strong, back end

Graceful and symmetrical topline

Attractive head

Modern pintos have good limbs

WORLDWIDE, THE **PHAA** HAS IN EXCESS OF **150,000 REGISTERED PINTOS;** THE **APHA** HAS **953,000.**

Beautiful markings
Some breeds, such as the Pinto, are valued for the patches on their coats. Breeders look for a good distribution of color and even markings on both sides of the body.

Appaloosa

HEIGHT AT WITHERS	ORIGIN	COLORS
14.2–15.2 hh (147–157 cm)	North America	Spotted—various patterns

Known for its colorful spotted coat patterns, this breed is practical, hardy, and versatile, with tremendous stamina.

Until recently, it was thought that all horses reached North America with the Spanish conquistadors in the late 15th and early 16th centuries. However, a New Zealand Appaloosa breeder theorizes that spotted Appaloosa-type horses may have already been there. Spotted horses are linked with the Nez Percé tribe of Oregon, eastern Washington, and western Idaho. Their lands included many fertile river valleys, one of which was that of the Palouse river, from which the name Appaloosa is derived.

The Nez Percé were skilful horse breeders and practiced a strict breeding policy, gelding male horses that were below standard and trading unsuitable females. Color was important, but the Nez Percé required, above all, hardy, practical horses, suitable for both war and hunting.

The Appaloosa breed was virtually wiped out in 1876–77, as US troops seized tribal lands. In 1938, when there were only a few surviving descendants of the Nez Percé horses, the breed underwent a revival, and the Appaloosa Horse Club was formed in Idaho, followed later by the British Appaloosa Society.

Today, the Appaloosa is widely used as a stock and pleasure horse, as well as for racing, jumping, and Western and long-distance riding. There is some divergence in type, particularly in the US, where there has been much outcrossing to the Quarter Horse (see pp.220–21). The best specimens look like well-bred cow ponies—compact, with very strong limbs. The breed is claimed to be innately hardy, very willing, and to have a very tractable temperament.

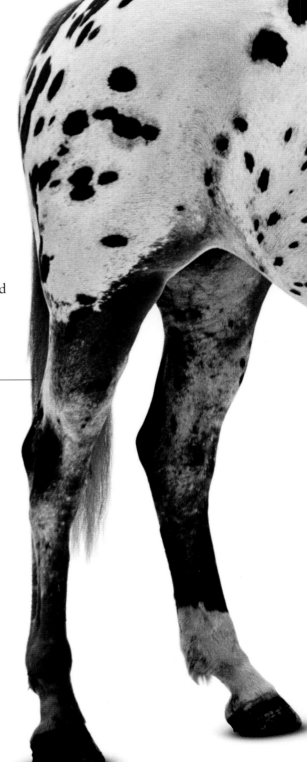

Thin, sparse tail

COAT PATTERNS

Five principal coat patterns are recognized in the breed: Leopard, characterized by a white area over all or part of the body, and dark, egg-shaped spots within the white area; Snowflake, in which white spotting occurs all over the body but is usually concentrated over the hips; Blanket, where the coat color over the hips can be either white or spotted; Marbleized, where there is a mottled pattern all over the body; and Frost, which consists of white specks on a dark background.

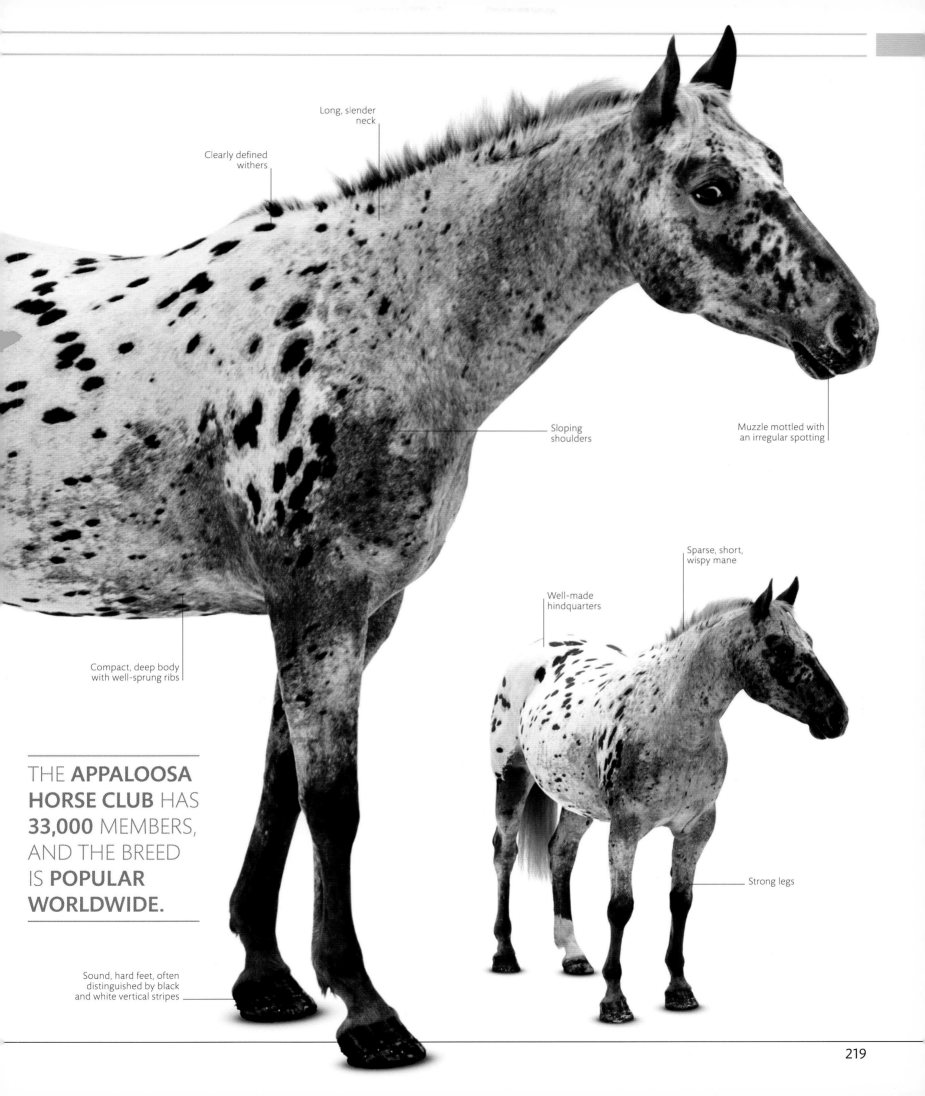

Long, slender neck

Clearly defined withers

Muzzle mottled with an irregular spotting

Sloping shoulders

Sparse, short, wispy mane

Well-made hindquarters

Compact, deep body with well-sprung ribs

Strong legs

THE **APPALOOSA HORSE CLUB** HAS **33,000** MEMBERS, AND THE BREED IS **POPULAR WORLDWIDE.**

Sound, hard feet, often distinguished by black and white vertical stripes

THE QUARTER HORSE CAN MOVE
AT SUCH HIGH SPEED IT CAN
**"TURN ON A DIME AND TOSS
YOU BACK NINE CENTS CHANGE"**
FROM A FLAT OUT GALLOP.

Quarter Horse

HEIGHT AT WITHERS	ORIGIN	COLORS
15–15.3 hh (152–160 cm)	Virginia, eastern US	Usually chestnut; any solid color is acceptable

The American Quarter Horse is famous for its speed over short distances, and its innate ability to work with cattle.

Settlers in eastern America inherited horses of mixed Spanish, Barb, and Arab blood. In 1611, crosses with imported British stock laid the foundation for the uniquely built American Quarter Horse. Compact, with massively muscled quarters, the horses were used for farm work, herding cattle, hauling timber, in light harness, and under saddle. By 1646, the Virginia settlers were racing their horses over a quarter of a mile, hence the breed's name.

Following the import of English Thoroughbreds (see pp.120–21), distance racing became popular and sprints declined. In the western states, however, the breed's speed, agility, and balance, combined with an instinct for working cattle, were appreciated by ranchers. It seems that breeding for particular requirements eventually created several distinct groups.

These are reflected in today's Quarter Horse, which has a variety of uses including trail-riding, rodeo, and racing. Recent studies found that the six subtypes of Quarter Horse can be divided into three genetically related groups: racing; pleasure and halter; and working cow, cutting, and reining. The most common 15 sires across the groups were all direct male descendants of the Thoroughbred Three Bars.

The Quarter Horse is a natural show jumper and a dressage performer. Quarter Horse racing is firmly established. Races, particularly the All American Futurity held in New Mexico, carry considerable prize money, often exceeding the sums on other events for Thoroughbred racing. The modern Quarter Horse is incredibly popular and the American Quarter Horse Association's register has millions of entries.

WRANGLING PARTNERS

The cowboy and his Quarter Horse are irrefutable icons of the old American West. Years of being bred to work cows have led to these horses having supreme confidence around cattle. They seem to second-guess the rider, making the work easier and leading to an enviable partnership between rider and horse.

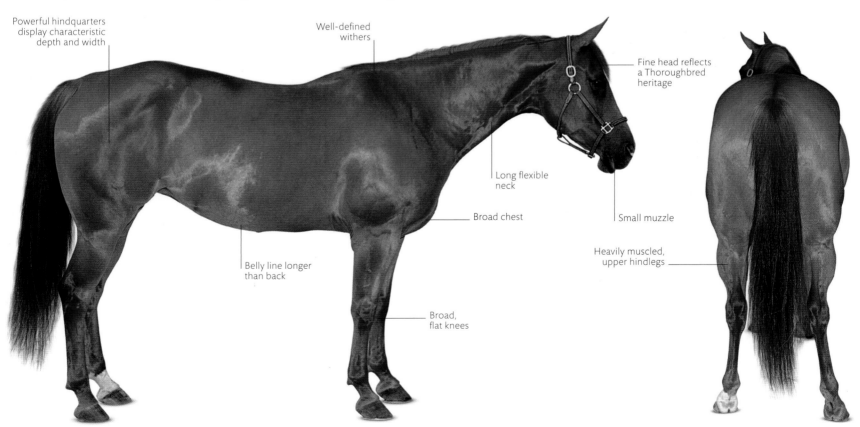

Powerful hindquarters display characteristic depth and width

Well-defined withers

Fine head reflects a Thoroughbred heritage

Long flexible neck

Broad chest

Small muzzle

Belly line longer than back

Heavily muscled, upper hindlegs

Broad, flat knees

Morgan

HEIGHT AT WITHERS	ORIGIN	COLORS
14.1–15.2 hh (145–157 cm)	Vermont, US	Chestnut, bay, black and brown

The Morgan is the first documented American breed and owes its existence to one celebrated stallion Justin Morgan.

The background of the Morgan's foundation sire, originally called Figure, remains unclear. Various theories about his ancestry have been advanced, including that he was a Thoroughbred (see pp.120–21) racehorse or a mix of Welsh Cob (see pp.291) with some Thoroughbred and Arab (see pp.92–93) blood. According to the American Morgan Horse Association, the teacher, composer, businessman, and horseman Justin Morgan acquired him as a colt of no more than 14 hh (142 cm), probably foaled in 1789 at West Springfield, Massachusetts. Reputedly the strongest, fastest horse in the area, Figure was used for general farm and agricultural tasks, as well as heavy draft work. He also competed in hauling contests and raced under saddle and in harness. He was never beaten. As a result, this diminutive horse was much in demand as a sire throughout the Connecticut River valley and in Vermont. All present-day Morgan horses can be traced back to Figure and his three most famous sons, Sherman, Woodbury, and Bullrush.

The present-day Morgan is larger than its ancestor and shows greater refinement, while retaining the distinctive conformation and proud carriage. Athletic, possessing great stamina and intelligence, and with a calm temperament, the Morgan is an excellent all-arounder. In the US, Morgans are still used for ranch work, but are popular under harness, for trail and pleasure riding, and their vigor and stamina are put to good use in eventing and endurance competitions. As well as the US, they are found in 20 countries worldwide.

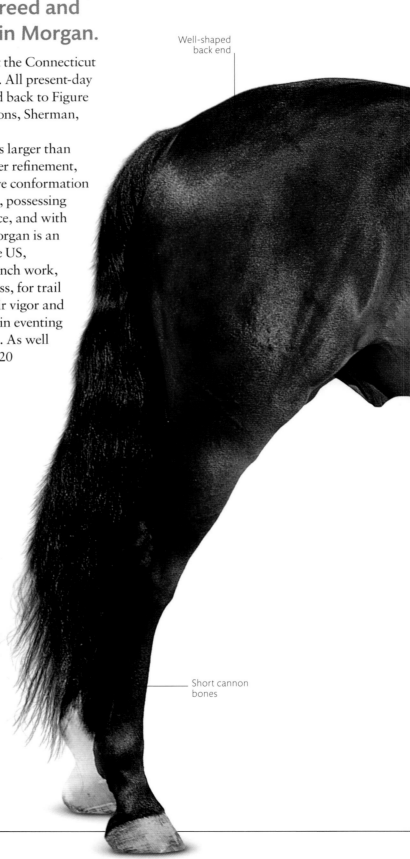

Well-shaped back end

Short cannon bones

SHOW MORGAN

Today Morgans are widely used for showing. They have a proud bearing and flashy style, but are easily trained and obedient. They can also be found in almost every discipline including eventing, dressage, cutting, and endurance. They make extremely good harness horses, and feature strongly in combined driving and carriage events. They were the first American breed to represent the US in the World Pairs Driving Competition.

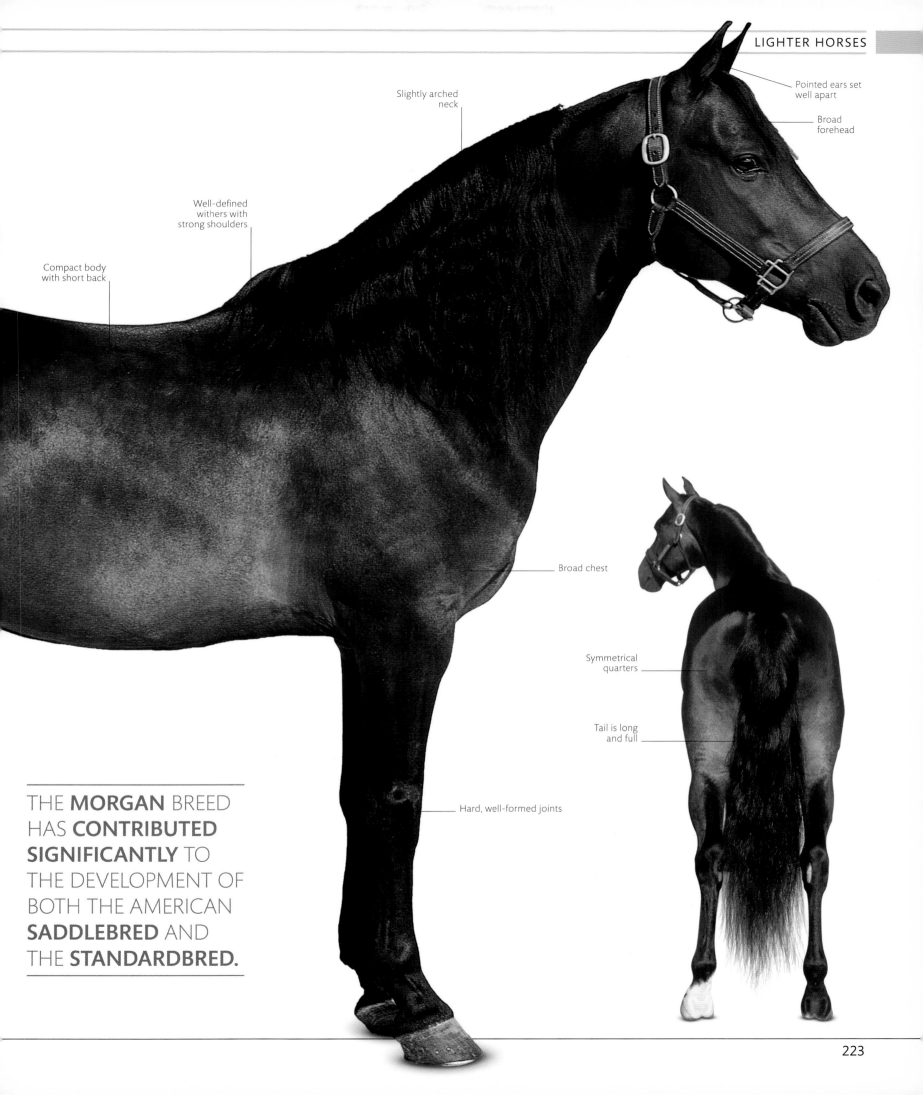

Pointed ears set
well apart

Broad
forehead

Slightly arched
neck

Well-defined
withers with
strong shoulders

Compact body
with short back

Broad chest

Symmetrical
quarters

Tail is long
and full

Hard, well-formed joints

THE **MORGAN** BREED
HAS **CONTRIBUTED**
SIGNIFICANTLY TO
THE DEVELOPMENT OF
BOTH THE AMERICAN
SADDLEBRED AND
THE **STANDARDBRED.**

American Saddlebred

HEIGHT AT WITHERS	ORIGIN	COLORS
14–17 hh (142–174 cm)	Kentucky, southern US	Chestnut and bay; also black, gray, and palomino

Long, extremely slender yet admirably strong legs are characteristic of this stylish and intelligent breed.

Like many American breeds, the Saddlebred started out as an all-purpose horse—ridden over rough terrain, used for plowing and farm work, and harnessed to a carriage for outings. It evolved in the southern US states, particularly around Kentucky, and was initially known as the Kentucky Saddler.

The breed's principal ancestor, the Narragansett Pacer, was the traditional mount of the New England plantation owners around Naragansett Bay, Rhode Island, on the eastern seaboard. The Pacer had the smooth, comfortable gait of its forebears—British ambling and pacing horses that were imported into America. Breeders in 19th-century Kentucky made selective crosses with the Morgan (see pp.222–23), an established breed in Vermont, and, in particular, with Thoroughbreds (see pp.120–21) to create the Saddlebred. One important sire was Gray Eagle. He was a Thoroughbred racehorse and most of today's Saddlebreds trace back to him. Other sires are Wagner and Lexington.

The modern American Saddlebred, with its arched neck and elegant, high-stepping gait is usually found in the show ring, both under saddle and in harness. The breed's pacing ancestry is clear in its action, while its speed, courage, and beauty of form derive from the Thoroughbred. In the US show ring, where Saddlebreds in competition are heavily shod, there are two classes in the saddle division: three-gaited and five-gaited. Three-gaited horses are shown at walk, trot, and canter, while the five-gaited horse, the supreme Saddlebred, performs an additional two gaits – one slow and the other at full speed (see also pp.18–19). The Saddlebred is also a fine harness horse, has achieved success in three-day eventing, and is used extensively for pleasure and trail riding.

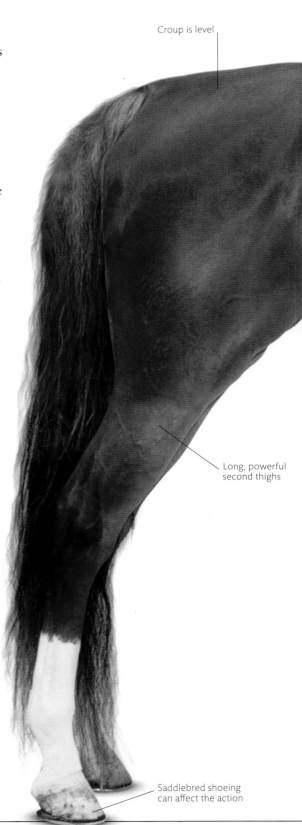

Croup is level

Long, powerful second thighs

Saddlebred shoeing can affect the action

SUPREME SULTAN

The Saddlebred Supreme Sultan (born in 1966) is immortalized in a bronze statue at the Kentucky Horse Park. The most important and influential sire of Saddlebreds in recent years, his offspring have proved successful in almost every sphere of Saddlebred competition. Canadian actor William Shatner, who played Captain James T. Kirk in the *Star Trek* series, owns Call Me Ringo (born in 1996) whose grandsire was Supreme Sultan.

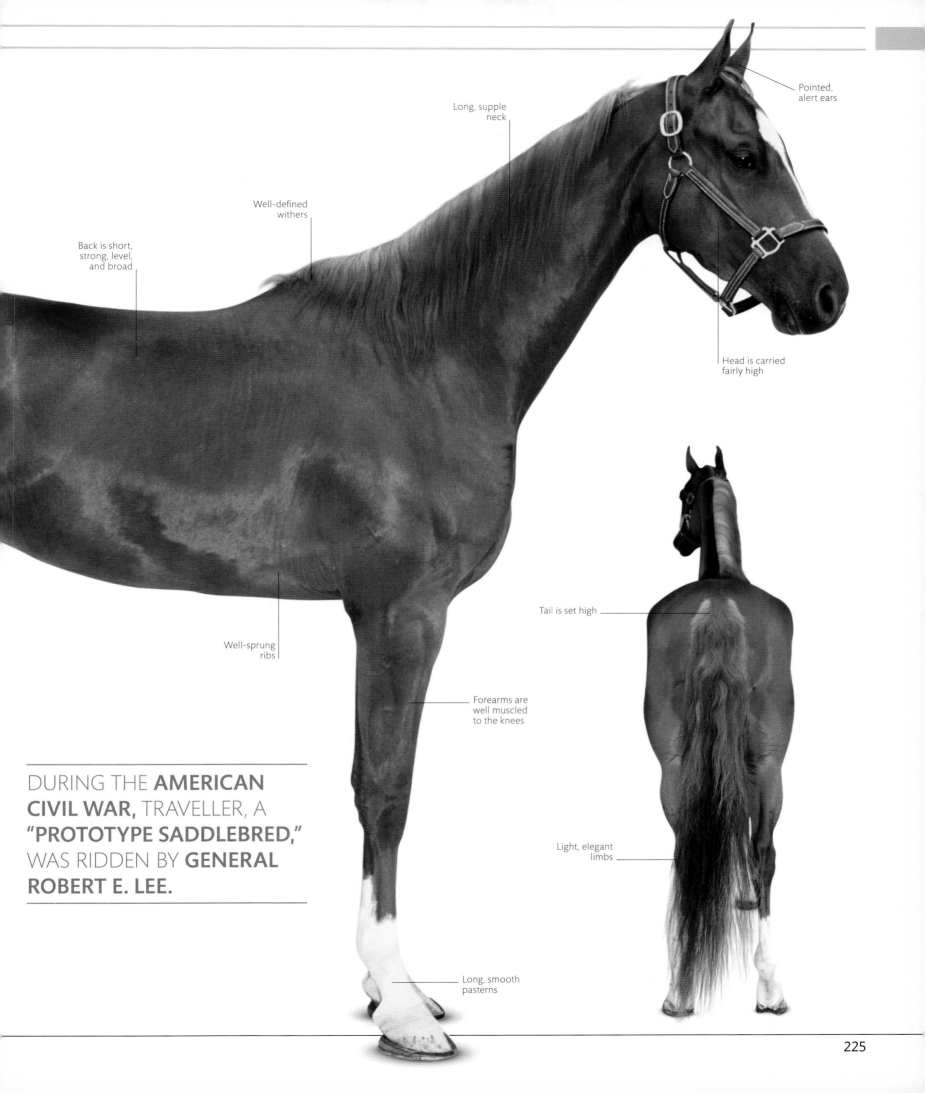

Pointed, alert ears

Long, supple neck

Well-defined withers

Back is short, strong, level, and broad

Head is carried fairly high

Well-sprung ribs

Tail is set high

Forearms are well muscled to the knees

Light, elegant limbs

DURING THE **AMERICAN CIVIL WAR,** TRAVELLER, A **"PROTOTYPE SADDLEBRED,"** WAS RIDDEN BY **GENERAL ROBERT E. LEE.**

Long, smooth pasterns

THERE ARE AROUND **52,000 MISSOURI FOX TROTTERS** LIVING ALL OVER **THE WORLD.**

Missouri Fox Trotter

HEIGHT AT WITHERS	ORIGIN	COLORS
14–16 hh (142–163 cm)	Missouri and Arkansas, US	All, primarily chestnut

HOW TO FOX TROT

The fox trot is such a smooth gait that riders have no need to rise in the saddle. The back remains level while the back feet can overstep the marks made by the front ones, so long as the forward movement is straight. Show classes are usually ridden in Western clothes and include all three of the Fox Trotters gaits. Artificial aids to accentuate the movement, such as excessive weighting of the feet with special shoes, are banned.

This breed is one of three North American gaited horses. The other two are the Saddlebred and the Tennessee Walker.

The Fox Trotter originated in the Ozarks, a mountainous region of southern Missouri and northern Arkansas. Settlers came here from Kentucky, Tennessee, and Virginia, bringing with them Thoroughbreds (see pp.120–21), Morgans (see pp.222–23), and Arabs (see pp.92–93). With the aim of creating a utility horse that could also race, they bred mares to the fastest sires. The prevailing Puritan religion, however, disapproved of racing, so they turned to producing a horse strong enough for farm work, but with a smooth action over rough ground.

Saddlebreds (see pp.224–25), Tennessee Walkers (see pp.228–29), and Standardbreds (see pp.232–33) were used to improve the breed. The result was a horse with a unique, characteristic gait: the "fox trot" is a broken gait in which the horse walks in front and trots behind. It is a sure-footed, sliding gait that produces very little movement in the back. The Fox Trotter can maintain this gait over long distances, so was the ideal trail riding horse for crossing the mountainous region. The breed was established in about 1820. A Fox Trotter studbook was opened in 1948 and was closed in 1982 (meaning it no longer allows any outside blood, resulting in pure bloodlines). In 2002 the breed became Missouri's official state horse.

The Fox Trotter's gait evolved naturally. In addition to the fox trot, horses and riders, perform the flat-foot walk and the canter. The walk is in strict four-beat time with distinct over-striding of the hind feet, while the canter is a broken, three-beat gait.

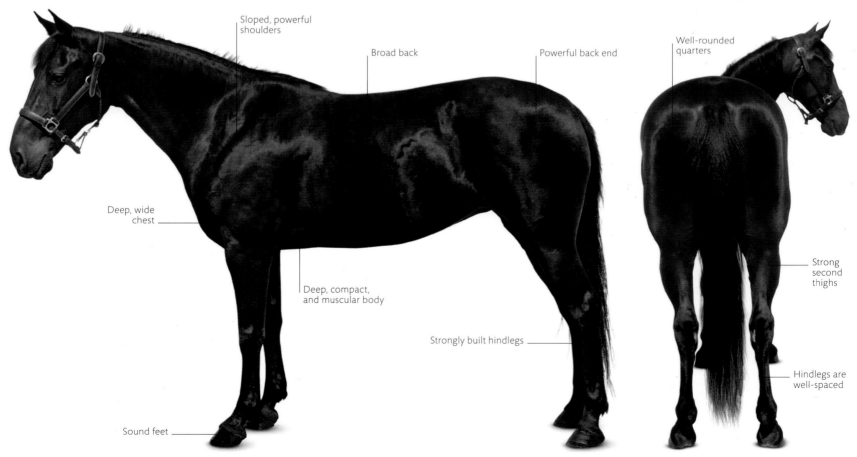

Sloped, powerful shoulders

Broad back

Powerful back end

Well-rounded quarters

Deep, wide chest

Deep, compact, and muscular body

Strongly built hindlegs

Sound feet

Strong second thighs

Hindlegs are well-spaced

Tennessee Walking Horse

HEIGHT AT WITHERS	ORIGIN	COLORS
14.3–17 hh (146–173 cm)	Tennessee, southern US	All colors

This breed was known as a "turn-row" horse because it could negotiate plantation rows without damaging young plants.

This gaited American breed evolved in Tennessee in the mid-19th century, after pioneers had crossed the Appalachian Mountains to establish outposts in Kentucky, Tennessee, and Missouri. The settlers aimed to breed a utility horse with endurance and stamina that could carry its owner for long hours when overseeing plantation work. Although great speed was not required, the horse did need to be able to cover long distances reasonably quickly.

Like other American gaited breeds, the Tennessee Walking Horse is descended from the Narragansett Pacer, with additional input from the Thoroughbred (see pp.120–21), Standardbred (see pp. 232–33), Morgan (see pp.222–23), and Saddlebred (see pp.224–25). The breed's foundation sire, the Standardbred stallion Black Allan, was descended from a line of Standardbred trotters (not pacers) and although he had no success as a harness racer, he passed on his distinctive walk to his progeny. The breed was officially recognized in 1947 by the United States Department of Agriculture.

Today, the Tennessee Walking Horse is primarily a show-ring and leisure horse. It has three distinct gaits: the flat walk, the running walk, and the canter. The flat walk is brisk with each foot hitting the ground separately. The running walk, for which the breed is renowned, is similar but much faster. It is described as "an extra-smooth, gliding gait" and "bounce-free." The canter is smoother than normal with a "rocking chair" motion. While performing the two walks, the Tennessee Walker nods its head conspicuously. The walks usually require special training. The breed has a gentle and docile disposition, making it suitable for nervous riders. The Tennessee Walking Horse Breeders' and Exhibitors' Association promotes the breed as "the ride of your life."

ELVIS AND HIS HORSES

Elvis Presley was a great fan of horses and owned many, keeping some of them on his 130-acre Circle-G ranch in Mississippi, not far from his house at Graceland. Among his collection were Bear and Colonel Midnight, both black Tennessee Walking Horses. The last horse Elvis bought was called Ebony's Double, also a Tennessee Walking Horse. Ebony's Double lived until he was 32 years old and died in January 2005, 27 years after the death of his famous owner. There are still horses at Graceland today.

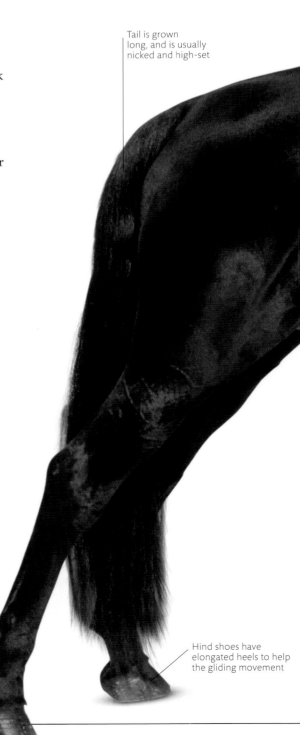

Tail is grown long, and is usually nicked and high-set

Hind shoes have elongated heels to help the gliding movement

Plain, large head

Short, strong back

Strong quarters

Barrel tapers toward back end

Powerful hindlegs

Legs are clean and hard

WHEN DOING THE **RUNNING WALK,** THIS HORSE CAN REACH SPEEDS UP TO **20 MILES (32 KM) AN HOUR.**

Hooves usually grown long and fitted with shoes that promote the lift in the action

Colorado Ranger Horse

HEIGHT AT WITHERS	ORIGIN	COLORS
Up to 15.2 hh (157 cm)	US	Any solid color or leopard spotting

The Colorado Ranger is a great working horse with tremendous strength, stamina, and athleticism.

The history of Colorado Rangers began in 1878 when Sultan Abdul Hamid of Turkey presented US General Ulysses S. Grant (see box, right) with two stallions—a gray, pure Siglavy-Gidran Arab called Leopard and a blue-gray, pure Barb called Linden Tree.

Initially these stallions were used in Virginia as the foundation sires for a breed of light harness horses. Later they spent a season on a ranch in Nebraska, siring stock from the native mares, some of which were spotted or colored. However, the Colorado Ranger breed was not created until 1934,

when Mike Ruby of Colorado's big Lazy J Bar Ranch used the descendants of the two Turkish stallions as foundation sires. The most notable of these were Patches, a great grandson of Leopard, and Max, a spotted descendent of the Leopard line.

Rangers were bred to be superlative working horses. They are refined, but compact, with powerful limbs and quarters, and most have a spotted pattern. Because of the spotted coat, a Ranger can be registered as an Appaloosa. However, Appaloosas cannot be registered as Rangers. Ranger outcrosses to Appaloosas, Araappaloosas (Arab cross Appaloosa), Quarter Horses, Thoroughbreds, and Lusitanos (born between 1980–87) are allowed.

ULYSSES S. GRANT

Although two of his horses were the foundation for the Colorado Ranger Horse, what General Grant would have made of the breed is anybody's guess, since it did not appear until 49 years after his death. He was renowned for this love of horses, however, and had a special affinity with them from childhood. According to his son Frederick, he "rode splendidly and always on magnificent and fiery horses."

COLORADO REMAINS THE **BREEDING CENTER,** BUT RANGERS ARE **ALSO** BRED **ELSEWHERE IN THE US.**

Undefined withers

Powerful quarters

Distinctive spotted patterning

Strong and athletic outline

Short legs are a notable feature

Compact frame

Tail can be sparse

Strong limbs

Sound, hard, open feet

American Standardbred

HEIGHT AT WITHERS	ORIGIN	COLORS
15–16 hh (152–163 cm)	Eastern seaboard, US	Bay, brown, and chestnut solid colors

High croup

The American Standardbred is the world's fastest harness racer and is often used to upgrade other trotting breeds.

The term Standardbred, first used in 1879, refers to the speed standard over a distance of one mile (1.6 km) that a horse had to attain to be listed in the breed register. The standard was originally 3 minutes, then it was reduced to 2 minutes 30 seconds for conventional trotters and 2 minutes 25 seconds for pacers. Today, speeds of under 1.55 minutes have been achieved. The breed's founding sire, a Thoroughbred (see pp.120–21) called Messenger, was imported into the US in 1788, having raced successfully on the flat in England. Although Messenger did not race in harness, he had trotting connections—through his sire, Mambrino—with the Norfolk Roadster. Messenger was bred to all sorts of mares, including Morgans (see pp.222–23) and Canadian and Narragansett Pacers. These last two breeds no longer exist, but their bloodlines included "ambling" horses, which introduced the pacing gait now favored in American harness racing.

Modern Standardbreds can be traced back to Messenger's descendant, Hambeltonian, who sired more than 1,300 offspring between 1851 and 1875. Although he never raced, he was croup high (quarters higher than the withers), by 2 in (5 cm), which contributed to his success as a sire of trotters and other trotting sires. Nearly all Standardbreds descend from Hambletonian's sons George Wilkes, Dictator, Happy Medium, and Electioneer. The US Trotting Association, founded in 1939, holds the registry and promotes this breed and harness racing.

Well-muscled second thigh

Iron-hard legs

THE RED MILE

The home of harness racing in the US is the famous Red Mile clay track in Kentucky. The second-oldest harness racing track in the world, it was founded in September 1875. The oldest track is Goshen in New York, founded in 1838. Harness racing is one of the most popular horse sports worldwide, attracting 30 million followers in the US alone. In Russia and Scandinavia it is much more popular than Thoroughbred racing.

THE **LATERAL GAIT** OF THIS BREED ENABLES **EASY, LONG-DISTANCE TRAVEL** WITHOUT TIRING THE RIDER.

Rocky Mountain Horse

HEIGHT AT WITHERS	ORIGIN	COLORS
14–16 hh (142–163 cm)	US	Any solid color, but mainly chocolate with flaxen mane and tail

THE ASSOCIATION

When the Rocky Mountain Horse Association was created in 1986 there were 26 horses in the register. By 2015, the total number registered through the years had reached 25,000. However, worldwide there are thought to be fewer than 15,000 horses, with under 800 registrations in the US each year. Rocky Mountain Horses can be found in most states of America and 11 countries worldwide. Today, foals are DNA-tested to verify their parentage and they must conform to the breed standard, which includes showing the lateral gait, before registration.

Sure-footed on rough ground, this remarkably hardy breed is ideally suited to mountainous terrains.

In common with much of the American equine population, the Rocky Mountain Horse (formerly referred to as a "pony") is said to have its origins in the early Spanish horses introduced to the New World in the 16th century by the conquistadores. Otherwise, the history of the breed is relatively obscure and to some degree based on hearsay and conjecture.

It is claimed that the Rocky Mountain Horse originated in the Appalachian foothills of eastern Kentucky in about 1890, but there is little evidence from this period to support this assertion. Nonetheless, the existence of a strain of horses with a comfortable ambling gait, sure-footed and well able to cope with the rough ground of the area, and to tolerate the Appalachian winters, is incontrovertible. In the 1960s, a stallion called Old Tobe, owned by Sam Tuttle of Kentucky, was used to develop the modern type, and today most Rocky Mountain Horses trace back to this stallion.

The outstanding characteristic of the Rocky Mountain Horse is the natural lateral gait, which is an easy, comfortable amble involving four distinct beats rather than the faster, two-beat pacing gait. Common among the early Spanish horses, this gait has been greatly favored since the Middle Ages. The breed is able to maintain a steady 7 mph (11 km per hour) over rough ground, and can reach speeds of 16 mph (25 km per hour) on better going.

The breed is suited for work on the farm as well as in harness and under saddle. Its temperament is said to be calm and kind, but it is not without spirit.

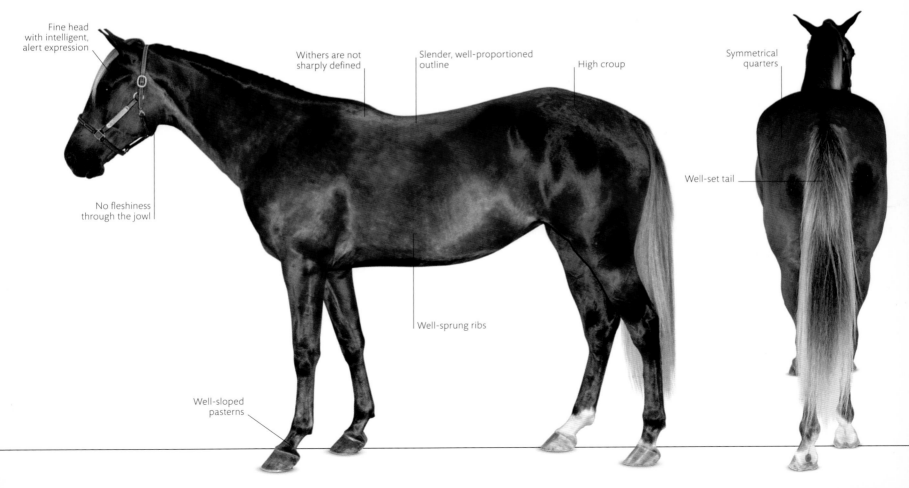

Fine head with intelligent, alert expression

No fleshiness through the jowl

Withers are not sharply defined

Slender, well-proportioned outline

High croup

Symmetrical quarters

Well-set tail

Well-sprung ribs

Well-sloped pasterns

Criollo

HEIGHT AT WITHERS	ORIGIN	COLORS
14–15 hh (142–152 cm)	Argentina	All colors except pintado (paint) and tobiano

TSCHIFFELY'S RIDE

Reliable packhorses, Criollos have incredible stamina and are able to cope with extreme conditions. In 1925, Argentine Professor Aimé Tschiffely (1895–1954) traveled 10,000 miles (16,090 km) from Buenos Aires to New York City with two Criollos: Gato and Mancha. The trip took nearly three years. The horses survived and went on to live to great ages.

Among the toughest horses in the world, Criollos can carry heavy weights over long distances and difficult terrain.

The word Criollo means "of Spanish origin" and is a generic term covering a variety of related South American horses, including the Crioulo Braziliero from Brazil, and the tough Llanero cattle horse from Venezuela, which is not dissimilar to the Argentine Criollo, with which it shares a common background.

The Argentine Criollo, however, descends from various Spanish horses shipped to South America by early explorers. It is the mount of the legendary gauchos—among the last of the world's horse people—and can withstand the most severe climatic conditions and lack of food and drink. In short, it has the ability to survive in near-impossible conditions and has been the mount of choice in at least two long-distance treks (see box, left).

Today, Criollos are used as cow horses as well as for pleasure and trail riding. The Argentine army also use them for many purposes and, when crossed with the Thoroughbred (see pp.120–21), they provide the base for the Argentinian polo pony (see pp.238–39)—the best in the world. A breed society for the Argentine Criollo was formed in 1918.

Elegant, muscular neck

Well-formed and muscular quarters

Strong, compact body

Typical Argentinian headcollar

Long, well-developed second thigh

Hocks joints are clean

A CRIOLLO NAMED **SUFRIDOR** UNDERTOOK AN **EPIC TREK** WITH TWO MEN ALONG **THE BEAGLE CHANNEL,** TIERRA DEL FUEGO, IN **1987–1993.**

Peruvian Paso

HEIGHT AT WITHERS	ORIGIN	COLORS
14–15 hh (142–152 cm)	Peru	All colors

This elegant, powerful breed is much loved for its easy-going temperament and ability to provide a smooth ride.

Also known as the Peruvian Stepping Horse, the Paso (meaning "step" in Spanish) is the most prominent of the Peruvian breeds. Its origins are not known. The first horses to arrive in Peru came from Spain with the conquistadors, and also from Jamaica, Panama, and other Central American areas. Then, when Peru became independent from Spain in 1823, other horses, including Arabs (see pp.92–93), Hackneys (see pp.126–27), Thoroughbreds (see pp.120–21), and Friesians (see pp.164–65), are thought to have been imported and bred to native stock. Any of these could have played a part in the foundation of Peruvian Paso. The Peruvian Paso breed is notable for its unique natural lateral gait, which is marked by a characteristically energetic, round, dishing action of the forelegs—rather like a swimmer's arms. Known as the *termino*, this gait is supported by a powerful movement of the hindlegs overstepping the prints of the forefeet. The quarters are held low, with the hocks well under the body, and the back is carried straight and rigid. Indeed, the Paso's action is said to be so smooth that a rider can carry a full glass of water without spilling it. This action makes for a comfortable ride over rough mountain terrain.

PASO FINO

The Puerto Rican Paso Fino is another naturally gaited breed. It has three gaits: *classic fino* or *paso fino* is rapid and collected; *corto* is slightly more extended and the speed of a trot; the *largo* is again extended, has four beats, and is lateral. Largo can reach speeds of canter or a slow gallop. Few horses can perform a correct *classic fino*.

Short, upright, and well-muscled neck

Compact, muscular body

Bulky chest muscles

Straight forearm and sloped shoulders

Exceptionally strong hindlegs

Strong quarters

Long, abundant tail of fine hair

THE PASO HAS A **HUGE HEART** AND **LUNGS** IN RELATION TO ITS SIZE.

Polo pony

HEIGHT AT WITHERS	ORIGIN	COLORS
15–15.3 hh (152–160 cm)	Argentina (modern version)	Any color

ARGENTINA AND POLO

Since the early 20th century, Argentina has dominated the polo scene. It produces the best polo ponies, which are sought the world over. The first match between US and Argentina, the Cup of the Americas, was held in 1928. The US team won, and again four years later, but since then Argentina has triumphed time and again.

Small horses that do not strictly belong to a breed, polo ponies have evolved a great deal and have many shared traits.

The first polo ponies originated in Asia and were no taller than 12.2 hh (127 cm). When polo was adopted as a pastime by British soldiers in India, British breeders crossed the native ponies with small Thoroughbred stallions and by 1870 the average height went up to about 13.2 hh (137 cm). A height limit of 14.2 hh (147 cm) was introduced by the Hurlingham Club in Britain in 1895. It was abandoned in 1919, probably because of what had happened once the game was introduced to the US in 1876. American breeders looked to Argentina for their polo ponies, and soon produced a distinctive polo pony using the tough native Criollo (see p.236) horses.

The Argentinians, who also liked polo, crossed their Criollos with Thoroughbreds (see pp.120–21) and eventually produced a distinctive, lean, wiry horse, which is very Thoroughbred in character with powerful quarters and strong hocks. The Argentinian polo pony displays the necessary qualities of speed, stamina, courage, and balance. Able to turn and twist at full gallop, the polo pony appears to have an inbred talent for the game, instinctively following the ball and making the quick stops and fast accelerations necessary for this sport.

In 2009, the famous polo pony gelding Califa was cloned. Today, polo ponies are increasingly produced in this way.

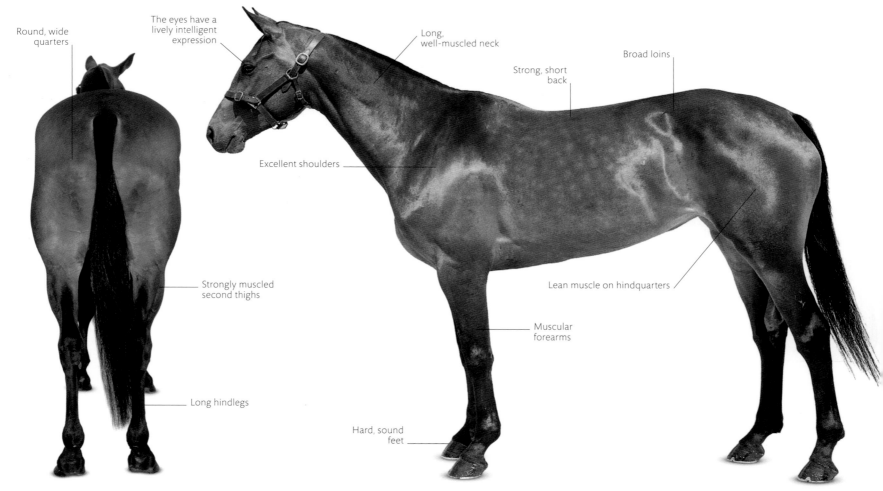

Round, wide quarters

The eyes have a lively intelligent expression

Long, well-muscled neck

Broad loins

Strong, short back

Excellent shoulders

Strongly muscled second thighs

Lean muscle on hindquarters

Muscular forearms

Long hindlegs

Hard, sound feet

THE WORLD'S NUMBER ONE POLO PLAYER, ARGENTINIAN **ADOLFO CAMBIASO,** HAS **CLONED** HIS BELOVED HORSE **CUARTETERA NUMEROUS TIMES.**

Brumby

HEIGHT AT WITHERS
14–15 hh
(142–152 cm)

ORIGIN
Australia

COLORS
All colors

IN THE WILD

As with the Mustang, the Brumby has an ongoing problem with overpopulation and overgrazing. However, Save the Brumbies has set out to help their cause and have sanctuaries where the public can get to know the horses. They also run sponsorship and adoption programs. In the wild, Brumbies have been found to be intelligent, healthy, and strong, and are said, in many cases, to be less inbred than the Thoroughbred.

Fast-moving and resilient, large numbers of these feral horses have spread all over the Australian outback.

After the great Australian Gold Rush of 1851, many horses—the imported forebears of the Walers and Australian Stock Horses—were released or escaped from mining settlements and were allowed to run wild in the scrublands. These horses came to be known as Brumbies, and they are the Australian equivalent of the American Mustang (see pp.212–13).

Over the years, Brumbies became increasingly feral and widespread and the herds grew ever larger while the horses degenerated in type and quality. However, having to fend for themselves in a difficult environment where there was little food, they developed a keen survival instinct that

enabled them to withstand the harsh climate and avoid the stockmen who hunted them.

They adapted very well and they eventually became so numerous that in the 1960s it was felt necessary to begin an extensive culling operation. The methods employed, however, were often inhumane and so unacceptable that Australia was condemned worldwide. Unlike some of the American Mustangs, there is little demand for Brumbies as riding horses in modern Australia, although they are said to be well suited to endurance and general riding and they make good companion animals.

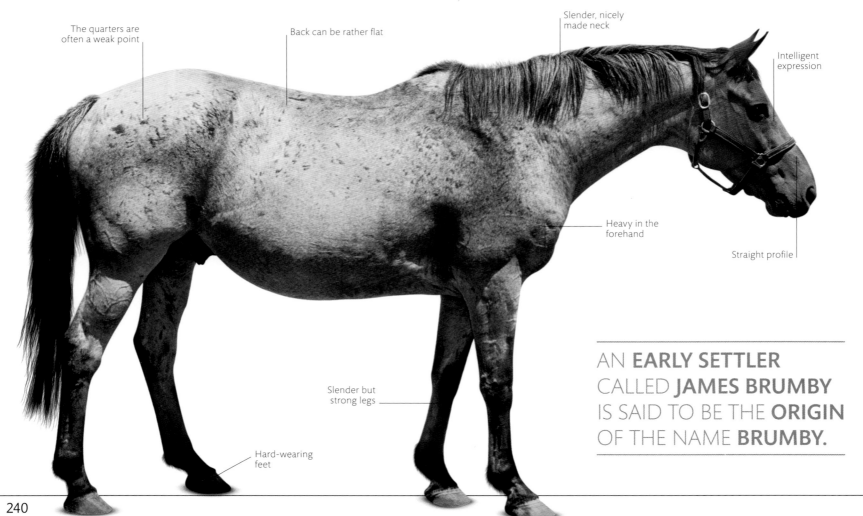

The quarters are often a weak point

Back can be rather flat

Slender, nicely made neck

Intelligent expression

Heavy in the forehand

Straight profile

Slender but strong legs

Hard-wearing feet

AN **EARLY SETTLER** CALLED **JAMES BRUMBY** IS SAID TO BE THE **ORIGIN** OF THE NAME **BRUMBY.**

Australian Stock Horse

HEIGHT AT WITHERS	ORIGIN	COLORS
15–16.2 hh (152–168 cm)	Australia	All solid colors

STOCK WORK

Across the world, where livestock is spread over a wide area, horses are often more useful than the best off-road vehicles. The Australian Stock Horse has evolved to work in the extreme conditions of the Australian outback. Campdrafting practices cow-working skills and involves cutting an animal from the "camp" or yard and moving it on a course. It requires cattle sense, speed, and bravery.

This breed is a great all-arounder with remarkable stamina, natural balance, and an amenable temperament.

The first horse bred in Australia—originally from Arab (see pp.92–93), Thoroughbred (see pp.120–21), and Anglo-Arab (see pp.148–49) stock—was the Waler, a working horse in New South Wales. Used in harness as well as under saddle, it was regarded as the world's finest cavalry horse because it had a sound constitution, great endurance and agility, and could carry a tremendous weight, even over rough ground. During World War I, Australia provided some 120,000 Walers for the Allied forces, and the Indian cavalry also took many until the 1930s. Many of these horses never returned, but numbers in Australia remained high.

The Waler's successor was the Australian Stock Horse. In the 1830s, Thoroughbred stallions were imported and these were bred to local mares. In the 1950s, Quarter Horse (see pp.220–21) and even some pony blood were introduced.

Today, the Australian Stock Horse Society works to promote and standardize the breed, but it remains of no set type and its appearance varies enormously. It is the largest single group of horses in Australia (the breed was first recognized in 1971), and its light build and reactive nature reflects the Australian preference for a versatile horse of Thoroughbred character.

Elegant, attractive head

Prominent Thoroughbred-type withers

Long, strong back

Thin, wiry neck

Lightweight hindquarters

Deep chest

Well-sprung rib cage

Strong second thighs

Excellent clean limbs

Hard, well-made feet

ESTABLISHED IN **1971**, THE **AUSTRALIAN STOCK HORSE SOCIETY** STUD BOOK CURRENTLY HAS **MORE THAN 180,000 HORSES** REGISTERED.

Environmental influence
Australia has no native horses. It is a testament to the enduring toughness of the Stock Horse and Brumby that they survive in conditions that are often testing for equines.

PONIES

All ponies are less than 15hh (152cm) high, anything taller is called a horse. However, ponies are so much more than small horses. Not only are their proportions different—they tend to have short stocky legs and comparatively sturdy bodies—but they are also renowned for their crafty intelligence and their survival instinct. Within this height limit, there are also equines that are more horselike in build, such as the various carefully developed riding ponies and the Caspian. Ponies are also incredibly strong, often being capable of carrying adults, despite their small size.

◀ **Perfectly adapted** Retaining some of the character of their ancestors, ponies are often capable of surviving without much human help. Semi-wild groups still exist around the world.

Caspian

HEIGHT AT WITHERS	ORIGIN	COLORS
10–12 hh (102–122 cm)	Iran	Bay, gray, chestnut; occasionally black or cream

Many claims have been made for this attractive little pony, which looks like a horse in miniature.

The Caspian is one of the most fascinating of all horse breeds. Genetically, it is most similar to Arabs—probably because of their geographical proximity and the likelihood of some interbreeding in the past. However, there is debate about which is the ancestor of which. A study of six Caspian ponies found they had 65 chromosomes rather than the usual 64 found in domestic horses. At the time, it was suggested that the extra chromosome was acquired due to crossbreeding with Przewalksi's horse, which has 66 chromosomes, but it is more likely that it was a genetic mutation. The Caspian also has several distinctive physical characteristics: a difference in the shape of the shoulder bone, and the rather odd formation of bones of the head, making the skull look vaulted; some also lack chestnuts.

The existence of Caspian horses was brought to the world's attention in 1965 when American traveler, Louise L. Firouz, found an alert, quick-moving pony type working in the narrow streets of Amol, on the shores of the Caspian Sea in northern Iran. She bought several and bred them. Ten years later, a stallion and seven mares were exported to the UK. Since then Caspians have been bred as far afield as North and South America, Australia, and New Zealand. Selective breeding and better quality food has led to the ponies increasing in height and having rather better conformation than their predecessors.

These excellent children's ponies have a long, low, free, and fast action and appear to "float." Natural jumpers, they are also easily trained to harness.

REACHING THE SEA

The Greeks recorded a race of miniature horses in ancient Medea, south of the Caspian Sea, and horse bones have been found in a Mesolithic cave, near Kermanshah, mid-way between Baghdad and Tehran. There are no indigenous horses here now; it seems that about 1,000 years ago, tribes were driven out from this region and fled to the Elborz mountains, which border the Caspian Sea. It is possible they took some horses with them.

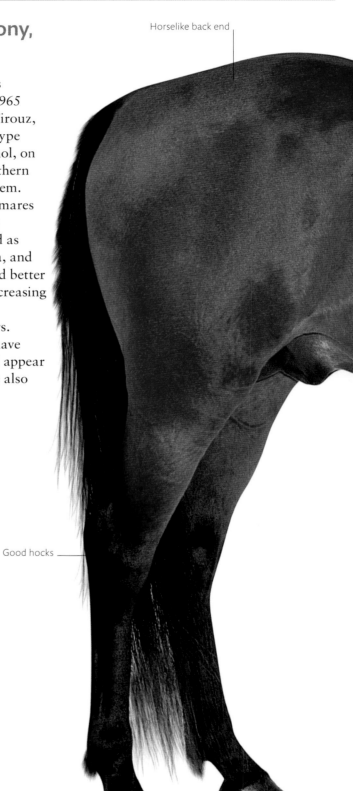

Horselike back end

Good hocks

Small, strong feet

Long, gracefully arched neck

Reasonable withers

Straight back

Short, pretty head

Sloped shoulders

Narrow and slim body

Strong quarters with unexpected length from hip to point of hock

Full, flowing tail and mane

CASPIANS CAN KEEP UP WITH **LARGER HORSES** AT **EVERY GAIT,** EXCEPT THE **GALLOP.**

Slim legs are sound and strong

Sumba

HEIGHT AT WITHERS
12.2 hh (127 cm)
ORIGIN Sumba, Indonesia
COLORS Most solid colors

The Sumba and related Sumbawa are most probably derived from ponies that originated in Central Asia. The Sumba takes its name from the island between Java and Timor, but it is found all over the archipelago, particularly in Sumatra. Docile and cooperative, Sumbas make good riding ponies and are used for the national sport of lance throwing. They are immensely strong and they can carry grown men as well as heavy pack loads. In the more rugged areas of the islands, this tough pony is a vital mode of transportation. Sumbas have been trained to perform in traditional dances, popular on some Indonesian islands.

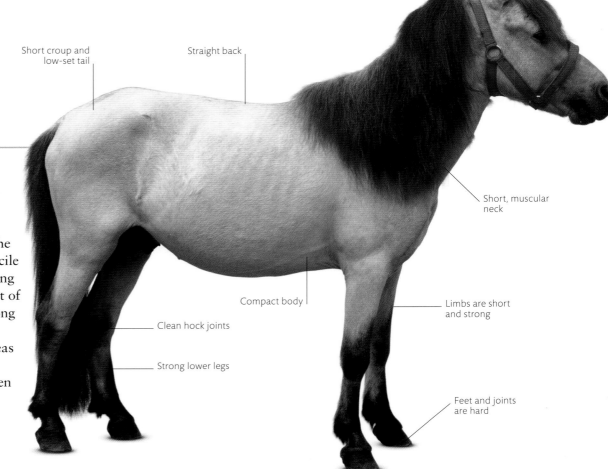

Short croup and low-set tail

Straight back

Short, muscular neck

Compact body

Clean hock joints

Strong lower legs

Limbs are short and strong

Feet and joints are hard

Sandalwood

HEIGHT AT WITHERS
Up to 13.1 hh (135 cm)
ORIGIN Sumba and Sumbawa, Indonesia
COLORS Wide range

Originally developed on the islands of Sumba and Sumbawa, the Sandalwood is named after the highly prized wood that is exported from Indonesia. It also contributed significantly to the economy of these islands. The pony owes much to Arab (see pp.92–93) stallions imported by the early Dutch colonists. Selected indigenous mares were sent to stallions established at the studs on Sumatra, and the youngstock was then dispersed to other islands for upgrading purposes. The Sandalwood is a refined, quality animal that has been used in the development the Kuda Pacu Indonesia, a racehorse that can thrive in a tropical climate.

Sloped shoulder

Long, straight back

Light, attractive head

Well-proportioned neck

Strong, thin legs

Hooves are tough and hard

Indian country-bred

HEIGHT AT WITHERS	ORIGIN	COLORS
14–15 hh (142–152 cm)	India	Any

INDIAN PONY CART

Called a *tonga* or *tanga*—or an *ekka* in northern India—these two-wheeled carts are drawn by a single pony and are mainly used for transporting passengers, sometimes rather more than seems fair to the pony. They may have a canopy overhead for protection from the sun. *Tongas* are also used for goods such as market produce. They are becoming rarer in the big cities, but are still a valued form of transportation in rural areas.

The term country-bred describes a variety of equines of mixed breeding, many of which are useful working horses.

Horses arrived in India from a variety of places. For several hundred years there was a constant flow of traders with their horses through the passes of the Hindu Kush and from Afghanistan. Many of these pack animals were steppe horses of Asian origin—Persians, Turkmenes, and Arab strains, Shirazi from southern Persia, Jaf, and Tchenarani, as well as Kabuli ponies from Afghanistan, and robust Baluchis. Early in the 19th century, there was a regular trade in Arab-type horses from the Arabian Gulf to Mumbai and Veraval.

In the north of India, where the people have a cultural connection with the tribes of Central Asia and the Middle East, there are several small pony types, including the Bhuti or Bhotia (from Sikkim) and the Spiti (from Himachal Pradesh). These tough mountain ponies were once important as riding and pack animals but today with increasing mechanization their numbers are falling. The Spiti has genetic similarities with the Zanskari pony (Kashmir, Leh, and Ladakh) and the Manipuri, which has a more obscure origin. The mixed ancestry of these ponies suggests they have interbred with each other and with the Tibetan pony.

Head is small

Long neck runs into clearly defined withers

Low-set tail

Quarters have a wiry quality

Weak second thighs

Chest is often narrow

Body often lacks depth

Feet are often upright and boxy

THE INDIAN COUNTRY-BRED PLAYS AN **IMPORTANT ROLE** IN THE **RURAL ECONOMY.**

Eagle hunters
The Kazakh people use Golden Eagles to hunt for small animals. Two annual festivals in Mongolia give them a chance to show-off their abilities on their wiry Tibetian ponies.

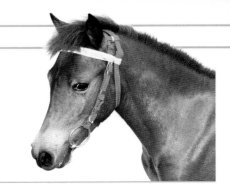

Timor

HEIGHT AT WITHERS	ORIGIN	COLORS
10–12 hh (102–122 cm)	Timor, Indonesia	Brown, black, and bay, occasionally gray

The smallest of the Indonesian ponies, this diminutive pony shows some Arab influence.

The Timor pony is an important element in the economy of the island of Timor. At one time, the population was estimated at one horse to every six people and the number per head of population remains high.

In the 16th and 17th centuries, the island came under the influence of first Portuguese and then Dutch colonists. Both introduced horses from Arabia and Persia to their colonies in Indonesia to upgrade the existing pony population, which had a background of Mongolian, Chinese, and Indian ponies (see p.249).

Despite the addition of desert-horse blood from the Middle East, and the existence of extensive savannah on the island providing wiry but nutritious feed, the Timor remains the smallest of the Indonesian ponies. Tough and agile, these ponies routinely carry full-grown men, who use them to work cattle. They are usually ridden in bitless bridles, which are traditional to the islands and reminiscent of those used in central Asia 4,000 years ago. Recognizable saddles are rarely seen, or required, and the riders' feet often touch the ground. The ponies are valued for driving, carrying packs, and other farm work.

Timors have been exported to Australia since 1803 and were first used to improve the stamina and toughness of existing Australian stock. They have also found work as children's ponies. Australian poet Banjo Paterson mentioned the Timor in his poem, *The Man from Snowy River*.

COFFIN BAY PONIES

Timors are tough enough to withstand the harsh conditions found in many parts of Australia. Sixty ponies were imported to Coffin Bay, South Australia, in 1839. The original stud saw many changes in ownership and the ponies interbred with other breeds until 2004, when they were moved to Brumbies Run, a nearby reserve. Here, about 35 ponies roam freely with little human contact except for an annual health check and auction to maintain the population.

Strong loins

WITH GREAT QUALITIES OF **ENDURANCE, AGILITY,** AND **STRENGTH,** THE TINY TIMOR IS A REMARKABLE EQUINE.

Full mane

Straight back with a level croup

Head is heavy and large

Short neck and upright shoulder

The tail is carried high

Well-muscled quarters

Narrow girth but well-sprung ribs

Strong second thighs

Hocks are correct though small

Fetlocks are acceptable

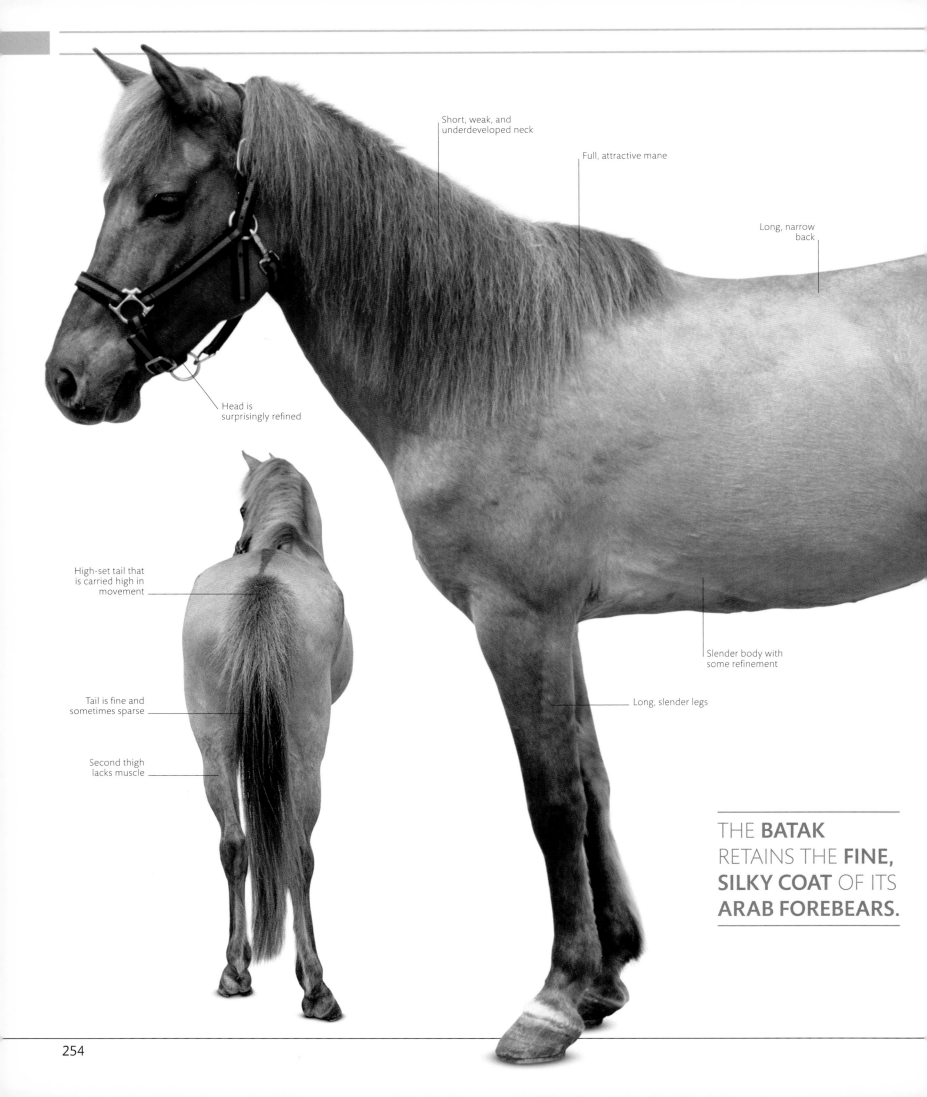

Short, weak, and underdeveloped neck

Full, attractive mane

Long, narrow back

Head is surprisingly refined

High-set tail that is carried high in movement

Tail is fine and sometimes sparse

Second thigh lacks muscle

Slender body with some refinement

Long, slender legs

THE **BATAK** RETAINS THE **FINE, SILKY COAT** OF ITS **ARAB FOREBEARS.**

Batak

HEIGHT AT WITHERS	ORIGIN	COLORS
Average 13 hh (132 cm)	Sumatra, Indonesia	Wide range

Excessively high "goose rump"

Humble, but attractive and tough, the Batak pony is inextricably linked to the Batak people.

The Batak shares its name with the indigenous people of north-central Sumatra. Made up of six distinct tribes, they traditionally ride ponies, race them, drive them in harness, and use them as pack animals. They also keep sacred horses for the purpose of sacrifice to the trinity of Toba gods, and eat horsemeat. Gambling has long been a popular pastime and if a man could not repay his debts it was said that he could be sold into slavery unless his creditor allowed him to provide a horse for the purpose of a public feast.

Most of the ponies of Indonesia have a similar mixed ancestry. They are not part of the original fauna of the islands, but were taken there over hundreds of years by people from China, India, and latterly by European colonists. This stock has been selectively bred by the islanders and Europeans to suit their needs. The Batak is a descendant of many types of horse and was certainly crossbred with Arabs to improve its quality. Not surprisingly, the Arab influence is very evident in this little equine, which has the reputation of being spirited but good-natured. It is both economical to feed and easily managed.

At one time there was a heavier strain of Batak called the Gayoe. Found in the north of the island, this pony was less Arab in character. It was used for transporting goods rather than for riding.

Today, the Batak is a working pony, and is widely used for riding. It also performs an important function as the core of Indonesian horse breeding, and is instrumental in upgrading poorer stock on the other Indonesian islands. Regular infusions of outside blood prevent the stock from degenerating and the ponies remain tough and constitutionally sound.

PONY POWER

The island ponies of Indonesia are small due to the difficult climate and lack of good grazing. However, they are all renowned for their strength—over the years, only those ponies tough enough do the work required of them under difficult conditions survived and were bred from. Batak ponies are capable of carrying adults and, being spirited and agile, are popular for racing.

Java

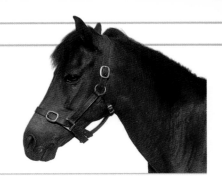

	HEIGHT AT WITHERS	ORIGIN	COLORS
	11.2–12.2 hh (117–127 cm)	Java, Indonesia	Any

KUDA LUMPING

Horses have had an influence on customs in Java. Kuda Lumping is a traditional spiritual dance performed by groups of up to eight men. They ride brightly painted "horses" made from bamboo or rattan, and are accompanied by musicians playing local instruments. Some dancers fall into trances and deliver prophecies. The dance is popular in Java although there are disputes about its origins. Nowadays, it is often done simply as an entertainment.

This diminutive horse has proved to be an enduring and tireless worker, much valued on its island home.

It is thought that the first ponies came to Java from southeast Asia. Local authorities believe that equines of Mongolian descent were brought to the islands as gifts in the 7th century, and Chinese ponies arrived in the 13th century. There also seem to have been crosses with desert-type horses brought to the island by early traders and later with those horses brought by 17th-century Dutch settlers. Although the Java is stronger and larger, and of a lighter build than other Indonesian breeds, the "desert" influence is not very apparent in the appearance of the modern Java pony. It has, however, inherited great stamina and resistance to heat. The Java is light in terms of conformation yet has good reserves of energy.

In rural areas, the pony was used in agriculture: due to the powerful input of the Dutch East India Company, the island has a long tradition of coffee, sugar cane, rubber, and tea cultivation. In the cities, the Java was used under harness for transportation and draft work, and it is still used to pull taxi carts carrying up to six people. The Java is also ridden, and the traditional rope stirrup, known as a "toe-stirrup" may still be seen.

Pronounced withers

Sloping croup

Long back

Head can be pretty

High-set tail

Weak, underdeveloped joints and legs

IN JAVA'S **THRIVING TREKKING INDUSTRY,** THE HORSES USED ARE OFTEN **THOROUGHBRED** CROSSED WITH **LOCAL PONIES.**

Hard and tough feet

Padang

HEIGHT AT WITHERS	ORIGIN	COLORS
12.2 hh (127 cm)	Sumatra, Indonesia	Any

CAPE HORSE

The Dutch East India Company brought the first horses to South Africa from Java in 1665. From these, Dutch settlers developed a tough little horse. Iranian desert horses were then imported to prevent inbreeding, and by 1800, there were about 200,000 Cape horses. Because of the addition of American Saddlebred (see pp.224–25) blood, today's Cape horses, also known as Boerperd, are often gaited.

The Padang is a lightly built pony of some quality and spirit, and is said to make a good riding pony.

The Padang pony of Sumatra is essentially no more than a type developed from the local Batak (see pp.254–55) strains. It originated through selective breeding by settlers of the Dutch East India Company. They established a stud at what was then the harbor town of Padang Mengabes on the island's west coast.

The predecessors of the ponies bred there may have been a little-known strain called the Preanger, which was basically a cross between local mares and imported horses of desert-type. It has also been suggested that there were two breeds in the area: the Batak and the Minangkabau (named after the inland valleys). They were used to transport gold to the coast and seem to have died out as population growth led to a lack of grazing. Whatever the history, the Dutch considered it to be a sound genetic base for further outcrosses to Arabs (see pp.92–93).

The Padang has had an improving influence on a number of Indonesian ponies, including the Java pony (see opposite). Like the Java, its strength and endurance seem out of all proportion to its size. The Padang does not sweat noticeably even when working hard in considerable heat. This strong pony is used for farm work and for riding and, like the Java, it also pulls heavily laden taxi carts.

Short, muscular neck

Fairly well-formed quarters without the customary goose rump

Thick tail

Second thighs lack muscle

THE **PADANG** PONY IS ONE OF THE **EIGHT PONIES** OF **INDONESIA.**

Long cannons

Light legs

Weak pastern

IN **EARLY JAPAN, MOUNTED WARRIORS** WERE PART OF THE **ARISTOCRACY.**

Hokkaido

HEIGHT AT WITHERS	ORIGIN	COLORS
12.3–13.1 hh (130–135 cm)	Japan	Most solid colors, but commonly roan

YABUSAME

At the end of the 19th century, bigger, faster horses were imported to Japan, and European riding became popular. Today, most Japanese riders use Thoroughbred-type horses, and adopt the European style. However, the old sport of *yabusame*, in which samurai on galloping horses fire arrows at a target, has survived as a Shinto ritual.

The Hokkaido—also known as Dosanko—is strong and resilient and probably the best of Japan's native breeds.

The first horses to arrive in Japan came from Central Asia in the 3rd century CE. In the 13th century, Mongolian ponies brought during Kublai Khan's attempted invasions may have supplemented the established local stock.

Over time most of Japan's islands have developed different horse types, probably from the same equines. Kyushu has three types: Misaki, Tokara (see p.261), and Taishu. The Miyako comes from Miyako-Jima, the Noma from Shikoku, and the Kiso (see p.260) and Tohoku from Honshu. The Yonaguni is from Yonaguni island (see p.261). It is thought that ponies were taken to Hokkaido from mainland Japan when it was settled in the 15th century and that they originated from the Tohoku breeding district.

Until the 1930s, horses in Japan were used in farming, for haulage, and under pack. The cavalry rode larger horses—crosses, or second crosses, with native ponies. A few ponies still work on farms and pull sleds, and, until recently, were used in coal mines.

Today, there are about 3,000 Hokkaidos, most of which roam freely in large grazing areas. They are rounded up once a year to check their health, deworm them, and so on. Others are being raised on farms under more controlled conditions. Hokkaidos are larger than many Japanese breeds. They are extremely hardy and strong and can survive and even thrive under very severe conditions. They are used for trail riding, as pack horses, and under harness. Many are natural pacers.

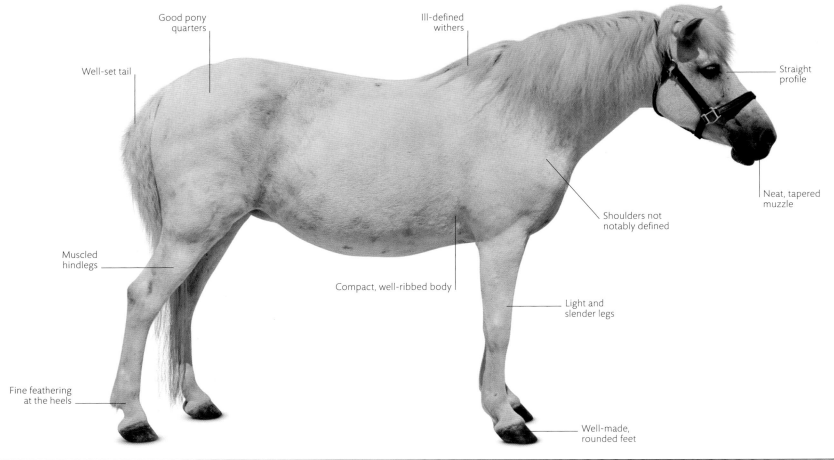

Good pony quarters

Well-set tail

Ill-defined withers

Straight profile

Neat, tapered muzzle

Muscled hindlegs

Shoulders not notably defined

Compact, well-ribbed body

Light and slender legs

Fine feathering at the heels

Well-made, rounded feet

Kiso

HEIGHT AT WITHERS	ORIGIN	COLORS
13 hh (132 cm)	Japan	Gray, brown

The Kiso is the only Japanese breed to have been bred selectively for military use.

The Kiso pony takes its name from the Kiso river valley and the mountainous region of Kiso-Sanmyaku in the Nagano prefecture, due west of Tokyo. It is said to be the only native breed on Japan's principal island, Honshu. The ancestry of the Kiso is uncertain but it is likely that the first horses introduced to the island originated from China or Central Asia.

The horses on Honshu were traditionally used for general agricultural work and as a pack animal. However, by the late Edo era (1600–1867) thousands were being bred for the army. During the reign of Emperor Meiji (1868–1912), the imperial Japanese army instituted a breeding program to develop horses of taller stature. The Kiso stallions were gelded and imported stock was used to cover the native Kiso mares. As a result, purebred Kisos almost died out. One stallion, which was kept at a religious shrine, is said to have escaped intact and his son, foaled in 1951, is the foundation sire of the modern Kiso. Despite efforts to preserve the breed, the population is still very small, numbering only a few hundred.

COMFORTABLE TRAVEL

Traveling Japanese civilian dignitaries sat on wide wooden saddles, which were covered with cloaks and bedding. The "horseman" sat cross-legged, or with his legs resting on either side of the horse's neck. Civilians rarely held the reins—that was the prerogative of the fighting man—so the horse was led by footmen.

IN 1904 THE JAPANESE AGENCY OF EQUINE AFFAIRS BANNED **BREEDING OF SMALL HORSES,** LEADING TO THE **NEAR DEMISE** OF THE KISO.

Short, thick neck

Low, flat withers

Thick tail and mane

Over-large head

Upright shoulders

Long trunk with short, sturdy legs

Strong, well-formed hooves

Tokara

	HEIGHT AT WITHERS	ORIGIN	COLORS
	13 hh (132 cm)	Kyushu, Japan	Mostly bay, brown, chestnut, roan

The Tokara is probably descended from horses brought to Japan from Korea and Mongolia in the 3rd century.

The Tokara Pony is named after its island home off the southwestern tip of Kyushu island in the Kagoshima prefecture. A small herd of ponies was discovered on one of these islands in the early 1950s by a Japanese professor from Kagoshima University. According to him, people from Kitaiga Island brought about 10 native horses with them when they moved to the islands in around 1897. Although the ponies were small owing to poor grazing, they were ridden, used for general farm work, and for sugar-cane processing.

In 1943, there were 100 ponies on the islands. In the 1960s, however, numbers declined owing to increased mechanization in farming. Some were taken to a local national park and others to a farm owned by the university's agricultural department. By the mid-1970s, the breed had almost disappeared on the islands so a breeding program was instituted using ponies that had been transferred to the mainland in the 1960s. A small population still exists in Kagoshima prefecture. Some of the ponies are kept at Hirakawa Zoo in Kagoshima.

YONAGUNI

This pony, developed in the Okinawa district of Yonaguni, is small, measuring about 11.1 hh (115 cm), and often chestnut. Its numbers dropped to about 60 in the late 20th century. A committee was formed to conserve them and now there are two herds totalling around 100 ponies. The islanders created a distinctive single-reined bridle to control their horses.

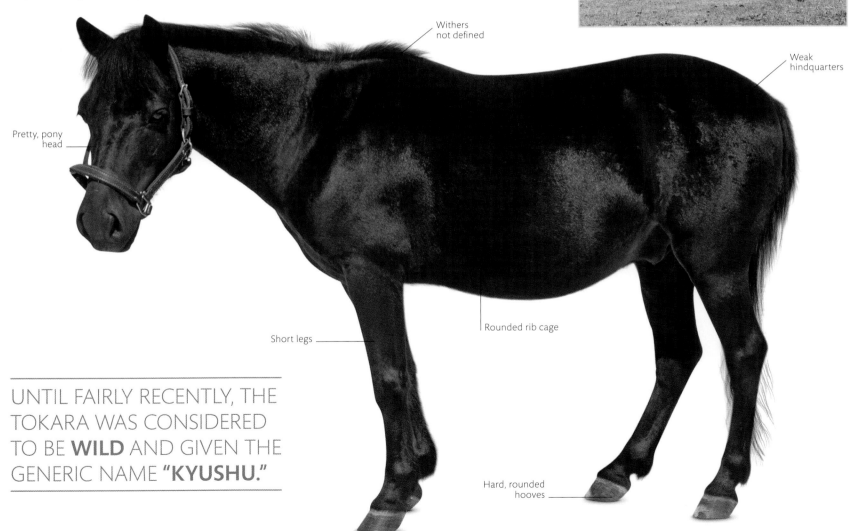

Withers not defined

Weak hindquarters

Pretty, pony head

Rounded rib cage

Short legs

Hard, rounded hooves

UNTIL FAIRLY RECENTLY, THE TOKARA WAS CONSIDERED TO BE **WILD** AND GIVEN THE GENERIC NAME **"KYUSHU."**

Australian Pony

HEIGHT AT WITHERS	ORIGIN	COLORS
12–14 hh (122–142 cm)	Australia	Any solid color, but mainly gray

With its exceptionally smooth action, long strides, and small size, this breed is ideal for children.

Horses are not indigenous to Australia, so the early Australians had to rely on imported horses and ponies to help them exploit the vast potential of their new country. In the 18th and 19th centuries, horses were brought into Australia from South Africa, Europe, particularly the UK, and elsewhere. These included Exmoors (see pp.276–77) and small, very hardy ponies from the nearby Indonesian island of Timor (see pp.252–53). A Hungarian pony, which apparently came to Australia in a circus in the mid-19th century, is also said to have had a marked influence. Several studs, based on these three breeds, were set up. Later to upgrade the stock, Arab (see pp.92–93) horses were imported from India, most of them shipped from the eastern port of Kolkata.

Other breeds that reached Australian shores included Thoroughbred (see pp.120–21), Hackney (see pp.126–27), Hackney Pony (see p.293), Welsh Mountain Pony (see pp.288–89), and Welsh Cob-types (see pp.136–37). These were crossbred, resulting in many different pony types being produced.

In 1931, the Australian Pony Stud Book Society was formed to establish a standard type. It included three sections: Shetland, Hackney Pony, and Australian. The Australian section included all the imported British mountain and moorland breeds, along with the Australian-bred stock. In 1950, a section was added for Welsh Mountain Ponies, and later volumes allowed for other imported pony breeds, such as Welsh Pony (see pp.290–91), Connemara (see pp.264–65), and New Forest (see pp.282–83).

Entry into the Australian section was upon inspection for type until 1960, when the section was closed to all stock but those from registered sires and dams.

AUSTRALIAN RIDING PONY

The seed of an idea for an elegant riding pony was sown in 1973, with the import of three pony stallions of Welsh descent. A group of Australian enthusiasts set up the Riding Pony Stud Book Society in 1975. They looked to the Welsh Pony, as well as Thoroughbreds and Arabs, to produce the type they wanted. Today the studbook has three sections, and the ponies are known for their outstanding show performances.

Well-rounded hindquarters

Well-set, perfectly straight tail

Short and straight cannon bones

Slightly crested, long and fine neck

Well-formed back and trunk

Fine head dominated by large eyes

Shoulders slope back to well-defined withers

Deep girth

ALL **AUSTRALIAN STATES** HAVE A **BRANCH** OF THE **AUSTRALIAN PONY STUD BOOK SOCIETY** WITH **11** BREEDS **REGISTERED.**

Strong, neat hooves

Connemara

HEIGHT AT WITHERS	ORIGIN	COLORS
12.2–14.2 hh (127–148 cm)	Connemara, western Ireland	Gray, black, bay, brown, dun; occasionally roan, chestnut, palomino, cream

Traditionally used for a variety of tasks on moorland farms, the hardy Connemara has tremendous staying power.

Ireland's only indigenous breed of pony originated in Connemara, a region of mountains, lakes, and moorland. Early Celtic settlers probably brought in horses, which would have interbred with native stock. Later, imported Spanish horses were crossed with this stock to produce the Irish Hobby, an ancestor of the Connemara. Barb (see pp.94–95) and Arab (see pp.92–93) blood was introduced in the 19th century.

The Irish potato famine of 1845 had a devastating effect on the Connemara, and by the 1860s, there were scarcely any left. The population picked up, however, and in 1923, when the Connemara Pony Breeders' Society was established, there were around 2,000 broodmares and 250 stallions. Government breeding programs brought in Welsh Cob (see pp.136–37) stallions, Arabs, Thoroughbreds (see pp.120–21), and Irish

Drafts (see pp.134–35). Major sires include Cannon Ball (born in 1904), Rebel (1922), and Golden Gleam (1932). Carna Dun (1950) was known for his exceptional daughters. There was also a line to the famous Arab, Naseel.

Since the closing of the studbook in 1964, it is feared that breeding with just a few popular stallions has had a negative effect. A genetic study (2003) reported that Thoroughbred was the most influential outside blood. Most ponies in the study also possessed Welsh Cob and Arab genes. About 50 percent had Irish Draft in their ancestry. The study concluded that the pony is being bred taller and losing some of its adaptation to the tough environment of its origins. There has also been a loss of genetic diversity.

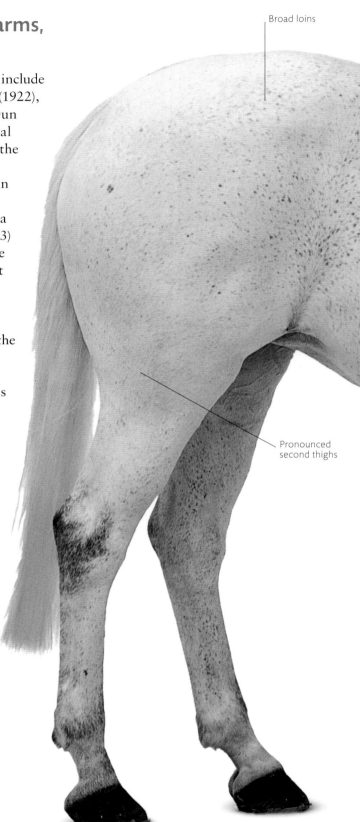

Broad loins

Pronounced second thighs

PERFORMANCE PONY

The Connemara is a brilliant performance pony—fast, courageous, and a remarkable jumper. It possesses a good, steady temperament, as well as intelligence and sure-footedness. Most of the breed also retain their physical hardiness and endurance derived from their wild, moorland environments. It is regarded as the ideal competition mount for young people and exported extensively to Europe, as well as to the US and Japan. There are breeders' societies in 16 countries.

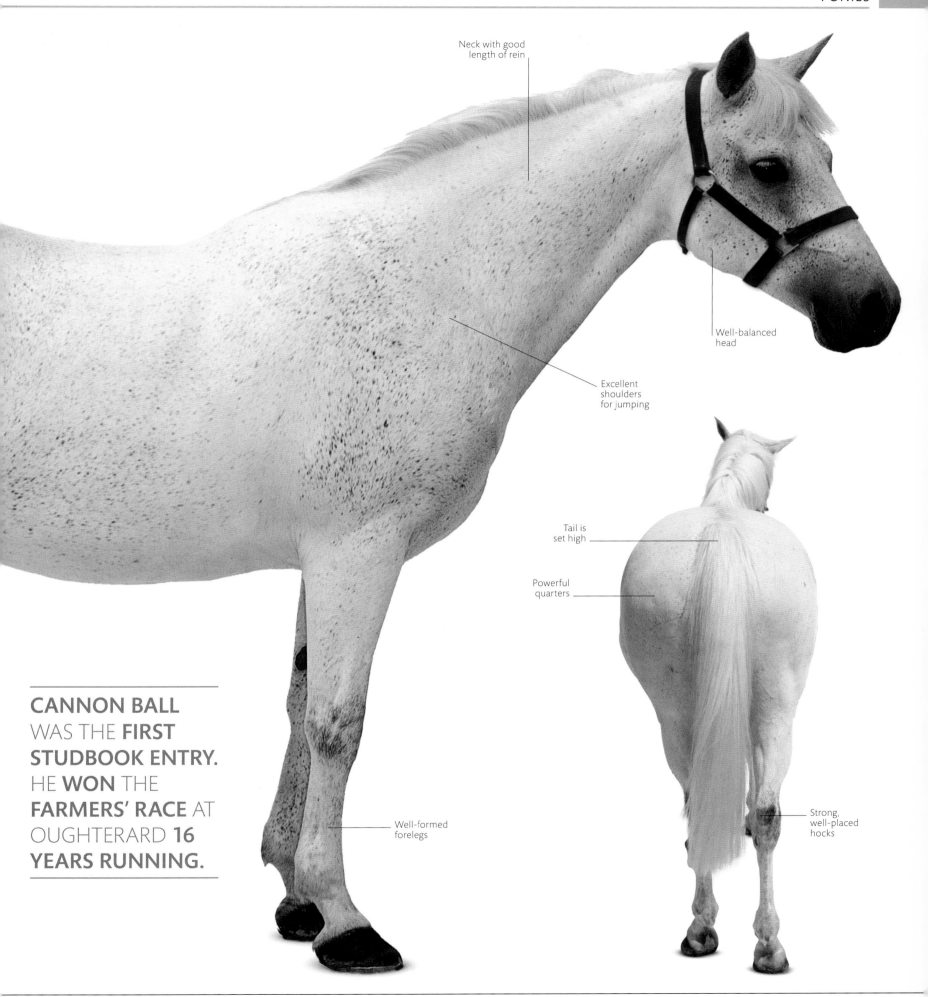

Neck with good length of rein

Well-balanced head

Excellent shoulders for jumping

Tail is set high

Powerful quarters

Well-formed forelegs

Strong, well-placed hocks

CANNON BALL WAS THE **FIRST STUDBOOK ENTRY.** HE **WON** THE **FARMERS' RACE** AT OUGHTERARD **16** YEARS RUNNING.

Learning from the land
The damp west coast of Ireland has produced a renowned pony breed. The Connemara is known for its jumping ability. Perhaps this is owing to its steep and rocky homeland.

Shetland

HEIGHT AT WITHERS	ORIGIN	COLORS
Up to 42 in (10.2 hh, 107 cm)	Shetland Islands	Any color except spotted

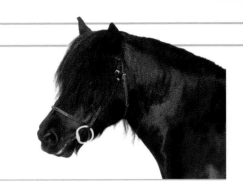

The Shetland's essential features are its general air of vitality, stamina, and robustness.

Small yet exceptionally strong and powerfully built, the Shetland Pony takes its name from the windswept Scottish islands in the far north of the UK. Excavations there unearthed bones of small ponies from the Bronze Age but the precise origins of today's breed are unknown. It appears to have genetic links with the Icelandic horse (see pp.302–303) and to some other Scandinavian breeds.

The harsh climate and rugged habitat of the Shetlands, where winters are cold and wet and forage is scarce, produced an equine of diminutive stature yet great strength and hardiness. Used to cultivate the land and to carry peat and seaweed, the Shetland was also ridden by adult males. Following the British Factories Act of 1847, which prevented women and children from working in coal mines, there was a huge demand for Shetlands as pit ponies. This docile and willing breed soon adapted to life underground, hauling heavy loads. Studs were established to develop a heavier type with the necessary bone and substance for pit work. A lighter type was popular in harness and as a children's mount.

Thousands of Shetlands were exported all over the world, many to the US and Canada. In North America, Shetlands were crossed with the Hackney Pony (see p.293) to produce the American Shetland (see pp.318–19).

The Shetland Stud Book Society was formed in 1890 and many ponies registered today are thought to trace their ancestry back to its first volumes. The two types of the 19th century have all but disappeared today, but a miniature type under 34 in (85 cm) is recognized.

Broad, exceptionally muscular loins

MINIATURE SHETLANDS

Miniature Shetlands are like their larger counterparts in every way. Away from their homeland, Shetlands make very popular children's ponies. They also go well in harness and may be seen in circus performances. They appear on stage in shows such as *Cinderella*, seemingly completely unfazed by being in the limelight. Worldwide, the Shetland has proved to be a successful breed, showing that there is still a market for an all-purpose pony of small size.

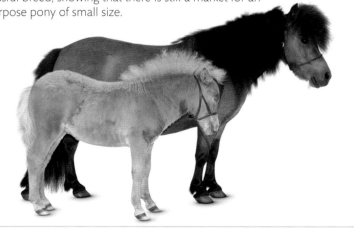

Sloped pasterns

THE **SHETLAND** GROWS A **"DOUBLE" COAT** THAT ENABLES IT TO SURVIVE **HARSH NORTHERN WINTERS.**

Small, neat ears

Well-shaped head with a broad forehead

Back is short and fairly wide

Powerful shoulders

Well-formed quarters

Thick-set, deep-ribbed body

Well-developed second thighs

Legs are short and muscular

Round, tough feet of hard blue horn

Highland

HEIGHT AT WITHERS	ORIGIN	COLORS
13–14.2 hh (132–148 cm)	Scottish Highlands and Islands, UK	All except broken colors

This is the all-purpose horse of the Scottish Highlands and Islands, particularly the Western Isles.

Ponies were living in northern Scotland after the last Ice Age and archaeological evidence shows Scandinavian horses were brought to Scotland during the Bronze Age, and later imported from Iceland. The modern Highland pony, however, is the result of numerous outcrosses.

Around 1535, King Louis XII of France gave some draft horses to James V of Scotland. These were used to improve the native breed. The Dukes of Athol introduced eastern horses in the 16th century. Spanish horses were added to the mix in the 17th and 18th centuries. In the late 19th century, John Munro-Mackenzie used the Arab Syrian to establish the Calgary strain. The first registered Highland pony was Herd Laddie by Highland Laddie, foaled in 1881. Most Highlands today have him in their pedigree.

Like the Shetland (see pp.268–69), the Highland evolved into an extremely tough, hardy breed. In the 19th century, the ponies, especially on the islands, were about 4 in (10 cm) smaller; the present size may have resulted from crossing with Clydesdales (see pp.50–51) to produce animals for forestry work. The Highland is sure-footed and strong enough to carry heavy red deer carcasses when herds are culled. It is also an ideal family pony, with a docile temperament. Very popular for pony trekking, the Highland is also shown in-hand or in riding classes. The colors are interesting and are often shades of dun: mouse, cream, yellow to gray, all with an eel stripe, and occasionally zebra markings on the upper legs and the shoulders.

A ROYAL CONNECTION

A keen horsewoman, Queen Elizabeth II, has both Highlands and Fells in the stables at Windsor Castle. Her great great grandmother Queen Victoria was fond of Scotland and spent many vacations there. In *Leaves from the Journal of our Life in the Highlands*, Queen Victoria describes a ride that must surely have been on Highlands: "We set off on ponies to go up one of the hills, Albert riding the dun pony and I the gray, attended only by Sandy McAra in the Highland dress."

Short cannons

Soft and silky feather on lower limbs

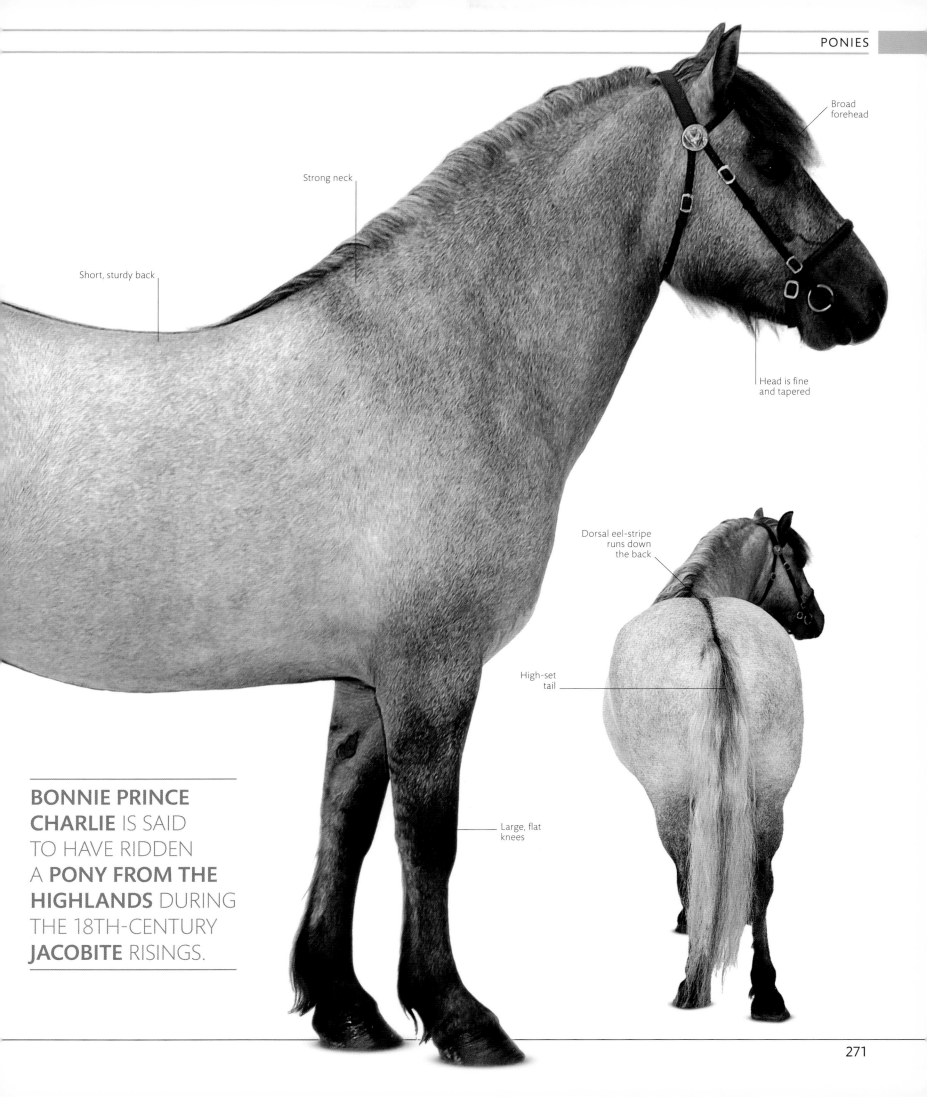

Broad forehead

Strong neck

Short, sturdy back

Head is fine and tapered

Dorsal eel-stripe runs down the back

High-set tail

Large, flat knees

BONNIE PRINCE CHARLIE IS SAID TO HAVE RIDDEN A **PONY FROM THE HIGHLANDS** DURING THE 18TH-CENTURY **JACOBITE** RISINGS.

271

Fell

HEIGHT AT WITHERS	ORIGIN	COLORS
14 hh (142 cm)	Northern England, UK	Black, brown, bay, gray is rare. No white markings

According to the breed standard, the Fell pony should be constitutionally as "hard as iron."

The Fell comes from the northern edges of the English Pennines and the wild moorlands of Westmorland and Cumberland, while the neighboring, and genetically related, Dales (see pp.274–75) belongs to the other side of the Pennines in North Yorkshire, Northumberland, and Durham. These ponies have the same origin but have developed according to the uses that have been made of them.

It is possible that the Friesian (see pp.164–65) was an early influence on the Fell. However, the greatest influence is the strong Scottish Galloway. This fleet-footed pony was the mount of raiders who operated on the Scottish borders and was later used by Scottish cattle drovers. The Galloway was a pony type produced between Nithsdale and the Mull of Galloway. Although it disappeared in the 19th century, the qualities it bequeathed to British stock are still evident. It stood between 13 hh and 14 hh (132 cm and 142 cm). It was hardy, sure-footed, possessed of great stamina, and very fast under saddle and in harness. It probably also formed part of the native horses that were bred with eastern sires during the 17th and 18th centuries and formed the basis of the English Thoroughbred (see pp.120–21).

Like the Dales, the Fell was used as a pack pony. However, the Fell is lighter than the Dales and a tremendous trotter so it was probably as popular under saddle as it was in harness. Today, it is sought after for both purposes and is, additionally, an excellent cross to produce horses of competition potential. Through the Wilson ponies, the Fell is part of the base stock of the modern Hackney Pony (see p.293).

Good pony
back end

Second
thigh is well
developed

Low,
powerful
hocks

BROUGH HILL FAIR

In its homeland, the Fell is often referred to as the Brough Hill Pony because of its association with the annual Brough Hill Fair, which was held on an open hill in Westmorland (Cumbria) between September 30 and October 1. Like the Appleby fair, it was a place for travelers to gather and sell all kinds of stock. The fair declined with the advent of the motorcar and had ceased by the 1960s, by which time Appleby had become the more important of the two fairs.

Not too fine at
the withers

Finely
chiseled
head

Tapering
muzzle

Sloped shoulders
give a long action

Strongly muscled
quarters

Deep, round-ribbed body

Luxuriant tail
and mane

FELLS CARRIED
PACK LOADS
OF ABOUT **224 LB**
(95 KG) OVER
240 MILES (384 KM)
EACH **WEEK.**

Fine feather
at the heels

Well-formed,
round feet

Dales

HEIGHT AT WITHERS	ORIGIN	COLORS
14.2 hh (147 cm)	Northern England	Mainly black, occasionally bay and brown, sometimes gray

Combining courage and stamina with a calm temperament, this super riding pony is well suited to trekking.

The Dales pony originates in northern England's eastern Pennines. It is the larger, heavier-built neighbor of the Fell (see pp.272–73). Like the Fell it has been crossbred to Friesians (see pp.164–65) and the Scottish Galloway.

In the 19th century, Dales ponies were used in lead and coal mines, as well as general farm work, and in pack trains. They are capable of handling loads well out of proportion to their size; on average they carried loads of 224 lb (100 kg).

The old-time Dales pony was noted as a great trotter in harness or under saddle, and was well able to travel 1 mile (1.6 km) in three minutes, while carrying considerable weight. To improve trotting ability, Welsh Cob (see pp.136–37) blood was introduced in the 19th century. The Dales was also crossed with Clydesdales (see pp.50–51), and by 1917 the breed was regarded as being two-thirds Clydesdale. However, its relationship with the Clydesdale was not successful and is no longer apparent. The Dales Pony Improvement Society was set up in 1916 and the Dales Pony Society in 1963.

The modern Dales pony retains the wonderful bone and clean limbs as well as the hard, blue feet for which it was justly famed. It is sure-footed, hardy, and strong. A brilliant and courageous performer in harness, it is also used as a riding pony.

UNDER THREAT

The Dales pony is listed as critical by the Rare Breeds Survival Trust. In Britain, there are fewer than 300 registered breeding mares. The Livestock Conservancy in the US records that there are fewer than 5,000 ponies worldwide. Like many native breeds, the Dales has much to offer both for riding and driving. Although enthusiasts will not allow the Dales to die out, any further reduction in the gene pool is very worrying for the future of the breed.

Large head is neat, and wide between the eyes

Strong, short back

Broad loins

Medium width muzzle

Deep girth with well-sprung ribs

Very hard feet

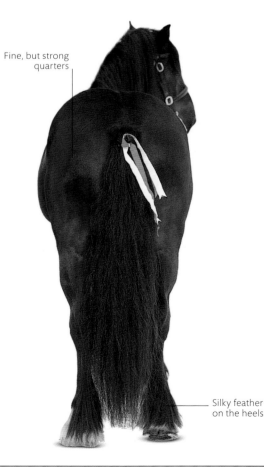

Fine, but strong quarters

Silky feather on the heels

DALES PONIES ARE EXCELLENT FOR **SNIGGING**, WHERE **TIMBER** IS **REMOVED** FROM FORESTS **WITHOUT MACHINERY**.

Double-layered, waterproof coat

Level back with breadth over the loins

Mealy-colored muzzle, with wide nostrils

Muscular development on underside of neck

Compact body, with depth through the girth

Deep, well-sprung rib cage

Short, well-spaced forelegs

Thick tail protects the hindquarters from rain and snow

BETWEEN **THE WORLD WARS,** THE **EXMOOR** WAS WIDELY USED AS **A CHILDREN'S PONY.**

Exmoor

HEIGHT AT WITHERS	ORIGIN	COLORS
12.2–12.3 hh (127–130 cm)	England	Bay, brown, or dun

The Exmoor pony is considered to be the oldest and purest descendent of Britain's native ponies.

Ponies have run wild on Exmoor in Devon for centuries. Unlike with most British native breeds, there have been few attempts to outcross them, probably due in part to the remoteness of their high moorland habitat. They have adapted to the harsh climatic conditions and relatively poor grazing, which means outcrosses to more refined breeds would not be beneficial. The Exmoor has a few characteristics that are signs of its adaptation to its harsh environment. These include fleshy "toad" eyes, "ice" tails, which have a thick, fanlike growth of short hair at the top, and a double-layered winter coat. It also has a distinctive jaw formation.

This pony is enormously strong, well balanced, and capable of carrying weight well out of proportion to its size, as well as galloping and jumping well. Today, it is less popular for children, but, if properly schooled, it does make a good, tough pony for a keen child or a small adult. As harness ponies, Exmoors have great stamina. They also make valuable base stock for breeding bigger horses.

The purity and quality of the herds still running on Exmoor are jealously safeguarded by the Exmoor Pony Society. Ponies bred away from the moor tend to lose type, so it is necessary for the breeders to return to the original stock to maintain the original character. In a sense, the Exmoor herds remain wild. Like many tough, native ponies, Exmoors have become appreciated for conservation grazing—they are turned out on scrublands to help restore or improve habitats and increase biodiversity.

Short, strong hindlegs

Hard, neat feet

BODMIN PONY

Unlike neighboring Devon, Cornwall has no true native ponies. The ponies that do live all year on Bodmin moor are not of any recognized breed or type. Taken off the moor and properly cared for, they can reach 14.2 hh (147 cm) or more and often make good riding ponies. In recent years, a collapse in the value of rough moorland ponies—fewer children are riding them—has led to these ponies being neglected, with some even dying of starvation.

THE **DARTMOOR** IS CONSIDERED TO BE ONE OF THE **MOST ELEGANT** RIDING PONIES IN THE WORLD.

Dartmoor

HEIGHT AT WITHERS	ORIGIN	COLORS
Not exceeding 12.2 hh (127 cm)	England	Bay, black, brown, and gray; occasionally chestnut and roan

DARTMOOR HILL PONIES

Long valued as wonderful children's ponies, the small, hill ponies that are still widely grazed on Dartmoor have recently lost popularity. However, they are vital for the management of the moor and there are several projects aimed at recreating a market for them. Recent efforts have been directed toward reducing foal numbers by using contraceptives, and selling the ponies for meat. There are also local enthusiasts who give them basic training which makes them more likely to find riding homes.

This breed is known for its strength and resilience, as well as its beauty.

This beautiful breed originated on the rough moorland of England's Dartmoor Forest. Unlike the Exmoor Pony (see pp.276–77), the Dartmoor has been influenced by different breeds and subjected to numerous outcrosses, partly because its environment was easily accessible by land and sea.

There is an early connection with the Old Devon Pack Horse, which was drawn from both Exmoor and Dartmoor blood, and the Cornish Goonhilly Pony. Both are now extinct. Up to the end of the 19th century, among the many breeds used as crosses with the Dartmoor were trotting Roadsters, Welsh Ponies, Cobs (see pp.130–31), Arabs (see pp.92–93)—particularly Dwarka, a bay stallion—small Thoroughbreds (see pp.120–21), and some Exmoors. There was also one disastrous experiment at the height of the Industrial Revolution using Shetlands (see pp.268–69), in an attempt to produce pit ponies. As a result, the tough Dartmoor of good riding type almost disappeared. However, the breed was saved by the introduction of Welsh Mountain Ponies, a Fell (see pp.272–73), and the polo pony stallion Lord Polo. During World War II, the moor was used for army training, and breed numbers fell drastically. It was saved by a few dedicated breeders.

There are still ponies on Dartmoor, but most are scrub stock. Today, the quality ponies are bred extensively at studs in the UK and mainland Europe. In 1988, the Duchy of Cornwall set up a program to help preserve the "wild" Dartmoor Pony, an endeavor supported by both Dartmoor National Park and the breed society.

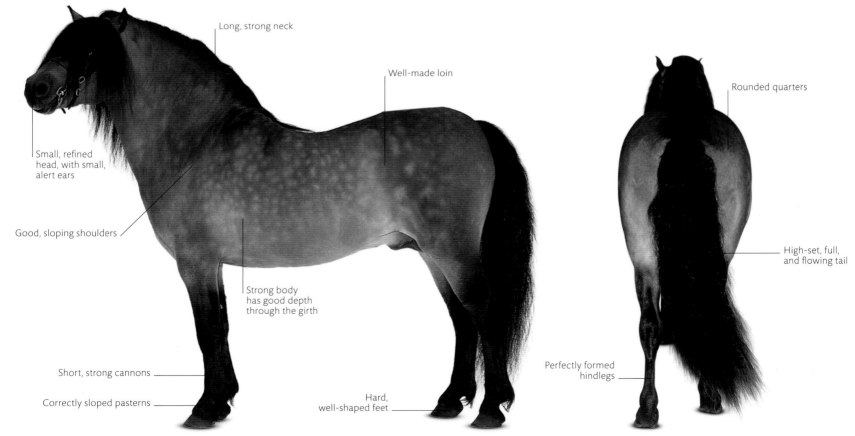

Long, strong neck

Well-made loin

Rounded quarters

Small, refined head, with small, alert ears

Good, sloping shoulders

High-set, full, and flowing tail

Strong body has good depth through the girth

Short, strong cannons

Correctly sloped pasterns

Hard, well-shaped feet

Perfectly formed hindlegs

Moorland nibblers
Small hardy ponies are part of the scenery on Dartmoor. They have contributed greatly to the open appearance of the moorland and are valuable conservation grazers.

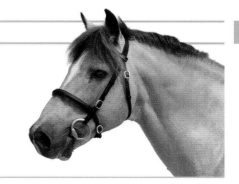

New Forest Pony

HEIGHT AT WITHERS	ORIGIN	COLORS
Up to 14.2 hh (148 cm)	New Forest, England	Any, except piebald, skewbald, spotted or blue-eyed cream

IN THE FOREST

There are around 3,000 ponies roaming the New Forest and although they may seem wild, they all have owners. The ponies are carefully watched over by agisters, specifically employed for the task. Every summer and fall the ponies are drifted (rounded up) to be checked. Colts are removed before they can breed, along with other ponies that are ready to be sold. Sales are held several times a year.

Ponies are said to have roamed the New Forest, an area of pastureland and forest, since the end of the last Ice Age.

The New Forest is an accessible tract of land that was once crossed by well-used travelers' routes. As a consequence, the New Forest Pony has very mixed origins. Although later the area became a royal hunting ground, forest-dwellers known as Commoners had the right to put their ponies out to graze, and the forest still supports herds of feral ponies.

In 1765, a Thoroughbred (see pp.120–21) stallion called Marske was brought to the forest after being sold by his owner, the Duke of Cumberland. The sire of Eclipse, possibly the greatest racehorse of all, Marske serviced forest mares for a short time until he went back to stud. In 1889, Queen Victoria lent an Arab and a Barb stallion to improve the stock, which had degenerated. Subsequently, Lords Cecil and Lucas introduced Highlands (see pp.270–71), Fells (see pp.272–73), Dales (see pp.274–75), Dartmoors (see pp.278–79),

Exmoors (see pp.276–77), and Welsh ponies (see pp.290–91). Another major influence was the polo pony (see pp.238–39) stallion, Field Marshall, out of a Welsh mare. By 1910 there was an established studbook.

The modern, commercially viable New Forest Pony is mostly stud-bred but retains the character and movement inherited from its natural environment. The ponies have sloped shoulders, making them good for riding, and a typically long, low action that is particularly marked at the canter, the Forester's best pace. They are sure-footed, excellent performers, and very strong; the larger ones can easily carry adults. The New Forest attracts many visitors and the ponies that roam at large have grown used to human contact. They have a calm temperament and are easily handled. They are said to be less sharp, or cunning, than some native breeds.

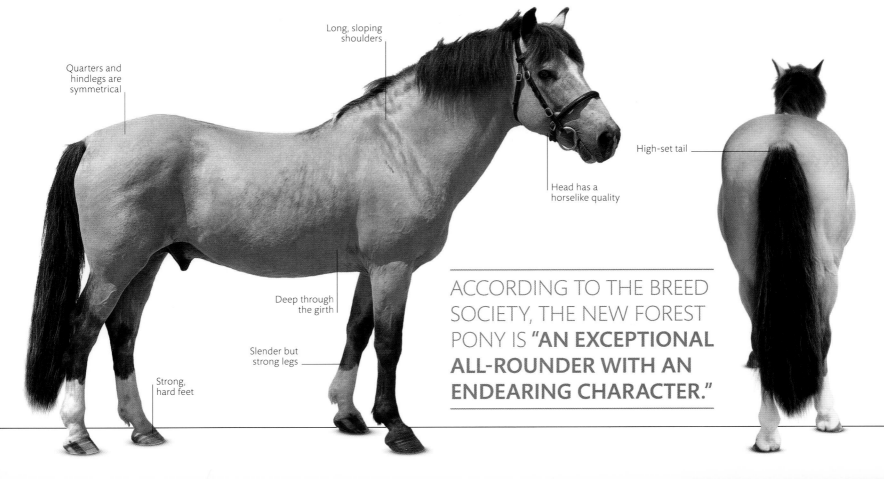

Quarters and hindlegs are symmetrical

Long, sloping shoulders

Head has a horselike quality

High-set tail

Deep through the girth

Slender but strong legs

Strong, hard feet

ACCORDING TO THE BREED SOCIETY, THE NEW FOREST PONY IS **"AN EXCEPTIONAL ALL-ROUNDER WITH AN ENDEARING CHARACTER."**

Lundy

HEIGHT AT WITHERS	ORIGIN	COLORS
13.2 hh (137 cm)	England	Mainly cream, dun, and bay

This distinctive breed evolved from a herd based on the island of Lundy off the coast of North Devon.

In 1928 the then owner of Lundy, Martin Coles Harman, brought a group of mainly New Forest (see pp.282–83) ponies to the island. After an eventful sea trip, the ponies had to swim from the boat to reach the shore. One of two stallions included in the group was of a finer type and, not surprisingly, he and his offspring did not thrive in the harsh winter conditions on the island. Later, Welsh (see pp.288–89) and Connemara (see pp.264–65) stallions were taken to Lundy and were far more successful in producing useful, hardy progeny. The Connemara cross is responsible for the distinctive Lundy pony-type seen today, although more New Forest stallions were also used in the 1970s. An influential Connemara sire was Rosenharley Peadar.

The Lundy herd was moved to Cornwall in 1980, and four years later the Lundy Breed Society was established. The ponies are bred in Cornwall and North Devon with selected mares and their foals sent back to the island to maintain stocking levels at about 20. Lundy ponies are hardy and good-tempered, and make excellent mounts for children.

LUNDY ISLAND

A granite outcrop 3 ½ miles (5.6 km) long by ½ mile (0.8 km) wide, Lundy Island rises out of the sea 12 miles (19 km) off the British coast of Devon, where the Bristol Channel meets the Atlantic. It is open to the prevailing south-westerly gales on the west side, but is more sheltered on the east. It is rich in flora and fauna, including seabirds and seals, as well as the Lundy pony. An area of the sea around it became Britain's first Marine Conservation Zone in 2010.

Adequately long and muscled neck

Sloping shoulders

Neat head with alert expression

Well-made quarters

Compact body

Muscled second thighs

Sufficient girth

Sound feet

THE ISLAND PONIES ARE **SEMI-FERAL** AND RECEIVE LITTLE **ATTENTION** APART FROM **VETERINARY CARE** AND **HOOF TRIMMING.**

Eriskay

HEIGHT AT WITHERS	ORIGIN	COLORS
12–13.2 hh (122–137 cm)	Scotland	Mainly gray, but occasionally black or bay

Sure-footed, active, and with a friendly temperament, the modern Eriskay is an ideal children's mount.

The ponies on Eriskay are thought to be final survivors of the original equines that populated many of Scotland's Western Isles. Until the mid-19th century, the ponies on these islands were the only form of transportation and would also have been used for every sort of task on the crofts (small farms) that enabled the islanders to eke out a living in this tough environment. The ponies carried peat and seaweed in creels, a kind of basketwork pannier fitted either side of the back, pulled carts over the rough ground, and carried children to school.

While on the other more accessible islands other breeds were imported including Fjords (see pp.306–307), Arabs (see pp.92–93), and Clydesdales (see pp.50–51), Eriskay's isolation meant that the ponies remained untouched. Even so, with mechanization their numbers decreased and by the 1970s, there were only around 20 ponies on the island. At this point, enthusiasts sought to reestablish the breed, setting up an active Eriskay Pony Society. The number of ponies has risen although the breed is still classified as critical by the Rare Breeds Survival Trust.

MADE TO ENDURE

Like many native British breeds, the Eriskay developed to withstand tough environmental conditions with little protection from the wet, wind, and cold. Any grass that does grow on the island is tough and lacks in nutrition, so the diet of the free-roaming Eriskay was meager. The ponies frequently augmented their food by eating the seaweed on the shoreline. Like the Shetland (see pp.268–69), they grow dense, waterproof coats and thick protective tails in winters and have unsurpassed qualities of hardiness and endurance.

FROM A LOW POINT OF JUST **20 PUREBRED PONIES,** THERE ARE NOW **ABOUT 420 ERISKAYS WORLDWIDE.**

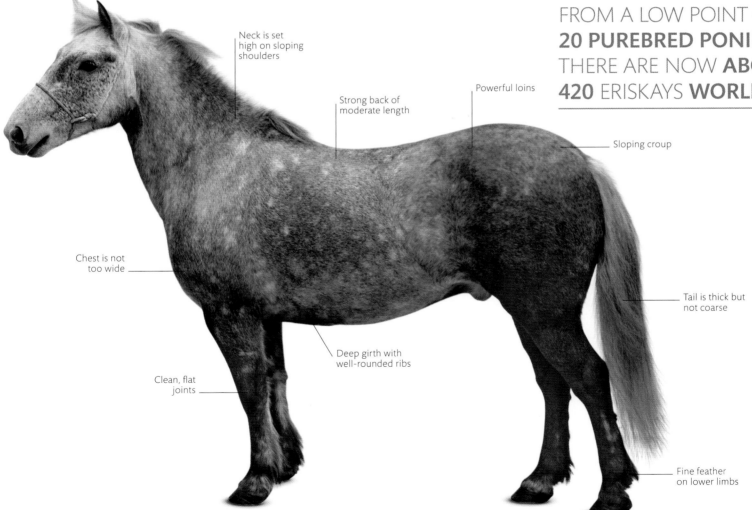

Neck is set high on sloping shoulders

Strong back of moderate length

Powerful loins

Sloping croup

Chest is not too wide

Tail is thick but not coarse

Deep girth with well-rounded ribs

Clean, flat joints

Fine feather on lower limbs

Enough to eat
It may not look like it, but there is plenty for these Eriskay ponies to live on. The ponies that live in extreme conditions around Britain are all adapted to survive on very poor grazing.

Welsh Mountain Pony

HEIGHT AT WITHERS	ORIGIN	COLORS
Up to 12 hh (122 cm)	Wales, UK	All solid colors, especially gray

THE COLOR GRAY

While there are many chestnut Welsh Mountain Ponies, gray remains the most common color. Glassalt—born in 1891—was black, but his sire, Flower of Wales was gray. After covering Dyoll Moonlight, he was gelded, presumably because he was considered "a little plain in the head" by Meuric Lloyd. This plainness may have been emphasized by the stallion's white blaze.

The Welsh Mountain is considered by many to be the most beautiful of the British native ponies.

The Welsh Pony and Cob Stud Book, established around 1901, is divided into four sections. The Welsh Mountain Pony, which is the smallest of the four Welsh breeds, occupies section A. It is considered the foundation for the three larger types.

Two sires of noted influence on this attractive pony were a small 18th-century Thoroughbred named Merlin, descended from the Darley Arabian, and Apricot, described as a Barb-Arab out of a Welsh mare. Since 1901, however, the refined and distinct appearance of the Mountain Pony has been produced by careful selection. The "founding father" of the modern breed was the stallion Dyoll Starlight, bred by Meuric Lloyd. He may have carried Arab blood through his dam Moonlight. After Dyoll Starlight, came Coed Coch Glyndwr, whose dam was Starlight's granddaughter.

The modern Welsh Mountain Pony is distinctive in appearance and notable for its powerful action, intelligence, and hardiness—a legacy of the rough terrain and harsh environment of the Welsh hills. It is a superb children's riding pony and is exceptional in harness. Exported all over the world, it is one of the finest foundations for producing bigger ponies and horses, passing on qualities of bone, substance, and constitutional soundness. Along with the Welsh Pony, section B (see pp.290–91), it is much used in the breeding of the Riding Pony (see p.292).

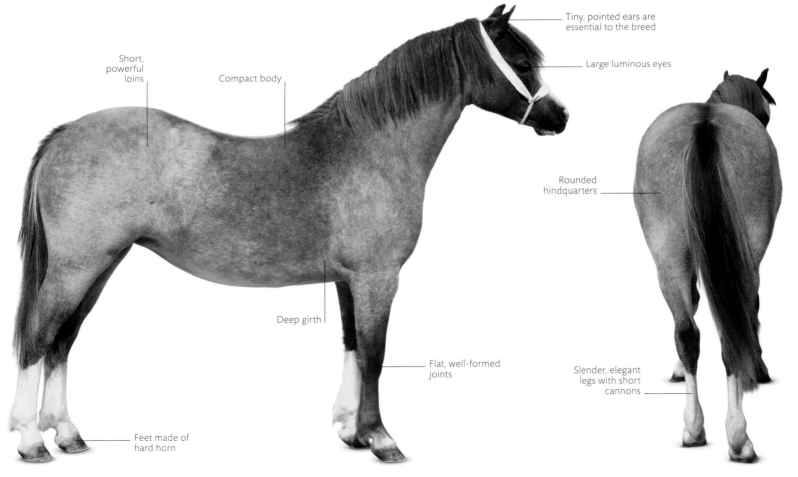

Tiny, pointed ears are essential to the breed

Large luminous eyes

Short, powerful loins

Compact body

Rounded hindquarters

Deep girth

Flat, well-formed joints

Slender, elegant legs with short cannons

Feet made of hard horn

DYOLL STARLIGHT'S SKELETON WAS PRESENTED TO THE **NATURAL HISTORY MUSEUM, LONDON** IN **1935**.

THE WELSH PONY HAS "QUALITY, **RIDING ACTION, ADEQUATE BONE** AND **SUBSTANCE,** HARDINESS AND CONSTITUTION."

Welsh Pony

HEIGHT AT WITHERS	**ORIGIN**	**COLORS**
Up to 13.2 hh (137 cm)	Wales, UK	All, except piebald and skewbald

WELSH PONY OF COB TYPE

This pony is listed in section C of the WPCS studbook. Like the section D, it is dual-purpose being suitable for both ride and drive. Section Cs are smaller than Ds, being up to 13.2 hh (137 cm), but they have every bit of the same determined character. Known for their ability to trot easily for miles, they are also comfortable to ride at canter. The Arab influence can often be seen in the section C's neat and attractive head.

A riding pony of quality, the Welsh Pony retains the spirited character that typifies the Welsh breeds.

This riding pony, which occupies Section B of the Welsh Pony and Cob Stud Book, is not as true to the original Welsh type as the Mountain Pony (see pp.288–89) and occasionally appears to be too close to the Thoroughbred-type Riding Pony (see p.292).

The early ponies of the "old breed" were often the result of crosses between Welsh Mountain mares and Cob-sized stallions, upgraded by the use of Arabs (see pp.92–93) and small Thoroughbreds (see pp.120–21). These ponies lived on the mountain and were ridden by shepherds and hunters. The modern ponies are much improved in quality, scope, and action—characteristics that can be traced back to two stallions: Tanybwlch Berwyn (1924) and Criban Victor (1944). The most important foundation sire,

Tanybwlch Berwyn, was by a Barb (see pp.94–95) called Sahara. His dam was the granddaughter of the Welsh Mountain Pony sire, Dyoll Starlight. Criban Victor had connections to the Mountain Pony through his grandfather Coed Coch Glyndwr (the foundation stallion of the famous Welsh stud, Coed Coch) and combined both substance and quality. Additional evidence of the strong eastern influence can be seen in the lines derived from the celebrated Arab sires Skowronek and Raseem, both owned by Lady Wentworth of the Crabbet Stud.

As a riding pony, the Welsh Pony's refinement and low, long-striding action have brought great success in the show ring and in competition. Most Welsh Ponies retain the hardiness of constitution that is a result of their native habitat.

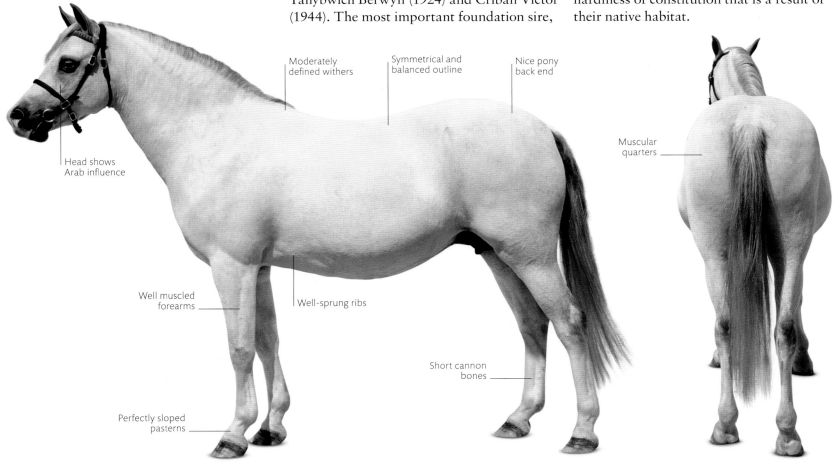

Moderately defined withers

Symmetrical and balanced outline

Nice pony back end

Muscular quarters

Head shows Arab influence

Well muscled forearms

Well-sprung ribs

Short cannon bones

Perfectly sloped pasterns

Riding Pony

	HEIGHT AT WITHERS	ORIGIN	COLORS
	12.2–14.2 hh (127–147 cm)	UK	All solid colors

SHOW PONY

Studs producing Riding Ponies are to be found throughout the UK and Ireland. Show classes for Riding Ponies are a prominent feature at all of the principal British horse shows. In the British show ring, Riding Ponies compete in three height divisions—up to 12.2 hh (127 cm), up to 13.2 hh (134 cm), and up to 14.2 hh (147 cm).

Arguably the most perfectly proportioned equine, the British Riding Pony was developed for the show ring.

Over a period of no more than half a century, a group of British breeders skilfully amalgamated various breeds and the resulting high-quality pony is a remarkable accomplishment. The foundation stock was largely a mix of Welsh ponies and, to a lesser extent, others ponies with Welsh blood, such as the Dartmoor (see pp.278–79). These were carefully crossed with small Thoroughbred (see pp.120–21) sires of polo pony type and Arab (see pp.92–93) blood was then introduced. At least one notable strain of Riding Pony is descended from a celebrated gray Arab stallion, Naseel, which originated in County Meath, Ireland.

Although the outline of the Riding Pony is that of a high-quality Thoroughbred in miniature and the action is similarly free and low, the Riding Pony should retain the bone and substance of a native pony. It is not a horse and there should be no loss of the essential pony look. The ponies also need to display perfect manners and have a good temperament as they are ridden by children. The breed standard calls for a pony to be elegant, particularly in motion, but to have quality bone. "The action should be true, straight and floating, covering the ground with effortless ease." The Working Hunter Pony is a derivation of the type.

Small, mobile ears

Skin covering the head is thin, with visible veins

Long, graceful neck

Back of medium length

High, well-set tail

Well-muscled quarters

Small muzzle with large nostrils

Soft, silky tail and mane

Long, well-sloped shoulder blade

Depth through girth

Long hindlegs

Short cannons

THE **RIDING PONY** IS THE **YOUNG RIDER'S EQUIVALENT** OF THE **THOROUGHBRED** SHOW HACK.

Hackney Pony

HEIGHT AT WITHERS	ORIGIN	COLORS
12.2–14 hh (127–142 cm)	Cumbria, UK	Solid colors from chestnut to black

AMERICAN HACKNEY PONY

The Hackney Pony has a huge following in the US, where there are various show classes aimed at slightly differently produced and turned out ponies: the speedy Roadster (below 13 hh; 132 cm), the high-stepping Cob Tail, the Long Tail, which is 12.2 hh (127 cm) or less, and the Pleasure Pony, which must be a pleasure to drive. They are also shown in hand. In the US the maximum height is 14.2 hh (147 cm)

This purpose-bred harness pony is small in stature but big in showiness and charisma.

In the UK, the Hackney Pony has the same studbook as the Hackney Horse (see pp.126–27). They share a great deal of common ancestry in that both are descended from the Norfolk and Yorkshire Trotters of the 18th and 19th centuries. However, the Hackney Pony is a real pony with pony character, not simply a little horse.

In essence, the Hackney Pony was the creation of Christopher Wilson of Kirkby Lonsdale in Cumbria. Using local Fell (see pp.272–73) ponies with occasional Welsh outcrosses, he had obtained a distinctive type by the 1880s. Wilson's most prized pony was his champion stallion, Sir George, who was by a Yorkshire Trotter. Via Norfolk Phenomenon, his line could be traced back to the first notable Thoroughbred racehorse, Flying Childers. Sir George's female progeny were mated back to their sire to produce elegant ponies with brilliant harness action. Their height was limited by wintering them on the fells, which also ensured they had a very hardy constitution. The modern Hackney Pony is confined largely to the show ring.

Well-muscled neck

Head often held high

Fine head with tapering muzzle

Low withers

Well-formed croup

Exceptionally strong, broad shoulders

Slender quarters

Fine forelegs

Hock joints set low for high action

Feet allowed to grow longer than usual

THE HACKNEY PONY HAS A **NATURALLY BRILLIANT, BRISK, HIGH-STEPPING ACTION** IN HARNESS.

Sorraia

HEIGHT AT WITHERS	ORIGIN	COLORS
14–14.2 hh (142–147 cm)	Portugal	Dun-gray (grulla)

ASTURCÓN

Standing at 11.2–12.2 hh (117–127 cm), the usually dark colored Asturcón originates in northern Spain and is thought to be a cross between Sorraias and Garranos. However, the Asturcón paces, meaning it moves both legs on one side then the other, which makes it a comfortable ride and indicates the presence of another ancestor since neither the Sorraia nor the Garrano pace naturally.

The Sorraia is thought to be a direct ancestor of the renowned Andalucian and Lusitano breeds.

It is probable that the indigenous horses of the Iberian Peninsula were the first to be domesticated in Europe. The Sorraia is considered to be one of their descendants and, as such, represents an important link to Iberian horses of the past.

The Sorraia once roamed the plains between the rivers Sor and Raia—running through both Spain and Portugal—from which it takes its name. For centuries, local "cowboys" rode the Sorraia and used it for a variety of light agricultural tasks. With mechanization, the ponies were no longer needed and the stock degenerated rapidly. Fortunately, in the 1930s, zoologist Dr. Ruy d'Andrade kept and studied a small herd of

Sorraias. His work led to efforts to conserve the breed. Today, are two separate herds, one each in Portugal and Germany. The Portuguese herd initially comprised only 10 individuals (one a pregnant mare) with a Criollo stallion being introduced in 1948. The German herd was created from three stallions and three mares—so the genetic diversity is very limited. The Sorraia remains critically endangered.

The modern Sorraia, though subject to inbreeding, retains the hardiness of its ancestors, is resistant to heat and cold, and thrives on sparse vegetation. It has a free, ground-covering stride with some knee action and subtle, elastic movements.

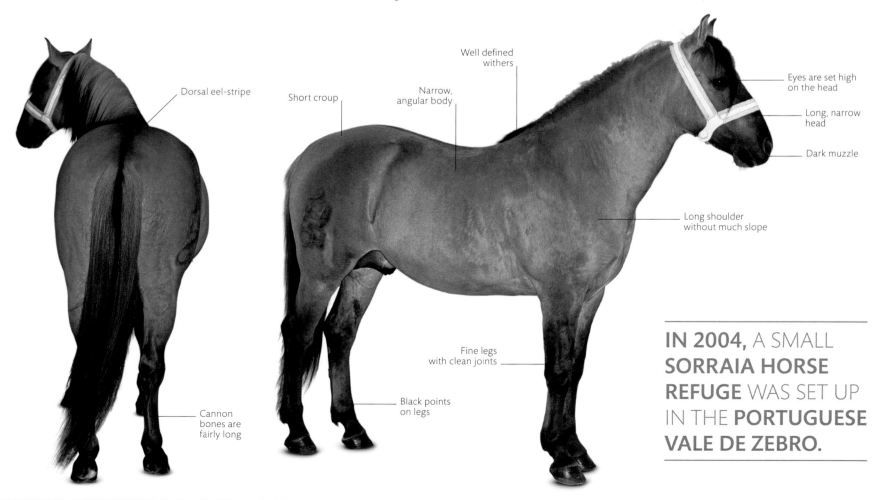

Dorsal eel-stripe

Short croup

Narrow, angular body

Well defined withers

Eyes are set high on the head

Long, narrow head

Dark muzzle

Long shoulder without much slope

Fine legs with clean joints

Black points on legs

Cannon bones are fairly long

IN 2004, A SMALL **SORRAIA HORSE REFUGE** WAS SET UP IN THE **PORTUGUESE VALE DE ZEBRO.**

Bardigiano

HEIGHT AT WITHERS	ORIGIN	COLORS
13.1–14.1 hh (134–145 cm)	Northern Apennines, Italy	Mostly bay

HIDDEN IN THE MOUNTAINS

It was important to find some purebred stock to rescue the Bardigiano from extinction. This was tricky because the ponies tended to stay in their mountain pastures for nine months of the year. Luckily, high in the mountains, local farmers had quietly maintained a small group of horses with the original characteristics of the breed and these were used to regenerate this pony.

The Bardigiano takes its name from Bardi, a small town in a hilly area to the west of Bologna.

The Romans are said to have introduced horses into Italy from Spain, Iran, and Noricum (a vassal province of the Roman Empire corresponding to modern Austria). The most attractive but least known of Italian breeds, the Bardigiano, is thought to have originally derived from these. There may be some eastern influence in the Bardigiano, which also resembles two other breeds: the Asturcón (see opposite) of the mountainous regions of northern Spain and the oldest of the British native breeds, the Exmoor pony (see pp.276–77).

After World War I, the military used these ponies to produce mules and the pure breed declined and almost died out. The situation worsened later when stallions of several different breeds were brought to the area, diluting the natural traits of the remaining animals. However, in 1972 the local agricultural association decided to try and resurrect the breed (see box, left). By the late 1970s, the Bardigiano was officially recognized and a breed standard set up.

The Bardigiano is a working mountain pony, physically equipped for use on rough, steep terrain at high altitudes. Hardy, quick-moving, and sure-footed in difficult mountain conditions, it is also strongly built and able to carry a pack saddle. Today, the Bardigiano is a popular trekking pony.

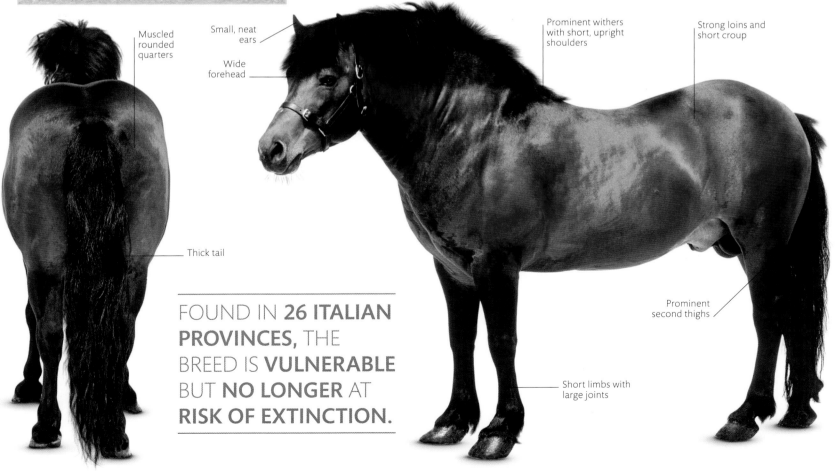

Muscled rounded quarters

Small, neat ears

Wide forehead

Prominent withers with short, upright shoulders

Strong loins and short croup

Thick tail

Prominent second thighs

Short limbs with large joints

FOUND IN **26 ITALIAN PROVINCES,** THE BREED IS **VULNERABLE** BUT **NO LONGER** AT **RISK OF EXTINCTION.**

Ariégeois

HEIGHT AT WITHERS	ORIGIN	COLORS
14.1–14.3 hh (145–150 cm)	France	Solid black

SUMMER PASTURES

Ariège is known for its annual transhumance (migration), a traditional practice that was revived in 2000. In June, cattle, sheep, and horses, including many Ariégeois ponies are moved to summer pastures at around 4,900 ft (1,500 m) above sea level. In October, they return to the valleys for the winter. An experienced mare, wearing a bell, leads the herd. Life in the high pastures maintains the constitutional toughness of the ponies and keeps them sure-footed and able to fend for themselves.

Tough, hardy, and able to withstand severe winters, the Ariégeois is a true mountain pony.

This black pony or small horse originated in the eastern Pyrenees, the snow-capped mountains separating France from the Iberian peninsula. At its source, the Ariège river, from which the breed's English name is derived, forms part of the border with Andorra and the old type of "unimproved" Ariégeois may still be found living semi-wild in the high valleys of this region.

Over the years, the Ariégeois was probably crossed with heavy pack horses, which would have passed through the region, to add substance, and the breed was also influenced by eastern blood. Later, the ponies were crossed with heavy draft breeds, such as the Percheron (see pp.62–63) and the Breton (see pp.68–69). Selective breeding started in around 1908, and the studbook was established in 1948 to conserve the breed. However, Arab blood was then used to upgrade the ponies.

The modern Ariégeois bears a very strong resemblance to the British Fell pony (see pp.272–73) and the native habitat of both is very similar. Such terrain is home to small wild ponies. With little breeding supervision, the ponies in this region would naturally be pony-sized, around 13–14.1 hh (132–145 cm). The size now given in the breed standard is probably due to crossbreeding for increased size.

The pony was traditionally employed on upland farms where the ground was rough and steeply sloping, and machinery was impractical. In its native region, the Ariégeois is still used in forestry, but it is primarily a recreational breed and very popular for trail-riding. Outside the Ariège department, the focus has changed to improving this agile breed for equestrian sports, such as harness driving, jumping, eventing, and stunt riding.

Flat forehead and bright, expressive eyes

Long, strong back

Sloped croup with low-set tail

Slightly heavy forehand

Short legs, with short cannons

Dense hoof makes shoeing unnecessary

Hindlegs tend to be cow-hocked

Waterproof, black coat with reddish highlights in winter

Thick tail protects against the cold

Slightly feathered heel

THIS BREED'S **FRENCH** NAME, *CHEVAL DE MÉRENS,* REFERS TO A **VILLAGE** IN THE UPPER **ARIÈGE VALLEY.**

Landais

HEIGHT AT WITHERS	**ORIGIN**	**COLORS**
11.1–13 hh (114–132 cm)	Landes, France	Bay, brown, chestnut, black, occasionally gray

FRENCH NATIONAL STUDS

In 1665, French politician Jean-Baptiste Colbert founded the first of 20 *Haras nationaux* with the aim of producing cavalry horses. Still funded by the state, the studs, now part of the IFCE (The French Institute of the Horse and Riding), focus on conserving French breeds, and introducing horses to new generations. Ariègeois (see pp.296–97), Landais, and Pottok are kept at Pau-Gélos (pictured here).

This rustic yet remarkable French native is now an endangered breed.

Also known as the Barthais, the Landais pony is derived from the semi-wild ponies that lived along the Ardour river valley in southwest France. Those from the Landais marshes around Dax were slightly smaller than those from Barthes plains, and it is this latter type that survived to the present day.

Arab (see pp.92–93) blood was introduced in the late 19th century, and again in 1913, when there were about 2,000 ponies in the Landes area. After World War II, the Landais came close to extinction, with only around 150 surviving ponies. Inbreeding became a problem and was remedied by outcrossing with Welsh Section B (see pp.290–91) stallions, with additional Arab blood. Today's Landais is the result of this

work and a more recent and much improved selective breeding program. A well-made riding pony, it is also hardy and frugal, adapts easily to heat and cold, and is docile and intelligent.

For a while, French pony clubs, formed in the early 1970s, encouraged Landais breeding. The pony also played a part as base stock of the Poney Français de Selle (see pp.300–301). Somewhat ironically, this new breed has now eclipsed the Landais in the show ring and threatens its existence, since breeders must choose between breeding the more popular Poney de Selle or the rather rustic Landais. Today, numbers are very low (36 foals born in 2013) and the breed is critically endangered.

IN 1976, A LANDAIS CALLED **DRAGON** WAS RIDDEN **AROUND FRANCE**—A JOURNEY OF **1,864 MILES** (3,000 KM), WHICH TOOK **100 DAYS**.

Short, pointy ears

Straight profile

Thick mane and silky coat

Strong shoulders with reasonable slope

Sloping croup

Rounded quarters

Broad, strong forehand

Well-muscled hindlegs

Low-set tail

Small amount of feather

Pottok

HEIGHT AT WITHERS	ORIGIN	COLORS
11.1–14.2 hh (115–147 cm)	Basque country of France and Spain	Black, bay, piebald

MOUNTAIN POTTOK

Born and raised in the mountains, the smaller of the two Pottok ponies is hardy and sure-footed. They were popular as circus ponies in the 16th century, and many were used as pit ponies in the mines of France and Britain. They may have been used to carry contraband over the steep Pyrenean trails before World War II.

This tough, but not unattractive, little pony originated in the Pyrenees on the borders between France and Spain.

Closest genetically to the Basque Mountain Horse, the Pottok is usually described as being wild or semi-feral, although it is perhaps less so today, since official bodies, such as the National Pottok Association and the French national studs, are responsible for its development. This breed is rather coarser than the Landais (opposite) and, like it, has been crossed to selected Arab (see pp.92–93) and Welsh Section B (see pp.290–91) stallions to reduce inbreeding and improve the stock.

Pottoks were recognized as a breed in 1970. The official French breed standard distinguishes two types: mountain and plains. The mountain ones (11.1–13 hh; 115–132 cm) roam free in the mountains for nine months of the year. They are now mostly piebald. The plains Pottoks are selections of the mountain ones. They are born and raised in better conditions, so they grow taller—11.3–14.2 hh (120–147 cm). They can also be piebald; other colors including bay, black, and chestnut are accepted, but not gray. The prairie ones are often not purebred.

Today, the Pottok is used as a child's pony and in harness. Like the Landais, it was used in the creation of the Poney Français de Selle (see pp.300–301).

Short, sloping croup

Widely spaced eyes

Short neck

Back tends to be long

Strong quarters

Straight shoulders

Well-sprung rib cage

Fine, short legs

Feet are well-made and very hard

THERE ARE NOW **FEWER** THAN **150 PURE POTTOK MARES** IN THEIR MOUNTAIN HOMES.

Poney Français de Selle

HEIGHT AT WITHERS	ORIGIN	COLORS
12.2–14.2 hh (127–148 cm)	France	All

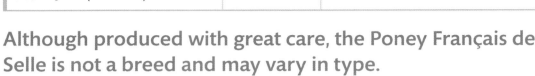

Although produced with great care, the Poney Français de Selle is not a breed and may vary in type.

Well-shaped back end

The attractive English Riding Pony (see p.292) inspired French breeders to develop their own miniature horse, the Poney Français de Selle (French Saddle Pony), for children to ride. The growth of Pony Clubs in France in the 1970s was additional encouragement. French native pony breeds were used as a base and crossed, with various pony stallions, particularly of British native breeds, such as Welsh Ponies (see pp.290–91) and New Forests (see pp.282–83), as well as Connemaras (see pp.264–65) and some Arabs (see pp.92–93). French breeders made less use of the Thoroughbred (see pp.120–21), which is usually an improving element, because they were more interested in developing an all-arounder suitable for lessons and Pony Club activities than a high-quality competition pony. The Landais (see p.298) proved a particularly popular base, although other French ponies, including the Pottok (see p.299) have been used. The Poney Français de Selle was originally called the Poney de Croisement (Crossbred Pony) due to the number of breeds used in its development. The breed organization, the Association Française du Poney de Croisement, was established in 1969 and the studbook opened in 1972. In 1991, the breed was relaunched as the Poney Français de Selle and the previous studbook closed to outside blood.

Described as "essentially a small horse," this small equine has the thick-set outline of a pony but the sporting capabilities of a horse, and is used for dressage, show jumping, and three-day eventing. Currently there is no defined breed standard owing to the differences between the various bloodlines, but the Poney Francais de Selle is, nevertheless, becoming a distinguishable type.

Strong legs with clearly defined tendons

GERMAN REITPONY

Developed from British native ponies, particularly Welsh Ponies, crossed with smaller Thoroughbreds, German warmbloods, and Arabs, this is the German version of the Poney Français de Selle. Bred to take child riders from beginner to national or even international competition level, these ponies stand at 13.2–14.2 hh (138–148 cm) and have a horse's conformation in miniature. Careful inspections ensure the best ponies are entered in the studbook. Above all, a pony character should be combined with a warmblood talent.

Long neck with prominent withers

Body is more thick-set than the English Riding Pony

Small head with convex or straight profile

Long, sloping shoulders

Sloping croup

Broad chest

Symmetrical quarters

Joints are inclined to roundness

Light feathering at the heels

THIS PONY CAN TAKE ITS **RIDER** FROM BEING A **COMPLETE NOVICE TO SERIOUS COMPETITION LEVEL.**

Icelandic

HEIGHT AT WITHERS	ORIGIN	COLORS
13–14 hh (132–142 cm)	Iceland	A wide range; chestnut is common

THE TÖLT

The *tölt* is a "running walk" that the Icelandic horse uses to swiftly cross broken ground. It can be done very slowly or very fast and is very comfortable for the rider and appears effortless on the part of the horse. FEIF (International Federation of Icelandic Horse Associations) sets the rules for breeding the Icelandic and it has had a strict assessment system since 1986.

Icelandic horses are known for their *tölt*, a four-beat walk at a fast or slow speed; some also pace.

The Icelandic horse is never referred to as a pony by Icelanders. The origins of the breed can be traced back to the 9th century, when settlers from the Scandinavian mainland brought animals to the volcanic island in boats. Since then, this little horse has played a central role in the lives of Icelanders.

The Icelandic horse retains an extreme purity of stock. There was an early attempt to introduce eastern blood but it proved so disastrous that the Althing (the world's oldest parliament) prohibited the import of horses. That law still stands, which means the bloodline has been preserved. From an early date, selective breeding seems to have been practiced, using fights between stallions as a basis for selection. More organized breeding began in 1879 in Skagafjordur in

northern Iceland. Initially based on preserving strength and stamina, the programs changed to focus on the quality of the five gaits peculiar to the breed. Many studs breed strictly to a specific color, of which there are about 15 basic types.

The Icelandic horse is often kept in semi-wild herds to preserve its character, with some shelter and feed during the severe winter. Farmers no longer travel on horses, but in the highland areas they still round up their horses and sheep on horseback at the end of summer. Trekking over Iceland is a well-established leisure activity and equestrian sports are also popular. Competitive events include racing, cross-country, dressage, and jumping. The horses are also bred for meat.

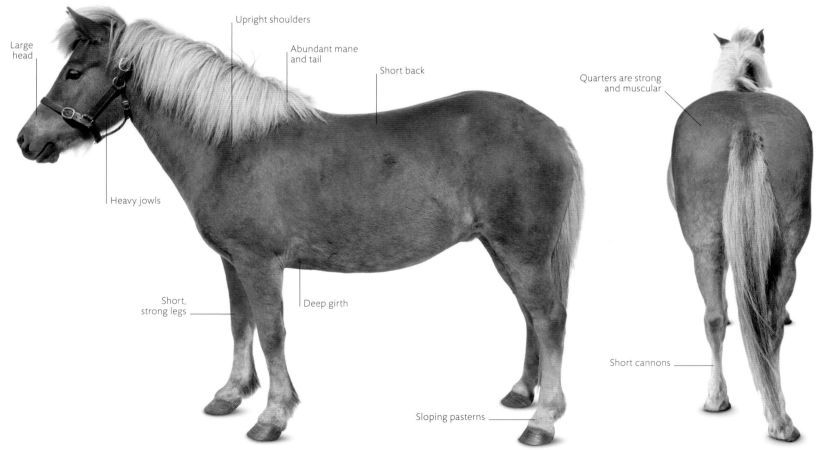

Large head

Upright shoulders

Abundant mane and tail

Short back

Heavy jowls

Quarters are strong and muscular

Short, strong legs

Deep girth

Short cannons

Sloping pasterns

IN ICELAND, **HORSES OUTNUMBER PEOPLE** BY MORE THAN **TWO TO ONE.**

Land of ice and snow
Strong enough to carry a fully grown adult for many miles across rough terrain, the Icelandic horse is a supreme example of how surroundings contribute to character.

Fjord

HEIGHT AT WITHERS	ORIGIN	COLORS
13–14 hh (132–142 cm)	Norway	Dun

Tough, hardy, and long-lived, the Fjord is one of the world's oldest and purest breeds.

Little is known about the origin of the Fjord, although it probably came from the east as there appear to have been wild horses in southern Sweden and in Denmark since the last ice age. Norse horses may have accompanied the Vikings on their travels, but these were not the same as the Fjords of today, although they may be their forbears.

The first deliberate breeding program in Norway began in the mid-1880s. Prior to this, the Fjord was smaller, at 12–12.2 hh (122–127 cm).

Breeding took place mainly in the western region of Norway (Vestlandet). The horse seems to have varied in size and type from the north to the south of Vestlandet. Those from Fjordane and Sunnmøre in the north were larger with a more profuse mane, tail, and feathering than those from Sunnhordland, which were lighter and more refined. The types from Sunnmøre and Fjordane are more predominant in today's breeding.

It is known that there were once Fjords in other colors: bay, brown, and chestnut and its shades. However, at the end of the 19th century, the breed almost died out. It was saved by a stallion called Njål (born 1891), from which all today's horses descend. This reduction in the gene pool seems to have made all Fjords dun colored.

The Fjord is used for plowing, as a pack pony, and under saddle. It excels in long-distance events, which suit its courage and stamina. It is a brilliant performer in harness and can hold its own in competitive events.

ASIATIC CONNECTION?

It is sometimes said that the Fjord is related to the Asiatic Wild Horse, also called Przewalski's horse, because the two share similar characteristics, such as their coat color and the black leg and back markings. However, this is not the case, because the Przewalski differs from domestic horses in that it has 66 chromosomes, while the Fjord has the usual 64. The only other horse with a different number is the Caspian (see pp.246–47).

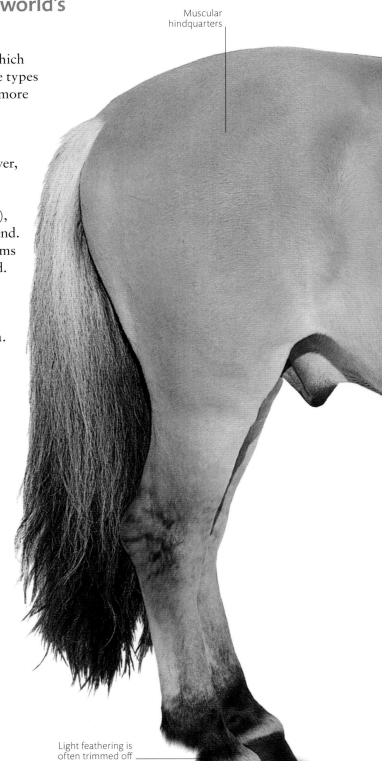

Muscular hindquarters

Light feathering is often trimmed off

Mane is cut in the shape of a crescent

Withers are often indistinct

Dun-colored coat

Heavy, strong shoulders

Dorsal stripe

Rounded barrel

Legs often have zebra bars

Tail is usually thick and full

THE **COARSE, ERECT** MANE IS TRADITIONALLY **HOGGED** TO SHOW THE **BLACK HAIRS** AT ITS CENTER.

Short, sturdy cannons

Hard, well-shaped hooves

Huçul

HEIGHT AT WITHERS	ORIGIN	COLORS
13–14 hh (132–142 cm)	Carpathians, Central Europe	Mostly bay, also dun, black, and chestnut

HUÇUL CLUB

In 1972, the Huçul Club was established in Czech Republic to save the Huçul. From owning only five purebreds in the beginning, it now has over 80, and the club has bred over 200 foals in that time. The Huçul Club was the first organization in Central Europe to create a center for riding for the disabled.

The hardy and enduring Huçul was renowned for carrying heavy loads over treacherous mountain paths.

The Huçul is native to the Carpathians, the high mountain chain that stretches from the Czech Republic through Slovakia, Poland, Hungary, and Ukraine to Romania. A recent scientific study suggests that the breed could have its origins in a large number of founders. The Huçul shows a relatively high genetic diversity, which can be connected to the breeding practices of the early Hungarians, who are known to have used horses from all over the continent. In addition, horse remains found in pagan Hungarian burial sites may have a common ancestry with the Huçul and are closely related to the extinct Tarpan, hinting that there is more to be learned about this breed.

In the 19th century, the Huçul was bred selectively in Romania, then later in Poland, and it was used as a mount by Austro-Hungarian troops. It was also used for light agricultural work and as a packhorse to provide transportation over mountain paths often covered in snow and ice.

Short and compact, the modern Huçul is a hardy, strong, and willing breed with a docile temperament. Most ponies are used in harness, although they can also be ridden. They are still employed on the highland farms of the Carpathians and used in forestry work as well. Today, Huçuls are bred all over Central Europe and it is thought that their numbers run into thousands.

Expressive head with large eyes

Short, muscular neck

Low withers

Strong back

Well-developed croup

Tail and mane is thick and coarse

Heavy forehand

Heavy, compact body

Sickle hocked

Small, hard hooves

THE **WORD HUÇUL** MEANS **OUTLAW** OR **REBEL** IN ROMANIAN.

Konik

HEIGHT AT WITHERS 12.3–13.3 hh
(130–140 cm)
ORIGIN Carpathians, Central Europe
COLORS Mostly dun, occasionally
black or chestnut

In the 1920s and 1930s, attempts to recreate
the extinct Tarpan resulted in the Konik,
which has some Tarpan characteristics, such
as the dun coloring and dorsal eel-stripe. In
Polish, konik means "pony" or "little horse."

The Konik feeds on tough bark and
invasive shrubs and this helps native flora
to reestablish. The breed is making a
significant contribution to the restoration
of delicate ecosystems, such as wetlands and
heavily farmed meadowland, across Europe.

The robust, attractive Konik is selectively
bred at Polish studs and is used under
harness and for light draft work. Its
kind and willing nature also makes it very
suitable for young riders.

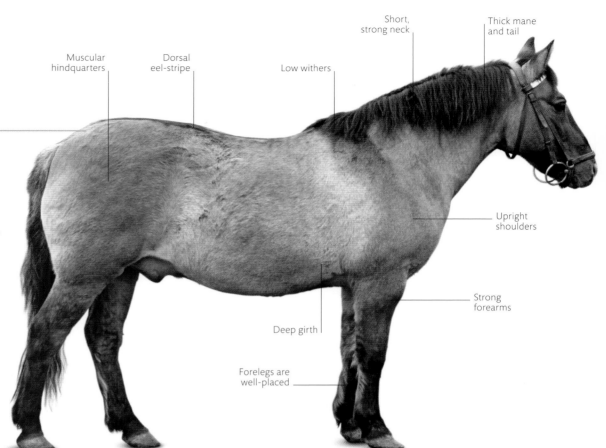

Muscular
hindquarters

Dorsal
eel-stripe

Low withers

Short,
strong neck

Thick mane
and tail

Upright
shoulders

Strong
forearms

Deep girth

Forelegs are
well-placed

Gotland

HEIGHT AT WITHERS
11.1–12.3 hh (115–130 cm)
ORIGIN Sweden
COLORS Mainly dun,
black, bay, and chestnut

Also known as the Skogsruss, which means
"little horse of the woods," the breed's first
pedigrees were listed in 1943. Influential
stallions include Welsh stallions Criban
Daniel and Reber General. There is also
Olle, a Syrian Arab–Gotland cross who
introduced the yellow dun coat color, and
the Arab (see pp.92–93), Khedivan, who is
responsible for the gray coloration. The
studbook was closed in 1971. Today,
Gotlands are bred throughout Scandinavia,
the US, as well as on Gotland.

Once used for general farm work, the
Gotland is now principally a riding pony and
is often used in riding schools, for children.
It is also a harness racing pony and excels at
show jumping, dressage, and eventing.

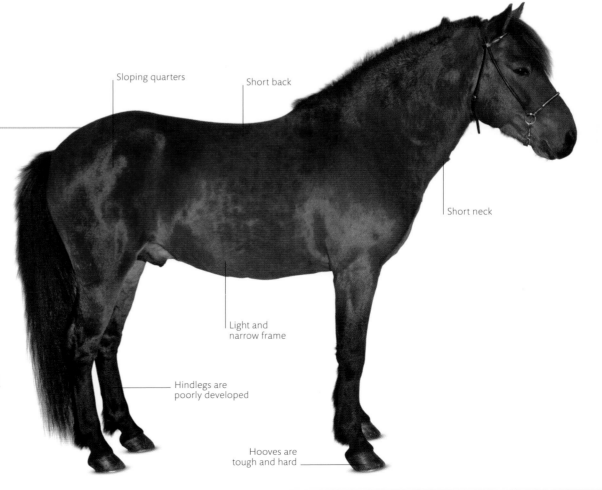

Sloping quarters

Short back

Short neck

Light and
narrow frame

Hindlegs are
poorly developed

Hooves are
tough and hard

Tough little horses
Natives of the Carpathian Mountains, Konik ponies are wiry, tough, and robust. Their thick woolly winter coat is more than capable of protecting them from the ice and snow.

Pindos

HEIGHT AT WITHERS	ORIGIN	COLORS
11.1–12.1 hh (115–125 cm)	Northern Greece	Mainly bay, brown, and gray

PENEIA PONY

The Peneia is bred in the Peloponnese in southern Greece. It is slightly larger than the Pindos and Skyrian, sometimes reaching 14 hh (142 cm). While its conformation is not perfect, it is a tough animal, capable of carrying an adult, and performs the usual tasks often required of a pony on small scale farms. Peneias are often trained to do a gait called aravani, which makes them comfortable to ride.

The small, hardy, and tough little ponies of northern Greece are named after the regions they are bred in.

The Pindos is bred in the traditional horse lands around the Pindos mountains—a range that runs along the border of Thessaly and Epirus in northern Greece. However, genetic analysis indicates that it may have an Asian origin. This pony is also, rather confusingly, called the Thessalonian.

Ponies have lived in this part of Greece for hundreds of years and are small in stature owing to the poor soil, sparse vegetation, and the harsh climatic conditions. The various types are named after the regions they are bred in, but as there are no breed associations or studbooks, it is likely crossbreeding has and continues to occur.

Today, the sure-footed Pindos is used as a pack pony, for light work on the small highland farmsteads, and in forestry. It is also a useful riding pony, able to travel fairly rapidly over rough terrain and along mountain tracks.

A tough, enduring pony, the Pindos can survive on minimal food supplies and is noted for its stamina. The breed does, however, have a reputation for being stubborn. As befits a mountain pony, the Pindos' feet are very hard and rarely need to be shod. Pindos mares are traditionally used for breeding mules.

Quarters appear weak

Head inclines to coarseness

Little muscle development on neck

Pronounced withers

Narrow body with long back

"Short-of-rib" appearance

Slender legs with small joints

TODAY, **BREED SOCIETIES** ARE **IMPROVING** THE **QUALITY OF THE GREEK PONIES.**

Skyrian

HEIGHT AT WITHERS	ORIGIN	COLORS
9.3–11.1 hh (100–115 cm)	Skyros, Greece	Mainly bay, also brown, chestnut, and gray; rarely dun

SKYRIANS ABROAD

There is a small herd of Skyrians in Scotland, UK. The ponies have lived there since 2005 and have been the subject of study by their current owner Sheilagh Brown, who is a veterinarian. She compared the genetics of the Skyrian, Caspian (see pp.246–47), and Exmoor (see pp.276–77). Her findings suggest that the Skyrian is not related to either of these breeds. Another small herd of Skyrians can be found on Corfu.

Ponies have lived on Skyros since ancient times, possibly even as far back as 2500 BCE.

This small breed may once have been spread across the Greek archipelago; it is now found only on the Aegean island of Skyros, and in one or two other places (see box, left). There are around 200 Skyrian ponies worldwide.

The Skyrian's overall proportions are more like those of a horse than a pony, and the breed is said to resemble the horses depicted in Ancient Greek statuary and on friezes, such as those on the Parthenon. This breed, unlike the Pindos (see opposite) and some other Greek breeds, displays no genetic affinity with Asian horses and appears to be quite distinct.

The Skyrian traditionally lived in small, wild herds around Mount Kohylas, from where it was brought down by the islanders to help with plowing and corn threshing, and used as a pack animal. The islanders also organized horse races, riding the ponies bareback, and later held village horse shows.

Today, the ponies are no longer used for farm work but still live in a semi-wild state in their natural habitat, which is now a conservation area. Although Skyrians are few in number, this sure-footed, good-tempered, and intelligent breed is ideal for children and young riders.

Supple neck with ample mane

Long sloped croup

Compact body

Weak but rounded quarters

Low-set tail

Deep girth

Short, tough limbs

Hoof of hard, black, dense horn

THE **SKYROS ISLAND HORSE TRUST** PRESERVES AND PROMOTES THE SKYRIAN.

Cayuse Indian Pony

HEIGHT AT WITHERS
14 hh
(142 cm)

ORIGIN
Oregon, US

COLORS
Any color

NATIVE AMERICANS

Horses enabled Native Americans to hunt buffalo and to follow their nomadic lifestyle more easily. Initially, Spanish settlers forbade them from owning horses. In time, however, they raided ranches and stole them. They were said to keep the best and eat the rest, thereby practicing selective breeding. Nowadays, the relationship they had with their horses is the stuff of legend.

This breed was developed by the Cayuse Native Americans who occupied territories in Oregon and Washington.

Since 1855, the Cayuse have lived on the Umatilla Indian Reservation. They were very skilled riders and horse breeders and their mounts were vital for their nomadic lifestyle, as well as for hunting buffalo. North American settlers referred to all horses that belonged to the Native Americans as "Cayuse Ponies," but, in fact, the Cayuse Indian Pony is a distinct breed thought to have originated in the 1800s. Although the Cayuse's ancestry is not clear, it may well be descended from French-Norman horses, possibly Percherons (see pp.62–63), imported into Canada. It seems likely that when French-Canadians crossed into eastern North America to trade, they bartered their horses with Indian tribes, particularly the Pawnee in the St. Louis area, and that horses were taken further west from here. The Cayuse practiced selective breeding, probably crossing the French-Norman horses with lighter Spanish Barbs (see pp.94–95).

The modern Cayuse is small and well-muscled with a stocky build. It has a broken walking gait, owing to well-sloped pasterns, which makes it comfortable to ride. Numbers are, however, very low and most Cayuses are found in California where enthusiasts have been trying to build up a herd.

NOTED FOR ITS **STAMINA AND SPEED,** THE **CAYUSE** WAS SAID TO BE SUPERIOR TO **US CAVALRY HORSES.**

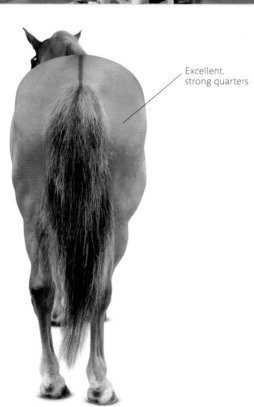

Excellent, strong quarters

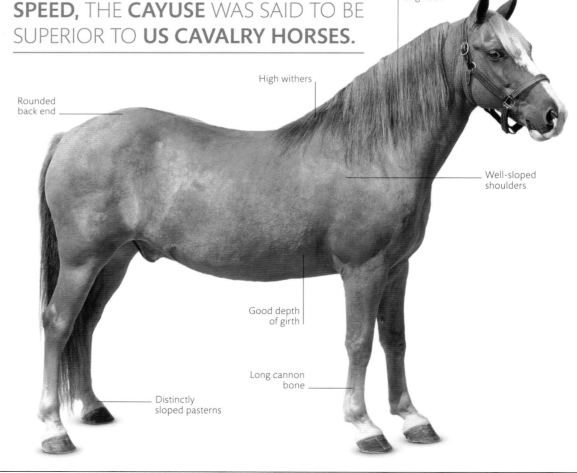

Strong, long neck

High withers

Rounded back end

Well-sloped shoulders

Good depth of girth

Long cannon bone

Distinctly sloped pasterns

Bashkir Curly

HEIGHT AT WITHERS	ORIGIN	COLORS
Average 15 hh (152 cm)	Nevada, US	Chestnut, bay

This incredibly tough mountain breed is distinguished by its thick, curly winter coat and luxurious mane and tail.

The origin of the Bashkir Curly is not known, although some of its genetic markers can be traced to Quarter Horses (see pp.220–21) and Morgans (see pp.222–23). Other unusual Bashkir Curly traits are found only in feral horses.

In 1898, Peter Damele and his father were riding in mountains in Central Nevada when they saw three horses with curled coats in a Mustang (see pp.212–13) herd. They took these home. In 1932, their descendants were among the few survivors of a severe winter. The Dameles moved to Dry Creek Ranch in Nevada in 1942.

Another winter storm ten years later killed all but four Curly mares and a colt called Cooper D—the first Curly stallion used for breeding. Later, the mares were bred to an Arab (see pp.92–93) called Nevada Red and a Morgan, Ruby Red King. Other breeds used included Appaloosa (see pp.218–19) and Saddlebred (see pp.224–25). Many of the American Bashkir Curly horses can be traced back to this original herd.

The American Bashkir Curly Horse registry opened in 1971. Curlies are good workers, as well as being highly intelligent, and are noted for their gentle disposition.

BENEFITS OF A CURLY COAT

The Bashkirs' curly hair is like mohair and said to be hypoallergenic. It can be spun into yarn. The curls are most obvious in the winter coat; summer coats may be quite straight. The winter coat grows in a variety of ways, which have been named: marcel wave, crushed velvet, curl, and micro curl. Manes and tails may fall in ringlets or be more like dreadlocks. The manes often split over the crest of the neck, falling on both sides.

Tail and mane are exceptionally thick

Flat, straightish back

Low, flat withers

Wide body with well-sprung ribs

Short limbs with 8 in (20 cm) bone below knee

Sloping pasterns

A **SIOUX WINTER COUNT** (CALENDAR) FROM THE **EARLY 19TH CENTURY** SHOWS **BASHKIR-LIKE CURLY-HAIRED** HORSES.

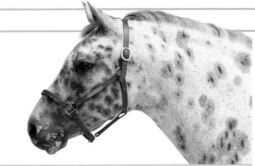

Pony of the Americas

HEIGHT AT WITHERS	ORIGIN	COLORS
11.2–14 hh (117–142 cm)	Iowa, US	Spotted

This breed's foundation stallion, Black Hand, was the offspring of a Shetland and an Appaloosa.

This is an all-American pony, and one of only three spotted horse breeds in the US; the other two are the Appaloosa (see pp.218–19) and the Colorado Ranger Horse (see p.230). The primary characteristic of this breed, and one of the main reasons for its development as a new breed, is the coat pattern.

In 1954, Leslie Boomhower, an Iowan lawyer bought an Appaloosa mare with a foal. The mare had been mated with a Shetland (see pp.268–69) stallion and the foal was white with a pattern of black spots. Boomhower decided to establish a new breed. He set up the Pony of the Americas Club in 1955. To ensure the highest breeding standards, the registry had strict conformation requirements, including height limit, head shape, and coat color, which had to be Appaloosa. As the breed's popularity grew, height limits were increased and Shetlands were replaced in the breeding program. Later, there were outcrosses to Arabs (see pp.92–93), Quarter Horses (see pp.220–21), and Welsh ponies (see pp.290–91).

There are two very common coat patterns: blanket and leopard. Ponies with blanket patterns have white markings over the loins and hips, while leopard types have spots covering the whole body.

Apart from color, the breeding focus is on substance, refinement, and a stylish, straight, balanced action. In the show ring, the ponies are ridden, driven, and jumped, and they are also said to be popular for trail and endurance riding.

PERFECT LEARNING PONY

Throughout the US, the Pony of the Americas fulfills its original purpose in that it is easy to train and is a gentle, placid mount for young children. Unlike Shetlands, which are wide over the back, this pony is shaped more like a small horse and is narrower. This makes it comfortable for children to sit on and easier for their legs to reach the stirrups, which in turn makes them more secure in the saddle.

Leopard spot coloring

Strong, striped hooves

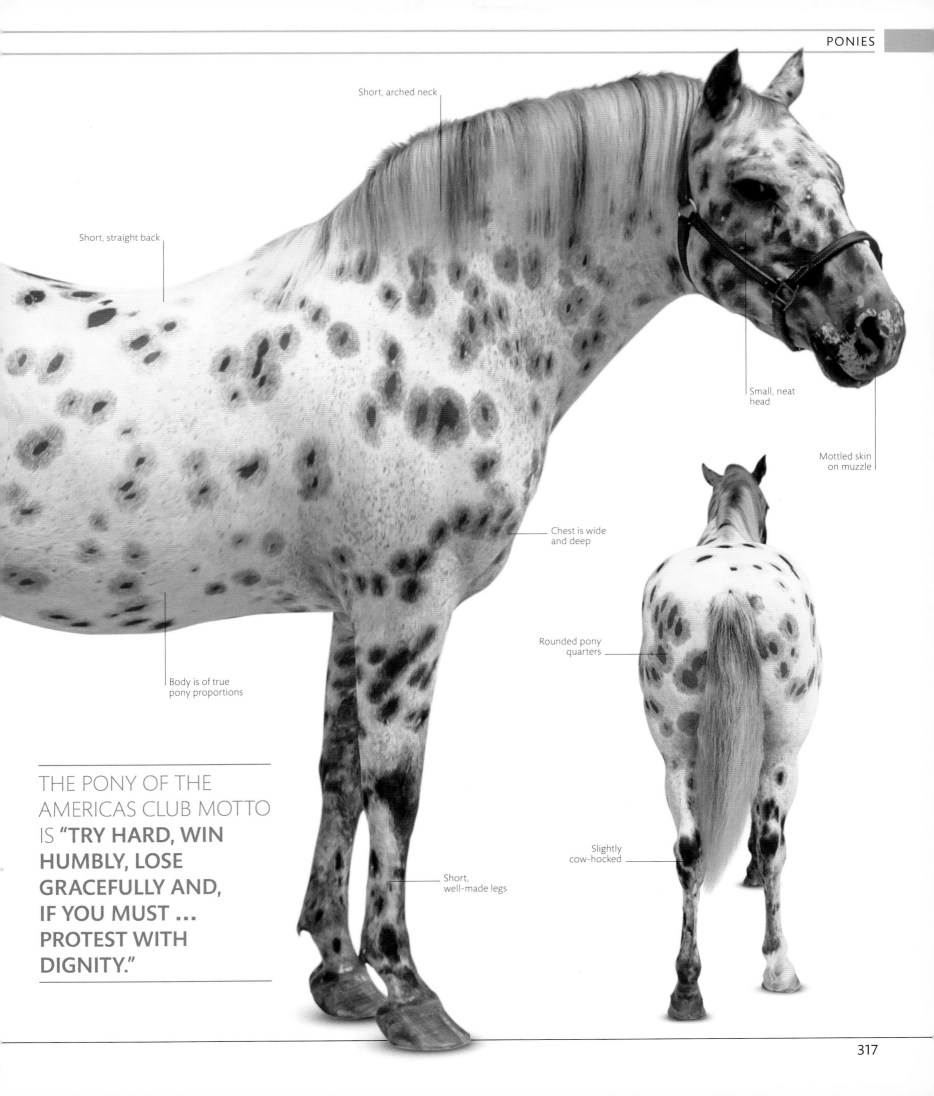

Short, arched neck

Short, straight back

Small, neat head

Mottled skin on muzzle

Chest is wide and deep

Body is of true pony proportions

Rounded pony quarters

THE PONY OF THE AMERICAS CLUB MOTTO IS **"TRY HARD, WIN HUMBLY, LOSE GRACEFULLY AND, IF YOU MUST ... PROTEST WITH DIGNITY."**

Short, well-made legs

Slightly cow-hocked

American Shetland

	HEIGHT AT WITHERS Up to 11.2 hh (117 cm)	**ORIGIN** US	**COLORS** All solid

WORKING IN HARNESS

Today's American Shetland is primarily a harness pony, drawing four-wheeled buggies and two-wheeled vehicles in roadster-pony classes (the equivalent of the British driving classes). Harness classes call for the high-stepping, flashy action for which this pony is bred. According to the American Shetland Pony Club, the modern Shetland "with its extreme action and spirited personality is truly at home in the show ring."

The American Shetland has been one of the best-loved ponies in the US for well over a century.

This pony is an American version of the hardy British breed that originated in the Scottish Shetland Islands. Robert Liburn of Wisconsin and Eli Elliot of Iowa imported the first Shetlands in 1884 and 1885, respectively. An American Shetland Pony Club was formed in 1888, and an American Shetland studbook was started in 1889. Within about 50 years, American breeders had started developing two Shetland-based breeds: the Pony of the Americas (see pp.316–17) and the most popular pony in the US, the American Shetland.

The original Shetland has been exported worldwide for well over 100 years, but only in the US has there been a deliberate attempt to cross the breed. Essentially a smart harness pony, the American Shetland was developed by selecting finer types from among the original island Shetlands and crossing them with Hackney (see p.293) and Welsh Ponies (see pp.290–91). Outcrosses were then made to Arabs (see pp.92–93) and small Thoroughbreds to produce what is a relatively distinctive type. The new-look Shetland is slightly taller and has a narrower frame and longer, finer limbs. It resembles the Hackney in outline, conformation, character, and action.

There are four distinct types of American Shetland: Foundation, which is shown in a natural state and is closest to the original Scottish Shetland; Classic, which is said to be a refined version of the Foundation; Modern, which has the high-stepping Hackney-style action, and Modern Pleasure, which is refined and elegant but not as extreme in its action as the Modern.

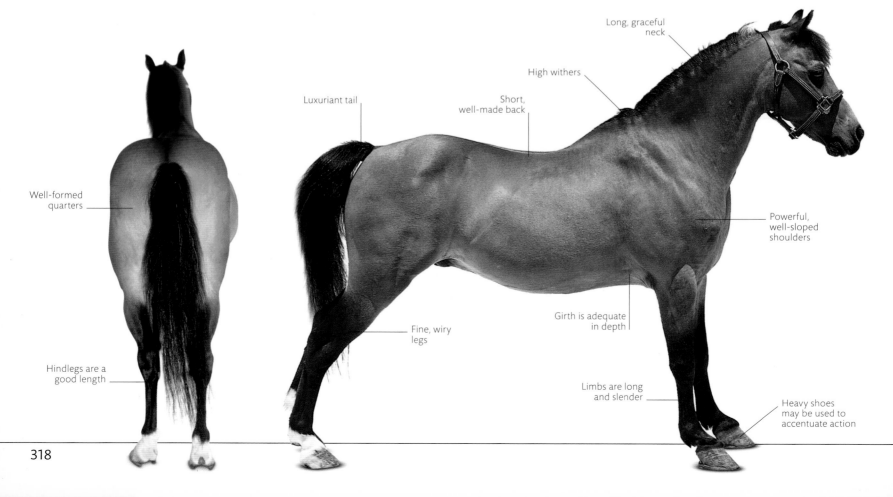

Long, graceful neck

High withers

Luxuriant tail

Short, well-made back

Well-formed quarters

Hindlegs are a good length

Fine, wiry legs

Powerful, well-sloped shoulders

Girth is adequate in depth

Limbs are long and slender

Heavy shoes may be used to accentuate action

THERE ARE **FOUR DIVISIONS** IN THE **AMERICAN SHETLAND REGISTRY** AND **TWO RELATED DIVISIONS** FOR **HALFBREDS.**

Chincoteague

HEIGHT AT WITHERS	ORIGIN	COLORS
12–13 hh (122–132 cm)	Assateague, Virginia, US	All

The island home of the Chincoteagues was set up as a refuge for the ponies in the 1920s.

Although this feral pony is named after Chincoteague Island off the east coast of the US, it originated and lives on neighboring Assateague. Straddling the boundary of two states, Maryland and Virginia, Assateague is home to two wild herds. The Maryland herd is managed by the National Park Service and the Virginia herd by the Chincoteague Volunteer Fire Company. A fence separates the two herds, which are kept to about 150 animals each to ensure they do not damage the island's ecology.

The ponies probably derive from animals abandoned by colonists in the 17th century to avoid fencing laws and livestock taxes. According to local folklore, however, horses of Moorish origin swam to Assateague from a shipwrecked Spanish galleon.

Pony Penning, a yearly roundup, was being practiced on both islands by the late 19th century. In the mid-1920s, the Chincoteague Volunteer Fire Company took an interest in the island stock and started holding fundraising events. Soon, visitors began to arrive to watch the festivities. Crowds still come to watch the ponies being corralled on Assateague and swum over to adjacent Chincoteague, where the yearlings are auctioned and sold to private owners.

In the 1960s, the stock had seriously degenerated and it was upgraded by the introduction of Shetland (see pp.268–69) and Welsh Pony (see pp.290–91) blood, as well as outcrosses to Pintos (see p.215). Officially registered in 1994, the stocky Chincoteague is said to be a good child's pony.

UNUSUAL DIET

Chincoteagues survive on a diet that most equines would not be able to stomach. It consists mainly of coarse marsh and beach grasses. For variety, the ponies also pick at greenbrier (*Smilax*), berberis, rose hips, seaweeds, and poison ivy. This diet contains a high concentration of salt. This results in the ponies drinking twice as much fresh water as domestic horses, which makes them look rather bloated. They sip at salt water but don't drink very much of it.

Strong hooves

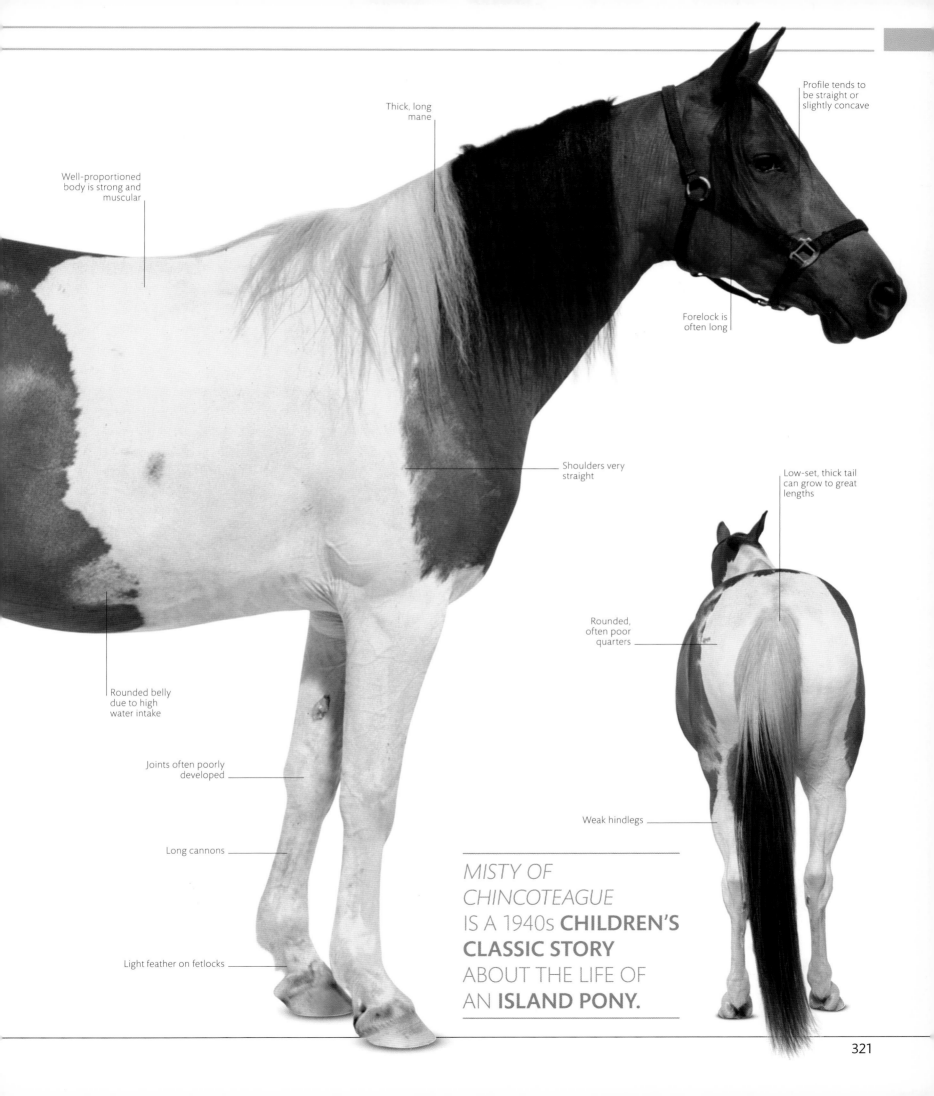

Profile tends to be straight or slightly concave

Thick, long mane

Forelock is often long

Well-proportioned body is strong and muscular

Shoulders very straight

Low-set, thick tail can grow to great lengths

Rounded, often poor quarters

Rounded belly due to high water intake

Joints often poorly developed

Weak hindlegs

Long cannons

MISTY OF CHINCOTEAGUE IS A 1940s **CHILDREN'S CLASSIC STORY** ABOUT THE LIFE OF AN **ISLAND PONY.**

Light feather on fetlocks

Sink or swim
The annual roundup on Assateague
ends with the ponies being swum
across the sea to Chincoteague. Strong
and fit, they are perfectly capable of
making the 10-minute trip.

Galiceño

HEIGHT AT WITHERS	ORIGIN	COLORS
12–13.3 hh (122–140 cm)	Mexico	Any solid colors

The Galiceño may have the small stature of a pony but its proportions are those of a horse.

The ancestry of this compact Mexican breed is thought to include descendants of the Iberian Sorraia (see p.294) and the northern Portuguese Garrano. The Galiceño takes its name from Galicia, the fertile province of northwest Spain where its ancestors originated. This area was renowned throughout Europe for its smooth-gaited horses, which were distinguished by their swift, running walk. In the 16th century, Spanish colonialists brought horses to Hispaniola and Cuba in the Caribbean and established breeding herds. Later, when the conquistadors invaded mainland America, and colonists and missionaries settled in Mexico, their horses came too. The Spanish are said to have used the Galiceños as pack animals in the silver mines and some went with Spanish missionaries to the American West, where they were acquired by Native Americans of the Great Plains.

The modern Galiceño was brought from Mexico to Texas in 1958, the same year it was officially recognized as a breed. Naturally quick, responsive, and agile, with a tough constitution, the Galiceño proved to be a good cattle horse and the breed is still used to a limited extent on ranches and for general farm work. In Mexico, the Galiceño is used as a riding pony and under draft. It is also used as a pack animal for light agricultural work. Many horses of this breed retain the running walk of their Spanish ancestors, making them popular for riding in the US, where they are also shown in harness and show jumped. In the US, numbers of Galiceños have declined but enthusiasts in some states, including Texas and Florida, preserve and promote the breed. Some of the present-day Galiceños in Mexico, especially the dun-colored types, still bear a strong resemblance to the Sorraia.

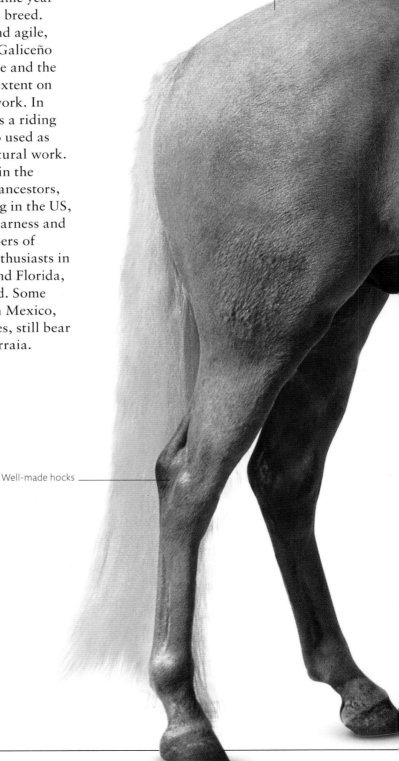

Sloping croup

Well-made hocks

GARRANO

Indigenous to northern Portugal, this pony, which is around 12.3 hh (130 cm) high, is built like a miniature horse. Like many of the small native ponies of Europe, it is threatened with extinction due to changes in agriculture—the disappearance of small farms—and also because of predation by wolves. Like the Galiceño, the Garrano is gaited. Bay in color, it has a thick mane and tail, and often has a concave (dished) profile.

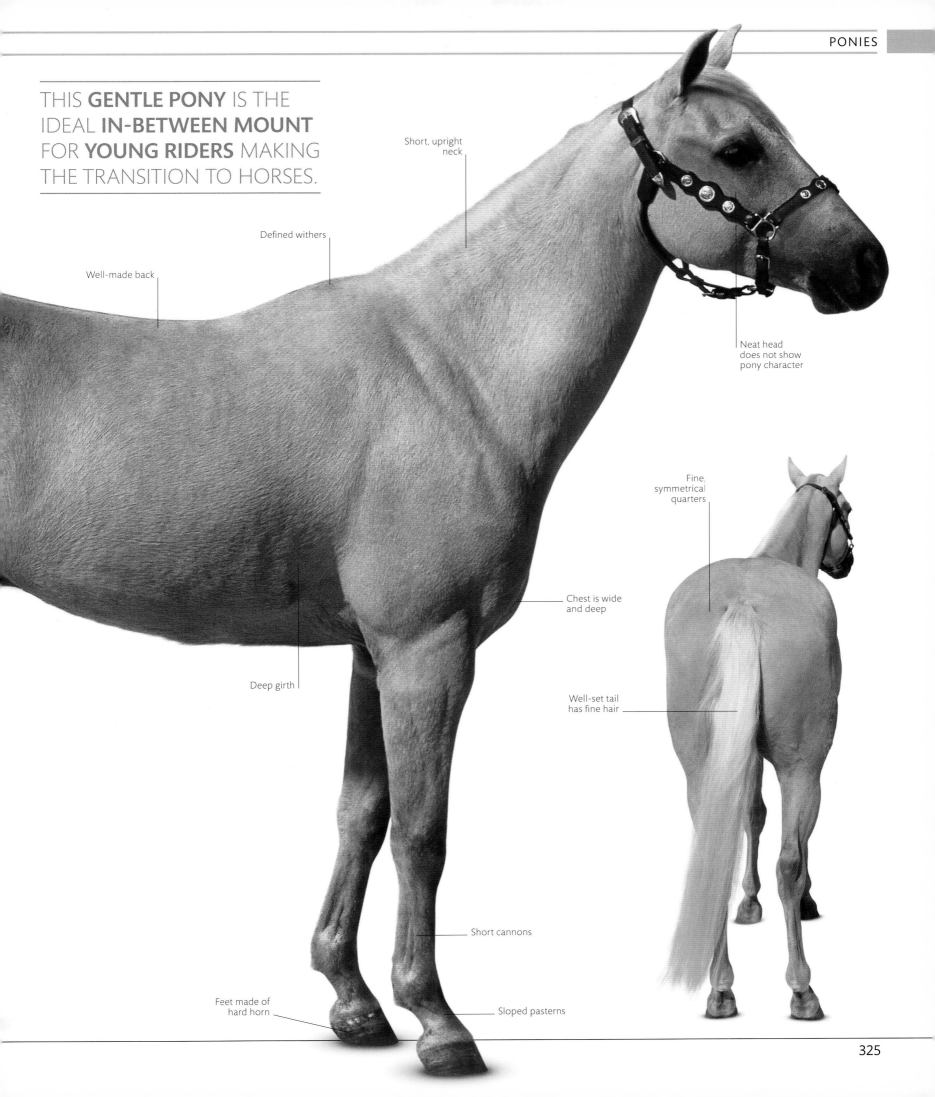

THIS **GENTLE PONY** IS THE IDEAL **IN-BETWEEN MOUNT** FOR **YOUNG RIDERS** MAKING THE TRANSITION TO HORSES.

Short, upright neck

Defined withers

Well-made back

Neat head does not show pony character

Fine, symmetrical quarters

Chest is wide and deep

Well-set tail has fine hair

Deep girth

Short cannons

Feet made of hard horn

Sloped pasterns

Falabella

HEIGHT AT WITHERS	ORIGIN	COLORS
Up to 8.3 hh (89 cm)	Argentina	All, including spotted

Purposely bred in the 19th century, this tiny horse is popular but numbers remain low.

Small ponies usually originate from environments where the climate is harsh and feed scarce. However, at various periods in equine history, miniature horses have been bred as pets and for curiosity value. Today, the best-known miniature is the Falabella.

In the mid-1850s, Patrick Newtall, an Irishman living in Argentina, created a herd from small horses brought from Pampas Indians. The herd passed through his family, along with details of his methods and information about the breeding lines. In 1927, Julio Cesar Falabella inherited the stud, which was based on a ranch outside Buenos Aires. In 1940, he created a breed registry, Establecimientos Falabella, and became the best known breeder of Falabellas. In 1991, this became the Asociación de Criadores de Caballos Falabella (Falabella Horse Breeders Association).

The breed was created by crossing the smallest Shetland (see pp.268–69) ponies with a very small Thoroughbred (see pp.120–21) stallion. Criollos (see p.236) and other breeds with pinto and appaloosa coats were then used to obtain the coat colors. The smallest and best-quality offspring were retained and intensive inbreeding took place to produce a near-perfect miniature horse. However, inbreeding often results in a lack of vigor and conformational weaknesses. In the Falabella, this can be seen in the legs.

In the 1960s, miniature horses were sent to the US, where they attracted publicity and proved very successful. In 1973, the Falabella Miniature Horse Association was formed in the US and the breed was registered. During the 1970s, small numbers of Falabellas were being exported to the US and countries all over the world.

PERFECT FOR KIDS

Although the horses are tiny, it is possible for small children to ride Falabellas and they are very popular when driven in harness at shows and in parades. As pets, they are said to be good-tempered and friendly, as well as easy to train. The best Falabellas may retain the better points of the Shetland but lack their tough constitution and the quarters are often weak

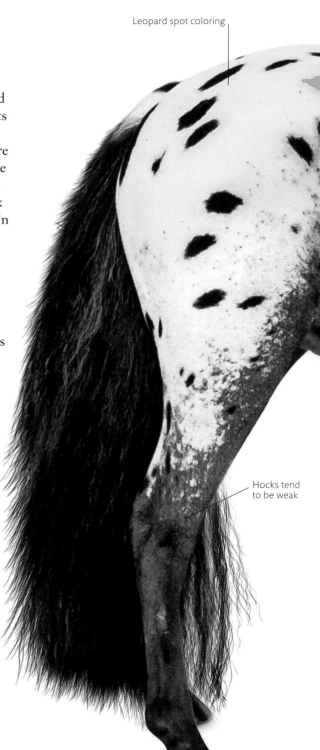

Leopard spot coloring

Hocks tend to be weak

Feet tend to be boxy

TOYLAND ZODIAC, A BLACK LEOPARD APPALOOSA, WAS ONE OF THE MOST **SUCCESSFUL FALABELLA** SIRES IN **THE US.**

Flat withers

Head is proportionate to the body in best specimens

Quarters and hindlegs lack strength

Coat is often long and silky

Bulky forehand and straight shoulders

Luxuriant growth of tail and mane

Short cannons, sometimes bow-legged

CHAPTER 4

CARE AND MANAGEMENT

A balanced diet

Horses living in natural conditions survive on grass and other plants. They graze for up to 20 hours a day to obtain the calories they need, so they do not waste energy unnecessarily, moving slowly as they eat. In winter, when their food is less freely available, they lose weight.

EAT TO WORK

When we ask horses to work, they have to move faster and for longer than they would do from choice. They are expected to carry or pull additional weight and perhaps do energetic athletic exercise such as jumping or dressage. In addition, these horses do not have as much time to eat and their natural diet—high in bulk and low in calories—may not provide sufficient energy to do the work required. To keep them fit and healthy, therefore, they need additional food in the form of forage, such as hay or alfalfa, and concentrated, processed feeds.

FORAGE AND OTHER FOODS

Hay, and other forage, such as haylage, is basically the horse's natural foodstuff dried to preserve it and ensure it is readily available throughout the winter and at other times when grazing is not possible. Grass or hay, and other forage, comprise the bulk of a horse's diet. The horse's gut has evolved to be able to obtain nutrients from this plant fiber (see pp.20–21). Hay and haylage are fed as they come and should make up the majority of a horse's supplementary food (see p.332–33).

In contrast, concentrated foods are mostly sold as mixtures of various ingredients in bags. They are based on chopped forage (chaff) or cereals and seeds (coarse mix), such as oats, maize, and linseed, or a combination of both. Most also contain added vitamins and micronutrients to ensure the horse receives everything it needs to be able to work, build muscle, and remain healthy. Coarse mixes look like a fruit- and nut-free granola and chopped forage consists of short-chopped dry stalks or hay, straw, or alfalfa. Both may contain additional small

Horses at work
When worked in a traditional way, draft horses expend a lot of energy. They need to be given concentrated feeds several times a day, after which they will need a break for digestion. They also need plenty of water.

pellets made of grains or chaffs, along with micronutrients and other ingredients. Larger pellets are often called "nuts" or "cubes." They are usually low in calories and intended for ponies and "good-doers" (equines that can survive on minimal rations).

There are a few other foods that are widely used. Sugar beet is an example. A by-product of the sugar industry and, in fact, low in sugar, it is easily digestible and a good source of fiber. There are also various supplements that can be fed to horses: vegetable oil and cod-liver oil provide calories and good

conditioners; cod-liver oil contains omega-3, which are good for joints. Horses are often fed a wide range of other supplements believed to have health-giving properties, such as garlic, seaweed, and brewer's yeast. There are also many multi-vitamin type products including "feed balancers," usually

Feeding hay
Grass, or hay, is the most natural form of food for a horse. Given a choice, horses will graze for many hours of the day, carefully picking what they want to eat.

in powder, granule, or pellet form, which contain vitamins, minerals, trace elements, prebiotics, and probiotics.

WHAT TO FEED

The type and the quantity of food required depend on the type of horse, its age, the work it's doing, and the availability of grazing. Native breeds, particularly ponies, should be able to survive on grass during the summer with additional forage in the winter. If they are working hard and losing condition, chaff-based feeds and sugar beet are suitable extras. For more highly bred horses, those that race, compete regularly, or do other hard work, such as plowing, coarse mixes are usually a necessity. These horses would never be able to consume enough forage to give them the calories they require.

Concentrated feeds are formulated for all types and ages of horses and a variety of work levels. Although the name of the food is a good indicator of its intended recipients, a label on the packaging will provide information on the ingredients, the digestible energy (calories), and an overall indication of the main constituents such as protein and fiber. When deciding what to feed a horse, the food's digestible energy is a helpful indicator since this is the energy the horse can make use of from the food. Competition feeds are higher in digestible energy than those for horses in moderate or light work. Feeds for veteran horses

contain prebiotics and other ingredients to make the food more palatable and more easily digestible. There are feeds for horses prone to laminitis (see p.348), for youngstock, and pregnant or lactating mares, among many others.

HOW TO FEED

Because of the horse's sensitive digestive system (see pp.20–21), it is important to feed concentrated foods with care. Sudden changes in diet can upset the delicate balance of the gut bacteria, while too much concentrated food can make horses excitable. Divide feeds into

Haynet
Overweight horses and ponies often need to have their food rationed. To ensure they don't eat it too quickly, it can be put into a haynet with small openings. This also avoids wastage.

Healthy treat
Carrots are among the top healthy treats for horses and may be fed in large quantites. They should be cut lengthwise, as round or square pieces can get stuck in the throat and cause choking.

WHAT'S IN FEED

Different feeds

Bagged mixes always have a label giving the digestible energy (calories), protein, fiber, and starch the food contains, along with any micronutrients. Coarse mixes are higher in calories than chaffs. Grains, such as oats and barley are always rolled or crushed before being added to feeds. Linseed must be cooked (usually labeled as micronized). Feeds may also include herbs and other ingredients such as molasses to make them smell and taste more interesting.

COD-LIVER OIL   CORN OIL   MOLASSES

FLAKED MAIZE   LINSEED   BARLEY   OATS   CHAFF

two or more small meals during the day and give forage ad lib if possible. Horses have evolved to eat almost continuously and not being able to do this can lead to digestive problems and behavioral issues, called stable vices (see also p.336). For all but the hardest working competition horses, forage (including grass) should make up between half and two thirds in weight of the overall diet.

Water is usually added to feed bowls to dampen the food and horses must also always have easy access to clean fresh water. They can be quite fussy and may not drink if the water they are offered tastes different to normal (if they are away from home, for example). It is important to keep an eye on them to make sure they are drinking sufficiently.

Horses that are working hard will sweat, losing both salt and fluids, so it is vital to give them salt to ensure they maintain the correct mineral balance in the blood. Salt licks are traditionally provided in the field and in stables, but some hard working horses may also require some salt in their feed. Electrolytes (liquids containing salt and trace elements) are often given to endurance horses during competition.

As with any other animal, it is possible to over- or underfeed horses, both of which can lead to serious health problems. The condition scoring chart can help in deciding if a horse is over- or underweight.

Feeding bucket
Food can be placed in a bucket on the ground, which helps keep it together and makes it easier for the horse to eat. Use buckets without handles so the horse cannot get its foot trapped.

HOW MUCH TO FEED

In the winter, a horse that lives outside uses more energy for warmth and will require supplements to make up for lower levels of nutrients in the grass. However, a horse that is stabled might not require more food in winter than in summer.

The total daily feed intake for a horse of 16 hh (163 cm) and over is usually recommended to be 24–26 lb (10.8–11.7 kg), whereas that for a pony of between 13–14 hh (132–142 cm) is about 18–20 lb (8.1–9 kg). Alternatively, a rough guide to the total food a mature horse needs daily is 2–2.5 percent of his weight (3 percent in youngstock). A weigh bridge is the best way to find out your horse's weight. Weigh tapes are reasonably accurate, but you can also get an estimate by measuring the horse's girth (largest part of the barrel) and length (point of the shoulder upward to the point of the buttock), then doing the calculation below.

WEIGHT CALCULATION
- Girth (in)^2 x length / 300 = weight in lb
- Girth (cm)^2 x length / 8700 = weight in kg

Pasture management

Horses are at their happiest when they are allowed to graze. It is important that their pasture is well kept and safe, and that they have a source of fresh, clean water, and, if possible, shelter from the worst of the weather. Most owners allow their horses plenty of grazing time.

GRASS

Grass is a horse's natural food and eating it keeps him healthy while providing him with hours of occupation and gentle exercise. Unlike most other plants, grass grows from its base, so its leaves can be constantly clipped off and it will continue to grow. It can also be walked over and, within reason, will continue to grow. Grass grows in a wide range of conditions, from dry to wet and hot to cold. This makes it a very economical food for all grazing animals, including horses.

Looking after grass is not difficult and will pay dividends. To begin with, the land should not be over-stocked: one horse per acre (0.4 ha) is the recommended maximum. Paddocks can be smaller as long as there are several of them and the horses are regularly moved between them to avoid overgrazing.

Horses produce a lot of droppings and don't like eating near them, so droppings must be regularly (daily or weekly) cleared from the paddock to avoid the development of areas of long coarse grass that never gets eaten. Droppings also contain worm eggs so picking them up will reduce the risk of parasite infestation in your horses. Fields often get badly damaged over the winter when the grass grows more slowly and the rain, snow, and ice create poached (muddy) areas. Most owners accept that the land will look dreadful by the end of the winter. When the weather improves, they move their horses into another pasture, allowing the winter fields to recover, which they will—grass is very tough. Harrowing and rolling (see box) speeds recovery, while large bare patches should be reseeded and the young grass seedlings protected for a few months.

WEEDS

Although, at first glance, a field just looks full of grass, it will usually contain several different grass species and plenty of other plants, including clover and weeds, as well. This is not a problem for most horses; they like a range of tastes and are not usually being fattened up so don't need high-quality grass. However, there are some weeds that are dangerous for them to eat. It is vital that paddocks are checked regularly for these and they are removed. Ragwort (see above)

Posts and rails
This type of fencing is strong and effective, but expensive. It is important to use good-quality, weather-proofed timber. Wooden fencing needs regular painting with wood preservative.

is one of the best known poisonous plants. Horses rarely eat it unless they are very hungry, but it should be dug out and burned, or otherwise destroyed, as it is palatable when dry. Buttercups are also poisonous. They are not often eaten, but the plants spread very quickly in damp conditions. Spraying with herbicide may be necessary to keep control of them since digging out is not really possible. Other weeds, such as docks and nettles are not poisonous, but can spread, especially where droppings aren't picked up. Horses don't eat them and they are unsightly. Topping (see box) is one way to keep them in check.

FENCES AND HEDGES

The best paddock boundary is post and rail fencing. This looks good and is safe for horses. However, it is expensive and must

Horse paddock
The key to maintaining a good horse paddock is to keep the grass topped (cut) to a uniform height and weed free. Trees and hedges are a good source of shade and shelter.

be maintained properly as broken rails can cause injury or allow escapes. Crib biters (see p.336) can damage it too.

Barbed wire can cause horrific injuries. If it is used, an inner barrier of electric fencing should be set up so the horses cannot come into contact with the barbed wire. Plain wire and wire meshes are acceptable, but must be taut and well-maintained. Horses can get a hoof or shoe stuck in mesh fencing, and electric fencing should be used to keep them a safe distance away.

Hedges and banks are good boundaries and provide some shelter from wind and rain, but they should usually be reinforced with fencing of some sort as horses can be very good escape artists, especially in winter when they are foraging for more food.

WATER

Fresh water in a trough or delivered in buckets must be readily available to all horses at all times. If you notice equine disagreements occurring at the water trough,

Water supply
Water troughs should be constructed of non-ferrous metal that will not rust. The trough should be placed at a site with good drainage to ensure the surrounding area does not become too muddy.

Purpose-built shelter
Field shelters—a shed with a large opening—are ideal for providing a horse with shelter from sun and rain. The back of the shelter should face the prevailing wind.

provide an alternative source. Some horses like to be in charge and water troughs and hay mangers are popular places for them to assert their authority.

SHELTER

While horses can often be seen outside in the most miserable of weather, standing with their bottoms to the rain, wind, or snow, in summer they happily spend all day inside a field shelter away from the heat and flies. It is vital to give them the choice of escaping from the elements should they wish to. A field shelter should be large enough to fit all the horses that are

in the paddock and have a big entrance so the boss can't patrol it, keeping out, or in, horses lower in the pecking order. Ideally, it should have a concrete or hardcore floor that extends outside by 10 ft (3 m) or so, otherwise the ground will get very poached.

GATES

Gates that are easy to open and close are essential, although they should not be easy for horses to open. Catches must be secure and without protruding parts as horses will gather around a gate at feed time: legs, eyes, and rugs are all vulnerable to damage. Depending on where the gate is in the field boundary, opening out is probably better than opening in. The hinges should be by the corner to avoid you and your horse getting caught in a tight squeeze. Gateways also get muddy and plenty of hardcore should help. Avoid using bark chippings or sawdust as these break down and then actually help the soil retain moisture.

GRASS MAINTENANCE

Harrowing—towing a chain harrow behind a tractor or ATV—allows air and moisture to get to the grass roots, which will improve growth. The "teeth" comb through the grass and other vegetation, stripping out dead material and loosening the soil surface. Winter paddocks can get badly poached. The quickest way to smooth off all the lumps and bumps, and help restore the health of the grass, is to use a roller in a process known as rolling. These are very heavy and usually need a tractor to tow them. Topping—mowing on a high cut—gets rid of long coarse grass and cuts weeds, such as nettles, down before they have a chance to set seed.

NETTLES

Stables and stable management

How horses are kept depends on what suits their owners, what they are used for, and the facilities that are available. The spectrum ranges from semi-feral herds that receive little or no regular attention, to carefully cosseted racehorses, housed in purpose-built stables and with personal grooms.

TIME TO GRAZE

Horses that are kept for recreation or competition are usually managed by dividing their time between being turned out to eat grass in fields and paddocks and being stabled. The amount of turn-out can vary considerably. Some horses live in grassy pastures all year with access to field shelters for protection against the weather and flies (see pp.336–37). This type of minimal management is often combined with occasional stabling—at night during the worst winter weather, for example.

STABLE TIME

A very common practice is to turn out during the day and stable at night for most of the year. Although this involves a bit more work for the owner, it makes it easier to feed individual horses specific diets and allows for daily grooming, health checks, and so on. However, horses at risk of laminitis (see p.346) are often stabled for longer periods to control their food intake.

Top-class competition horses and racehorses are traditionally stabled for most of the time with only short periods of turn-out. With valuable performance

horses, one of the reasons for more or less continuous stabling is the worry that they might injure themselves if they are allowed to take unsupervised exercise. However, living in a stable is not natural for a horse. Horses that are confined to a stable get frustrated and bored and may develop stable vices (see box). Even just a daily hour or two at liberty, ideally with companions, is very beneficial for a horse's mental and physical health.

The stableyard
Being able to see other horses in the stableyard creates a limited opportunity to socialize. Horses are, by nature, herd animals so this is an important contributing factor to their psychological health.

STABLE DESIGN

Where there are lots of horses living in a herd-type arrangement, the easiest form of stabling is an open barn with plenty of bedding on the floor, mangers full of hay around the edges or in the middle, and access to water. In some cases, the horses can be allowed to come and go from the barn as they wish. Alternatively, they can be kept in during bad weather. However, in many cases, especially where horses are kept in smaller numbers, it is more convenient to keep them in individual stables.

Most stables have the same basic design. Today, the most common types of stables are loose boxes and stalls. The loose boxes are larger, like individual rooms, and they may be enclosed within a larger barn. They consist of a square or rectangular box, ideally about 12 x 14 ft (3.7 x 4.3 m), with a large, outward-opening door, split into two, on one side. Traditionally, these boxes are in rows with

STABLE VICES

■ Windsucking: the horse ingests air and flexes the underside of it's neck in a sucking action. This gives it digestive problems, including ulcers.
■ Crib-biting: the horse grasps a stable door or fence with its teeth, gripping and grinding them. This damages the teeth, as well as property, and causes digestive problems.
■ Weaving: the horse shifts its weight from one leg to another while also waving its head to and fro. This stresses the front legs and the neck muscles. It may wear out the floor of the stable.
■ Box-walking: the horse constantly circles around the stable and may paw the ground or kick the stable door. Again, this places stress on the front legs and hooves and may damage the stable floor.

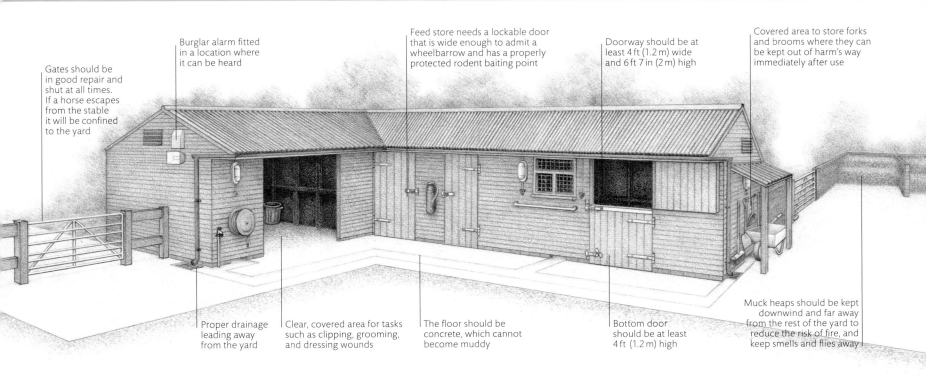

Gates should be in good repair and shut at all times. If a horse escapes from the stable it will be confined to the yard

Burglar alarm fitted in a location where it can be heard

Feed store needs a lockable door that is wide enough to admit a wheelbarrow and has a properly protected rodent baiting point

Doorway should be at least 4 ft (1.2 m) wide and 6 ft 7 in (2 m) high

Covered area to store forks and brooms where they can be kept out of harm's way immediately after use

Proper drainage leading away from the yard

Clear, covered area for tasks such as clipping, grooming, and dressing wounds

The floor should be concrete, which cannot become muddy

Bottom door should be at least 4 ft (1.2 m) high

Muck heaps should be kept downwind and far away from the rest of the yard to reduce the risk of fire, and keep smells and flies away

American barn
In this type of stabling, boxes face each other across a central aisle. The entire area is covered to provide protection, which creates a better environment for horses: they can see and communicate.

the doors looking out onto a yard, which may be lined with stables on two or three sides. The best kind of stabling is probably the American barn method. In American barns, rows of boxes face into the center of the building, which provides better protection against the weather. Increasingly there are grills between stables so that the horses can see each other, which is very important for their psychological well-being.

Stalls, a variation on stables, are less suitable for long-term occupation. They tend to be narrower than stables and the horses are often tied up when in them because there are no doors. In some, the horses

are tied facing the wall, which restricts their vision, too. They are useful as temporary accommodation for horses that have been brought in to be ridden, such as during a horse show or polo match. Stalls are also used in army barracks.

Whatever their design, stables must be well ventilated, but not drafty. Top doors must be left open at all times when the box is occupied. They should be reasonably insulated since the horse inside cannot move much to keep warm; in addition, stabled horses are often also clipped (see p.341). Most stabled horses are rugged in winter for this reason. Drainage is vital for cleaning stables and to ensure they do not get over-wet from urine or spilled water when in use.

Mucking out
Mucking out is usually done with a fork, a shovel, a broom, and a wheelbarrow, although there are additional tools that can be used depending on the choice of bedding.

Ideal site and buildings
The ideal yard has easy access to paddocks and covered areas for horses, feed, and storage. It should be built on two or more sides of a square and the site should be level.

BEDDING AND MUCKING OUT

The traditional bedding material is wheat straw. Nowadays, wood shavings and other wood-based materials, along with shedded paper, hemp, and miscanthus, are more popular. These newer materials have several advantages over straw. They are dust-free and horses don't eat them. They are also more absorbent, making it easier to see and remove urine-soaked areas. Rubber flooring is widely used, often in conjunction with softer bedding materials. It is easily cleaned and labor-intensive. Although comparatively expensive to install, rubber flooring reduces the amount of soft bedding required, so there is less waste to put on the muck heap.

The best practice is to clean out beds every day, removing all damp and soiled bedding and remaking the bed with some additional fresh bedding. A variation, known as deep littering, is removing droppings daily and doing a thorough muck out once a week or at longer intervals. This saves some time each day, but the thorough muck out will take longer. It can also lead to the bedding becoming smelly and moldy, which affects the horse's health. Dirty bedding can cause hoof and breathing problems.

Comfortable companions
Although horses don't need to be stabled, they like to be safe and with other horses. In hot countries and those with harsh winters, stabling can provide a comfortable refuge.

Grooming and care

Domesticated horses are groomed and usually shod to keep them healthy and capable of doing the work required of them. They need regular visits from the farrier and equine dentist, and at least annual vaccinations to protect them from tetanus and other diseases.

GROOMING

Most horses are groomed before being worked so that the horse looks tidy and the tack doesn't rub against dirt on the skin, causing sores. Grooming also helps to keep the skin healthy and the tack clean. The extent of the grooming depends on how dirty the horse is, whether it has a winter or summer coat, and how clean the rider or driver wants their horse to be. Horses that are stabled for much of the time are usually groomed before and after exercise, which helps to keep them occupied and their

coats healthy. Horses that are turned out often prefer a good roll in a dusty or muddy patch after being worked, and this does seem to deter flies.

Although there are electric groomers and vacuum cleaners, most people still brush their horses by hand. It is an opportunity to pamper your horse and bond with him too. First, remove any mud using a plastic curry comb and a dandy brush. These are quite rough, so avoid delicate areas, such as the face. Take care when brushing the legs and belly. These are sensitive and you are in a

vulnerable position if the horse reacts badly to being brushed here. Next, use a body brush to remove dust, loose hair, and skin, and to produce a shine on the coat. A soft body brush can be used carefully on the face and around the ears. There are smaller brushes that can make this job a bit easier. Some horses love having their ears brushed inside and out, but don't assume this will be the case when you first groom a horse.

Brush out the mane and tail with a comb or dandy brush. There are spray-on liquids that help to detangle this longer hair and

GROOMING EQUIPMENT

Grooming kit consists of various brushes for different purposes and a few other items, such as hoof picks and combs. These are best stored in a tray (above). Each horse should have its own grooming kit, which should be kept clean.

Dandy brush
This stiff-bristled brush is used to remove mud from the legs and body.

Body brush
Soft bristles are good for cleaning the coat and brushing the more sensitive parts of the body.

Plastic curry comb
This plastic-bristled comb is used for breaking up caked mud on the body and for cleaning dandy brushes.

Metal curry comb
A metal curry comb is for cleaning other brushes only and should never be used on a horse.

Rubber curry comb
This curry comb is useful when a horse is shedding its winter coat, as the rubber draws out the hairs.

Water brush
A damp brush is used for "laying" (smoothing down) the hairs of the mane and tail. Detangler sprays can be used instead.

Soft sponge
Use separate sponges to wet and clean the face and dock (tail area).

Massage pad
This is used to massage the horse after riding.

Hoof pick
This hooked metal tool is for removing mud from the hooves.

Metal comb
This is for combing and "pulling" (removing long hairs with a quick tug) the mane and tail.

Stable rubber
Actually a linen cloth, the stable rubber is used to give the coat a final polish.

make the job easier for you and more pleasant for the horse; they also give the hair more body and produce a good shine. Longer hairs can be trimmed or pulled to tidy the overall appearance.

Pick out the soles of the hooves removing mud and grit. It is recommended that the hoof pick is used from the back to the front of the hoof to avoid knocking the sensitive areas around the heel and lower leg.

BRAIDING

When horses are being shown or tidied up for driving, for instance, the mane and tail are often braided. The mane is divided into 9–12 short braids, plus one on the forelock. Once braided, these are usually rolled up into a neat ball. The tail hair may simply be trimmed around the top or it can be braided by bringing small sections of hair from each side and braiding them together in the middle. This type of braid continues about a third of the way down the tail, the rest of which is left loose. More complicated designs can be used, depending on the desired end result.

Braiding the tail
The hairs of a horse's tail grow around the dock, so you cannot simply divide the hair into three as you would human hair. You have to bring in successive sections of hair from each side as you braid down the tail.

CLIPPING THE COAT

In the winter, horses in cold countries grow a thick coat for protection against the cold weather. Horses that work hard, such as jumping or galloping, are often clipped to remove much or all of this coat. This reduces sweating and makes it easier to keep them clean. There is a wide variety of rugs that can be used to keep them warm when they are at rest. There are no hard and fast rules about how much hair to remove when clipping. Usually it is a matter of the taste of the rider or owner. The lightest clip is a trace clip, which removes the hair on the underside of the neck and belly. A blanket clip takes more off, leaving the back unclipped, while a hunter just leaves a saddle patch.

Most of the coat is left unclipped

When a horse is in harness (side straps), the traces usually run along this line

Trace clip
The aim of a trace clip is to remove hair only from areas where sweat accumulates when a horse is worked, which are the underside of the neck, the chest, the top of the legs and the belly. If you prefer, you can just clip the hair from the underside of the neck and the belly.

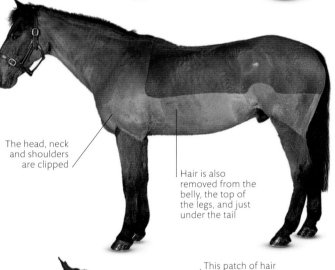

The head, neck and shoulders are clipped

Hair is also removed from the belly, the top of the legs, and just under the tail

Blanket clip
The effect of this clip is the same as a horse wearing an exercise sheet during long periods of slow work as it allows sweat to evaporate, but prevents the horse's hindquarter muscles from getting cold.

This patch of hair protects the skin from friction with the saddle

Hunter clip
For a hunter clip, you should leave only the saddle area and the horse's legs unclipped. The horse will need to wear a rug whenever it isn't being exercised.

In all three clips, hair is left on the legs to give some protection from the cold and mud

HOOF CARE AND SHOEING

A horse's hoof is composed of the wall, sole, and frog. The wall, which is the part of the hoof that can be seen when a horse has its feet on the ground, consists of horn. Horn is made of a tough material called keratin—the same material that human finger- and toenails are made of—and, like nails, is produced continuously.

Working horses usually have metal shoes on their hooves, but increasingly people have "barefoot" horses, or make use of rubber boots to protect the hooves when riding. The shoe protects the hoof from being worn away more quickly than it can be replaced by natural growth, and it also improves the grip of the foot. When shoeing, it is vital that the farrier takes into account the horse's natural action, but in some cases, shoeing can also remedy conformational defects, enabling the horse to work more correctly and so avoid problems such as tripping or overreaching (see p.346).

Horses are reshod every 4–6 weeks. The old shoe is removed and the hoof trimmed to remove the excess growth that would be worn away if the horse was barefoot. Most farriers carry a range of shoe sizes and designs, but the final fitting is usually done by heating

Removing a shoe
Farriers have a range of specialist tools, some of which are only used for shoeing a horse. This farrier is using a buffer and hammer to remove a worn metal shoe.

the shoe in a forge and shaping it to suit the individual hoof. It is pressed to the hoof while still hot to check the fit. This is known as hot shoeing. The shoe is nailed to the hoof, which, just like a human nail, is insensitive.

Although metal shoes have been used for centuries, their disadvantage is that they restrict the natural working of the hoof. The shoe prevents the hoof from expanding and contracting as it hits the ground and this often results in the frog shrinking and no longer touching the ground. The frog has an elastic consistency and helps to absorb the shock of impact. It also helps to pump the blood up the legs, so if the frog shrinks, it will affect the blood flow to and from the foot.

Barefoot horses are worked without shoes and their owners know that they need to watch for excess wear of the exposed horn. There are many different designs of rubber boot that can be used to protect hooves that are overworn or those that are sensitive to hard surfaces, which is often the case when the shoes are first removed. Once they are accustomed to going without shoes, most leisure horses cope very well since they are often worked on soft surfaces and for fewer hours compared to a working horse in the past.

TEETH CARE

Horse teeth grow continuously and, in a natural environment, they are worn down when horses chew coarse food, such as stalky grasses and scrubby vegetation. Domesticated horses require regular dental care because their diet usually lacks these coarser elements. In addition, uneven wear, sometimes caused by eating hard feeds and hay, leads to the teeth developing sharp edges that can ulcerate the insides of the cheeks. Equine dentists use rasps to remove sharp edges and rebalance the grinding surfaces. Perhaps surprisingly, most horses tolerate this work, which requires the mouth to be held open with a gag.

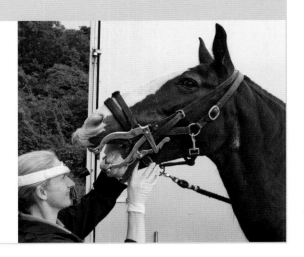

DEWORMING

It used to be standard practice to give horses an anthelmintic (dewormer) every six to eight weeks throughout the year to ensure that they were free of gut parasites (worms). However, it was found that regular deworming was leading to resistance in the parasites to the chemicals in anthelmintics. Studies also showed that up to 80 percent of horses have resistance to worms, especially horses that are well looked after and kept on healthy ground. Nowadays, a combination of dung removal from pasture to reduce the spread of worms and twice yearly deworming is considered to be sufficient for most horses. Cross grazing with other animals, such as sheep and cattle can also reduce the spread of parasites in pasture.

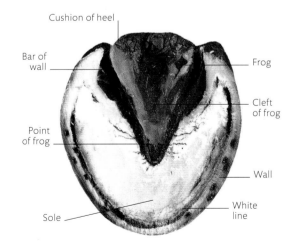

Underside of a healthy hoof
The white line separates the insensitive wall from the concave sole of the hoof. It is the hard horn wall that bears the horse's weight and to which the shoe is fixed.

Cushion of heel
Bar of wall
Point of frog
Sole
Frog
Cleft of frog
Wall
White line

Brushing with care
Most horses love being brushed, but most have one or two areas, such as the belly or ears, where they find it ticklish or irritating. A haynet, which they also enjoy, will help to distract them.

Signs of health

You can recognize a healthy horse by its shiny coat, bright eyes, pricked ears, and contented demeanor. Watching it walk, trot, and canter will help you to judge whether it is fit. Most owners regularly run their hands over their horse's body and legs to check for lumps and signs of discomfort.

KNOW YOUR HORSE

One of the best ways to be sure that your horse is healthy is to get to know him very well. Watch him grazing in the field; observe him in the stable. Get to know all his little character traits, along with all existing lumps and bumps and every ticklish spot, then you'll notice if anything changes. Watch how he eats and whether he drinks afterward or, perhaps, at a different time.

It is very important that horses have a good drink every day, so if you notice he is not drinking then that's a sure sign something is up.

Once they have settled in and know their surroundings and companions, most horses are fairly calm so long as their daily routine stays the same. Get to know your horse's habits. If he is usually unflappable then you should be alert to other problems if he

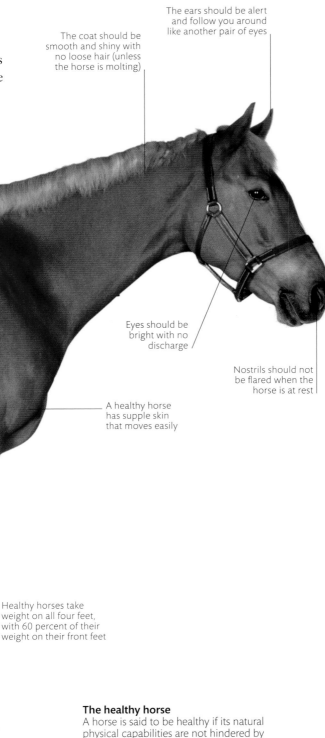

The ears should be alert and follow you around like another pair of eyes

The coat should be smooth and shiny with no loose hair (unless the horse is molting)

Eyes should be bright with no discharge

Nostrils should not be flared when the horse is at rest

A healthy horse has supple skin that moves easily

The tail should be clean, without rubbed patches on the dock. It should be relaxed, not clamped between the legs or held to one side as the horse trots

Healthy horses take weight on all four feet, with 60 percent of their weight on their front feet

The hooves should not have any horizontal grooves or vertical cracks. The horn should not be broken or split where it meets the ground

The healthy horse
A horse is said to be healthy if its natural physical capabilities are not hindered by disease or accident. There are many signs of health that can be observed.

VITAL SIGNS

Pulse and resting respiration vary between horses, so it is important to get to know your horse's particular vital signs. Pulse should be 36–42 a minute, slightly more in younger animals. Temperature 100.5°F (38.5°C); over 103°F (39.5°C) indicates a serious problem. Breathing rate is around 12 breaths per minute.

To measure your horse's pulse, place the tip of your fingers on the artery that passes over the edge of the cheek bone

To check your horse's circulation, press hard with a finger on his gum. It should take no more than four seconds for the white area to regain its pink color

starts box-walking (see p.336) or goes off his food. Similarly, suspect a problem if a horse that is usually alert and lively becomes quiet and withdrawn.

Droppings are a good reflection of a horse's overall health. They do vary from horse to horse (get to know yours), but in general they should be well-formed but soft. Very loose or dry hard droppings may

Observing your horse
It is important to observe your horse when he is grazing and observe his eating habits. Most horses have fixed eating habit and if they change their behavior it is a sign that something is wrong.

be a sign of intestinal problems. If your horse does not pass droppings for several hours, this can indicate colic (see p.346). If he shows other signs of discomfort as well it is vital to call your vet.

The distinction between healthy and unhealthy domestic horses is far less clear than in the wild. Equally, a horse may be healthy but this doesn't mean it is fit.

Obesity
Being overweight is a particular problem in horses in good pastures and doing little work. It causes many health problems.

HEALTHY WEIGHT

The general appearance of a horse will tell you a lot about his health and fitness. Condition scoring considers condition (fat cover) in more detail. It is based on a scale that ranges from 0—where the horse is emaciated and his ribs and pelvis are clearly visible—to 5—where the horse is obese with fat deposits on his neck, shoulders, and

hindquarters. Diseases such as laminitis (see p.346) and equine metabolic syndrome (similar to diabetes) are closely linked to condition, so it is important to check your horse regularly and take steps to avoid him becoming very overweight. Well kept horses should never be thin or emaciated, so a very low bodyweight is often a sign of an underlying health problem.

SIGNS OF PROBLEMS

Observing your horse and its behavior will allow you to spot any deviations from its normal habits. The following signs may indicate health issues.
- Dark-colored urine
- Front leg lameness (nodding the head in walk or trot)
- Hind leg lameness (dropping one hip more than the other in walk or trot)
- Continual shifting of weight from one leg to another

- Pain, heat, and swelling, particularly in the legs or hooves
- Refusing to eat or stopping eating
- Straining while trying to swallow during eating
- Lying down and unable or unwilling to get up
- Persistent rolling, often accompanied by sweating and pawing the ground
- Raised temperature, pulse, and breathing rate
- Lowered temperature, pulse, and breathing rate
- Coughing and nasal discharge

- Abnormal sound during breathing
- Swelling or an unusual lump on the body
- Wound of any size
- Heat or swelling in a joint
- Swollen eye or eyelids
- Unintentional weight loss
- Loose droppings
- Loss of coat in patches
- Scratching and rubbing mane or tail
- Retaining winter coat year-round

Equine health

Despite their great size, horses are comparatively delicate creatures and are prone to a range of health issues. Some are related to the fact that horses are worked, which puts undue pressure on the limbs and back. They can also stem from the digestive system, which is very sensitive in horses.

LEGS AND BACK

Riding horses puts extra stress on an animal that is already carrying its own not insignificant weight on four slender limbs. Strained tendons are common, along with bruising of the soles of the hooves. Arthritic changes and inflammation in various leg joints or in the small bones of the legs and feet, such as the sesamoids or the navicular, also cause lameness. Some problems can be eased with rest and treatment, others are more or less permanent. Overreach injuries, where the toe of a hind foot hits the heel or pastern of the front leg, cutting it, sometimes quite deeply, can be avoided by protecting the front feet and lower legs with various designs of wraparound "boots." These are also used to avoid "brushing" injuries, where one foot catches the leg beside it as the horse moves.

Laminitis is a serious condition that affects the feet. The tissues of the hoof become inflamed and because there is no room for swelling this causes a great deal of pain. In bad cases, the pedal bone (see p.15) drops, requiring extensive veterinary treatment over a long period. Laminitis occurs in overweight horses and is linked to a disease similar to diabetes, called equine metabolic syndrome. Horses often suffer recurring bouts. Another painful hoof problem is abcesses, where pus builds up in the foot. This is relatively easily relieved by making a hole in the sole of the foot for the pus to drain out.

Back problems often stem from a poorly fitted saddle, which restricts the movement of the shoulders or rubs the back. It is vital to have saddles fitted by an expert and checked annually to ensure the fit is still good. Some back problems and non-specific muscle discomfort can be relieved by equine chiropractors, who offer manipulation and massage.

DIGESTION

All horse owners dread colic. Basically stomachache, colic ranges from a mild attack, which can be eased with muscle relaxants, to twists and torsions, which require surgery to remove affected parts of the bowel and often result in death. Colic has many causes, but can be triggered by a simple change in diet, parasitic worms, or stress. Other possibilities are ingestion of sand, dental problems, and lack of water. Signs of colic include sweating, pawing the ground, rolling, stretching, and restless behavior.

Choke is a problem that is associated with eating too fast. Food gets stuck in the throat and the horse becomes distressed as it tries to swallow; mucus can run from its nose and mouth. Although horrible to see, choke often resolves itself within a few minutes. If not, then veterinary treatment may be needed.

SKIN

Sweet itch is among the most common skin disorders in horses. An allergic reaction to midge bites, it causes itching on the neck and tail, which the horse relieves by rubbing until the skin is raw. Fly sheets, sprays, and lotions can reduce the effects, but the most successful way to avoid sweet itch, which is not curable, is to stable a horse in the mornings and evenings, when midges are at their most active.

Sarcoids and melanomas are two other common skin problems. Sarcoids are skin cancers that can be treated by freezing, immune therapy (injecting with BCG),

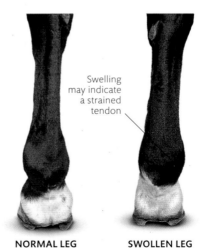

Swelling may indicate a strained tendon

NORMAL LEG   **SWOLLEN LEG**

Always treat a swelling
Never ignore a swollen leg, even if the horse is not lame. Use a cold treatment, such as a freeze pack, on the swelling until the problem has been diagnosed.

Rolling
Rolling is normal horse social and grooming behavior—they often roll in the company of other horses or they might just be scratching an itch. However, if a horse rolls persistently it may have colic and will need to be treated.

or creams, or by using radiation or lasers. This can be successful, although some sarcoids recur and may then grow aggressively. Melanomas are skin lumps that affect mostly gray horses. They can also grow internally. Although not as dangerous as the human equivalent, they are particularly likely to develop around the anus, which they can eventually block, meaning the horse has to be euthanized. There are various treatments, but these are not always successful.

Other horse skin problems include sunburn on the pink skin of the face, which can be avoided by using sunblock cream, ringworm, rain scald, and mud fever (pastern

Washing legs
A horse's fetlocks and pasterns are prone to mud fever, and washing the legs with antiseptic shampoo helps to soften the scabs. The legs should be dried thoroughly and antibiotic cream applied.

dermatitis). Ringworm is a fungal infection. It causes hair loss and is highly contagious, including to humans, and is treated with antifungal creams and medicines put into feed. Rain scald and mud fever are bacterial infections of the body and legs. They are associated with warm, wet weather and are treated by keeping the affected area clean and dry and using creams.

CUSHING'S DISEASE

Older horses (over 15 years) may develop long curly coats that do not shed completely in spring. They can become potbellied with fat along the crest of their neck. These are classic signs of Cushing's disease, which is caused

by degeneration in the hypothalamus in the brain. Horses with Cushing's disease are more prone to laminitis. There are medical treatments for Cushing's disease, which can be managed quite well, although it will still develop and eventually lead to the death of the horse.

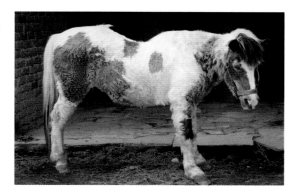

Poorly pony
The thick curly coat of this pony is a sign it has Cushing's disease. The way it is standing, with its front legs leaning back, indicates it also has laminitis.

Glossary

ABOVE THE BIT When the horse carries the mouth above the level of the rider's hand. This practice reduces the rider's control.

ACTION The movement of the skeletal frame in respect of locomotion.

AIDS Signals made by the rider or driver to communicate their wishes to the horse. The "natural" riding aids are the legs, hands, body-weight, and voice. The "artificial" aids are the whip and the spurs.

AIRS ABOVE THE GROUND High School movements including the capriole, courbette, and levade, in which the horse has either the forelegs or all four feet off the ground. These movements, due to their complexity, are usually performed only by classical riding schools, such as the Spanish Riding School and Cadre Noir.

ALLELE Alternative forms of a gene that influence characteristics, such as coat color, depending on whether the allele is dominant or recessive relative to the other alleles.

AMBLE The slower form of the lateral pacing gait. *See* Pacer.

ARTICULATION Where two or more bones meet to form a joint.

ASIAN HORSES A loosely applied term referring to horses of Eastern origin, either Arab or Barb, in use during the formative years of the English Thoroughbred.

BARREL The body between the forearms and the loins.

BEHIND THE BIT When the horse tucks its nose behind the vertical, avoiding the bit.

BLUE FEET Dense, blue-black coloring of the horn of the hooves.

BONE (i) The measurement around the leg just below the knee or hock. The bone measurement determines the horse's ability to carry weight. (ii) The individual components of the skeleton.

BOW-HOCKS Hocks turned in at the points. *See also* cow-hocks.

BOXY FOOT A narrow, upright foot with a small frog and a closed heel. Also known as club, donkey, or mule foot.

BREAKING The early schooling or education of a horse for the various purposes for which it may be required; also called backing if the horse is intended for riding.

BREED An equine group that displays consistent characteristics and/or levels of performance and whose pedigrees are entered in a studbook.

BROOD MARE A mare used for breeding.

BY Used in conjunction with the name of a sire, i.e. by so-and-so. A horse is said to be "out of" a mare.

CABALLINE A term used to distinguish the domestic and Przewalski's horses from the other equids.

CANNON BONE The bone of the foreleg between the knee and the fetlock. Also called the "shin bone." The corresponding bone in the hind leg is the called the shannon, or shank.

CARRIAGE HORSE A relatively light, elegant horse for private or hackney carriage use.

CART HORSE A coldblood draft horse.

CAVALRY REMOUNT A horse used for service in an army unit. Also called a "trooper."

CHESTNUTS (i) Small, horny excrescences (outgrowths), also called castors, on the inside of all four legs of most domestic horses and Przewalski's horse. They are only present on the forelegs of zebras and asses. (ii) A rich brown coat color.

CHIN GROOVE The indent above the lower lip. When a horse is bridled, this is where the curb chain of the bit lies so it can also be called the curb groove.

CHROMOSOME A threadlike structure within cells that carries genetic information. All domestic horses have 64 chromosomes whereas the donkey has only 62.

CLEAN-LEGGED Without feather on the lower limbs. This is particularly used to describe draft and harness horses, many of which do have feathering. For example, the Cleveland Bay and Suffolk Punch are clean-legged.

CLOSE-COUPLED Usually means a short back, which is particularly desirable in a dressage horse since it allows collection. Also indicates a strong, weight-carrying build.

CLOSED STUDBOOK New registrations are only accepted if bred from mares and stallions already listed in the studbook or breed registry. No outside blood is allowed.

COACH HORSE A powerful, strongly built horse capable of drawing a heavy coach.

COLDBLOOD The generic name for the European heavy breeds.

COLLECTION The concentration of the horses's forces toward the center as a result of a shortened base line accompanied by a lowered croup, a raised carriage of the neck, and the head held on the vertical plane.

COLT An uncastrated male horse up to four years old. Male foals are called "colt foals."

CONFORMATION The manner in which the horse is "put together" with particular regard to its proportions.

COW-HOCKS Hocks turned in at the points like those of a cow. *See also* bow-hocks.

CROSSBREEDING The mating of individuals of different breeds, types or species.

CROUP This extends from the highest point of the topline as it meets the hindquarters to the top of the tail. A "croup-high" is a horse where the highest point of the croup is higher than the withers.

DAM A horse's female parent.

DEPTH OF GIRTH The measurement from the withers to the elbow. "Good depth of girth" describes generous measurements between the two points.

DESERT HORSE The term used to describe horses bred in desert conditions or horses bred from such desert stock. They are resistant to heat and able to cope with a minimal water intake.

DIPPED BACK A hollow back between the withers and the croup. A dipped back often occurs in old age.

DILUTION GENE The name given to genes in which the recessive allele, when inherited from both parents, lightens color. Dilution genes can influence coat color, and sometimes eye and skin color too.

DISHED FACE A concave head profile, particularly found in Arab horses, but also in some other breeds.

DISHING The action of the foreleg when the toe is thrown outward in a circular movement. Usually considered to be faulty action.

DNA (deoxyribonucleic acid) The material that makes up chromosomes. It is found in cells and carries the genetic information necessary for making and maintaining an organism.

DOCK The part of the tail on which the hair grows. Also the hairless underside.

DOCKING Amputation of part of the tail. This used to be done to draft horses to avoid the tail being caught in harness. It is now banned in many countries.

DOMINANT ALLELE An allele that masks the effect of a recessive allele. The feature it influences tends to be more common in a population because it is seen when the allele is inherited from both parents (homozygous condition) or from only one (heterozygous condition).

DORSAL-EEL STRIPE A continuous strip of black, brown, or dun hair extending from the neck to the tail. It is most usually found in dun-colored horses and other equids.

DRAFT A term applied to a horse drawing any vehicle but more usually associated with the heavy breeds.

DRY Sometimes used to describe the lean fine-skinned appearance of the head of desert-bred stock. There is an absence of fatty tissue and the veins stand out clearly on the skin.

ENGAGEMENT The hind legs are engaged when they are brought well under the body.

ENTIRE A term used to describe an uncastrated male horse (stallion).

EQUID A term used for all members of the horse family. Living species of equids are all of the *Equus* genus.

ERGOT The horny growth on the back of the fetlock joint.

EWE NECK A neck that is under-developed on its upper edge, sometimes due to the horse carrying its head high. The lower side of the neck often appears overdeveloped as a result.

EXTENSION The extension of the paces is the lengthening of the stride and outline. The opposite of collection.

EXTRAVAGANT ACTION High knee and hock action like that of the Hackney Horse and Pony, and the American Saddlebred.

FALSE RIBS The 10 asternal ribs to the rear of the eight "true" (sternal) ribs.

FEATHER Long hair on the lower legs and fetlocks. Usually abundant on heavy horses and found on some horses and ponies.

FILLY A female horse under four years old.

FIVE-GAITED An American term for the American Saddlebred, shown at walk, trot, and canter, as well as the rack (a fast walk) and slow lateral pace (a two-beated gait).

FLANK Area of the horse between the last rib and the hindquarters, and below the loins.

FLEXION i) The horse shows flexion when it yields its lower jaw to the bit, bending its neck softly at the poll. ii) The full bending of the hock joints.

FLOATING i) The action associated with the trotting gait of the Arab horse. ii) Rasping the teeth is also called floating.

FOAL Colt, gelding, or filly up to one year old.

FOREARM The foreleg above the knee and below the elbow.

FOREHAND The horse's head, neck, shoulder, withers, and forelegs.

FORELOCK The mane between the ears, which hangs over the forehead.

FOUR-IN-HAND A team of four harness horses.

FROG The rubbery pad of horn in the sole of the foot, which acts as a shock absorber.

FULL MOUTH A horse at six years with permanent teeth has a "full mouth."

GAITED HORSE American term for horses schooled to artificial as well as natural gaits.

GASKIN *See* Second thigh.

GELDING A castrated male horse.

GENE The basic unit of inheritance that determines what a horse's body looks like and how its body works.

GIRTH The circumference of the body measured from behind the withers around the barrel.

GOOSE-RUMP A steep slope from the croup to the top of the tail, thought to shorten stride length. Sometimes called the "jumper's bump."

HACK (i) A recognized type of light riding horse. (ii) "To hack", i.e. to go for a ride.

HALFBRED A cross between a Thoroughbred and any other breed. A Thoroughbred crossed with an Arab is an Anglo-Arab, a breed in its own right.

HAMES Metal arms fitting into the harness collar and linked to the traces.

HAND A unit of measurement of medieval origin, which describes a horse's height. One hand equals 4 in (10 cm).

HARNESS The collective term for the equipment of a driven horse. Not applicable to riding equipment.

HARNESS HORSE A horse used in harness with the associated conformation, such as straight shoulders and wide, strong chest, and having an elevated "harness action."

HAUTE ÉCOLE The classical art of advanced riding. *See also* Airs Above the Ground.

HEAVY HORSE Any large draft horse.

HEAVYWEIGHT A horse that, by virtue of its bone and substance, is judged capable of carrying weights of over 89 kg (196 lb).

HEMIONE A name used to distinguish the Asian wild asses from other equids.

HETEROZYGOUS A term given to the inheritance of a recessive gene allele from one parent and a dominant gene allele from the other.

HIGH-CROWNED TEETH Refers to teeth that grow some way above the gum line and are subject to significant wear from abrasive vegetation such as grass. In horses, the teeth are also open-rooted and so grow continually until well into old age.

HIGH SCHOOL *See* Haute École.

HINDQUARTERS The body from the rear of the flank to the top of the tail down to the top of the second thigh (gaskin).

HINNY The offspring of a female donkey (jenny) and a male horse (stallion). They are much rarer than mules.

HOGGED MANE A mane that has been removed by clipping.

HOLLOW BACK *See* Dipped Back.

HOMOZYGOUS A term given to the inheritance of the same gene allele (either recessive or dominant) from both parents.

HOTBLOOD A term used to describe Arabs, Barbs, and Thoroughbreds.

HYBRID A cross between any two equid species, such as a horse and an ass.

INBREEDING The mating of sire/daughter, son/dam, or brother/ sister to fix or accentuate a particular characteristic.

IN HAND When a horse is controlled from the ground rather than ridden.

JIBBAH The traditional name for the formation of the forehead of the Arab.

JOG TROT A short-paced trot.

LEADER Either of the two leading horses in a team of four, or a single horse harnessed in front of one or more horses. The "near" leader is the left-hand horse, and the "off" leader is the right-hand one.

LEVADE A classical air above the ground in which the forehand is lifted with bent forelegs on deeply bent hind legs—a controlled half-rear.

LIGHT HORSE A horse, other than a heavy horse or a pony, that is suitable for riding or carriage work.

LIGHT HORSEMAN Light cavalry capable of swift movement as opposed to heavily armed cavalry (heavy cavalry), relying principally upon the shock tactic of the charge.

LIGHT OF BONE Lack of bone below the knee. Considered a serious fault, it means the horse is less able to support a rider's weight without strain.

LIGHTWEIGHT A horse that, by virtue of its bone and substance, is judged capable of carrying weights up to 174 lb (79 kg)

LINE-BREEDING The mating of individuals with a common ancestor some generations removed to accentuate particular features.

LOADED SHOULDER When the forehand appears over-developed and heavy with upright shoulders and flat withers. This type of build usually gives the horse a short, choppy stride.

LOINS The area on either side of the spinal vertebrae lying just behind the saddle.

LOPE Slow Western canter performed with a natural head carriage.

LOW-CROWNED TEETH Refers to teeth with an enamel cap that only extend a short way above the gum line. The root is well defined and closed, so the teeth cannot grow continually. *Hyracotherium* had teeth like this.

MANÈGE An enclosure used for teaching and schooling horses.

MARE A female horse aged four or over.

MEALY NOSE Oatmeal-colored muzzle, like that of the Exmoor pony.

MIDDLEWEIGHT A horse that, by virtue of its bone and substance, is judged capable of carrying weights of up to 196 lb (89 kg).

MONODACTYLY Having only one toe on each foot.

MITBAH The traditional name for the angle between the head and the neck of the Arab.

MULE Offspring of a male donkey (jackass) and a female horse (mare).

NARROW BEHIND When weak muscling in the croup and thighs gives a too-slight appearance from behind.

NATIVE PONIES Ponies that live in semi-wild herds, particularly in the British Isles. Also another name for the British mountain and moorland breeds.

NICK The cutting and resetting of the muscles under the tail to give an artificially high carriage.

NON-CABALLINE A term that encompasses all equids except domestic and Przewalski's horses.

ON THE BIT A horse is "on the bit" when it relaxes its jaw to the bit and responds softly to the rein aids, carrying its head so that its profile is nearly vertical.

OPEN STUDBOOK Horses can be registered in an open studbook, regardless of their parentage, as long as they meet the criteria set out by the breed society. Qualities needed for entry can be stringent and relate to conformation, performance, or both. Color "breeds," such as Palomino, need only conform in respect of their color.

OUTCROSS The mating of unrelated horses; introduction of outside blood to the breed.

OUT OF Used in conjunction with the dam, i.e. out of so-and-so. A horse is said to be "by" a sire.

PACER A horse that has a lateral action at trot rather than the conventional diagonal movement, i.e. near fore and near hind together followed by the offside pair.

PACK HORSE A horse used to transport goods in packs carried on either side of its back.

PARIETAL BONES The bones on the top of the skull.

PARTBRED Progeny of a Thoroughbred and another breed, e.g. Welsh partbred.

PEDIGREE Details of ancestry recorded in a studbook.

PIEBALD English term for body coloring of black and white patches.

PIGEON TOES A conformational fault in which the feet are turned inward. Sometimes called pin-toes.

PLAITING A potentially dangerous fault in the action when the feet cross over each other in movement.

POINTS (i) External features of the horse comprising its conformation. (ii) Relating to color, e.g. bay with black points, meaning a bay with black lower legs, mane, and tail.

POLL Part of the head between or just behind the ears.

POLYDACTYLY In horses, having more than one toe on each foot.

POSTILLION A rider driving a harness horse, usually one of a pair or team, from the saddle.

PREORBITAL The part of the face below the eye of a horse extending to the end of the muzzle.

PREPOTENCY The ability consistently to pass on character and type to the progeny.

PUREBRED Horse of unmixed breeding.

QUALITY The element of refinement in breeds and types, usually due to Arab or Thoroughbred influence.

QUARTERS *See* Hindquarters.

RACEHORSE A horse bred for racing, usually a Thoroughbred but also other breeds.

RACK The fifth gait of the American Saddlebred. "A flashy, fast, four-beat gait," unrelated to pacing.

RAM-HEAD A convex profile like that of the Barb. Similar to Roman nose.

RANGY Description of a horse having size and scope of movement.

RECESSIVE ALLELE A gene allele that must be inherited from both parents for the feature to appear in their offspring.

RIDING HORSE A horse suitable for riding with the conformation associated with comfortable riding action (as opposed to draft or carriage).

ROACHED MANE American term for hogged mane.

ROADSTER (i) The famous Norfolk Roadster, a trotting saddle horse, ancestor of the modern Hackney. (ii) In the US, a light harness horse, usually a Standardbred.

ROMAN NOSE The convex profile as found in the Shire and other heavy breeds. *See also* Ram-head.

RUNNING HORSE English racing stock, also called Running Stock, which provided the base for the Thoroughbred when crossed with imported Eastern sires.

SADDLE HORSE (i) A riding horse. (ii) A wooden trestle to support saddles.

SADDLE MARKS White hair under the saddle area probably caused by a poorly fitting saddle.

SCHOOL MOVEMENTS The gymnastic exercises carried on within a school. Also "school figures" involving movement patterns. *See also* Airs Above the Ground and Manège.

SCOPE Capability for freedom of movement to a special degree.

SECOND THIGH The muscle extending from the stifle down to the hock. Also called the gaskin.

SET TAIL A tail broken or nicked and set to give an artificially high carriage.

SHANNON BONE Hind cannon bone. Also called the shank.

SHORT-COUPLED *See* Close-Coupled.

SHOULDER The horse's shoulder has no bony attachment to the rest of the skeleton. *See also* Upright Shoulder and Sloped Shoulder.

SICKLE HOCKS Weak, bent hocks resembling a sickle shape.

SIRE A horse's male parent.

SKEWBALD English term for body color of irregular white and colored patches other than black.

SLAB-SIDED A horse with flat ribs.

SLOPED SHOULDER Shoulders that have a long slope from the top by the withers to the joint with the humerus give the horse a long, smooth stride.

SOUND HORSE A horse that is not lame. It can also refer to one that has an excellent conformation and is in good health, has no blemishes or defects, and moves straight in all limbs.

STALLION An uncastrated male horse of four years old or more.

STAMP A prepotent stallion is said to stamp his stock with his own character and physical attributes. *See* Prepotency.

STAMP OF HORSE A recognizable type, or pattern, of horse.

STUD (i) A breeding establishment—a stud farm. (ii) A stallion.

STUDBOOK A book kept by a breed society in which the pedigrees of stock eligible for entry are recorded. Some breed societies have a closed studbook. Others have an open studbook. Some may have both.

SUBSTANCE The physical quality of the body in terms of its build and general musculature.

TACK Saddlery; an abbreviation of "tackle."

TOPLINE The line of the back from the withers to the end of the croup.

TURNOUT Standard of dress and accoutrements of a horse and rider, or of a driven vehicle.

TYPE A horse fulfilling a particular purpose (such as a Cob, a Hunter, and a Hack) but which does not necessarily belong to a specific breed.

UPRIGHT SHOULDER A shoulder that falls steeply from the withers to the humerus produces a short, choppy stride. This may be considered a desirable trait, in the Icelandic horse and draft horses, for example, and was once very fashionable in riding horses.

UP TO WEIGHT A term describing a horse that, on account of its substance, bone, size, and overall conformation, is capable of carrying a substantial weight.

WARMBLOOD In general terms, a half- or partbred horse, the result of an Arab or Thoroughbred cross with other blood or bloods, usually coldbloods.

WEIGHT CARRIER A horse capable of carrying 209 lb (95.2 kg). Also called a heavyweight horse.

ZEBRA BARS Dark, striped markings on the forearms and occasionally on the hindlegs as well.

Index

QR

S

T

Acknowledgments

The publishers would like to thank the following people:

Duncan Turner, Alex Lloyd, Steve Woosnam-Savage, Sharon Spencer, Rohit Bhardwaj, and Sanjay Chauhan, for design help; Frankie Piscitelli, Rupa Rao, Riji Raju, Nisha Shaw, Antara Moitra, Priyanjali Narain, and Ira Pundeer for editorial support; Elizabeth Wise for the index; Kaiya Shang for proofreading; Joanna Weeks and Kim Bryant for additional text; Jagtar Singh, Ashok Kumar and Sachin Singh for technical support; and Magdalena Strakova for images and additional text.

Picture Credits

The publisher would like to thank the following for their kind permission to reproduce their photographs:
(Key: a-above; b-below/bottom; c-center; f-far; l-left; r-right; t-top)

1 Alamy Stock Photo: Juniors Bildarchiv GmbH. **2–3 Getty Images:** Kelly Bowden. **4–5 Dreamstime.com:** Jeanne Provost. **6–7 Alamy Stock Photo:** Juniors Bildarchiv GmbH. **8 Dorling Kindersley:** Royal Veterinary College, University of London (tr). **13 123RF.com:** Kongsak Sumano (cl). **Alamy Stock Photo:** Norman Owen Tomalin (c); tbkmedia.de (cr). **Dreamstime.com:** Christian Degroote (clb). **14 Dorling Kindersley:** Irish Draught Foal- Gort Mill Mr R J Lampard (tr). **22 Dorling Kindersley:** Appaloosa (photographed by Stephen Oliver) Golden Nugget Sally Chaplin (tr).

23 Dreamstime.com: Terry Alexander (ca). **24 Fotolia:** Pixel Memoirs (cra). **25 Alamy Stock Photo:** Granger Historical Picture Archve (tr). **26 Dreamstime.com:** Nigel Baker (tr). **Jo Weeks:** (b). **28 123RF.com:** Tracy Fox (cra). **Fotolia:** Eric Isselee (tr). **29 Alamy Stock Photo:** Juniors Bildarchiv GmbH (ca). **30–31 Getty Images:** Gary Alvis. **32 Dorling Kindersley:** Barnabas Kindersley (b); Durham University Oriental Museum (tr). **34 Dorling Kindersley:** University of Pennsylvania Museum of Archaeology and Anthropology (clb). **35 123RF.com:** Tomas Hajek. **36 123RF.com:** jorisvo (bl). **37 Alamy Stock Photo:** Lordprice Collection (crb). **Getty Images:** Universal History Archive / UIG (t). **38–39 Alamy Stock Photo:** Gary Calton (b). **39 123RF.com:** FSergio (crb). **Alamy Stock Photo:** Juniors Bildarchiv GmbH (tc). **40 Dorling Kindersley:** Durham University Oriental Museum (tr). **41 Dorling Kindersley:** The University of Aberdeen (cl). **Getty Images:** Universal History Archive / UIG (cb). **42 Alamy Stock Photo:** Niday Picture Library (b). **43 123RF.com:** Keith webber Jr. (cb). **Alamy Stock Photo:** Chronicle (tl). **45 Dorling Kindersley:** Highland – Fruich of Dykes Countess of Swinton (tr). **46–47 Getty Images:** Darrell Gulin. **48 Alamy Stock Photo:** David Elliott. **50 Dreamstime.com:** Christopher Halloran (bl). **50–51 Dorling Kindersley:** Clydesdale– Blue Print Mervyn and Pauline Ramage, Mount Farm Clydesdale Horses, Tyne and Wear. **51 Dorling Kindersley:** Clydesdale – Blue Print Mervyn and Pauline Ramage, Mount Farm

Clydesdale Horses, Tyne and Wear (br). **52–53 Dorling Kindersley:** Shire – Duke im Lockwood, Courage Shire Horse Centre, Berks. **53 Alamy Stock Photo:** WENN Ltd (br). **Dorling Kindersley:** Shire – Duke im Lockwood, Courage Shire Horse Centre, Berks (tr). **54 Alamy Stock Photo:** geogphotos (bl). **54–55 Dorling Kindersley:** Suffolk Punch Laurei Keepsake II P Adams and Sons. **60 iStockphoto.com:** Robertobinetti70 (bl). **62 Dorling Kindersley:** Percheron – Tango Haras National de Saint Lo, France (tr). **Bob Langrish:** (bc). **63 Dorling Kindersley:** Percheron – Tango Haras National de Saint Lo, France (br). **64 Dreamstime.com:** Martina Berg (bl). **66 Alamy Stock Photo:** Richard Becker (cla). **67 Alamy Stock Photo:** Hemis (cla). **Dorling Kindersley:** Bob Langrish / Boulonnais – Urus Courtesy of Haras National de Compiegne, France (tr); Bob Langrish / Haras National de Compiegne, France / Boulonnais (bl). **70 Dorling Kindersley:** Norman Cob – Ibis Haras National de Sa in t L6, France (bl). **70–71 Dorling Kindersley:** Norman Cob – Ibis Haras National de Sa in t L6, France. **71 Dorling Kindersley:** Norman Cob – Ibis Haras National de Sa in t L6, France (tr). **Kit Houghton / Houghton's Horses:** (br). **74 Dorling Kindersley:** Jutland – Tempo 0rgen Neilsen, Denmark (bl, tr); Jutland – Tempo 0rgen Neilsen, Denmark (bl, tr). **78 Alamy Stock Photo:** Juniors Bildarchiv GmbH (bc). **80 Alamy Stock Photo:** Mikael Utterström (bl). **82 Annelise Wara (www. hesteliv.com):** (cl). **88 Alamy**

Stock Photo: Mikhail Kondrashov "fotomik" (cla). **89 Dreamstime. com:** Georgios Kollidas (cl). **90 Getty Images:** Konrad Wothe / Minden Pictures. **96–97 Dreamstime.com:** Amskad. **100–101 Dreamstime.com:** Mikle15. **103 Alamy Stock Photo:** Arterra Picture Library (cla). **Dorling Kindersley:** Karabakh- Moscow Hippodrome (bl, br, tr); Karabakh- Moscow Hippodrome (bl, br, tr); Karabakh- Moscow Hippodrome (bl, br, tr). **104 Alamy Stock Photo:** Roger Arnold (cla). **106 Alamy Stock Photo:** Theodore Kaye (cla). **107 Dorling Kindersley:** Tersk- Moscow Hippodrome (bl, bc, tr); Tersk- Moscow Hippodrome (bl, bc, tr); Tersk- Moscow Hippodrome (bl, bc, tr). **Photoshot:** UPPA (cla). **108–109 123RF.com:** Yulia Chupina. **110 Alamy Stock Photo:** Mikhail Kondrashov "fotomik" (bl). **112 Alamy Stock Photo:** horsemen (cla). **113 Bridgeman Images:** Private Collection / The Stapleton Collection (cr). **Dorling Kindersley:** Don- Baret (bl, br, tr); Don- Baret (bl, br, tr); Don- Baret (bl, br, tr). **114 Alamy Stock Photo:** Art Directors & TRIP (cla). **116 Magdalena Strakova** (cb, tr). **122 Dorling Kindersley:** Cleveland Bay – Oaten Mainbrace Mr and Mrs Dim mock (tr). **122–123 Dorling Kindersley:** Cleveland Bay – Oaten Mainbrace Mr and Mrs Dim mock. **124 Alamy Stock Photo:** Farlap (bc). **Dorling Kindersley:** Hunter – Hobo Robert Oliver (tr). **124–125 Dorling Kindersley:** Hunter – Hobo Robert Oliver. **125 Dorling Kindersley:** Hunter – Hobo Robert Oliver (br). **128 Dorling Kindersley:** Hack – Rye Tangle Robert Oliver (tr).

Dreamstime.com: Mille19 (bl). **128–129 Dorling Kindersley:** Hack – Rye Tangle Robert Oliver. **129 Dorling Kindersley:** Hack – Rye Tangle Robert Oliver (br). **130 Dorling Kindersley:** Cob – Silvester and r Hunter Ovation both owned by Robert Oliver (tr). **Dreamstime. com:** Lynn Bystrom (bc). **130–131 Dorling Kindersley:** Cob – Silvester and r Hunter Ovation both owned by Robert Oliver. **131 Dorling Kindersley:** Cob – Silvester and r Hunter Ovation both owned by Robert Oliver (br). **132–133 Alamy Stock Photo:** Mark J. Barrett. **134 Dorling Kindersley:** Irish Draught – Miss Mill (bl). **134–135 Dorling Kindersley:** Irish Draught – Miss Mill. **135 Dorling Kindersley:** (tr). **136–137 Dorling Kindersley:** Welsh Cob – Trejlys Jacko Mr and Mrs L E Bigley. **137 Dorling Kindersley:** Welsh Cob- Trejlys Jacko Mr and Mrs L E Bigley (tr). **138–139 Alamy Stock Photo:** Manfred Grebler. **140 Dorling Kindersley:** Andalucian– Adonis-Rex Welsh pool And a lucian Stud, Powys (bl). **142 Dorling Kindersley:** Alter Real– Casto Portuguese National Stud, Portugal (br, tr); Alter Real– Casto Portuguese National Stud, Portugal (br, tr). **Kit Houghton / Houghton's Horses:** (cla). **143 Dorling Kindersley:** Hispano-Arab - Ultima Mr & Mrs Davies (cla). **145 Dreamstime.com:** Wessel Cirkel (cl). **146–147 Alamy Stock Photo:** Marion Kaplan. **148 Alamy Stock Photo:** Hemis (bc). **150 Dorling Kindersley:** Camargue – Redounet Mr Contreras, Les Saintes Maries de Ia Mer, France. **151 Dorling Kindersley:** Camargue – Redounet Mr Contreras, Les Saintes Maries de Ia Mer, France (bl, bc, tr); Camargue – Redounet Mr Contreras, Les Saintes Maries de Ia Mer, France (bl, bc, tr); Camargue – Redounet Mr Contreras, Les Saintes Maries de Ia Mer, France

(bl, bc, tr). **152–153 123RF.com:** Sergei Uriadnikov. **154 Dorling Kindersley:** Selle Français – Prince D'elle Haras National De Saint L6, France (tr). **154–155 Dorling Kindersley:** Selle Français – Prince D'elle Haras National De Saint L6, France. **155 Dorling Kindersley:** Selle Français – Prince D'elle Haras National De Saint L6, France (br). **156–157 Dorling Kindersley:** French Trotter – Pur Historien Haras National De Compiegne, France. **157 Dorling Kindersley:** French Trotter – Pur Historien Haras National De Compiegne, France (tr). **Wikipedia:** (br). **159 Dorling Kindersley:** Gelderlander – Spooks Peter Munt, Ascot Driving Stables, Berks (br). **164 Dorling Kindersley:** Friesian – Sjouke Sonia Gray, Tattondale Carriages, Cheshire. **165 Dorling Kindersley:** Friesian – Sjouke Sonia Gray, Tattondale Carriages, Cheshire (tr, br); Friesian – Sjouke Sonia Gray, Tattondale Carriages, Cheshire (tr, br). **Bob Langrish:** (cra). **166 Dorling Kindersley:** Kit Houghton / Claes Oldenburg (bc). **168 Bob Langrish:** (cla). **169 Bob Langrish:** (cl). **170 Dorling Kindersley:** Holstein - Lenard Sue Watson, Trenawin Stud, Cornwall (tr). **Bob Langrish:** (bl). **170–171 Dorling Kindersley:** Holstein – Lenard Sue Watson, Trenawin Stud, Cornwall. **171 Dorling Kindersley:** Holstein - Lenard Sue Watson, Trenawin Stud, Cornwall (br). **176 Dorling Kindersley:** Knabstrup – Femiks Poul Elmerkjrer, Denmark (br). **Getty Images:** Monty Fresco / Topical Press Agency (bc). **176–177 Dorling Kindersley:** Knabstrup – Femiks Poul Elmerkjrer, Denmark. **178 Dorling Kindersley:** (bl, br, tr); Frederiksborg – Zarif LanglfJkkegard Harry Nielsen, Denmark (bl, br, tr);

Frederiksborg – Zarif LanglfJkkegard Harry Nielsen, Denmark (bl, br, tr). **Getty Images:** Holger Leue (cla). **179 Dorling Kindersley:** Danish Warm blood – Rambo orgen Olsen, Denmark (bl, tr); Danish Warm blood – Rambo)orgen Olsen, Denmark (bl, tr). **183 iStockphoto. com:** Sitikka (cla). **184 Animal Photography:** Venyamin Nikiforov (cla). **185 Bob Langrish:** (cla). **190 Kit Houghton / Houghton's Horses:** (cla); **Magdalena Strakova** (cl). **192 Alamy Stock Photo:** Prisma Bildagentur AG (cla). **194 123RF.com:** Ina van Hateren (bc). **Dorling Kindersley:** Haflinger- Nomad Miss Helen Blair, Silvretta Haflinger Stud, W Midlands (tr). **194–195 Dorling Kindersley:** Haflinger- Nomad Miss Helen Blair, Silvretta Haflinger Stud, W Midlands. **195 Dorling Kindersley:** Haflinger- Nomad Miss Helen Blair, Silvretta Haflinger Stud, W Midlands (br). **198 Alamy Stock Photo:** Marka (bc). **200 Alamy Stock Photo:** Odyssey-Images (cla). **201 Alamy Stock Photo:** Juniors Bildarchiv GmbH (cl). **Dorling Kindersley:** Murgese – Obscuro Istituto Incremento lppico di Crema, Italy (bl, br, tr); Murgese – Obscuro Istituto Incremento lppico di Crema, Italy (bl, br, tr); Murgese – Obscuro Istituto Incremento lppico di Crema, Italy (bl, br, tr). **202–203 Dorling Kindersley:** Lipizzaner - Siglavy Szella john Goddard Fenwick & Lyn Moran, Ausdan Stud, Dyfed. **203 Dorling Kindersley:** Lipizzaner – Siglavy Szella john Goddard Fenwick & Lyn Moran, Ausdan Stud, Dyfed (tr). **Dreamstime.com:** Azham Ahmad (br). **204 Magdalena Strakova** (tr, cr, b). **206–207 Alamy Stock Photo:** Andrea Kornfeld. **210 Dorling Kindersley:** Nonius- Pampas owned by A G

Kishumseigi, Hungary (cla, bc, tr, br); Nonius-owned by A G Kishumseigi, Hungary (cla, bc, tr, br); Nonius- Pampas owned by A G Kishumseigi, Hungary (cla, bc, tr, br); Nonius- Pampas owned by A G Kishumseigi, Hungary (cla, bc, tr, br). **211 Dorling Kindersley:** Furioso – Furioso IV A G Kishumseigi, Hungary (tr). **213 Rex by Shutterstock:** Gravitas Ventures / Everett (br). **214 Dorling Kindersley:** Palomino – Wychwood Dynascha Mrs G Harwood, Wychwood Stud, Glos (bl, tr, br); Palomino – Wychwood Dynascha Mrs G Harwood, Wychwood Stud, Glos (bl, tr, br); Palomino – Wychwood Dynascha Mrs G Harwood, Wychwood Stud, Glos (bl, tr, br). **215 Dorling Kindersley:** Dan Bannister (cla). **216–217 Alamy Stock Photo:** Juniors Bildarchiv GmbH. **218 Dreamstime.com:** Zuzana Tillerová (bl). **218–219 Dorling Kindersley:** Appaloosa – Golden Nugget Sally Chaplin. **221 Alamy Stock Photo:** Outdoor-Archiv (cra). **222 Dorling Kindersley:** Morgan – Fox Creek's Dynasty Darwin Olsen, Kentucky Horse Park, USA (tr). **223 Dorling Kindersley:** Morgan – Fox Creek's Dynasty Darwin Olsen, Kentucky Horse Park, USA (br). **228 Bob Langrish:** (bl). **232 Dorling Kindersley:** Standardbred- Rambling Willie Farrington Stables and the Estate of Paul Siebert, Kentucky Horse Park, USA (bl). **232–233 Dorling Kindersley:** Standardbred- Rambling Willie Farrington Stables and the Estate of Paul Siebert, Kentucky Horse Park, USA. **233 Dorling Kindersley:** Standardbred- Rambling Willie Farrington Stables and the Estate of Paul Siebert, Kentucky Horse Park, USA (tr). **235 Bob Langrish:** (cl). **236 Photoshot:** Gabriele Boiselle / Woodfall (cla). **237 Alamy Stock Photo:** Efrain Padro (cra).

238 123RF.com: joetex1 (cla). 240 Dreamstime.com: Tanya Puntti (cla). 242–243 Alamy Stock Photo: Regien Paassen. 244 Alamy Stock Photo: Juniors Bildarchiv GmbH. 246 Dorling Kindersley: Caspian-Hopstone Shabdiz Mrs Scott, Henden Caspian Stud, Wilts (tr). Dreamstime.com: Robert Wisdom (bl). 246–247 Dorling Kindersley: Caspian- Hopstone Shabdiz Mrs Scott, Henden Caspian Stud, Wilts. 247 Dorling Kindersley: Caspian-Hopstone Shabdiz Mrs Scott, Henden Caspian Stud, Wilts (br). 250–251 Verne Crawford. 254 Dorling Kindersley: Batak – Dora Tung Kurniawan, Sumatra, Indonesia (bl). 254–255 Dorling Kindersley: Batak – Dora Tung Kurniawan, Sumatra, Indonesia. 256 Alamy Stock Photo: ZUMA Press, Inc. (cla). 259 iStockphoto. com: winhorse (cla). 260 Getty Images: Universal History Archive (cr). 261 Alamy Stock Photo: Silvia Groniewicz (cra). 262 Kerry Dunstan / Malibu Park Stud, Victoria Australia: (bl). 264 Dorling Kindersley: Connemara- Spinway Bright Morning Miss S Hodgkins, Spinway Stud, Oxon (tr). Bob Langrish: (bl). 264–265 Dorling Kindersley: Connemara – Spinway Bright Morning Miss S Hodgkins, Spinway Stud, Oxon. 265 Dorling Kindersley: Connemara – Spinway

Bright Morning Miss S Hodgkins, Spinway Stud, Oxon (br). 270 Alamy Stock Photo: Chronicle (bl). Dorling Kindersley: Highland – Fruich of Dykes Countess of Swinton (tr). 270–271 Dorling Kindersley: Highland – Fruich of Dykes Countess of Swinton. 271 Dorling Kindersley: Highland – Fruich of Dykes Countess of Swinton (br). 272 Bridgeman Images: South Shields Museum & Art Gallery, South Shields, UK (bl). Dorling Kindersley: Fell – Waverhead William Mr and Mrs S Errington (tr). 272–273 Dorling Kindersley: Fell – Waverhead William Mr and Mrs S Errington. 273 Dorling Kindersley: Fell – Waverhead William Mr and Mrs S Errington (br). 274 Dorling Kindersley: Dales – Warrenlane Duke Mr Dickson, Millbeck Pony Stud, Yorks (bc, br, tr); Dales – Warrenlane Duke Mr Dickson, Millbeck Pony Stud, Yorks (bc, br, tr); Dales – Warrenlane Duke Mr Dickson, Millbeck Pony Stud, Yorks (bc, br, tr). Bob Langrish: (cr). 275 Dorling Kindersley: Dales – Warrenlane Duke Mr Dickson, Millbeck Pony Stud, Yorks. 276 Dorling Kindersley: Exmoor – Murrayton Delphinus June Freeman, Murrayton Stud, Herts (bl). 276–277 Dorling Kindersley: Exmoor – Murrayton

Delphinus June Freeman, Murrayton Stud, Herts. 277 Dorling Kindersley: Exmoor – Murrayton Delphinus June Freeman, Murrayton Stud, Herts (tr). 278 Dorling Kindersley: Dartmoor – Allendale Vampire Miss M Houlden, Haven Stud, Hereford. 279 Dorling Kindersley: Dartmoor – Allendale Vampire Miss M Houlden, Haven Stud, Hereford (br, tr); Dartmoor – Allendale Vampire Miss M Houlden, Haven Stud, Hereford (br, tr). 286–287 Alamy Stock Photo: Scottish Viewpoint. 292 Dorling Kindersley: Riding Pony – Brutt Robert Oliver (bl, br, tr); Riding Pony – Brutt Robert Oliver (bl, br, tr); Riding Pony – Brutt Robert Oliver (bl, br, tr). Bob Langrish: (cla). 293 Bob Langrish: (cl). 295 SuperStock: Marka / Marka (cl). 296 Bob Langrish: (cl). 300 Getty Images: Patrik Stollarz / AFP (bc). 302 Dreamstime.com: Daria Medvedeva (cl). 304–305 Getty Images: Arctic-Images. 306–307 Dorling Kindersley: Fjord – Ausdan Svejk john Goddard Fenwick and Lyn Moran, Ausdan Stud, Dyfed. 307 Dorling Kindersley: Fjord – Ausdan Svejk john Goddard Fenwick and Lyn Moran, Ausdan Stud, Dyfed (br). 308 Alamy Stock Photo: Juniors Bildarchiv GmbH

(cla). 310–311 Alamy Stock Photo: Terry Whittaker. 312 Kit Houghton / Houghton's Horses: (cl). 313 Dreamstime.com: Dimitris Kolyris (cla). 314 Photoshot: Nativestock (cl). 315 Alamy Stock Photo: Mark J. Barrett (cra). Dorling Kindersley: Bashkir – Mel's Lucky Boy Dan Stewart Family, Kentucwky Horse Park, USA (b). 320 Dreamstime.com: Steve Cole (bl). 322–323 Alamy Stock Photo: Prisma Bildagentur AG. 324 123RF. com: Zacarias Pereira da Mata (bl). 326 Dorling Kindersley: Falabella – Pegasus of Kilverstone (tr). iStockphoto.com: Andy Gehrig (bl). 326–327 Dorling Kindersley: Falabella – Pegasus of Kilverstone. 327 Dorling Kindersley: Falabella – Pegasus of Kilverstone (br). 328–329 Getty Images: Somogyvari. 330–331 Dreamstime. com: Conny Sjostrom. 337 Bob Langrish: (cl). 338–339 Getty Images: Gregory T. Smith. 342 Alamy Stock Photo: Agencja Fotograficzna Caro (bc). 347 Alamy Stock Photo: Juniors Bildarchiv GmbH (cra)

Endpapers: naturepl.com: Kristel Richard 0

All other images © Dorling KindersleyFor further information see: www.dkimages.com